UNCLOISTERED VIRTUE

Uncloistered Virtue

English Political
Literature, 1640–1660

THOMAS N. CORNS

CLARENDON PRESS · OXFORD

1992

Oxford University Press, Walton Street, Oxford OX2 6DP
Oxford New York Toronto
Delhi Bombay Calcutta Madras Karachi
Petaling Jaya Singapore Hong Kong Tokyo
Nairobi Dar es Salaam Cape Town
Melbourne Auckland
and associated companies in
Berlin Ibadan

Oxford is a trade mark of Oxford University Press

Published in the United States
by Oxford University Press, New York

British Library Cataloguing in Publication Data
Data available

Library of Congress Cataloging in Publication Data
Corns, Thomas N.
Uncloistered virtue: English political literature, 1640–1660 /
Thomas N. Corns.
Includes bibliographical references.
1. Great Britain—History—Puritan Revolution, 1642–1660—
Literature and the revolution. 2. Great Britain—History—Civil
War, 1642–1649—Literature and the war. 3. English literature—
Early modern, 1500–1700—History and criticism. 4. Politics and
literature—Great Britain—History—17th century. 5. Great Britain—
Politics and government—1642–1660. 6. Political poetry, English—
History and criticism. I. Title.
PR435C67   1992
820.9'358—dc20   92–13022
ISBN 0–19–812883–5

Typeset by Pentacor PLC, High Wycombe, Bucks.

Printed and bound in
Great Britain by Bookcraft Ltd
Midsomer Norton, Bath

To Martha
and
Joseph Corns

Sit memorasse satis

Preface

THIS IS a work of literary criticism, not a political or social history, nor even a literary history, though debts to historians of the Civil War period pervade it. Hill, Underdown, Worden, and Hutton, among others, radically shape my perception of the period and with it my interpretation of its political literature. My purpose, however, unwaveringly remains the development of critical readings of major texts, rather than the advancement of our understanding of the origins, nature, or political consequences of the war.

Some debts are personal and more direct. Nigel Smith and David Loades read and commented on every chapter, alerting me to errors and infelicities and deeply enriching my sense of Civil War historiography. I am very grateful too to Michael Wilding, who read the Marvell chapter, to David Lindsay, who read the chapters on poetry, and to David Loewenstein and Peter Kitson, who both read some of the chapters on radical prose. I appreciated their generally encouraging remarks and valued their specific observations and suggestions. The readers appointed by Oxford University Press to assess the typescript made a number of helpful comments which I have sought to address.

I am grateful to the staff of a number of libraries, including the Bodleian Library, the British Library, the Rylands Library, the Manchester Central Library, the Newberry Library, and, above all, the Library of the University of Wales, Bangor. The secretarial staff of my department have been unflinchingly resilient in face of the dreary tasks of printing out and of copying several drafts of a bulky typescript. Robert Corns assisted in the preparation of the index.

Sections of this book appeared previously in *Eighteenth Century Life*, *Modern Language Review*, and *Freedom and the English Revolution*, edited by R. C. Richardson and G. M. Ridden. I am grateful for the permission of the publishers to draw on that material. I also acknowledge the kind permission of Oxford University Press, to quote from *Poems of Richard Lovelace* and *The Complete Poems and Letters* of Andrew Marvell; of Yale University

Press, to quote from the *Complete Prose Works* of John Milton; of the Longman Group, to quote from *The Poems of John Milton*; and of Cornell University Press, to quote from *The Works of Gerrard Winstanley*.

Contents

Abbreviations

ELR	*English Literary Renaissance*
Hist. Jnl.	*The Historical Journal*
HLQ	*Huntington Library Quarterly*
JEH	*The Journal of Ecclesiastical History*
JHI	*Journal of the History of Ideas*
MLR	*The Modern Language Review*
P & P	*Past and Present*
PMLA	*Publications of the Modern Language Association of America*
Proc. Brit. Acad.	*Proceedings of the British Academy*
SP	*Studies in Philology*
YES	*Yearbook of English Studies*
Acts and Ordinances	C. H. Firth and R. S. Rait (eds.), *Acts and Ordinances of the Interregnum, 1642–1660* (London, 1911)
Brailsford	H. N. Brailsford, *The Levellers and the English Revolution*, ed. Christopher Hill (1961; Nottingham, 1976)
Carew, *Poems*	*The Poems of Thomas Carew*, ed. Rhodes Dunlap (1949; Oxford, 1964).
Corns	Thomas N. Corns (ed.), *The Literature of Controversy* (London, 1987).
Cowley, *Poems* (1656)	Abraham Cowley, *Poems* (London, 1656)
Cowley, *Poems* (1905)	Abraham Cowley, *Poems*, ed. A. R. Waller (Cambridge, 1905)
CPW	*Complete Prose Works of John Milton*, ed. Don M. Wolfe et al. (New Haven, 1953–82)
Davis, *Fear*	J. C. Davis, *Fear, Myth and History: The Ranters and the Historians* (Cambridge, 1986)
Dryden, *Poems and Fables*	*The Poems and Fables of John Dryden*, ed. James Kinsley (1958; Oxford, 1961)
EB	Charles I (attrib.), *Eikon Basilike: The Pourtraicture of his Sacred Majestie in his Solitudes and Sufferings* ([London], 1649)
Gardiner	S. R. Gardiner, *History of the Great Civil War* (London, 1889)

Greaves and Zaller	Richard L. Greaves and Robert Zaller, *Biographical Dictionary of British Radicals in the Seventeenth Century* (Brighton, 1982)
Hardacre	Paul Hardacre, *The Royalists during the English Revolution* (The Hague, 1956)
Healy and Sawday	Thomas Healy and Jonathan Sawday (eds.), *Literature and the English Civil War* (Cambridge, 1990)
Herrick, *Hesperides*	Robert Herrick, *Hesperides* (Scolar Press Facsimile, 1969; Menston and London, 1973)
Herrick, *HNN*	Robert Herrick, *His Noble Numbers* ibid.
Herrick, *Poetical Works*	*The Poetical Works of Robert Herrick* ed. L. C. Martin (Oxford, 1956)
Lieb and Shawcross	Michael Lieb and John T. Shawcross (eds.), *Achievements of the Left Hand: Essays on the Prose of John Milton* (Amherst, 1974)
Loewenstein and Turner	David Loewenstein and James Grantham Turner (eds.), *Politics, Poetics, and Hermeneutics in Milton's Prose* (Cambridge, 1990)
Lovelace, *Luc.*	Richard Lovelace, *Lucasta* (London, 1649)
Lovelace, *Poems*	*The Poems of Richard Lovelace*, ed. C. H. Wilkinson (Oxford, 1930)
Lovelace, *Selected Poems*	Richard Lovelace, *Selected Poems*, ed. Gerald Hammond (Manchester, 1987).
LR	J. Milton French (ed.), *The Life Records of John Milton* (1948–58; New York, 1968)
Marvell, *Poems and Letters*	*The Poems and Letters of Andrew Marvell*, ed. H. M. Margoliouth, 3rd edn., rev. Pierre Legouis with E. E. Duncan-Jones (Oxford, 1971)
Milton, *Divorce*	John Milton, *The Doctrine and Discipline of Divorce* (London, 1643)
Milton, *Poems*	*The Poems of John Milton*, ed John Carey and Alastair Fowler (London, 1968)
Nyquist and Ferguson	Mary Nyquist and Margaret W. Ferguson (eds.), *Re-membering Milton: Essays on the Texts and Traditions* (New York and London, 1987)
Pennington and Thomas	Donald Pennington and Keith Thomas (eds.), *Puritans and Revolutionaries* (Oxford, 1978)
Plomer	Henry R. Plomer, *A Dictionary of Book sellers who were at Work in England,*

	Scotland and Ireland from 1641 to 1667 (London, 1907)
Ranter Writings	Nigel Smith (ed.), *A Collection of Ranter Writings from the 17th Century*, foreword by John Carey (London, 1983)
Rochester, *Poems*	*The Poems of John Wilmot, Earl of Rochester* ed. Keith Walker (Oxford, 1984)
Winstanley, *Law of Freedom*	Gerrard Winstanley, *The Law of Freedom and Other Writings*, ed. Christopher Hill (1973; Cambridge, 1983)
Winstanley, *Works*	*The Works of Gerrard Winstanley*, ed. George H. Sabine (Ithaca, NY, 1941)
Worden	Blair Worden, *The Rump Parliament* (1974; Cambridge, 1977)

1

Introduction

THIS is a critical study not only of the tracts and pamphlets of the literature of controversy but also of works within other literary genres of a non-controversial kind, such as the love lyric and devotional poem. To the former it attempts to bring a new sense of its polemical ingenuity, its powerful integration of literary artifice and political cunning, and an enhanced awareness of its relationship both with other texts and with the political crises which it engages. For the latter, the study offers a new precision in the interpretation of its ideological implications and a new sense of how seemingly creative, intimate or recreational writing relates to the circumambient political intertext. It juxtaposes the overtly controversial with other kinds of writing in ways intended to illuminate both. Confronting closely similar issues, Wilding defined his programme as 'to politicise and historicise';[1] in a sense, I see mine to be to repoliticize, to return to texts the political potency they once possessed, by means of reanimating an awareness of those contexts which they engaged.

Besides the critical readings, a number of wider theses emerge, about the capacity of literature to preserve an ideology in periods of eclipse; about the ways in which new literary forms develop to meet changed circumstances, and in which old forms like the love lyric may mutate to carry more complex social and political values; and about the transformations that occur in the English literary tradition over the middle decades of the seventeenth century.

Repoliticizing the literature of the Civil War and Interregnum requires that it be located in the wider context of contemporary press output, of ways of perceiving and representing the contending forces, and of attitudes to the role and importance of the press. The 1640s and 1650s constitute an extraordinary period for the written

---

[1] M. Wilding, *Dragons Teeth: Literature in the English Revolution* (Oxford, 1987), 2.

word in England. George Thomason, a London bookseller of remarkable foresight, set himself the objective of building a collection of the books and pamphlets as they were published. He ended with over 15,000 separate titles and about 9,000 periodical parts, though it would seem likely that he collected only about two-thirds of the total output of the press.[2] The most striking thing about the collection, besides its general size, is the extraordinary surge in the work of the press in the early 1640s. A third of the individual items were published in the period 1641–5; approximately 2,000 were published in 1642 alone.[3] This has several implications. In part it shows the effect of the sudden release of those controls which had held the press in check over the 1630s and earlier. In part, too, it shows both a strong market for written material, much of which related directly to the developing crisis, and an associated belief that it was worth while, politically as well as commercially, to address that market. Political publication had been a prominent aspect of the work of the press at least since the Elizabethan period,[4] but securing the opinion of the reading public became almost an obsession in the political life of the nation in the 1640s, facilitated at least temporarily by a collapse in effective measures for control. From its inception the press had been obliged to operate within a repressive legal framework. Though that foundered with the suspension of the power of the Star Chamber

[2] For a history of the collection, see G. K. Fortescue, *Catalogue of the Pamphlets, Books, Newspapers, and Manuscripts relating to the Civil War, the Commonwealth, and the Restoration Collected by George Thomason* (London, 1908), i, pp. iii–xix. The most pessimistic assessment of the exhaustiveness of the collection seems to be that of S. Lambert, who observes that 'three separate calculations show that the Thomason tracts . . . contain at most 63% of papers in each of the categories considered' ('The Beginnings of Printing for the House of Commons, 1640–42', *The Library*, 6th ser. 3 (1981), 45). Her estimates, however, are based on a period which may not be representative of his performance overall. In 1640, Thomason was just starting out; in 1642, the peak year for press production, he may well have been swamped. On the formation and history of the collection, see L. Potter, *Secret Rites and Secret Writing: Royalist Literature, 1641–1660* (Cambridge, 1989), 1–7.

[3] For a statistical account of the collection, see T. N. Corns, 'Publication and Politics, 1640–1661: An SPSS-Based Account of the Thomason Collection of Civil War Tracts', *Literary and Linguistic Computing*, 1 (1986), 74–84.

[4] For a descriptive bibliography of controversial writing of the Elizabethan and Jacobean periods, see P. Milward, *Religious Controversies of the Elizabethan Age* (London, 1977), and *Religious Controversies of the Jacobean Age* (London, 1978). Milward lists 764 items from the period 1603–25, and, though Thomason collected other material besides religious controversy, the comparison with the size of the press output in the 1640s and 1650s is nevertheless suggestive.

decree of 1637, subsequent Governments each introduced some measures on broadly similar lines to regain control.[5] Once loosed, however, the genie of press freedom proved hard to return to its legislative bottle.

This study issues some challenges to the received canon of seventeenth-century literature, most significantly in the claims it makes for the writings of Winstanley and some of the Ranters. But much of the material collected by Thomason, though vital in contextualizing texts which do reward a close reading, is trivial, ephemeral, repetitive, sometimes dull (although often not without a robust appeal). Collectively, it presents a fascinating version of English political life as deeply fissured along clearly demarcated ideological lines. What it offers is a number of politically useful constructs which negotiate a complex relationship with the intricacies and uncertainties that historically obtained, but which are remote from the nuances, the elusiveness, the discrimination manifest in much of the better writing of the period.

We know that even among the propertied classes with a direct stake in the political life of the country, neutralism was a powerful element in the early years of the conflict between king and Parliament. Morrill, for example, has found evidence of 'attempted neutrality pacts' in twenty-two English counties and in many boroughs, and Hutton has demonstrated how some areas resisted the mobilization of 1642.[6] Neutralism constituted an active and coherent political position, though it finds relatively little expression in contemporary publications, which are dominated, rather, by the development of powerful and politically damaging stereotypes, pre-eminently, the parliamentarian image of the Cavalier and the royalist image of the Roundhead;[7] images with which writers as diverse as Milton and Herrick negotiate a complicated relationship.

If the accounts of the parliamentary press were reliable, it should have been an easy thing to recognize a Cavalier, distinguished sharply by his hair, his clothing, and his language. A 'spy' reports,

---

[5] For a brief account of the framework of legislation, see *CPW* ii. 158–64.

[6] J. S. Morrill, *The Revolt in the Provinces* (London, 1976), 36–7; R. Hutton, *The Royalist War Effort 1642–1646* (London, 1982), 7–8, 11–13.

[7] For a broader history of these figures, see T. N. Corns, W. A. Speck, and J. A. Downie, 'Archetypal Mystification: Polemic and Reality in English Political Literature, 1640–1750', *Eighteenth Century Life*, 7 (1982), 1–27; for another account of stereotyping, see W. Lamont and S. Oldfield, *Politics, Religion and Literature in the Seventeenth Century* (London and Totowa, NJ, 1975), ch. 3.

rather improbably, on a visit to a Cavalier camp at York, where 'I perceived many of these *Cabalieroes* richly deck'd with long shag hair, reaching down to their heels . . . the *Coronet* [i.e. Cornet] bearing these words in the Banner, *Damme we'll win the day*.'[8] A theologian explains the significance of the distinctively long hair thus: 'Your shag pole locusts originall was the opening of the bottomlesse pit, *Rev*: 9: the smoaky pit, out of the smoake, came those shag pole locusts that weare hair like women.'[9] In a spoof account of a Cavalier Parliament, they are made to admit that they are 'old beaten souldiers of *Bacchus*', recognizable by 'the manner of our Periwigs, the length of our curled or crisped haire, by the pearle or ribbins at the eares', by the 'nicety and curiosity of the habit', by 'the gingling of the Coach-wheel roweld spurs', and by 'the French troubled stradling of the legges'.[10] That gait finds ready explanation, for the parliamentary press exhibits a recurrent fascination with the excess of Cavalier sexual mores: twenty whores cannot sate a Cavalier,[11] and in the areas around their camps 'we have scarce a good Maid within ten miles . . . we can scarce keepe our wives from being overrun'.[12]

Blasphemous execration, frenzied lust, and a hatred of property characterize Cavalier conduct and motivation. Swearing receives a striking prominence, and in the lists of atrocities, which constitute a common feature of parliamentarian reportage, it assumes equal status with stripping, whipping, arbitrary executions, and mutilations.[13] Sexual outrage appears less as a contingency of war than as a Cavalier policy. To Lord Wentworth, son of the Earl of Strafford, is attributed an address to his troops in which he urges them to 'ravish their Virgins; force the timorous maides to clip you in dalliance, and wreake your utmost spleen upon the roundheads'.[14] Again, in a singularly prurient fantasy, a Cavalier discusses raping goldsmiths'

---

[8] Anon., *Nocturnall Occurrences, or, Deeds of Darknesse Committed by the Cavaleers in their Rendevous* (London, 1642), sig. A2ᵛ.

[9] Anon., *A Short, Compendious, and True Description of the Round-Heads and the Long-Heads* (n.p., 1642), 5.

[10] Anon., *A Witty Answer to a Foolish Pamphlet, Intituled New Orders New* (London, n.d.), sig. A3ᵛ.

[11] Anon., *The Wicked Resolution of the Cavaliers* (London, 1642), 1.

[12] Anon., *Sad and Fearful Newes from Beverley* (London, n.d.), sigs. A3ᵛ-A4ʳ.

[13] See e.g. William Warren, *Strange, True and Lamentable Newes from Exceter* (London, 1643), sig. A4ʳ, and Anon., *Prince Ruperts Burning Love to England: Discovered in Birminghams Flames* (London, 1643), 4.

[14] Anon., *A Barbarous and Inhumane Speech spoken by the Lord Wentworth* (London, 1642), sig. A4ʳ.

wives once London has fallen: 'nay we will make them [the husbands] to hold up their wives smocks, and after this, they shall kneele downe and thank us, for taking pains to inlarge their hornes.'[15] Cavaliers fight, also, to repair fortunes damaged by earlier excesses:

you may remember, that though we say, we fight for the King, yet we respect nothing but our own private pockets, and plundering of houses for gold, for it is fitter that we that are men of metall, and know how to spend money in a most damnable manner, should have plenty of gold and silver.[16]

Those not prompted by lust or avarice act out of hatred of the godly. The royalist army is an instrument of the Pope, made up of papists, many of them Irish. Thus, a Cavalier officer is represented as complaining:

because I am a Protestant, I must not like nor owne that many of the Kings guard troops are Papists, and there are some Popish Commanders, how this came about I know not, specially seeing it is a principle with the wisest, that no Papist should have command, for feare of the ill report it would make among the Kings Liedge people.[17]

Another, cruder text simulates a petition of Catholics, urging Rupert to use his army in extirpation of the godly:

Prince looke about thee, here is much adoe,
'Tis time to looke and lay about thee too;
Send obstinate Offenders to their graves,
That neither will be Catholicks nor slaves.[18]

The stereotype bears little scrutiny as a fair representation of Parliament's enemies. The appearance of the Cavaliers was much less distinctive. Indeed, throughout the hostilities the officer corps of each side favoured long hair (as we may see from contemporary portraits), and though some of Puritan rank and file wore their hair short at the start of the war (as Presbyterian divines advocated) their hair soon became indistinguishable from that of their opponents.[19] Clothing scarcely distinguished enemies of the same rank (except in

---

[15] Anon., *Wicked Resolution*, 2–3.   [16] Ibid. 1.

[17] Anon., *A Private Letter, from an Eminent Cavalier* (London, 1642), 7.

[18] Anon., *The Catholikes Petition to Prince Rupert . . . with a Draught of a Proclamation Presented to His Highnesse, for the More Speedy Recruting his Army, Destroying the Protestants, and Gaining a Crowne*, (London, 1644), sig. A1ʳ.

[19] L. Hutchinson, *Memoirs of the Life of Colonel Hutchinson*, ed. J. Sutherland (London, 1973), 62–3; C. H. Firth, *Cromwell's Army*, 3rd edn. (London, 1921), 231.

so far as regiments developed a system of uniform); when Rupert broke through to the parliamentary baggage train at Naseby, he was approached by the officer guarding it, who had mistaken him for Fairfax, the parliamentary commander, and decided to ask him how the battle was going.[20] Contemporary woodcuts scarcely distinguish parliamentarian and royalist commanders in terms of dress or hairstyle. Swearing was particularly censured in the armies of the king, and the King's Regulations are clear and severe.[21] There is some evidence that the royalist forces seem generally to have been characterized by the display of piety; they had considerably more chaplains than the parliamentarian armies, attendance at prayers and sermons was compulsory, and they prayed before battle.[22] Personal greed can scarcely explain the motivation of senior officers, who were expected largely to raise regiments out of their own resources. Fortunes were lost, not revived, in the service of the king.[23] Royalist troops would seem to have been more restrained than their adversaries in taking plunder,[24] and, though certainly there were some outrages, royalist cruelty scarcely matched the New Model Army's wanton mistreatment of captured camp-followers after Naseby.[25] The charge of popery is harder to assess, since we have no consensus among historians about either the extent of Catholicism in seventeenth-century England or the level of Catholic commitment to the royalist cause,[26] though clearly Catholics were in a small minority and certainly could not have dominated the royalist forces in the way in which the parliamentarian press liked to suggest.

[20] E. Scott, *Rupert Prince Palatine*, 2nd edn. (London, 1904), 173.

[21] Anon., *Military Orders and Articles, Established by His Majestie* (Oxford, n.d.), sig. A3ᵛ.

[22] Firth, *Cromwell's Army* 313–17; Anon., *Military Orders*, sig. A3ᵛ; Scott, *Rupert*, 149.

[23] P. R. Newman, 'The Royalist Army in Northern England, 1642–1645', D.Phil. diss., (York, 1978), *passim*.

[24] Scott, *Rupert*, 65; Firth, *Cromwell's Army*, 294–5; Hutchinson, *Memoirs*, 67.

[25] Gardiner, ii. 217.

[26] The technical difficulties in assessing the level of Catholicism nationally are considered by J. Bossy, *The English Catholic Community 1570–1850* (New York, 1976), 182–94. He tentatively suggests that Catholics in the mid seventeenth century constituted no more than 2% of the total population of England. K. Lindley argues that Catholics were inclined to neutrality in 'The Part Played by the Catholics', in B. Manning (ed.), *Politics, Religion and the English Civil War*, (London, 1973), 127–76; whereas P. R. Newman claims they were generally much more active than the Anglican population and made up a considerable fraction of the officer corps of at least the Northern armies of the king ('Catholic Royalists of Northern England, 1642–1645', *Northern History*, 15 (1979), 88–95).

The construction of the stereotype repays study. In part, propagandists reactivate an established pejorative image of the professional soldiery available well before the spiral into open warfare, the constituent elements of which are well indicated by the ponderous *double entendres* of an anonymous pamphlet of 1641, *The Brothers of the Blade: Answerable to the Sisters of the Scaberd, or, A Dialogue betweene two Hotspurres of the Times, Serjeant Slice-Man, alias Smell-Smock of Coney-Court in Chick-Lane, and Corporall Dam-Mee of Bell-Alley neer Pick-Hatch* (London, 1641). The topographical allusions are to notorious resorts of prostitution. In the dialogue, which makes no allusion to the imminent civil war, professional soldiers returned from the abortive Scottish campaign and from service in the Netherlands discuss poverty, pillage, highway robbery, whoring, and drinking. A woodcut, rather more accomplished than the text, shows a soldier and a prostitute embracing on a bed. All the elements of this military stereotype recur in parliamentary accounts of the Cavaliers, and can be traced back at least to the Elizabethan period—they occur, for example, in Shakespeare's representation of Falstaff and his associates. A second powerful element comes from the ancient and widespread tradition of anti-court writing, which represented the monarch's courtiers as ruthless, foppish, esurient, and lecherous. Such attacks were fairly commonplace in Continental Europe from the late Middle Ages, and found numerous English manifestations. In the Elizabethan and Jacobean period, this perspective informed much of the stage representation of the courtier class, from the foppish affectation of Shakespeare's Osric to the murderous carnality of *The Revenger's Tragedy*.[27]

To this legacy parliamentarian propaganda gives a polemical function and a clearer social direction. Most simply, whoring is an affront to godly decency. Atrocities, which are the common matter of all partisan accounts of wars, are potently linked with Catholicism and with the taking of plunder. There is a strong suggestion of a continuity between the struggle in England and assaults on the Reformation taking place on the European mainland, and more especially with the current revolt in Ireland. As John Goodwin put

[27] S. Anglo, 'The Courtier', in A. G. Dickens (ed.), *The Courts of Europe: Politics, Patronage and Royalty, 1400–1800*, (London, 1977), 33–53. On anti-court sentiment on the Jacobean stage, see M. Heinemann, *Puritanism and Theatre: Thomas Middleton and Opposition Drama under the Early Stuarts* (Cambridge, 1980), *passim*.

it, the royalists 'threaten you with the utmost insolencies they can execute upon you [the people of London], and (in effect) to stretch the line of miserable and wofull *Ireland* over you and your City, and whole Nation.'[28] These texts persistently target the anxieties of the man of property:

For your Estates, these are already designed, by your enemies, for a reward and recompence for their labour and travell in procuring your ruine. Your silver, and gold, your houses, and lands, with all your precious and pleasant things besides, must call you Master no more, if you fall into the hands of these devourers . . . . I beseech you consider this, you that have lived at ease, and in all fulnesse hitherto, and have wanted nothing of all that your hearts could desire, to make your lives comfortable . . . tell me how, or what will you do in such a day, wherein your fair necks, that never had yoke upon them to this day, shall be wrung and galled, and torne with those Iron yokes, of poverty, nakednesse, hunger, cold, contempt, want of all things.[29]

Such writing constitutes an important intertext to the work of several major authors. Thus, the sexual libertinism of Herrick and Lovelace in some ways mocks the received image, much as their version of the selfless sufferings of the Cavalier challenges parliamentarian insistence on Cavalier greed and self-interest. Milton purposefully stoops to adopt the image of the Cavalier bravo, using it to discredit Charles I's march on Parliament and to frighten backsliders from restoring Charles II, and he frequently draws upon the easy certainties of anti-Catholic sentiment to discredit prelates and even Presbyterians by association, to demonstrate the godliness of the Rump's policy towards Ireland, and to raise prejudices against royal courts.

Royalist propaganda represented the armed forces of Parliament (including the officer corps) as a rabble drawn from the unpropertied classes and as subscribers to the views and practices of the most extreme sects. Their commanders are men of low birth and high ambition:

> Thus doe the froth of all the earth,
> A spawne sprung from a dunghill birth,
> now Prince it in our Land:

[28] John Goodwin, *Anti-Cavalierisme, or, Truth Pleading as well the Necessity, as the Lawfulness of this Present War* (London, 1642), 12.
[29] Ibid. 37.

A people come the Lord knowes how,
Both Fame and nameless will just now,
must everyone command.[30]

Their intellectual and spiritual leaders are 'The Felt-maker, and Saucie stable Groome . . . Sow-gelders and Coblers',[31] while the officer corps, especially after the new modelling, consists of ambitious working men, such as Colonel Hewson, 'a Shoe-maker', and ex-drayman Colonel Pride, 'thou every brought'st good Beere'.[32] Roundheads generally subscribe to the sexual licentiousness attributed to the more extreme sects. Thus, a 'roundhead parliament' resolves 'That everything is to be common amongst the Brethren, one Mans Wife for another, when the candle of iniquity is extinguished, and the Spirit moves, as to the Exposition of that place in the Scripture, *Increase and Multiply*'.[33] Solid Presbyterianism and its grave ranks of accomplished and sober divines scarcely appear in royalist propaganda.

Again image relates in highly mediated fashion to reality. The social distinction between royalist and parliamentarian troops for the most part defies definition. Gentry and nobility raised the earliest Roundhead regiments. Although a professional officer corps, largely promoted through ability and sometimes drawn from the tradesman class, evolved much later (long after the stereotype had been established), even the New Model Army was officered by gentlemen:

It has been calculated that out of the thirty-seven colonels and general officers twenty-one were commoners of good family, nine were members of noble families, and only seven were not gentlemen of birth. A large number of the inferior officers belonged to the minor landed gentry, and came from families whose pedigrees and arms were registered in the visitations of heralds.[34]

As late as Naseby, Independents and sectaries were a minority, and Presbyterians predominated. Indeed, on Kishlansky's controversial account, religious radicalism was only one element within the

[30] Humphrey Willis, *Times Whirligig, or, the Blew-New-Made Gentleman Mounted* (n.p., 1647), sig. B1ʳ.
[31] T. J., *The World Turn'd Upside Down, or, A Briefe Description of the Ridiculous Fashions of these Distracted Times* (London, 1647), sig. A3ʳ.
[32] Anon., *The Cities Welcome to Colonell Rich and Colonell Baxter, with their Solemne Invitation to the Sainted Commanders in the Army* (n.p., 1648).
[33] Anon., *New Orders, New, Agreed upon by a Parliament of Round-Heads* (London, 1642), 5. [34] Firth, *Cromwell's Army*, 46–7.

theological orientation of the New Model Army, and its later
revolutionary intervention into English political life reflected, not
the victory of that sectarian radicalism, but the radicalization of the
army through the failures of the Long Parliament to maintain their
pay and find a settlement with the king.[35] The Long Parliament
itself, once its royalist members had withdrawn, was probably quite
solidly Presbyterian in orientation, and the Westminster Assembly of
Divines, convoked to work out a new church settlement, contained
very few Independent Congregationalists and no sectaries.[36]

The political advantage of the royalist stereotype lies in the appeal
it makes to the propertied and in the anxieties it arouses about the
release of ill-disciplined forces which thereafter may become
uncontrollable. That image has a fascinating later history, as
Presbyterians and similar elements within the Puritan opposition to
the king adopt it as part of the campaign to limit toleration and to
enforce a Presbyterian settlement.

The manœuvre proved astonishingly effective and shaped the
self-representation of several major figures. That caricature of the
propertiless *enragé* stalks Milton's prose, stimulating autobiographical excursions in his earliest tracts, strongly influencing his
polemical strategy in his tracts of 1643–5, and recurring as an
undercurrent in his defence of republicanism. It affects, too, much
more radical figures. Lilburne's assertion of his own social status,
Winstanley's insistence on the Digger movement's quietism, reflect
it; Coppe and Clarkson generate a *frisson* by taking it on and
seemingly validating it. In general, it shapes the radicals' persistent
assertion of their own respectability and their representation of
radical change as if it were some kind of restoration.

---

[35] M. A. Kishlansky, *The Rise of the New Model Army* (Cambridge, 1979), 72–4,
291, and *passim*. Some historians, however, feel Kishlansky overstates his case or that
it is inherently implausible. C. Hill outlines some of the arguments that have been
raised against it in *A Turbulent, Seditious, and Factious People: John Bunyan and his
Church* (1988; Oxford, 1989), 381.   [36] See below, Ch. 3.

2

Milton and the Bishops

THE Long Parliament assembled on 4 November 1640. Many issues exercised those Lords and Commons who were unsympathetic to the court, among them, apparent malpractices by the king's ministers, pre-eminently Thomas Wentworth, Earl of Strafford, and a cluster of serious issues relating to the government of the country over the previous decade, issues which pointed towards the most profound constitutional questions about the relationship of the monarchy to the nation. At the outset, though, ecclesiastical matters seemed to head the agenda of the most vocal opponents of the court. Four days after the opening, one relatively moderate MP declared, 'Let religion be our *primum quaerite*, for all else are but *etceteras* to it', a sentiment which was widely echoed and which was manifest in several of the Parliament's earliest measures.[1] But 'religion' covered a considerable range of issues, some relating to changes in the prevailing doctrinal concerns of the Church of England, some to matters of ceremony, some to individual acts of malpractice by clergymen, pre-eminently, Archbishop William Laud, and the spurious charge that he favoured a softening of relations with Rome, and some to the larger and more theoretical question of the power structure within the government of the Church.[2]

[1] C. Carlton, *Archbishop William Laud* (London and New York, 1987), 197–8; the speaker was Sir Benjamin Rudyerd, a vociferous though relatively moderate critic of prelatical church government, who drew back from the attempt to abolish, rather than to reform, episcopacy (*DNB*).

[2] See J. F. H. New, *Anglican and Puritan: The Basis of their Opposition, 1558–1640* (London, 1964), for a wide-ranging review of the issues; Carlton, *Laud*, 214–24, for the case made against Laud at his trial; N. Tyacke, 'Puritanism, Arminianism and Counter-Reformation', in C. Russell (ed.), *The Origins of the English Civil War* (London and Basingstoke, 1973), 119–43, and *Anti-Calvinists: The Rise of English Arminianism, c.1590–1640* (Oxford and New York, 1987), 181–247, for an account of the role of the Arminian controversy in the developing political crisis and for the relationship between Arminianism and ceremony; and H. R. Trevor-Roper, *Catholics, Anglicans and Puritans: Seventeenth Century Essays* (London, 1987), 113–19, for an assessment of 'the Laudian experience as a whole' (p. 113).

Milton's earlier controversial prose all relates to the Puritan attack on prelatical church government. His interests were quite narrowly focused on the historical justification for episcopacy and on its shortcomings. Indeed, in the context of the wide range of outrage manifested by opponents of the court in the early 1640s, Milton's concerns seem very restricted and in a sense relatively detached from the particularity of the case that others were constructing against the conduct of Laud and of Strafford, though they closely engaged episcopalian propaganda. Not until 1649 did Milton persistently shift his regard from ecclesiastical and doctrinal matters. Furthermore, as we shall see, his political writings remained characterized by a reluctance to develop the large argument, to connect discrete elements of his critique, and to operate at the level of theorectical abstraction.[3]

Of Reformation[4] was published in May 1641 as a contribution to a broad and by then possibly senescent Puritan campaign against prelacy that may have begun to lose some of its sting. The arguments it rehearses have been interpreted as an extension of the history of prelacy suffixed as a postscript to the *Answer to a Booke Entituled, An Humble Remonstrance* (London, 1641), written by Smectymnuus, a consortium of Presbyterian divines who had undertaken the refutation of Bishop Joseph Hall's studiedly urbane *Humble Remonstrance to the High Court of Parliament*.[5] The historical moment of *Of Reformation* is the attempt to recapture the buoyancy, six months earlier, of the first actions of the Long Parliament. The pamphlet proceeds on assumptions of unity of purpose and of the imminence and certainty of success, and it culminates in a seemingly ecstatic prayer:

O how much more glorious will those former Deliverances appeare, when we shall know them not onely to have sav'd us from greatest miseries past, but to have reserv'd us for greatest happinesse to come. Hitherto thou hast but freed us, and that not fully, from the unjust and Tyrannous Claime of thy Foes, now unite us intirely, and appropriate us to thy selfe, tie us everlastingly in willing Homage to the *Prerogative* of thy eternall *Throne* (*Of Reformation*, CPW i. 615).

Milton's apocalyptic voice, no doubt appropriately, has attracted

---

[3] See below, Ch. 6.

[4] All references to Milton's prose, unless otherwise stated, are to *CPW*.

[5] Smectymnuus is an acronym from the names Stephen Marshall, Edmund Calamy, Thomas Young, Matthew Newcomen, and William Spurstow.

some critical attention. Fixler speaks of the 'remarkable fervency' of this apocalyptic prayer and its counterpart in his third antiprelatical tract, rightly identifying 'an assurance far greater than anything in his later prose',[6] and Mueller, too, considers the ways in which he recasts 'native apocalypticism as a unitary framework where a divine design finds realization in and through the struggles of the English people'.[7] Mueller recognizes a tension between the apocalyptic vision and the ambitions and role of the individual, though perhaps without engaging the complexity with which Milton and his contemporaries regarded the imminence of the Apocalypse while continuing their day-to-day lives. My concerns, however, are more with his polemical strategy, and with the ways in which he developed a voice to achieve a historically determined objective of manipulating an identifiable readership. No matter how confident he may have been of the onrush of last things, he addressed with considerable guile the problems contemporaneously faced by puritanism in its most militant form. The proximity of Christ's coming in no sense relaxed the responsibilities of the godly in the current struggle.

Unusually within the Milton prose *œuvre*, *Of Reformation* takes the form of correspondence; the title-page carries the phrase 'Two Bookes, Written to a Freind [*sic*]'. The epistolary stance, though lightly and improbably assumed, suggests the tentativeness of the neophyte pamphleteer who may have taken too literally a Smectym-nuan request that he write something for them. The posture, however, assumes a central significance in the strategy of the pamphlet.

Through the figure of this 'friend' Milton produces within his discourse a character which fills the space the intended reader should occupy, a 'you' who may be persistently invoked as comrade, as esteemed equal (Milton calls him 'Sir'), as co-worker in the proposed completion of the Reformation in England. Thus, the reader-friend is invited to collaborate in reviewing the case against prelacy: 'Mark Sir here how the Pope came by S. *Peters* Patrymony, as he feigns it, not the donation of *Constantine*, but idolatry and rebellion got it him. Yee need but read *Sigonius*' (i. 578). He is urged to consider recondite evidence which Milton, rather flatteringly,

---

[6] M. Fixler, *Milton and the Kingdoms of God* (London, 1964), 101.
[7] J. Mueller, 'Embodying Glory: The Apocalyptic Strain in Milton's *Of Reformation*', in Loewenstein and Turner, 35.

assumes he is already familiar with: 'You know Sir what was the judgement of *Padre Paolo* the great Venetian Antagonist of the *Pope*' (i. 581). At times, perhaps, the mechanism creaks a little; after all, if one knew the judgement of Padre Paolo, one would certainly know he was a Venetian opponent of the Pope. Milton's parenthetic supplement concedes that the knowing Sir is not his only reader.

Yet, generally, the fiction works fairly well, and as the reader is produced, so too is the author, who appears as friend and aide, furnishing information for the process of co-discovery: 'Hitherto Sir you have heard how the *Prelates* have weaken'd and withdrawne the externall Accomplishments of Kingly prosperity . . . now heare how they strike at the very heart, and vitals' (i. 592). Thus, Milton constructs an image of the author as disinterested servant of truth, though occasionally he protests that role perhaps too stridently:

wherever I have in this BOOKE plainely and roundly (though worthily and truly) laid open the faults and blemishes of *Fathers*, *Martyrs*, or Christian *Emperors*; or have otherwise inveighed against Error and Superstition with vehement Expressions: I have done it, neither out of malice, nor list to speak evill, nor any vaine-glory; but of meere necessity to vindicate the spotlesse *Truth* from an ignominious bondage (i. 535).

Such open asseverations, though, are crude compared with the way in which, pervasively, seeming performatives function to shape the reader's perception of the kindly author, who abbreviates document-ation ('I will not run into a paroxysm of citations again in this point, only instance *Athanasius*' (i. 566)); who presents translations ('*Dante* in his 19. *Canto* of *Inferno* hath thus, as I will render it you in English blank Verse' (i. 558)); and who anticipates objections with a timely tendered citation ('Now lest it should bee thought that something else might ayle this Author thus to hamper the Bishops of those dayes; I will bring you the opinion of the famousest men for wit and learning' (i. 558)). The text assembles a comfortable relationship between the author and the reader it produces, but besides this 'I' and 'you' Milton offers, somewhat ambiguously, a 'we'.

The pronominalization usually replaces a configuration of author and reader in their collaborative enquiry into the destructive role of prelacy in the history of the Church. 'We' are frequently involved in the consideration of evidence and in agreeing conclusions:

But since hee [Constantine] must needs bee the Load-starre of *Reformation* as some men clatter, it will be good to see further his knowledge of *Religion* what it was, and by that we may likewise guesse at the sincerity of his Times (i. 555).

Lastly, we all know by Examples, that exact *Reformation* is not perfited at the first push (i. 536).

Now certaine if Church-government be taught in the Gospel, as the Bishops dare not deny, we may well conclude of what late standing . . . (i. 574).

Yet the pronominalization cannot always be thus interpreted. The 'we' must sometimes embrace agents outside the simple duality of author and reader, extending to include all decent, Protestant English people groaning under the prelates' tyranny and struggling to be free:

yet me thinkes the *Precedencie* which GOD gave this *Iland*, to be the first *Restorer* of *buried Truth*, should have beene followed with more happy successe, and sooner attain'd Perfection; in which, as yet we are amongst the last . . . Certainly it would be worth the while therefore and the paines to enquire more particularly, what, and how many the chiefe causes have been, that have still hindred our *Uniforme Consent* to the rest of the *Churches* abroad, (at this time especially) when the *Kingdome* is in a good *propensity* thereto; and all men in Prayers, in Hopes, or in Disputes, either for or against it (i. 526–7).

The passage is deeply suggestive of how Milton works the relationship with his readers. The 'we' that must perfect Reformation must include all England while the national Church remains deviant from Continental Protestant models. This 'we' surely includes not only Milton and his reader-friends but also the more sound of his countrymen. Milton presumes to speak for England, incorporating into the first person plural all but a few.

Those few are the chief enemies of the nation, the bishops and their supporters, and are persistently referred to in the third person and prominalized as 'they' and 'them' (though occasionally Milton apostrophizes them (i. 551)):

And for the *Bishops*, they were so far from any such worthy Attempts, as that they suffer'd themselvs to be the common stales to countenance with their prostituted *Gravities* every Politick Fetch that was then on foot, as oft as the Potent *Statists* pleas'd to employ them. Never do we read that they made use of their Authority and high Place of accesse, to bring the jarring Nobility to *Christian peace* (i. 530–1).

And a cosy polarity develops between 'them' and 'us':

Having fitted us only for peace, ánd that a servile peace, by lessening our numbers, dreining our estates, enfeebling our bodies, cowing our free spirits by those wayes as you have heard, their impotent actions cannot sustaine themselves the least moment, unlesse they rouze us up to a *Warre* fit for *Cain* to be the Leader of (i. 595–6).

II

By the spring of 1641 the broad Puritan opposition to the court had scored some significant political successes. It had a majority of sorts in the House of Commons; gradually London's institutions were falling under its control; and it had released its Caroline martyrs and imprisoned Laud. Strafford was executed in the same month that *Of Reformation* appeared. But such moments of triumph are often characterized by anxiety and hesitation, and indeed, retrospectively, we can discern how unstable that broad coalition of puritanically inclined groups proved to be. Moreover, contemporaneously, it was evident that the campaign against the bishops had begun to lose its impetus. Debate focused on how rigorously episcopacy should be treated. Should it be utterly extirpated, or could it be reformed? In December 1640 the Commons had received the London Petition, signed by 15,000 citizens, which advocated root-and-branch extirpation.[8] Some parliamentarians and divines, however, sensed that such a course would provoke a reaction or destabilize the social fabric, and sought instead a more limited revision. A compromise formula, embodied in a petition of seven or eight hundred ministers, among them two of the Smectymnuans, was presented to the Commons. Although in March 1641, two months before the publication of *Of Reformation*, the Commons passed resolutions to strip bishops of their temporal power and to undermine their economic position, the root-and-branch movement had run into the sand; Milton's tract addresses that failure.

At the same time the public face of episcopacy was in transformation. With Laud in jail, where he would remain until his execution, John Williams, bishop of Lincoln, emerged as most influential. He was a figure with a long and well-known record of public

---

[8] *CPW* i. 63.

antagonism to Laud, who had conducted a vendetta against him. His elevation to the archbishopric of York later in 1641 marked his new status. Joseph Hall, who as bishop of Exeter had assumed a conciliatory attitude to his own Puritan ministers, took over the role of leading press apologist for prelacy. He too was rewarded, moving to the more prestigious see of Norwich in the autumn. James Ussher, archbishop of Armagh, seconded his efforts, publishing a learned defence of episcopacy in the month that *Of Reformation* appeared. Ussher, widely known to have opposed concessions to Irish Catholicism, was the only scholar of international repute among the bishops, and he was 'untainted by Laudian extremism'.[9] He, like Hall, made a formidable adversary of hard-line Puritanism. None of them were Arminians, and together they entered into formal negotiations with moderate Puritan divines, among them three of the Smectymnuans. By late spring 1641, more amenable Presbyterians could be heard expressing confidence that the Laudian model had gone for ever.[10]

In this context the purposefulness of Milton's management of his readers emerges. His own position was not in doubt. Whatever compromise his Smectymnuan associates may have been entertaining, he stood among the most militant advocates of root-and-branch extirpation. *Of Reformation* ends in a rather foam-flecked flourish of vindictive eschatology in which he seems to be anticipating the execution of the bishops, for that is the likeliest interpretation of his phrase a 'shamefull end in this *Life* (which *God* grant them)' (i. 616). Thereafter he envisaged them:

thrown downe eternally into the *darkest* and *deepest Gulfe* of HELL, where under the *despightfull controule*, the trample and spurne of all the other *Damned*, that in the anguish of their *Torture* shall have no other ease then to exercise a *Raving* and *Bestiall Tyranny* over them as their *Slaves* and *Negro's*, they shall remaine in that plight for ever, the *basest*, the *lowermost*, the *most dejected*, most *underfoot* and *downe-trodden Vassals* of *Perdition* (i. 616–17).

It was difficult, perhaps, to think of the learned Ussher and the witty Hall in quite those terms, but it was *Of Reformation*'s intention to involve a broad spectrum of Puritan opinion in that uncompromising vision of prelacy, and that process relied heavily

[9] Trevor-Roper, *Catholics, Anglicans and Puritans*, 149.
[10] *CPW* i. 69–70, 1031.

on making convincing the polarity between author and reader, the godly you–me–us, and the unredeemably ungodly them, the bishops.

The argument of the tract contains a lacuna which had been present in the analogous postscript to the Smectymnuan *Answer*.[11] It offers a historical rhapsody in which English Protestant bishops are equated with pre-Reformation ones and indeed with the bishops of Constantine's day. Distinctions of period and denomination are tacitly suppressed; all represent the same perversion in the same way—English and Protestant share the same category as Catholics and foreigners, a category separate in every way from the godly. Barker and Lieb have remarked on the way in which Milton, to tidy up any blurring between the categories, evaluates Constantine and the Marian martyrs more hostilely than was customary in the Puritan tradition.[12] We are urged to regard all bishops as creatures apart, their alienness pronounced in terms which set them at times not only outside the ranks of the godly but outside the human species. With an aggression that redefines the decorum of the debate, in ways which invoke the idiom of the Elizabethan Marprelate campaign,[13] Milton offers them to us as grotesque ingestion machines, reduced to 'many-benefice-gaping' mouths, to 'canary-sucking' and 'swan-eating' palates (i. 249). Wolfe's comment, that Milton does not give credit to 'such an admirable man in private life as Ussher or Hall',[14] somewhat understates the position. Rather, he tries to sweep away the common ground, leaving the compromisers to build their new consensus over an abyss.

Of Reformation cannot work on a sensibility that is not already Puritan. Milton creates a location for the reader to occupy, but an episcopalian would find it untenable. Its full title signals its intended audience: *Of Reformation touching Church-Discipline in England: and the Causes that hitherto have Hindered It*. A supporter of prelacy would not have accepted that the English Reformation was

---

[11] *CPW* i. 961–75.

[12] A. Barker, *Milton and the Puritan Dilemma, 1641–1660* (Toronto, 1942), 33–4; M. Lieb, 'Milton's *Of Reformation* and the Dynamics of Controversy', in Lieb and Shawcross, 58.

[13] See T. Kranidas, '"Decorum" and the Style of Milton's Antiprelatical Tracts', *SP*, 62 (1965), 176–87, reprinted in S. E. Fish (ed.) *Seventeenth Century Prose: Modern Essays in Criticism* (New York, 1971), 475–88; and T. N. Corns, 'Obscenity, Slang and Indecorum in Milton's English Prose', *Prose Studies*, 3 (1980), 5–14.

[14] *CPW* i. 113.

less complete than elsewhere. Throughout, Milton assumes that the Church of England is corrupt and deviant—assumes, but never proves, because the audience he addresses already shares those assumptions. For the episcopalian, the image of bishops is unrecognizable, and the author's insistence on comradeship is denied: he knows Milton is no friend of his, nor he of Milton, and he turns away in shock and contempt. Indeed, we have some evidence of exactly that response. Thomas Fuller, a conciliatory episcopalian, remarked of the tract, 'One lately hath traduced them [bishops of the reformed Church of England] with such language, as neither beseemed his parts (whosoever he was) that spake it, nor their piety of whom it was spoken';[15] and John Bramhall, Ussher's eventual successor in the see of Armagh, observed, 'With what indignation doe all good Protestants see those blessed Men, now stiled in Print by a young novice, *halting and time-serving Prelates* . . . It was truely said by *Seneca*, that the most contemptible Persons ever have the loosest tongues.'[16] But the Puritan reader is secured, addressed as friend and comrade, and inserted alongside the author in the ranks of the godly. The charges of ignorance, corruption, brutality, and popish leanings, central to Milton's vision, had been commonplaces of the antiprelatical tradition since the Elizabethan period.[17] Even Puritan compromisers were weaned on such images, and, as the tract does its work, they are obliged to accept the polarization it postulates. Compromise with prelacy is to be taken off the agenda, but the friendship that Milton offers more than compensates for this constraint; for all the godly, he defines the prospect of a celestial triumph, when they 'shall clasp inseparable Hands with *joy*, and *blisse* in over measure for ever' (i. 616).

III

Milton's second antiprelatical pamphlet, *Of Prelatical Episcopacy* (London, 1641), engaged more directly some recent episcopalian texts, specifically, Joseph Hall's *Episcopacie by Divine Right*

[15] T. Fuller, *The Holy State* (London, 1642), 291–2; quoted in *LR* ii. 52–3.
[16] J. Bramhall, *The Serpents Salve, or, A Remedie for the Biting of an Aspe* (London, 1643); quoted in *LR* ii. 83.
[17] Corns, 'Obscenity', 7–8; R. A. Anselment, *'Betwixt Jest and Earnest': Marprelate, Milton, Marvell, Swift and the Decorum of Religious Ridicule* (Toronto, Buffalo, and London, 1979), 61–93.

Asserted (London, 1640), James Ussher's *Judgement of Doctor Rainoldes touching the Originall of Episcopacy* (London, 1641), and perhaps also *A Compendious Discourse, Proving Episcopacy to be of Apostolicall and Consequently of Divine Institution* (London, 1641) by Peloni Almoni.[18] The titles of the last two indicate well enough the strategy of these publications. Theirs was a defence of episcopal church government based very largely on the demonstration, documented from patristic accounts, of its antiquity. Milton's purpose in *Of Prelatical Episcopacy* is clear and alarmingly simple, and that is to discredit such arguments by discrediting the sources on which they are premissed. Patrick, the Yale editor, offers this sympathetic appreciation of what Milton does:

The greatness of Milton's tract lies less in his scholarship and reasoning than in his brilliant debating. Although he chose to be no more exact in method than as the citations of his opponents led him, he utilized almost all the rhetorical skills and devices of classical oratory. Consequently his total effect is so satisfying and so overwhelming that the opposing arguments tend to be forgotten. He was attempting to address a wider public than the erudite theologians and scholars to whom Ussher's pamphlet would have appealed. As a result, Milton pleads the case for the equality of presbyters and bishops as if he were a lawyer defending a client.[19]

This seems a curious combination of great astuteness and ethical special pleading. Certainly, we may savour the well-observed paradox that in this debate Milton is the populist, seeking out a larger audience than the divines Ussher may primarily be addressing. More significantly though, Milton, edging towards Independency, was incubating disruptively radical notions about the role of the laity in the work of completing the Reformation, nor was he himself in holy orders for all his evident obsessions with matters of doctrine and church government. Milton sensibly speaks to the Puritans in Parliament and to those who constituted the metropolitan ground swell against prelacy. The objective remains, as in *Of Reformation*, of so souring the political atmosphere that reconciliation becomes impossible. But Patrick, quite literally, takes Milton's word for the validity of the way in which he handles evidence, echoing closely his promise, 'I shall not strive to be more exact in Methode, then as their citations lead mee' (*Of Prelatical Episcopacy*, *CPW* i. 627).

---

[18] *CPW* i. 618–19.
[19] Ibid. 619.

Patrick endorses the 'greatness' of a pamphlet which, on his own account and Milton's, relegates the meticulous appraisal of evidence and dismisses a proper consideration of opposite views ('opposing arguments tend to be forgotten'), and which locates the discourse in the context, not of academic investigation where it belongs, but of forensic rhetoric. Some may regard these as unusual traits for a scholar to value.

Discussions of the antiquity of episcopal church government depended largely on the interpretation of a nucleus of patristic texts to which controversialists persistently reverted. With some justice Hall referred, perhaps for once rather impatiently, to 'The testimonies of *Irenoeus, Tertullian, Cyprian, Basil, Theodoret, Hierome, Ambrose, Augustine, Sidonius,* and others . . . so familiarly quoted by all Writers, that I shall not need to urge them'.[20] Milton considered a good few of these patristic writers, or rather he took their evidence, for, except when he was considering the process of transmission (and thus the possibility of corruption), he proceeded as if the books were living men to be summoned, interrogated, and dismissed:

Now come the Epistles of *Ignatius* to shew us first, that . . . (i. 635).

Next follows *Irenoeus* Bishop of *Lions* (i. 639).

Tertullian accosts us next (for *Polycrates* had his answer) (i. 644).

Persistently he adopted the familiar forensic mechanism of discrediting the evidence by discrediting the reliability of the witness in other contexts.

Consider his treatment of Irenaeus, whose testimony was widely regarded as proof of the apostolic status of episcopacy.[21] Hall interpreted the evidence straightforwardly and with characteristic clarity:

Polycarpus, saith he [Irenaeus], was not only taught by the Apostles, conversed with many of them who saw our Lord Christ, but also was by the Apostles made Bishop in *Asia*, in that Church which is at *Smyrna*, whom we our selves saw in younger age, for he lasted long, and being old, he most nobly and gloriously suffering Martyrdome, passed out of this life! Lo here was but one ages difference, *Polycarpus* saw, and conversed with the Apostles, *Irenoeus* saw *Polycarpus*; by their hands was he ordained Bishop, constantly lived and dyed a Martyr in that holy function.[22]

---

[20] Joseph Hall, *Episcopacie by Divine Right Asserted* (London, 1640), sig. Ll4ᵛ.
[21] *CPW* i. 639.
[22] Hall, *Episcopacie*, sig. Ll4ᵛ.

Irenaeus's evidence related not to matters of doctrine or interpretation but to the recollection of historical fact: Polycarpus told him that he had been apostolically ordained bishop of Smyrna. While Hall's account is simple and lucid, Milton's response is complex and specious. He begins with a point Hall conceded: yes, indeed, when he met Polycarpus, 'he was a Boy' (i. 640), and a child's testimony is perhaps not necessarily as trustworthy as an adult's. Milton, though, shifts very rapidly to a larger attack on Irenaeus and the age he lived in. He locates in another patristic writer (whose objectivity and motivation, this time, he chooses not to question) a hint of scandal. Eusebius writes about one Papias, 'a very ancient writer, one that had heard St. *Iohn*' but who 'fill'd his writings with many new doctrines, and fabulous conceits'. According to Eusebius, Irenaeus subscribed to some of these heresies. Now Hall and his confrères cited him not as a touchstone of doctrinal authenticity but as a witness to a fact. But Milton concludes, 'if *Irenoeus* were so rash as to take unexamin'd opinions from an Author of so small capacity, when he was a man, we should be more rash our selves to rely upon those observations which he made when he was a Boy' (i. 641). Milton, I feel sure, understood the difference between trusting opinions and making observations: a heretic can report honestly and accurately what somebody once told him. Moreover, as Kranidas points out, Milton's use of the evidence of Eusebius is further complicated since his testimony 'follows a touching injunction to "keep those truly saintly men of an earlier generation in mind, as a splendid example of meticulous accuracy"',[23] which runs somewhat counter to Milton's practice. The case well illustrates the utter ruthlessness with which Milton picks over the evidence; patristic testimony has no validity except as a source of invalidating patristic evidence.

Milton's dismissal of Irenaeus depends on a personal attack, despite his cool assurances to his readers that it was a fault with the immediately post-apostolic age that believers were more concerned with personalities than with appraising texts; they 'heeded more the person, then the Doctrine' (i. 641). With verve he constructs a vision of life in an early Christian community:

with less fervency was studied what Saint *Paul*, or Saint *Iohn* had written

---

[23] T. Kranidas, 'Words, Words, Words, and the Word: Milton's *Of Prelatical Episcopacy*', *Milton Studies*, 16 (1982), 159.

then was listen'd to one that could say here hee taught, here he stood, this was his stature, and thus he went habited, and O happy this house that harbour'd him, and that cold stone whereon he rested, this Village wherein he wrought such a miracle, and that pavement bedew'd with the warme effusion of his last blood, that sprouted up into eternall Roses to crowne his Martyrdome (i. 641–2).

Note the schema of mounting grandiloquence: an exclamation ('O happy this house'), an antithetical and pathetic arrangement of 'that cold stone' and the 'warme effusion', the poetic word ('bedew'd'[24]), and the absurd hagiographical detail of the eternal roses. Milton's reconstruction appears unsupported by evidence. He does not (and could not) prove that the average early Christian subordinated Bible-study to story-swapping. Rather, the account inhabits the easy ground of commonsensical assumption that generally feeds such smears.[25] The real issues are subordinated to a rhapsody exploiting what Milton would have readers believe they know about village life and about earlier times.

Milton's final assault on Irenaeus involves associating him with Catholicism. Alluding to his statements about the Virgin Mary, he claims, 'if *Irenoeus* for his neerenesse to the *Apostles*, must be the Patron of *Episcopacy* to us, it is no marvell though he be the Patron of Idolatry to the Papist, for the same cause' (i. 642). The Yale editor quotes anonymous seventeenth-century marginalia to a copy of *Of Prelatical Episcopacy* which recognize that Milton's case rests on a tendentiously hostile reading: 'As for those 2. places out of Irenaeus. Let any sober man peruse them and they are capable of a faire and harmles interpretation. But this writer doth purposely twist in the worst sense to discredit the Father.'[26] The taint of popery completes the character assassination, though even if Irenaeus had been a proto-Catholic he could still have remembered what Polycarp said to him. Milton's asseveration, that 'wee have cause to thinke him lesse judicious in his reports from hand to hand of what the *Apostles* did, when we find him so negligent in keeping the *faith* which they writ' (i. 642), is brazenly illogical, but convincing to those ready to be convinced.

---

[24] Marked as characteristically used in poetic or rhetorical discourse (*OED*).

[25] For an interesting analogue, compare the attack on the presentation of petitions on behalf of John Wilkes, in Samuel Johnson, *The False Alarm*, in *The Political Writings of Dr Johnson*, ed. J. P. Hardy (London, 1963), 54–5.

[26] *CPW* i. 642 n. 57.

Milton's comments in the 1640s on the practice of law are generally rather negative, despite (or perhaps because of) his friendship with jurists, his family connections with the profession—brother Christopher was a lawyer—and his family's enthusiasm for litigation.[27] Yet the construction of a forensic frame of reference organizes the dialectic of *Of Prelatical Episcopacy*, in sharp contrast with the three texts he primarily engages, all of which present a straightforward, scholarly exposition of the historical evidence. But the forensic context implied in Milton's pamphlet is not the open courtroom of English common law, with trial before an impartial judge and a jury of one's peers, but rather Milton speaks as if he and we, the readers, constitute together the body before whom malefactors and witnesses are interrogated. The discourse model is not a common-law court but an equity court such as the by then defunct Star Chamber committee.

Once more, pronominalization crucially defines the relationship. Here Milton scarcely ever addresses his readers as 'you'; rather, he makes statements about what 'we' know and how 'we' perceive the evidence:

That other legendarie piece found among the lives of the Saints, and sent us from the shop of the Jesuites at *Lovain*, does but bear the name of *Polycrates*, how truly who can tell? and shall have some more weight with us, when *Polycrates* can perswade us of that which he affirms in the same place of *Eusebius* 5. Book, that St. *John* was a Priest, and wore the golden brestplate: and why should he convince us more with his traditions of *Timothy's* Episcopacie, then he could convince *Victor* Bishop of *Rome* with his traditions concerning the Feast of Easter, who not regarding his irrefragable instances of examples taken from *Philip*, and his daughters that were Prophetesses; or from *Polycarpus*, no nor from St. *Iohn* himselfe, excommunicated both him, and all the Asian Churches for celebrating their Easter judaically: he may therfore go back to the seaven Bishops his kinsmen, and make his moane to them that we esteem his traditionall ware, as lightly as *Victor* did (i. 633–4).

Milton establishes for his readers a set of positions which he articulates on our behalf. He voices our scepticism about a text of Polycrates, involving us in a seemingly shared set of assumptions about Continental Catholic scholarship ('the shop of the Jesuites at

---

[27] See e.g. *Of Reformation*, *CPW* i. 539 and *Eikonoklastes*, *CPW* iii. 403; on his father's court-cases, see e.g. *LR* ii. 13–14; on his brother, called to the Bar in 1640, see W. R. Parker, *Milton: A Biography* (Oxford, 1968), i. 189.

Lovain'). He establishes a series of reservations about the authenticity or orthodoxy of other views attributed to Polycrates. He raises to our collective recollection his excommunication by Victor, bishop of Rome, for his heterodox views on the calculation of Easter, and offers as our agreed resolve ('that we esteem') the dismissal of his evidence for apostolically sanctioned episcopacy. Milton speaks as if from within a configuration of authorized enquirers whose collective values and assumptions he voices. A little later, like a good colleague, he manifests impatience with people who are wasting our time: 'I wonder that men teachers of the Protestant Religion, make no more difficulty of imposing upon our belief a supposititious ofspring of some dozen Epistles' (i. 635).

Generally, when Milton does speak of 'I', he shifts rapidly to incorporate his readers into a 'we' of shared belief or response, as in:

but this I purpose not to take advantage of, for what availes it to wrangle about the corrupt editions of Councells, when as we know that many yeares ere this which was almost 500. years after *Christ*, the Councels themselvs were fouly corrupted with ungodly Prelatisme (i. 629).

The 'we' that regards episcopacy as a corruption and as 'ungodly' cannot include any who do not already share a Puritan theory of church government. The location which Milton leaves for his readers and which he asserts he shares is already deeply polarized from the writers he attacks and admits of no real dialogue with them.

Of Prelatical Episcopacy has attracted infrequent but sometimes very acute critical responses. Kranidas has developed an astute argument around the apparent paradox that Milton's case is really made in the opening page: 'The battle is won in the first twenty lines. Episcopacy is either of divine constitution or human. If only human, we can take it or leave it. If divine, the only authority is Scripture. But nowhere in Scripture . . . is there found "any difference betweene a Bishop, and a Presbyter" [i. 625]. Ergo, we can leave it.'[28] Fish, building on Kranidas's interpretation, views it as a tract about supplementarity, about Milton's argument against attaching supplement to the divine Word, which is fraught with paradoxical implications:

My thesis . . . is that Milton . . . is uneasy about his performance . . . In a

---

[28] 'Words', 154–5.

word, that performance is superfluous, and because it is superfluous, it is also, potentially at least, impious. If the scripture is fully able to satisfy us, there is no need to say anything else, and since the fullness of scripture is the tract's first assertion, it is over before it begins. At the same time that the opening sentences promise to adjudicate between the respective claims of scripture and tradition, scripture is declared to be the judge of the dispute, and almost immediately the tract finds itself all dressed up with nowhere to go. Indeed going somewhere is precisely the error it wishes to avoid, as from the very first danger and impiety are associated with movement.[29]

Kranidas and Fish comment very acutely, though their interpretations need contextualizing historically. For Fish, who remarks (accurately, I feel—I had missed the point) that 'we never notice that the *scripture is nowhere cited*',[30] Milton's practice not only seems curiously fissured but also contrasts sharply with the exegetical impulse manifest two years later in *The Doctrine and Discipline of Divorce*. I believe it points rather to the utterly negative and reactive way in which Milton characteristically develops his argument. As we shall see, only rarely in his prose does he address an issue as if unprompted by the exigencies of debate, and when he does so he is at once at his most open and vulnerable. Very often, the reader must reconstruct what his thesis is from the dismantled remains of the thesis he has destroyed. Thus, though he removes the historical argument for prelacy, he leaves the argument for alternative systems of church government implied but not stated. Here, the case for regarding the evidence of Scripture without regard to apostolic and patristic tradition remains to be reconstructed by Fish and other astute interpreters. But the reader, too, is a historically determined entity, and Milton's target readership is not among those who need conviction—he seeks the assent only of Puritan confrères in *Of Reformation* and *Of Prelatical Episcopacy*—rather they need reassurance of the rightness of their cause and they need motivation to translate theory into practice. Much of Milton's dialectic has been directed towards the excitement of prejudices, opinions, and values latent within his readers.

Milton strikes a similar author–reader relationship and a similarly negative and reactive posture in his third tract in the antiprelatical campaign, *Animadversions upon the Remonstrants*

---

[29] S. Fish, 'Wanting a Supplement: The Question of Interpretation in Milton's Early Prose', in Loewenstein and Turner, 44.   [30] Ibid. 52, his emphasis.

Defence against Smectymnuus (London, 1641), the title of which marks the battlefields of the controversy. This is a point-by-point reply to Joseph Hall's reply to Smectymnuus's reply to his *Humble Remonstrance to the High Court of Parliament* (London, 1640), an ingenious and urbane attempt to persuade the new Puritan ascendancy to treat episcopacy in a more conciliatory fashion than root-and-branch militants would have wanted.

Once more Milton offers himself in an intimately co-operative role:

> if it bee ask't why this close and succinct manner of coping with the Adversary was rather chosen, this was the reason, chiefly that the ingenuous Reader without further amusing himselfe in the labyrinth of controversall antiquity, may come the speediest way to see the truth vindicated, and Sophistry taken short at the first false bound (*Animadversions, CPW* i. 664).[31]

Hall had objected that his first pamphlet had been countered not by one scholar but by a consortium of Smectymnuans.[32] Milton, too, persistently speaks this language of 'we' and 'us', but he does so on behalf of something rather more potent than a group of divines: Milton speaks for godly England. Once more, the readership is remorselessly incorporated into his denunciation of episcopacy.

Of Reformation had simulated some of the conventions of personal epistolary address, and *Of Prelatical Episcopacy* those of forensic oratory; *Animadversions* gestures towards simulating those of academic disputation, with Milton as spokesman of a configuration which insistently embraces the readers:

> Ere a foot furder we must bee content to heare a preambling boast of your valour . . . shew us any one point of your *Remonstrance* that do's not more concern superiority, pride, ease and the belly, then the truth and glory of God, or the salvation of souls. . . . Doe not think to Perswade us of your undaunted courage (i. 665).

'You' and 'your' refer to Bishop Hall. Though Milton occasionally detaches the reader from the 'we' that speaks, the severance is only temporary:

---

[31] 'Ingenuous', here, is probably a vague term of approbation, 'noble in nature, character, or disposition' (*OED*, sig. 2).
[32] See *CPW* i. 664–5 for Hall's comment and Milton's response.

We see you are in choler, therefore till you coole a while wee turne us to the ingenious[33] Reader. See how this *Remonstrant* would invest himselfe conditionally with all the rheume of the Towne, that he might have sufficient to bespaul his Brethren. They are accus'd by him of uncharitable falshood, whereas their onely crime hath beene that they have too credulously thought him if not an over-logicall, yet a well-meaning man; but now we find him either grossly deficient in his principles of *Logick*, or else purposely bent to delude the Parliament (i. 693–4).

Milton turns to his reader, suspends him from his assumed consent, smooths him with compliments ('ingenious Reader'), directs his attention ('See how'), and feeds him with evidence ('whereas their onely crime'), before he is finally reabsorbed into the appropriate way of perceiving Hall ('but now we find him').

Animadversions engages Hall with a level of aggression Smectymnuus never aspired to. After all, they were junior ministers of the ecclesiastical community of which Hall was a bishop; moreover, even as they refuted him, some of them were in secret negotiation to find a compromise with his version of post-Laudian episcopacy. In any case, in a sense, Hall simply outclassed them. The so-called 'English Seneca', he brought a distinctive and accomplished prose style into the service of a well-conceived polemical strategy. Never discourteous, but exuding an effortless superiority, he talks to the Smectymnuans as brothers—but as younger brothers.[34] While Hall could despatch with a wristy elegance the gentle medium-pace of Smectymnuus's attack, Milton's faster, shorter, merciless bodyline deliveries are a tougher prospect:

Remon. [i.e. Hall] Brethren [the Smectymnuans] whiles yee desire to seeme Godly, learne to be less malitious.

Ans. Remonstrant, till you have better learnt your principles of Logick, take not upon you to be a Doctor to others.

Remon. God blesses all good men from such charity.

Ans. I never found that Logicall maxims were uncharitable before, yet should a Jury of Logicians passe upon you, you would never be sav'd by the Book.

Remon. And our Sacred Monarchy from such friends.

Ans. Adde, as the Prelates.   .

---

[33] Probably an alternative form of 'ingenuous' (*OED*); see above, n. 31.

[34] 'Brethren' is Hall's customary recurrent term for the Smectymnuans (*A Defence of the Humble Remonstrance* (London, 1641), *passim*).

Remon. If Episcopacy have yoked Monarch, it is the Insolence of the Persons, not of the Calling.

Ans. It was the fault of the persons, and of no Calling, we doe not count Prelatry a Calling (i. 673).

Though it assumes some aspect of a dialogic form, such writing works to exclude real dialogue, a point epitomized perhaps in the exchange:

Remon. No one Clergie in the whole Christian world yeelds so many eminent schollers, learned preachers, grave, holy and accomplish'd Divines as this Church of *England* doth at this day.

Answ. Ha, ha, ha (i. 726).

Scarcely a Wildean response, but adequate for the purpose in that it excludes a polite reply. People in the posture Milton strikes cannot be argued with rationally, but Milton does not seek argument: rather, he looks to advance the campaign beyond negotiation into the irreversible destruction of episcopacy.

We have no evidence how the Smectymnuans perceived Milton's contribution. The episcopalian response was the heavy-handed character assassination attempted in the anonymous[35] *Modest Confutation of a Slanderous and Scurrilous Libell, Entituled, Animadversions* (London, 1642), which attempts to construct a pejorative image of Milton from the internal evidence of his tract. He is represented through a mishmash of elements familiar from traditional anti-Puritan propaganda, as an ignorant, hungry divine, looking for a fat living and a prosperous widow, denouncing the corruption of prelates while disclosing his own familiarity with the whore-house.[36] Milton felt stung to respond, but in a sense the episcopalian response was a triumph for the strategy of *Animadversions*, in that he had drawn his adversaries out from the posture of sweet reasonableness they had assumed into a crudely adversarial attack, not really upon Milton, but rather upon a ghost of Milton, a stereotypical Puritan divine, and their hostility to that figure subverts the conciliatory approaches Williams, Hall, and Ussher were developing: evidently, the leopard had not changed its spots. Milton revived a stereotype too. If his enemies' image of him could

---

[35] Milton thought it was probably the work of Hall and one of his sons; for a review of the evidence, see *CPW* i. 863.

[36] Anon., *A Modest Confutation of a Slanderous and Scurrilous Libell, Entituled, Animadversions* (London, 1642), 9, 34, 36–7, sig. A3^{r-v}. The text is reproduced in W. R. Parker, *Milton's Contemporary Reputation* (1940; New York, 1971), 123–69.

have been scripted by Ben Jonson, his version of Hall owed much to
Marprelate. Critically, however, Milton gained by the exchange. A
polarization along the lines of the 1580s or the early Jacobean
period served his case as surely as it undermined Hall's.

IV

For over six months after the publication of *Animadversions* Milton
was silent. His next pamphlet, *The Reason of Church-Government
Urg'd against Prelaty*, constituted a subtle but crucial development
in the way in which he presented himself to his readers. Previously,
he had offered himself in the role of collaborator in the final phase
of a Puritan reformation conceived in terms of the extirpation of
prelacy and the establishment of Presbyterianism on the Genevan
model. He appears as the embodiment of a collective voice,
distinguished only by his eloquent vehemence. Though this posture
persists into *The Reason of Church-Government*, a new role
emerges. The speaker produced within the text is no longer the
anonymous acolyte of Presbyterianism. A distinct self-image is
produced in terms of youth, integrity, and creativity. The author, as
he speaks, describes the process of his thoughts, how he has come
by his perceptions and how they are developing. At times, he
seemingly soliloquizes. Nor does this figure so straightforwardly
assume the complicity of his readers in his system of values.

Superficially, much about the tract is familiar. Like *Of Prelatical
Episcopacy* and *Of Reformation*, it is a response in the name of
Presbyterian Puritanism to a particular episcopalian initiative,
*Certain Briefe Treatises, Written by Diverse Learned Men, concerning
the Ancient and Modern Government of the Church* (Oxford,
1641), a compilation, 'perhaps assembled by archbishop Ussher
himself', of short works by eight divines, of whom only Ussher and
John Dury were still living.[37] Milton takes us through our
evaluation of their arguments: 'We may returne now from this
interposing difficulty thus remov'd, to affirme, that since Church-
government is so strictly commanded in Gods word, the first and
greatest reason why we should submit thereto, is . . .' (*The Reason
of Church-Government*, *CPW* i. 761). He concedes points, engages
arguments, and develops a case in our name: 'We acknowledge that
the civill magistrate weares an authority . . . But to make a King a

---

[37] *CPW* i. 738.

type, we say is . . .' (i. 771). In this collective mode, he establishes an ersatz dialogue with the episcopalians: 'But how O Prelats should you remove schisme . . . ? The remedy which you alledge is the very disease we groan under; and never can be to us a remedy but by removing it selfe' (i. 791).

Compared with *Animadversions*, *The Reason of Church-Government* characteristically operates at some remove from the object of its attack. In contrast with the pattern of quotation and observation, allusion here is generally vague. Rather than dismantling *Certain Briefe Treatises* sentence by sentence, he produces a collective prelatical position which offers an easier target: 'For wherein, or in what worke is the office of a Prelat excellent above that of a Pastor? in ordination you'l say; but flatly against the Scripture, for there we know . . .' (i. 767). The 'you' seems to be no identifiable speaker, nor does what 'you'l say' correspond very closely to what anyone actually says in *Certain Briefe Treatises*. It is on offer as the response of a typical episcopalian. Chess is a less demanding game when one may move one's opponent's pieces.

Yet the author produced in the text cannot be contained within the comfortable reader-relationship posited in the earlier tracts. As many have remarked, this was the first pamphlet to carry Milton's name on the title-page. Caution can scarcely explain its earlier omission, since all three bore the name of the bookseller Thomas Underhill.[38] If the Puritan revolution had been rapidly reversed, reinstated Laudian authorities could have tracked Milton down and dealt with him easily enough. Nor can it simply be that he felt he had finally produced something worth putting his name to. He always had an almost reverential respect for the product of his own pen,[39] and he made sure that copies of the first three tracts were lodged in the Bodleian Library. He gave George Thomason a copy of *Of Reformation* for his collection, and Thomason's copies of the other two are possibly gifts also.[40] It is unlikely then that Milton put his name to *The Reason of Church-Government* simply because he thought it worthier than the others.

But the authorial acknowledgement accords completely with the radically new self-image produced within it, no longer the collective

---

[38] On Underhill, who was new to the trade, see Plomer.

[39] T. N. Corns, 'New Light on the Left Hand: Contemporary Views of Milton's Prose Style', *Durham University Journal*, 72 (1980), 177–9.

[40] *LR* ii. 138–9, 35, 38.

spokesman, but an individual asserting his difference from the broad movement and developing an argument with it.

Through the central motif of the author agonistes, Milton stresses the importance of struggle and personal enlightenment in the active search for purity: 'if any man incline to thinke I undertake a taske too difficult for my yeares, I trust through the supreme inlightning assistance farre otherwise; for my yeeres, be they few or many, what imports it?' (i. 749). While *Of Prelatical Episcopacy*, as Fish remarks, offers ultimately an argument for the Scripture unsupplemented by human endeavour, *The Reason of Church-Government* presents the work of reformation in much more complicated terms, as the action of the inner light of the Holy Spirit on both the evidence and the prevailing political circumstance. Yet it is curious that Milton should thus emphasize his youthfulness, with its suggestion of inexperience.

Adversaries had already accused him of immaturity.[41] In fact, Milton was 34, not an especially young age for participating in religious controversy in the mid seventeenth century. Of the fifty members of the Westminster Assembly of Divines whose ages Masson supplies, 12 per cent were in their thirties and 2 per cent in their twenties,[42] and many prominent activists of the 1640s were Milton's junior. Fairfax was commanding the New Model Army by the time he was 34; Prince Rupert of the Rhine commanded the royalist cavalry at 23.[43]

Yet the alleged youthfulness fits a self-portrait of the author in tentative enquiry, relying not on received Puritan dogma nor even on unmediated Scripture but on personal illumination: 'I shall use such light as I have receav'd' (i. 765). Sometimes the present tense connotes searching as an active, continuous process: 'the more I search, the more I grow into all perswasion to think . . . that . . .' (i. 782). The organicism of 'grow into all perswasion' suggests at once the involuntary working of the Holy Spirit within and the provisional nature of his current position: growth admits the possibility of future change. Occasionally Milton seems to stand outside his ratiocination as if to comment upon it:

But heer again I find my thoughts almost in suspense betwixt yea and no,

---

[41] John Bramhall had called him 'a young novice' (ibid. ii. 83); the Modest Confuter adopted a similar line (Anon., *Modest Confutation, passim*).

[42] D. Masson, *The Life of John Milton* (London, 1877–94), ii. 516–23.

[43] *DNB*.

and am nigh turning mine eye which way I may best retire, and not proceed in this subject, blaming the ardency of my mind that fixt me too attentively to come thus farre (i. 830).

Writing of such introversion appears rarely in contemporary controversy. Milton turns from the conflict to consider the working of his own mind, to assess the state of his own knowledge and his uncertainty, in a way that relates to the long autobiographical digression at the heart of the text. Here Milton spends about 3,000 words in describing his poetic ambitions, his dedication to Christian poetry, the experience of his tour of Italy and the reception of his poetry there (i. 804–23). The account itself manifests some ambivalence in that Milton at once proclaims utter commitment to the vocation of the poet and his frustration at losing the chance of ecclesiastical preferment because of discrimination against Puritans— his notion that he has been 'Church-outed by the Prelats' (i. 823)— though, of course, poets as diverse as Herbert and Herrick contemporaneously combined both vocations. Whatever its limitations as a source of biographical information (understandably, it has been frequently picked over), the passage establishes a powerful image of the reluctant participant in controversy, cherishing a sense both of his uniqueness and of his separateness from entrenched partisanship:

I trust hereby to make it manifest with what small willingnesse I endure to interrupt the pursuit of no lesse hopes then these, and leave a calme and pleasing solitarynes fed with cherful and confident thoughts, to imbark in a troubl'd sea of noises and hoars disputes, put from beholding the bright countenance of truth in the quiet and still air of delightfull studies to come into the dim reflexion of hollow antiquities sold by the seeming bulk, and there be fain to club quotations with men whose learning and belief lies in marginal stuffings (i. 821–2).

A new polarity emerges; in place of the distinction between the godly and the prelates, he offers a distinction between withdrawn liberal and humanistic enquiry and the scuffles of controversy, the former characterized by gentlemanly contemplation, the latter really no more than a trade, where learning, like more physical produce, is 'sold by the seeming bulk'. The phrase, 'troubl'd sea of noises and hoars disputes', implying reservations about the dialectic of both sides in the debate, surely suggests disenchantment with his co-workers. Only with reluctance and regret has he enlisted, in obedience to a higher and inner prompting that makes grave demands of its servants: 'But were it the meanest under-service, if God by his Secretary conscience injoyn it, it were sad for me if I should draw back' (i. 822).

The Reason of Church-Government is characterized by an uncertain transition from the voice that speaks collectively from within the Presbyterian position to the assertion of the centrality of individual perception and conscience. As such, it accords well with Milton's position in the developing crisis. By the summer of 1642, the fragile nature of the united Puritan opposition to the old order had been disclosed. Milton had come to recognize problematic elements in his own alignment.

The ostensible object of the pamphlet, the refutation of *Certain Briefe Treatises*, is elbowed aside by the urgent emergence of another issue, scarcely mentioned by Ussher or his associates, but of growing significance: the status of sects. The topic is almost new to Milton's writing. The words 'sect(s)', 'sectaries', 'schism(s)', 'schismatic(s)', and 'schismatical' altogether occur only six times in the first three antiprelatical pamphlets, and seventy times in *The Reason of Church-Government*.[44] Milton returns almost neurotically to the subject, and as he writes a welter of scarcely compatible positions emerge.

At times he concedes that sects constitute unacceptable heterodoxies. He speaks of 'sects and heresies', 'sects and errors' (i. 795). He suggests their persistence is useful only in that, by offering resistible temptations, they permit the godly to remain, duly exercised, in their true faith: 'These are but winds and flaws to try the floting vessell of our faith whether it be stanch and sayl well' (i. 794). He claims that there are too few sectaries to concern sober Christians and that their numbers are exaggerated by prelatical propaganda:

As for those many Sects and divisions rumor'd to be amongst us, it is not hard to perceave that they are partly the meere fictions and false alarmes of the Prelates, thereby to cast amazements and panick terrors into the hearts of weaker Christians that they should not venture to change the present deformity of the Church for fear of I know not what worse inconveniences (i. 794).

A minor problem, then, tendentiously distorted to cause panic,

---

[44] Information drawn from L. Sterne and H. H. Kollmeier (eds.), *A Concordance to the English Prose of John Milton* (Binghamton, N.Y., 1985).

though Milton here still acknowledges the sects to be a problem. A little later, he suggests that deviations from orthodoxy are the temporary concomitant of reform which may later be tidied up:

No wonder then in the reforming of a Church which is never brought to effect without the fierce encounter of truth and falshood together, if, as it were the splinters and shares of so violent a jousting, there fall from between the shock many fond errors and fanatick opinions, which when truth has the upper hand, and the reformation shall be perfeted, will easily be rid out of the way, or kept so low, as that they shall be only the exercise of our knowledge, not the disturbance, or interruption of our faith (i. 796).

Milton clearly indicates a hostility to sects—they are the litter produced incidentally to the important conflict with prelacy, 'fanatick', associated with 'errors', and evidently scheduled for elimination ('rid out of the way'). Those which survive will remain rather like specimens in a rare breeds park, and function as material for the intellectual games of the godly, a category ('our faith') which once more embraces author and reader.

   Yet elsewhere in the pamphlet Milton discloses warmth for sectarian dissent. As he meets the claim that prelacy alone can control heresy and schism he produces a complex image of a cultural revolution:

The Winter might as well vaunt it selfe against the Spring, I destroy all noysome and rank weeds, I keepe downe all pestilent vapours. Yes and all wholesome herbs, and all fresh dews, by your violent & hidebound frost; but when the gentle west winds shall open the fruitfull bosome of the earth thus over-girded by your imprisonment, then the flowers put forth and spring, and then the Sunne shall scatter the mists, and the manuring hand of the Tiller shall root up all that burdens the soile without thank to your bondage (i. 785).

Opinions suppressed by the prelates could grow into weeds or into 'wholesome herbs'. Major doctrinal issues may not be simply resolved once and for all. Milton argues for patience and scepticism: a tolerationalist approach will permit what is necessary for reformation to manifest itself. The image of the Tiller, clearly derived from the parable of the tares,[45] retains its chiliastic implications, anticipating the millenary completion of the reformation in which deviance will be suppressed but only by divine intervention. Christ alone can determine surely the relative status of

[45] Matt. 13: 24–30.

heterodoxies, some of which may be essential for the work in progress.

Milton envisages that the constituents appropriate for the reformed religion will include believers currently outside Presbyterian Calvinism, a sentiment most radically and adversarially expressed in 'Noise it till ye be hoarse; that a rabble of Sects will come in, it will be answer'd ye, no rabble sir Priest, but a unanimous multitude of good Protestants will then joyne the Church, which now because of you stand separated' (i. 787–8). He means, not Presbyterians like the Smectymnuans still within the Church of England, but the 'Brethren of the Separation', those former Brownists who had withdrawn from a church they believed incapable of reformation, a position that was contemporaneously mutating into Congregational Independency. Milton offers a vision of a national church much looser in its management of doctrinal disagreement and capable of permitting the fruitful coexistence of dissenting voices and beliefs.

Milton's attitudes towards the crisis developing within Puritanism were as complex and confused as his attitudes towards his readers or his notion of his place in the larger movement. Fish was nearly right when he remarked of this tract, 'The silent claim made by the logical superstructure merely marks out areas within which the reader, or at least one class of reader, experiences a series of recognitions (or rememberings) of what he has always known to be true; and these recognitions occur independently of the pressure exerted by numbered chapters, divisions into books, first or second reasons, "thuses" and "therefores".'[46] But the work, at its core, has little of the declaratory certainty that he attributes to it. This jittery, jumbled tract does not 'jump up and down', in the phrase Fish adopts,[47] so much as back and forth, shifting between irreconcilable alternatives. He still adopts the collective language of Puritan orthodoxy and he still asserts the validity of Presbyterianism—no one can find 'any crookednes, any wrincle or spot . . . in presbyterial government' (i. 834)—but simultaneously he offers the voice of individual conscience and inner light and the associated case for the toleration of heterodoxy. In the latter mode, Milton articulated surprisingly early a kind of licence for personal illumination that was to become the characteristic of theological radicals in

[46] S. E. Fish, *Self-Consuming Artifacts: The Experience of Seventeenth-Century Literature* (Berkeley, Los Angeles, and London, 1972), 280–1.
[47] Ibid. 290.

the later 1640s and in the 1650s. His personal agenda appears confused: one moment he contemplates, with seeming confidence, the completion of the work of reformation; the next, he regrets the necessity of his participation and wishes himself elsewhere, writing poetry. The unconcealed confusions make it a more open and curiously vulnerable pamphlet, representing microcosmically the crisis in the Puritan movement in the early 1640s.

His last tract in the antiprelatical group, *An Apology against a Pamphlet call'd A Modest Confutation of the Animadversions upon the Remonstrant against Smectymnuus* (London, 1642), could scarcely be more determined by the exigencies of the by now attenuated debate. Polemical exigencies required Milton once more to narrow the focus and to behave with the care that the proximity of cunning adversaries required, while at the same time the form of the personal apologia permitted development of his new concern with establishing and managing an image of himself. Thereafter, from April 1642 to August 1643, Milton published nothing. Certainly, the spiral into civil war marginalized the issue of the reform of church government.[48] When he returned to print, however, a new voice articulated a new radical perspective.

[48] Corns, 'Publication and Politics', 78.

3

Milton as Heretic and Poet

MILTON published nothing between April 1642 and August 1643. In August 1642, probably despairing of alternative strategies, Charles I had raised his banner to muster a royal army, practically and symbolically initiating the English Civil War. October saw the gory stalemate of Edgehill; November, Rupert's march on London, halted at Turnham Green when he decided against engaging the trained bands that had advanced to meet him; thereafter both sides campaigned actively over numerous theatres of war. Milton made no explicit allusion to the war in print before November 1644, nor is there any evidence that he joined or sought to join any unit of the parliamentary army. Indeed, the only composition with political implications that can with confidence be attributed to the period between his last antiprelatical pamphlet and the first divorce tract is the extraordinary sonnet which begins 'Captain or colonel, or knight in arms'.

This appears in the Trinity Manuscript under the heading 'On his door when the City expected an assault', which is crossed through and 'When the assault was intended to the City' substituted in Milton's own hand, with the date '1642', later deleted:[1]

> Captain or colonel, or knight in arms,
>> Whose chance on these defenceless doors may seize,
>> If deed of honour did thee ever please,
>> Guard them, and him within protect from harms,
> He can requite thee, for he knows the charms
>> That call fame on such gentle acts as these,
>> And he can spread thy name o'er lands and seas,
>> Whatever clime the sun's bright circle warms.
> Lift not thy spear against the muses' bower,
>> The great Emathian conqueror bid spare
>> The house of Pindarus, when temple and tower

---

[1] *Poems*, 284–5; all references to Milton's poems are to this edn. unless otherwise stated.

Went to the ground: and the repeated air
Of sad Electra's poet had the power
To save the Athenian walls from ruin bare.[2]

Milton speaks as if to a successful royalist commander—there is a
scheme of opposition between beleaguered poets (Milton, Pindar,
Euripides) and attacking forces (royalists, Alexander, and the
Spartans). What is Milton thinking of? I have argued that the poem
illustrates very well the instability of his political utterances.[3] In
part, no doubt, the exigencies of the genre, the sonnet with its
requirement of simple symbolic structures often of a binary form,
shape the argument. Yet the poem nevertheless requires serious
political interpretation. It concedes the possibility that the side
Milton had formerly seen as poised to usher in the new age in a
millenarian frenzy stands open to defeat; moreover, should the
troops arrive, Milton has fashioned an image of himself as Cinna the
poet, not Cinna the conspirator. To that extent, it completes
perhaps the journey from active partisanship towards a self-
regarding detachment, towards that bardic contemplation valorized
in the autobiographical section of *The Reason of Church-Government*.[4] Troops, pressed men and volunteers, facing the pikes and
cannon of the king's army may not have appreciated the irony of
the newly acquired pacificism of one formerly so implacably
insistent on the extremest of measures against the king's bishops.
When Milton first published it, in October 1645, four months after
the decisive victory at Naseby, he decontextualized it, omitting all
reference to the circumstance of its composition and merely heading
it with the roman numeral VIII as a part of a series of sonnets.

He returned to pamphleteering with *The Doctrine and Discipline
of Divorce* (London, 1643), which represents his first unmistakable
deviation from the prevailing orthodoxies of Calvinist Presbyterianism, his first pamphlet written outside a polemical exchange, and his
first real gesture towards intellectual independence and originality.
But in civil war polemic nothing is made from nothing. Biographers

---

[2] Ibid. 285.
[3] T. N. Corns, ' "Some Rousing Motions": The Plurality of Miltonic Ideology', in
Healy and Sawday, 117–20. For rather different readings, see J. Mueller, 'On Genesis
in Genre: Milton's Politicizing of the Sonnet in "Captain or Colonel" ', in B. K.
Lewalski (ed.), *Renaissance Genres: Essays in Theory, History, and Interpretation*
(Cambridge, Mass., 1986), 213–40; Parker, *Milton*, i. 232–3.
[4] See above, Ch. 2.

have insistently discussed his motivation in terms of his own apparently unhappy marriage,[5] though explanations that see the tract as in some sense programmatic—first Milton persuades the State to stand the existing law on its head; then he benefits from it— are somewhat crude: there were surely easier and more practical ways to assuage the discomforts of marital disharmony. No doubt one may construct a biographical explanation for his initial interest in the topic and for the vehemence with which he sometimes addressed it. For my argument, however, two other aspects are more pertinent, its direction of address and its relationship to current controversies within English Puritanism.

The title-page bears as epigraph the text of Matthew 13: 52, 'Every Scribe instructed to the Kingdom of Heav'n, is like the Maister of a new house which bringeth out of his treasurie things old and new.' It suggests, primarily, that Milton's thesis is founded on arguments which are both 'old and new', though it may be secondarily significant that the text follows a series of eschatological parables, including that of the tares which Milton had earlier invoked to support his notion that unusual ideas, both sound and suspect, should be allowed to bloom together.[6] The title-page presents the tract as 'Seasonable to be now thought on in the Reformation intended', which is most naturally interpreted as an allusion to the inception of the work of the Westminster Assembly of Divines, which met for the first time on 1 July 1643, a month before the pamphlet was published. The Assembly, predominantly Presbyterians but with a sprinkling of Congregational Independents— episcopalians, who had been nominated, did not attend—had been constituted by Parliament to effect the work Milton had earlier regarded so optimistically, the completion of the reformation in England.[7]

Despite the denominational differences, the Assembly began its work in a genuine spirit of scholarly collaboration, as, in long plenary and committee sessions, they addressed first the redrafting of the Thirty-Nine Articles. Here were some of the cleverest and

---

[5] See e.g. the comments of Parker, that 'His self-respect cried for restoration. . . . Now, without reference to his own particular case, he made a general assault upon the Canon Laws governing marriage. . . . he stood to profit indirectly' (*Milton*, i. 235–6).

[6] In *The Reason of Church-Government*, *CPW* i. 785.

[7] Masson, *Life*, iii. 509–27.

most learned men of the age, met together in circumstances, seemingly, of open and liberal enquiry. Quite probably Milton, though aware of the internal disagreements gestating within Puritanism, thought them tractable to persuasion by a relatively plain and rational exposition of his case for divorce reform (and by implication for a reconsideration of the notion of Christian marriage).

The intellectual and imaginative economy of *The Doctrine and Discipline*, elegantly analysed by Fallon, discloses a fascinating tension between the action of 'Milton the marrier', who 'unites body and spirit into one substance', and 'Milton the divorcer', who 'creates order by separation, by circumscribing a world for gentle, wise, and monist individuals and setting it apart from the chaos of disordered dualism'.[8] Milton's thesis is blunt: companionable marriage best serves the end God defined for the institution; if a marriage is emotionally, intellectually, spiritually unrewarding (and no longer to God's ends) it should be annulled. The starkness of the argument is striking because it is inscribed in a discourse that eschews rhetorical flourish. Though the threads of his argument are intertwined, Milton sharply differentiates the alternatives of the honourable separation and the dishonourable marriage, of the higher legitimacy of divorce for non-carnal reasons and the illegitimacy of a marriage that functions only at the level of sexual competence. Arguments from the concept of companionship have a striking freshness in discussions of Christian marriage.

Milton develops a radically new idiom. Whereas the imagery of the antiprelatical tracts was characterized by its high density and elaborate structure, the first edition of *The Doctrine and Discipline*, in proportion to its length, has far fewer similes and metaphors and their structure is much simpler, rarely developing into the flamboyant conceits he favoured earlier.[9] Moreover, for the first time, Milton writes uninfluenced by the skittish frenzy of the Marprelate tradition. No specific enemies are hunted through these pages. Opposing opinion, cited for the most part anonymously, appears countered with respectful patience: 'But some are ready to object, that . . . But let them know again, that . . .'; 'Upon these principles, I

---

[8] S. M. Fallon, 'The Metaphysics of Milton's Divorce Tracts', in Loewenstein and Turner, 70.

[9] T. N. Corns, *The Development of Milton's Prose Style* (Oxford, 1982), 85–8.

answer, that . . .'[10] The old tetchiness only occasionally intrudes: 'Others are so ridiculous to allege that . . .'; 'Yet *Beza's* opinion is that a politick law, but what politick law I know not, unlesse one of *Matchiavel's*, may regulate sin' (*Divorce*, 31, 33).

Exposition is explicitly and formally logical, generally eschewing rational hiatuses, the insinuation of morally loaded terms, and the oblique denigration of opposite views:

Lest therefore so noble a creature as man should be shut up incurably under a worse evill by an easie mistake in that ordinance which God gave him to remedy a lesse evill, reapplying to himselfe sorrow while he went to rid away solitariness, it cannot avoyd to be concluded, that if the woman be naturally so of disposition, as will not help to remove, but help to encrease that same God-forbidd'n lonelines which will in time draw on with it a generall discomfort and dejection of minde, not beseeming either Christian profession or moral conversation, unprofitable and dangerous to the Common wealth, when the houshold estate, out of which must flourish forth the vigor and spirit of all publick enterprizes, is so ill contented and procur'd at home, and cannot be supported; such a mariage can be no mariage whereto the most honest end is wanting: and the agrieved person shall doe more manly, to be extraordinary and singular in claiming the due right whereof he is frustrated, then to piece up his lost contentment by visiting the Stews, or stepping to his neighbours bed, which is the common shift in this mis-fortune, or else by suffering his usefull life to wast away and be lost under a secret affliction of an unconscionable size to humane strength (*Divorce*, 6–7).

Note how clearly Milton enunciates the assumptions about God and man on which he establishes his argument—that God legislates for man's happiness (I shall consider the gendering of these remarks shortly), that marriage was conceived as a mitigation of loneliness, that an unhappy marriage is at least as bad as that loneliness. If the purpose of the institution is to remove an evil, and if the miscarriage of that institution is worse than the evil it was designed to assuage, then, indeed, 'it cannot avoyd to be concluded' that a remedy must be sought. Again, he defines the possible outcomes of a bad marriage—protracted unhappiness, marital infidelity, or divorce: divorce alone, of course, provides the potential for fulfilling God's

---

[10] John Milton, *The Doctrine and Discipline of Divorce* (London, 1643), 8, 14. All references to the first edn. are to this edn. *CPW* offers both versions distinguished by a complicated typographical system which does not really allow the reader a proper appreciation of the lean elegance of the first edition once it is swathed in the accretions of the second.

purpose through subsequent and successful marriage. At the start of the tract, Milton states his thesis, helpfully italicized, and the method that he will adopt; and he does very much as he says he will do, ticking off the points in an orderly, scholarly manner: 'Seventhly . . . Eighthly . . . Ninthly . . . Next . . .' (*Divorce*, 18–20).

Milton's divorce tracts obviously lie at the heart of any discussion of his sexual ideology and of mid-seventeenth-century gender politics. Nyquist speaks of 'the deeply masculinist assumptions at work in Milton's articulation of a radically bourgeois view of marriage'.[11] Of the two versions of *The Doctrine and Discipline of Divorce* Patterson observes, 'Both title-pages declare that the institution of marriage in England at the time demands revision "for the good of both sexes", a claim easily refuted by today's readers of both sexes, who quickly discover the passages of masculinist bias that, no matter what happened later in *Paradise Lost*, cannot be explained away.'[12] Turner discourses on those ideological elements which distinguish the divorce tracts from the depiction of Edenic marriage.[13] The assumptions, both about the politics of the relationship between the genders and about the role of marriage in supporting and developing, profitably and safely, the household economy paradigmatic of urban bourgeois society, lie very close to the surface of the passage quoted above.

Both in Milton's masculinism and in his denigration of human sexuality, another central concern of the tract, the polemical context in which he operates strictly controls the range of options open to him. We must remember the probable intended audience of the first edition, namely the Assembly, composed in the main of figures of a strict Presbyterian orthodoxy. To such an audience Milton's thesis is already potentially quite outrageous. To say that in a sexual relationship he looks not simply for relief from the imperatives of his sexual appetite but for spiritual companionship is to attribute to the ideal wife considerable status in the devotional life of the wayfaring Christian. In a sense, we must recalibrate our political expectations: in a context in which some males, in the words of

---

[11] M. Nyquist, 'The Genesis of Gendered Subjectivity in the Divorce Tracts and in *Paradise Lost*', in Nyquist and Ferguson, 106.

[12] A. Patterson, ' "No Meer Amatorious Novel?" ', in Loewenstein and Turner, 85.

[13] J. G. Turner, *One Flesh: Paradisal Marriage and Sexual Relations in the Age of Milton* (Oxford, 1987), esp. ch. 6.

'Loves Alchymie', 'Hope not for minde in women',[14] Milton's perspective may be perceived as almost decent.

His expression, of course, remains unrelentingly masculinist. But then his target readers, all male and for the most part orthodox, belonged to a group which was rapidly coming to view the uppity woman as symptom and symbol of a larger malaise threatening the social fabric. For example, Thomas Edwards, whose *Gangraena*, published in three parts in 1646,[15] catalogued (albeit somewhat disingenuously, as we shall see later in the chapter) the variety of heresy among sectaries, made much of women taking a prominent part in religious discourse, and anecdotes proliferate throughout.[16] Edwards speaks of women sectaries rather than of women in general, and relationships with the latter are Milton's concern; but his writing may be cited in evidence of the extreme difficulties Milton faced in securing a proper reception for his arguments. Indeed, Edwards represents Milton's pamphlet as a bad influence on the would-be woman-preacher, citing this otherwise unsubstantiated anecdote:

There are two Gentlemen of the Inns of Court, civil and well disposed men, who out of novelty went to hear the women preach, and after Mistris *Attaway* the Lace-woman had finished her exercise, these two Gentlemen had some discourse with her, and among other passages she spake to them of Master *Miltons* Doctrine of Divorce . . . saying, it was a point to be considered of; and that she for her part could look more into it, for she had an unsanctified husband.[17]

Edwards fished the same polemical waters as Milton, targeting the same body of broad Puritan orthodoxy with whom it can scarcely have helped one's reception to be admired by women of heretical orientation. If Milton seems in *The Doctrine and Discipline of Divorce* to speak in the familiar harsh tones of a masculinist and patriarchal sexual ideology, he may be no more than adjusting his argument to soften the response of his target readers (though he

[14] John Donne, 'Loves Alchymie', l. 23, *Songs and Sonets*, in *Poetical Works*, ed. Sir H. Grierson (1933; London, 1968), 34.

[15] Thomas Edwards, *Gangraena, or, A Catalogue and Discovery of Many of the Errours, Heresies, Blasphemies and Pernicious Practices of the Sectaries of this Time* (London, 1646); *The Second Part of Gangraena* (London, 1646); *The Third Part of Gangraena* (London, 1646); a facsimile of all three parts bound together has been published with an introduction by M. M. Goldsmith and I. Roots (Exeter, 1977).

[16] See e.g. the table of contents to *The Third Part*.

[17] Edwards, *The Second Part*, 10–11; *LR* ii. 145.

may simply subscribe to that position). In a sense, his treatise is perhaps as provocative as it dare be without the further incitement a less masculinist timbre might provoke.

A similar point may be made about his attitudes to the sexual act. Differences between the enthusiastic encomiums in *Paradise Lost* to the 'rites | Mysterious of connubial love' (iv. 742–3, *Poems*, 657) and its representation in the tract are plainly apparent. There it is variously associated with clumsy mechanicalism, bestiality, and slime. However, it is unlikely that the imagery of one so skilled as Milton in some sense discloses more deeply held beliefs than the associated exposition. Milton's imagery here relentlessly serves the argument. In part the attitude he expresses towards sexuality supports his case that Christian marriage should be founded on spiritual, intellectual, or emotional compatibility. Moreover, it wisely attempts to pre-empt analysis of his pamphlet that would interpret it as a libertine argument in favour of loosing the marriage bonds in order to facilitate promiscuous carnality. If Milton appears as a man who does not much care for coitus, then the charge that he advocates liberalized divorce to facilitate a wider sexual experience is (or should be) pre-empted—though, as we shall see, Milton's new enemies were not thus to be forestalled. Incidentally, however, Milton does admit the power of at least the male sexual urge. We should recall that the man frustrated with his marriage[18] steps to the stews or his neighbour's bed, not to talk to, but to copulate with, another woman.

Milton's final area of pre-emptive manœuvre concerns the manner of address he develops towards his target readership and the now familiar matter of pronominalization. He speaks to his readers as though they share his concern for the current phase of the reformation and as participants in the process of rediscovering hidden truth, fellow-toilers under the burdens of postlapsarianism:

For though it were granted us by divine indulgence to be exempt from all that can be harmfull to us from without, yet the perversnesse of our folly is so bent, that we should never lin hammering out of our owne hearts, as it were out of a flint, the seeds and sparkles of new miseries to our selves, till all were in a blaze againe. And no marvell if out of our own hearts, for they are evil (*Divorce*, 1).

That 'we', however, narrows from all fallen people to the comrades

---

[18] Quoted above.

in a struggle for the alleviation of misery through completing the
work of reformation: we explore the question of divorce together,
'we think', 'we find', 'we may further see', and so on (pp. 6, 8). But
in distinction from the old, perhaps rather specious, consensus
Milton claimed with his readers in the antiprelatical tracts, here he is
at pains to produce an 'I' within the text that stands against the
common run of received opinion. Anticipating hostility, he
advances pleas for patience and rationality: 'This onely is desir'd of
them who are minded to judge hardly . . . that they would be still
and heare all out, nor think it equall to answer deliberate reason
with sudden heat' (p. 4). He would scarcely have asked episcopalian
adversaries to stay their 'sudden heat'. His edginess, however,
frequently manifests itself: 'I may erre perhaps in soothing my selfe
that this present truth reviv'd, will deserve to be not ungently
receiv'd on all hands' (p. 4). But he shows too the kind of moral
courage which will characterize his most dangerous prose writing
up to 1660; whatever polemical guile he may adopt, he remains
always prepared to accept the risk of association with the causes he
espouses. The 'I' that speaks in the first divorce tract actively seeks
out orthodoxy and confronts it squarely:

I conceive my selfe exhorted among the rest to communicate such thoughts
as I have, and offer them now in this generall labour of reformation, to the
candid view both of the Church and Magistrate: especially because I see it
the hope of good men, that those irregular and unspirituall Courts have
spun their utmost date in this Land (p. 3).

The first person recurs persistently, citing, arguing, refuting, seizing
the moment vouchsafed by the collapse of the Caroline instruments
of control—and seeking too to stand in the full gaze, 'the candid
view', of those who now wield power.

II

The reception of Milton's first divorce tract dispelled whatever
illusions he may have entertained about the capacity of his pre-
emptive strategy to secure a fair hearing from fellow Puritans.
  Others attempted that same irenic approach, looking to establish
a dialogue with Presbyterian Calvinism within the framework of a
general agreement relating to a community of antipathies to

episcopalianism. About five months after the publication of his first divorce tract, five members of the Westminster Assembly who had been ministers of Independent congregations in American colonies published a pamphlet of similar tone,[19] describing how Congregationalism worked in North America and attempting to demonstrate that such a system need not foster anarchy. In trying to establish a perimeter to reasonable and respectable religious practice which will include those of their own persuasion as well as the narrower circle of Presbyterianism, they attempt to realize what they term 'the hopefull expectation we have been entertained with of an happy *latitude*'.[20]

Yet by the time they write, their perception of their cultural environment has become distinctly pessimistic. They complain, 'We found . . . our opinions and wayes . . . environed about with a cloud of mistakes . . . and our persons with reproaches . . . as of *Schisme*.'[21] Their response, unsurprisingly, invokes the past community of suffering under Laud, asserting that the differences that divide them from Presbyterianism are slighter than those that separate both from Laudian episcopalianism, and they conclude with in effect a desperate plea for 'the allowance of a latitude to some lesser differences with peaceableness, as not knowing where else with safety, health, and livelyhood to set our feet on earth'.[22] Their approach received, at least initially, a sympathetic response—the licenser of the tract, while affirming his own Presbyterian loyalty, speaks of '*This* Apologeticall Narration *of our Reverend and deare Brethren . . . full of peaceablenesse, modesty, and candour: and . . . so seasonably needful*'.[23] Milton's divorce tract received from the outset a much tougher response.

In a sense the *Apologeticall Narration* defined quite well the theoretical difficulty. How may the 'latitude to some lesser differences' that they claim be distinguished from heresies and schisms which may not be tolerated? The Presbyterian position, with its model in Calvin's Geneva and its notion of the clear determination and maintenance of doctrinal unity by means of an unambiguous classic system, had both a theoretical coherence and

---

[19] Thomas Goodwin, et al., *An Apologeticall Narration, Humbly Submitted to the Honourable Houses of Parliament* (London, 1643); Thomason dated his copy 'Jan. 13th' (i.e. 13 January 1644).

[20] Ibid. 26.

[21] Ibid. 23.

[22] Ibid. 31.

[23] Ibid., sig. A1ᵛ.

an embryonic organizational capacity which Congregational Independency lacked. Negotiating a middle way between universal toleration and the doctrinal control central to Presbyterian church government offers a challenge to which Milton never rose, either in the confusion and uncertainty first manifest in *The Reason of Church-Government* or in the lofty contradictions of *Areopagitica*.[24] Moreover, Presbyterianism, by virtue of the organizational control at the heart of its ideology, went into the debate with Congregational Independency and the kind of heterodoxy Milton espoused with a political structure which gave it an unassailable advantage. The Presbyterian position on the central issues dividing Puritanism was clear, and the Presbyterians were organized. Moreover, they were further augmented by the support of others, such as the Erastian William Prynne and the anti-Laudian and Calvinist episcopalian Daniel Featley, who shared an anxiety about the control of groups outside the perimeter that the authors of the *Apologeticall Narration* sought to define.

Milton's tract rapidly assumed a central role in a sudden and rather dirty campaign characterized by a polemical strategy as effective as it was simple. Presbyterian apologists and their auxiliaries presented a vision of London as a city profoundly threatened by an epidemic of heresy, a single disease manifest in many symptoms. The general title of Edwards's tracts of 1646, *Gangraena*, indicates the way of regarding radicalism which had broadly developed in the mid-1640s. Heresy emerges as a complex syndrome, embracing social disorder (the propertiless and uneducated now preach), disorder between the sexes (women now preach), sexual libertinism, and unacceptable blasphemous heresies which impugn central tenets of Protestant doctrine. Congregational Independency provides the organizational conditions necessary for the disease, and tolerationism its ideological prerequisite. The campaign rested largely on often anecdotal evidence of contemporary practices and on the analysis (or at least consideration) of heretical publications. By 1643–4, however, some elements could be substantiated much less well than others. Though Daniel Featley makes much of the bizarre licentiousness alleged of the Münsterian Anabaptists and attempts to implicate contemporary radicals in similar conduct, sexual libertinism seems a difficult charge to substantiate before the

---

[24] See above, Ch. 2; *Areopagitica* is considered below.

anecdotes associated with the Ranter movement emerge in 1649–51.[25] This is probably why Milton's first divorce tract assumed such a high media profile, since it could be represented to those who had never read it (possibly by others who had never read it either) as exactly the sort of libertine manifesto Milton had struggled to distance himself from. Moreover, the publication of his tract served as evidence for one specific proposal that more conservative Puritan opinion was eager to press on the Long Parliament, namely the revival of the licensing system that had obtained under Laud as a primary element in the control of hostile texts.

Milton's tract, after something of a lull, attracted pulpit condemnation, printed vituperation, a petition from the Stationers Company, and the attention of Parliament. Herbert Palmer's sermon to Parliament, just over a year after the publication of *The Doctrine and Discipline*, published as *The Glasse of Gods Providence towards his Faithfull Ones* (London, 1644), while not mentioning the tract or Milton by name, seemingly denounces it as an argument 'for Liberty to *marry incestuously*' and a clear example of a book that could appropriately be suppressed.[26]

The printed attacks on Milton, save for the anonymous *Answer to a Book, Intituled, The Doctrine and Discipline of Divorce* (London, 1644), show a striking homogeneity of approach. There is some justice in Milton's tart objections in *Colasterion* (London, 1645) to the 'light arm'd refuters . . . pelting thir three lines utterd with a sage delivery of no reason, but an impotent and wors then *Bonner*-like censure to burn' (*CPW* ii. 724). The usual response handled Milton by distorting the content or the title into some terse but misleading phrase and incorporating it in a list of other apparently outrageous heresies as evidence of the extremism blossoming in a climate of toleration. Daniel Featley's comments exemplify the approach:

For they [i.e. Anabaptists] print not onely *Anabaptisme*, from whence they take their name; but many other most damnable doctrines, tending to carnall liberty, Familisme, and a *medley* and *hodg-podge* of all Religions. Witness the book . . . called *The Bloudie Tenet* . . . Witnesse a Tractate of Divorce, in which the bonds of matrimony are let loose to inordinate lust . . . Witnesse a Pamphlet . . . inituled, *Mans Mortality*.[27]

---

[25] Daniel Featley, *The Dippers Dipt* (London, 1645), 209–10; see below, Ch. 5.
[26] *LR* ii. 106; Parker, *Reputation*, 20, 73–4; *CPW* ii. 142, 144.
[27] Featley, *Dippers*, sig. B2ᵛ.

Mathew Simmons and Thomas Payne, printers of Milton's first divorce tract, certainly became beneficiaries of the triumph of Independency after 1649,[28] but we have no evidence to connect either with Anabaptism (nor, one suspects, had Featley, beyond his own obsession with that tendency as *fons et origo* of all sectarian evils). More interesting is the company that Milton's tract is made to keep. Roger Williams's *Bloudy Tenent of Persecution for Cause of Conscience* (London, 1644) and Richard Overton's *Mans Mortallitie* (Amsterdam, 1643; London, 1644) recur alongside *The Doctrine and Discipline* in several attacks on Independency and the sects.[29] Williams's tract constitutes a grand statement of the case for toleration; Overton's elegantly rehearses, with a measured control that no doubt infuriated the orthodox, the arguments in favour of a heresy Milton came to espouse, mortalism or the belief that the body and soul die together, remain indissolubly linked in the grave, and are resurrected together, a notion that subverted many contemporary views about the nature of death and immortality.

In a sense, Milton is flattered by the company he is associated with. In particular, Williams was a high-profile figure who had returned from the American colonies with a considerable reputation for political and intellectual vigour. But two points about Milton's new notoriety must be stressed. He appears in the public eye through a Presbyterian campaign which associates him (in his capacity as advocate of an outrageous opinion) not only with luminaries like Williams but also with women preachers and with uneducated tradesmen-preachers. Secondly, while the campaign elevates Milton's profile, it simultaneously and paradoxically marginalizes him: he appears not at the centre of an important initiative to reform Christian marriage but rather as a symptom of a larger malaise.

Both considerations radically inform Milton's response, not only in the ways in which he attempts to extricate himself from the attack but also in the ways in which he revises the presentation of himself in his writing.

---

[28] Plomer.

[29] The attribution of *Mans Mortallitie* to Overton, the future Leveller, was once controversial; see R. O., *Mans Mortalitie*, ed. H. Fisch (Liverpool, 1968), pp. xii–xv. All three tracts recur e.g. in the Sion College Ministers' *Testimony to the Truth of Jesus Christ* (London, 1648), 19, 22, and *passim*, and on the anonymous broadsheet *These Tradesmen are Preachers in and about the City of London* (London, 1647). On the contemporary association of the three works, see W. Haller, *Liberty and Reformation in the Puritan Revolution* (New York, 1955), 124, 134, 178.

III

The Presbyterian campaign rests upon a tendentious view of the history of the Reformation, which distinguishes the tradition of Luther and Calvin both from lower-class fanaticism, usually exemplified by the Anabaptist group which seized Münster in 1534–5 and whose heresies Luther excoriated,[30] and from dangerous and blasphemous intellectuals like Michael Servetus, the anti-Trinitarian polymath executed in Calvin's Geneva.[31] Milton challenges that history, suggesting that the Lutheran and Calvinist Reformations constituted a period of fervid but fraternal debate and dissent and that the views of Luther, Calvin, and their associates constitute a more open and controversial body of opinion than English Presbyterians would pretend.

Milton's two strongest initiatives against the Presbyterian view of Reformation history come in *The Judgement of Martin Bucer* (London, 1644) and *Tetrachordon* (London, 1645). The latter, his most ambitious attempt so far at biblical exegesis, closes with two sections of citations. The first, a list of 'Who among the fathers have interpreted the words of Christ concerning divorce, as is heer interpreted; and what the civil law of Christian Emperors in the primitive Church determin'd' (*CPW* ii. 692), may seem a curious compilation, given his earlier strictures on both patristic writing and the early Christian emperors,[32] though it serves his turn to demonstrate the antiquity of his proposal: thus, he is no mere fanatical innovator. The readmittance of the Fathers into the ranks of godly scholarship, a surprising turn-around, evidences the flexibility of Miltonic opinion in the service of the polemical moment. The second section brings him into close engagement with his assailants. It is a long list of witnesses, among them such cardinal figures as Wycliffe, 'the first preacher of a general reformation to all *Europe*', Luther, and Melanchthon, 'the third great luminary of reformation' (ii. 707–8), each of whom is cited endorsing some case for divorce on grounds other than those that obtained in English canon law.

[30] N. Cohn, *The Pursuit of the Millennium*, 2nd edn. (London, 1970), ch. 13; for a contemporary account, see the anonymous *Short History of the Anabaptists of High and Low Germany* (London, 1644), which makes explicit connections between 16th-cent. Germany and contemporary London.

[31] R. H. Bainton, *Hunted Heretic: The Life and Death of Michael Servetus, 1511–1553* (1953; Boston, 1960), chs. 9–11.

[32] See above, Ch. 2.

Milton layers the manœuvre in *The Judgement of Martin Bucer*. The body of the text is a translation of part of *De Regno Christi* by the sixteenth-century German divine, Martin Bucer, which has the added cachet of being addressed to Edward VI as a contribution to the latter's commitment to the English Reformation.[33] Milton may thus represent it as a text still working to achieve its author's original objectives long after his premature death (*Judgement*, *CPW* ii. 430). Not content, though, with associating his own position with Bucer's, Milton links Bucer to his sixteenth-century context by prefacing the translation with 'Testimonies of the high approbation Which learned men have given of *Martin Bucer*', among them Foxe, Beza, Sir John Cheke, and, probably most significantly, Calvin himself (ii. 422–9). Milton is not arguing that such figures agreed with Bucer and with himself on divorce; what he is demonstrating is that Bucer argued as he did and yet retained the respect of and a dialogue with those very figures English Presbyterians regard so highly. Milton's contemporary opponents may claim such notions put one outside the pale of theological respectability; but he can show that Bucer was perceived differently and that he should be perceived differently too.

Milton insists on his right to address his readers not as an outcast but as an educational and ethical peer. The second edition of *The Doctrine and Discipline* explicitly addresses 'The Parlament of England, with the Assembly' of Divines (*CPW* ii. 222). *The Judgement of Martin Bucer* has an introductory epistle to Parliament (ii. 430–40); *Areopagitica* (London, 1644) simulates a speech before Parliament. Though his enemies may traduce him in sermons to Parliament, though the Stationers Company may petition Parliament against him, he persists in addressing that same audience.

His assertion of his membership of the political nation and of his distinction from tub-preachers receives its fullest expression in *Colasterion* (London, 1645), which with cruel brilliance exploits a fortuitous circumstance. Milton has discovered—or at least claims to have discovered—that the only considerable engagement of his first divorce tract, *An Answer to a Book, Intituled, The Doctrine and Discipline of Divorce*, was written by a serving-man who had managed to become a solicitor. Milton, thus, may demonstrate his own distance from those propertiless men with whom the Presby-

---

[33] *CPW* ii. 416–18.

terians associated him by the curiously fitting remedy of ridiculing the social status of his presumably Presbyterian refuter. Moreover, he may do so in terms which persistently declare his own community with an intended readership drawn from the propertied and liberally educated:

the cheif [opponent] . . . was intimated to mee, and since ratif'd to bee no other, if any can hold laughter, and I am sure none will guess him lower, then an actual Serving-man. This creature, for the Story must on, (and what though hee be the lowest person of an interlude, hee may deserv a canvasing,) transplanted himself, and to the improvment of his wages, and your better notice of his capacity, turn'd Sollicter (ii. 726–7).

Milton, who drew wages from no one till he entered the service of the Council of State in 1649, distinguishes his adversary's esurient insistence from his own disinterestedness. But note the way Milton prompts his readers to align with him against an intrusive social outsider.

We have no real evidence of how Milton perceived the working classes. Elsewhere in *Colasterion* he defends the rights of those whose expression is 'flat and rude' (ii. 725). Indeed, Wilding has demonstrated that in *Areopagitica* Milton conceives of the heroic task of completing the Reformation in England in imagery relating to the building of the Temple of the Lord in which 'the physical labours of the common people are . . . properly represented as dignified, noble, beautiful'.[34] Milton's views on central areas of human experience at times seem chillingly labile as arguments are assumed and abandoned to serve the polemical moment.

Dozens of jokes about the serving-man-turned-solicitor permeate *Colasterion*, appropriating the Presbyterian notion that the uneducated may not debate religion: 'this is not for an unbutton'd fellow to discuss in the Garret, at his tressle' (ii. 746). His would-be confuter does not know Greek or Hebrew, yet he presumes to quote them (ii. 724–5); he does not understand Roman law (ii. 736); 'I mean not to dispute Philosophy with this Pork, who never read any', Milton avers (ii. 737); 'Came this doctrin out of som School, or som stie?' (ii. 739). Milton persistently declines to engage his adversary except at this level of abuse, for to do so would be to compromise the tactical notion that people of that social echelon

---

[34] M. Wilding, 'Milton's *Areopagitica*: Liberty for the Sects', *Prose Studies*, 9/2 (1986), 17; reprinted in Corns, 17.

have no business meddling in this debate. Thus, the confuter had raised a reasonable practical objection to the ease of divorce Milton advocated, namely that it made provision difficult for offspring *in utero* at the time of separation. Milton replies that such objections 'must needs be good news for Chamber-maids, to hear a Serving-man grown so provident for great bellies' (ii. 734), which trades off assumptions about servant-class sexual morality.

The jokes serve as part of a caste rite to celebrate the social solidarity of Milton and his readers and to exclude their inferiors from the debate. As such, it ingeniously responds to the kinds of representation that Milton's adversaries had directed towards him. Whereas once Milton had invoked the community of the godly, now he invokes the community of the educated and propertied.

Tetrachordon manifests the same kind of spare functionalism of style that Milton developed in the first edition of *The Doctrine and Discipline*, an idiom characterized by the infrequency and relative simplicity of imagery. Evidently, though, he tapped a richer vein for *Areopagitica*, with its careful presentation of the heroic role of the controversialist, and material added to the second edition of *The Doctrine and Discipline* brings the average incidence of similes and metaphors into line with his stylistic practices in the antiprelatical tracts. Indeed, as I have argued elsewhere,[35] some of the additions he makes in the second edition are so highly charged with imagery that the reader struggles to find their plain sense. In some parts of the new prefatory epistle almost every sentence has a simile or metaphor, and sometimes, perplexingly, he reworks and reapplies the same vehicle. Thus the reader confronts on the same page, in the 1644 edition:

Error and Custome: Who with the numerous and vulgar train their followers, make it their chiefe designe to envie and cry-down the industry of free reasoning, under the terms of humor, and innovation; as if the womb of teeming Truth were to be clos'd up, if shee presume to bring forth ought, that sorts not with their unchew'd notions and suppositions (ii. 224)

and:

For Truth is as impossible to be soil'd by any outward touch, as the Sun beam. Though this ill hap wait on her nativity, that shee never comes into the world, but like a Bastard, to the ignominy of him that brought her

---

[35] These statements about Milton's imagery are based on the analysis fully described in Corns, *Development*, ch. 10.

forth: till Time the Midwife rather then the mother of Truth, have washt and salted the Infant, declar'd her legitimat, and Churcht the father of his young *Minerva*, from the needless causes of his purgation (ii. 225).

First Milton offers the reader a somewhat disturbing image of gynaecological morbidity, of the prolific female balked in the process of parturition through some clumsy kitchen surgery, a hideous infibulation. In that scheme, Truth is conceptualized as the parturient female; but in the second passage Truth must be conceptualized as a newly delivered child. Milton reorganizes the same complex image into a tenor in which Truth has become the object, not the subject, of childbirth, the child not the mother. The second passage shows how insistently Milton crams imagery into the supplementary material he adds, as the reference to childbirth follows hard upon an undeveloped comparison of Truth and sunshine and mutates into a literary grotesque which, as the Yale editor notes,[36] mingles classical myth with the Anglican service of churching women after childbirth.

IV

Areopagitica, easily the most widely read of Milton's prose works in the twentieth century, has been curiously appropriated as an icon of humanistic liberalism. Its most famous maxim, 'a good Booke is the pretious life-blood of a master spirit' (ii. 493), adorns a plaque in New York Public Library and the endpapers of a once popular series of school texts, and the whole text appears on the walls of Hart House Great Hall of the University of Toronto.[37] Moreover, the history of its translation indicates that oppressed liberal opinion has sometimes sought to support its position with it at various times of crisis in various cultures.[38]

Counter-arguments, however, have been sometimes heard. Illo, reviewing the debate from his own clearly defined opposition to the liberal iconizing of *Areopagitica*, has some sharp comments on the

---

[36] *CPW* ii. 225.

[37] I am indebted to Jeremy Maule for a postcard of the library motto and to Ian Lancashire for confirmation of a recollection concerning Toronto; the school texts were published by E. P. Dutton in New York and by J. M. Dent & Sons in London and Toronto.

[38] For translations of *Areopagitica* see C. Huckabay, *John Milton: An Annotated Bibliography 1929–1960*, rev. edn. (Pittsburgh, 1969), 45.

partisan special pleading Milton's text has produced from writers whom one might have expected to exercise a greater scepticism.[39] Palpably, Milton's position, with its exclusion of Catholic and maybe episcopalian voices from free expression, appears less radical than the kind of untrammelled tolerationism Roger Williams advocated in *The Bloudy Tenent of Persecution*. However, the debate about how libertarian or radical a voice we hear in *Areopagitica* may be significantly advanced if we contextualize Milton's argument appropriately and if we recognize what by now should clearly have emerged from a study of Milton's prose, namely that his exposition of large and general principles is persistently shaped and compromised by his polemical awareness. To look for philosophical coherence in Milton's controversial prose is merely to mistake the decorum of its genre.

On 14 June 1643, about six weeks before the publication of his first divorce tract, the Long Parliament passed legislation that placed publishing on the same footing it had had under the Star Chamber decree of 1637. Most significantly, it required that all books must bear the name of author and printer, and that all books must be approved for publication by a licenser. Since the appointment of such licensers rested with the new Presbyterian establishment (as earlier it had rested with the bishop of London), an effective control over dissent should have been secured. The outcome of the legislation was, however, paradoxical. While 40 per cent of texts hostile to Independency and the sects scrupulously obeyed the law, the people it was intended to silence continued to transgress. The Presbyterians, having achieved the reintroduction of a machinery for press control, evidently used it, even though it was ignored by their enemies whom it was designed to frustrate. Radicals defied as well as broke the law. While printers often withheld their names from title-pages, authors generally did not.[40] Milton followed the radical paradigm. His first divorce tract carried the initials of its printer, but not of its author; the second carried Milton's initials, but not the printer's; so too did *Colasterion* and *Tetrachordon*; more defiantly still, *Areopagitica* carried his full name (though neither name nor initials of the printer) and constitutes a challenge to the new ascendancy to take him to court.

---

[39] For an account of the issues, see J. Illo, 'Areopagiticas Mythic and Real', *Prose Studies*, 11 (1988), 1–23.

[40] Corns, 'Publication and Politics', 80.

None of those tracts was licensed, though the less dangerous
Judgement of Martin Bucer (after all, merely a translation) and the
wholly innocuous *Of Education* (London, 1644) were.[41]

We have no evidence to indicate why Milton, after simply defying
the Licensing Order for almost eighteen months, decided to
campaign for the review and withdrawal which *Areopagitica* calls
for (ii. 491–2, 570). Not only does his pamphlet explicitly address the
Long Parliament, but its arguments also purposefully address the
constituent elements within it, as Sirluck has brilliantly demonstrated.[42] Yet internal contradictions abound. He at the same time
addresses the largest of issues and the meticulous detail of recent
legislation; the grandiose principles he seemingly advances conflict
with the controls he advocates for Catholics and episcopalians; and
there are incoherencies in what he has to say about the role of books
in the pursuit of godly wisdom. While he seeks an adjustment in
legislative procedure so that censorship may be carried out by
prosecution after publication rather than by a process of licensing,
he talks as if he were defending the most cherished rights of a liberal
democracy on the classical model. Moreover, he justifies attack on
licensing by invoking a view of its role in Western history which he
should have known (and probably did know) to be irreconcilable
with the facts.

Fish prises open one set of contradictions to disclose an ingenious
reading of the tract:

In short, the argument against licensing, which has always been read as an
argument *for* books, is really an argument that renders books beside the
point; books are no more going to save you than they are going to corrupt
you; by denying their potency in one direction, Milton necessarily denies
their potency in the other and undercuts the extravagant claims he himself
makes . . . Whatever books are, they cannot be what he says they are in
those ringing sentences, the preservers of truth, the life-blood of a master
spirit, the image of God.[43]

Certainly, Fish has identified a point of real significance: Milton

---

[41] For an intelligent account of Milton's centring of the author in *Areopagitica*, see
A. Blum, 'The Author's Authority: *Areopagitica* and the Labour of Licensing', in
Nyquist and Ferguson, 74–96.

[42] *CPW* ii. 170–8; see also N. Smith's valuable '*Areopagitica*: Voicing Contexts,
1643–5', in Loewenstein and Turner, 103–22.

[43] S. Fish, 'Driving from the Letter: Truth and Indeterminacy in Milton's
Areopagitica', in Nyquist and Ferguson, 238.

makes very large claims for the power of books to preserve the
truths discovered by great authors and at the same time speaks of all
books as things which may be used wisely or badly as their readers
are godly or depraved, and moreover speaks of godliness and
depravity as dependent on the inner working of the Spirit: 'ye
cannot make them chaste that came not hither so' (ii. 527). But Fish
forgets the polemical context and understates the levels of contradiction.

Milton needs to suggest that the impact of the publishing
legislation is sufficiently important for Parliament to reconsider a
matter which it probably felt had been satisfactorily resolved.
Hence, the grandiloquent phrase-making to which Fish alludes and
which others have found so memorable: 'Books are not absolutely
dead things', and so on (ii. 492). He needs also to suggest that the
circulation of apparently inimical material is not profoundly
threatening to the state. Hence his assertions about the invincibility
of truth against falsehood, 'Let [truth] and Falshood grapple; who
ever knew Truth put to the wors, in a free and open encounter' (ii.
561), a notion related to his views that virtue must be tested to be
meritorious (ii. 514–15) and that 'bad books' may be useful to 'a
discreet and judicious Reader' (ii. 512).

Those are arguments in favour of complete toleration: if
falsehood openly expressed may always be beaten, why then restrict
any publications? It is a logic that Williams was prepared to follow.
But Milton knows whom he addresses and he knows what would be
utterly unacceptable to them. Once more he arrives at the familiar
impasse of Independent theory: if the movement seeks to widen the
perimeter of acceptability, who is to say how widely? Milton does
not duck the question, but he answers it only in pragmatic and
rhetorical (rather than philosophical terms). Sectaries, like the
heterodoxies characteristic of religious radicals, are to be allowed.
In a polemical *tour de force*, the endeavours of the unorthodox are
recast into the heroic mould:

Yet these are the men cry'd out against for schismaticks and sectaries; as if,
while the Temple of the Lord was building, some cutting, some squaring
the marble, others hewing the cedars, there should be a sort of irrationall
men who could not consider there must be many schisms and many
dissections made in the quarry and in the timber, ere the house of God can
be built (ii. 555).

As Wilding observes, 'What had been harsh and ugly terms of abuse and contempt . . . are now resituated in this beautiful account of the building of the Temple of the Lord.'[44] The heterodox emerge as the Stakhanovites in the reconstruction of Puritan England. At the same time, Milton excludes from freedom to publish royalists (he deprecates the circulation of *Mercurius Aulicus* (ii. 528)), Catholics, and quite probably episcopalians. Exactly what he means by 'I mean not tolerated Popery, and open superstition' (ii. 565) remains uncertain. It may be a hendiadys; alternatively it may allude to two categories, one popery, the other superstition, a term that he uses freely with reference to both prelacy and Catholicism.[45] Certainly, though, Milton offers up to orthodox Puritanism its more long-standing enemies as victims for uncompromising suppression by any means necessary. Moreover, he insists that the civil magistrate may retain authority to discipline any opinion found to be unacceptable after trial in a court of law. Though the phrasing once more retains an unfortunate (for his exegetes) ambiguity, he seemingly recommends that all books be issued with the printers' names and preferably with the authors', and that any 'found mischievous and libellous' should be suppressed (ii. 569).

Milton wraps his argument in the thickest cloak of anti-Catholic sentiment he has assumed so far. It works in two ways. Firstly, he labours to establish that the mechanism of licensing originated in the Counter-Reformation and that it was adopted by prelates from that source, and that it now threatens to corrupt the revival of the English Reformation: 'this project of licencing crept out of the *Inquisition*, was catcht up by our Prelates, and hath caught some of our Presbyters' (ii. 493). Though this flourish may be successful at the level of rhetoric, its inadequacy as an account of press control in the early modern period is now well known,[46] and the advantages of licensing as a way of regulating dissent convinced every Government of the mid seventeenth century (including those Milton served, sometimes with a responsibility for the implementation of the legislation) of its preferability to any other system, such as prosecution after publication. It was an appealing measure to have at one's disposal. Secondly, Milton persistently links the process of

---

[44] 'Milton's *Areopagitica*', 16–17.
[45] Compare e.g. *The Reason of Church-Government*, *CPW* i. 766 and 787.
[46] *CPW* ii. 158–9.

licensing by means of his imagery to Catholicism and to episcopalianism.[47]

Thus, his analogy between censorship and the suppression of souls about to enter the world moves from its initial classical referents—'*Radamanth* and his Colleagues'—to a side-swipe at Catholic eschatology that seeks out 'new limbo's and new hells wherein they might include our Books also' (ii. 505–6). Again, 'they either condemn'd in a prohibition, or had [an unorthodox book] strait into the new Purgatory of an Index' (ii. 503). The repetitive nature of the series of formulaic imprimaturs placed before a licensed work is associated with the repetitions of the liturgy and in turn with priests and prelates:

Sure they have a conceit, if he of the bottomlesse pit had not long since broke prison, that this quadruple exorcism [a series of imprimaturs] would barre him down . . . Sometimes 5 *Imprimaturs* are seen together dialoguewise in the Piatza of one Title page, complementing and ducking each to other with their shav'n reverences . . . These [imprimaturs] are the prety responsories, these are the deare Antiphonies that so bewitcht of late our Prelats (ii. 504).[48]

Milton binds with a silken thread of imagery the process of censorship and those he would identify as its initiators. The censor is a remote and hierarchical figure, like an 'Archbishop over a large dioces of books' (ii. 540). Censorship adds physical restraint to spiritual affairs. It implies

that all the Sermons, all the Lectures preacht, printed, vented in such numbers, and such volumes, as have now wellnigh made all other books unsalable, should not be armor enough against one single *enchiridion*, without the castle St. *Angelo* of an *Imprimatur* (ii. 537).

Note that he selects as his vehicle not an unspecified fortress but the very arsenal and garrison of the bishop of Rome. Clearly, Milton knows very well the prejudices and assumptions of his target readership and he manipulates them relentlessly.

---

[47] A. F. Price, 'Incidental Imagery in *Areopagitica*', *Modern Philology*, 49 (1952), 218; T. N. Corns, 'Imagery in Civil War Polemic: Milton, Overton and the *Eikon Basilike*', *Milton Quarterly*, 14 (1980), 1–2.

[48] On Italian influences in his anti-papal writing, see Smith, 'Voicing Contexts', 111, who discusses this passage.

V

Milton published his first collection of poems, *Poems of Mr. John Milton, Both English and Latin* (London, 1645), probably over the Christmas period, 1645. George Thomason dated his copy 'Jan: 2ᵈ'. It stands in a complex relationship to his earlier vernacular prose and especially to the tracts of 1643–5.

The volume contains only three slight pieces written later than 1640.[49] We may only guess at why he chose to publish now, rather than in the previous lustrum. Quite probably Humphrey Moseley, his publisher, was a major influence in his decision. Moseley, who had recently published Waller, could well have regarded Milton's collection, which included the previously published *Comus*, as a sound addition to a rapidly expanding list, which would soon include works by Crashaw, Denham, Cowley, Davenant, Suckling, and Donne, and which ensured his easy pre-eminence as the major publisher of non-controversial and creative writing in the mid-century period. Moseley, whose own orientation is frequently disclosed in prefatory material as solidly royalist, generally eschewed the kinds of vituperative and relatively ephemeral writings that Milton had engaged in during the early 1640s. Milton's appearance in his list constitutes a curious cultural cachet for a writer so frequently represented as a radical *enragé*. Curiously, Moseley speaks in the preface he affixes to Milton's poems of his own commitment to promoting fine literature in an age of polemic.[50]

Although almost all of Milton's poems in the collection relate to the period before 1640, their presentation possibly reflects his emerging concern with the presentation of himself in terms that contradict the image his adversaries had produced. Historical ironies emerge sharply. His early poems variously commemorate the Catholic Marchioness of Winchester, Dr Felton, bishop of Ely, and Launcelot Andrewes, bishop of Winchester and a champion of episcopacy ('English Poems', *Poems* (1645), 23; 'Poemata', 56, 16). By 1642, Milton was sarcastically alluding to Andrewes as 'a man so much bruited for learning', as if that judgement were superficial

---

[49] Sonnets viii–x; I follow the dating of Carey and Fowler, *Poems*, 284–8.

[50] *Poems of Mr. John Milton, Both English and Latin* (London, 1645), sig. A3ʳ⁻ᵛ. The pagination is not continuous between the English section of the collection and the 'Poemata', compositions in other languages. On Moseley, see Plomer, and J. C. Reed, 'Humphrey Moseley, Publisher', *Oxford Bibliographical Society Proceedings and Papers*, 2 (1927–30).

(*The Reason of Church-Government*, *CPW* i. 768). His headnotes
to the aristocratic entertainments proclaim their association with the
aristocrats whom they celebrated and who patronized their author
('English Poems', 51, 67), though the Bridgewater family were
solidly and actively royalist. *Comus* is further introduced by a letter
to Milton from Sir Henry Wooton, while Provost of Eton, in praise
of the masque (pp. 71–3). Wooton also pays tribute to Milton's
scholarship and to his planned Grand Tour, thus alluding to his
learning, his high cultural aspirations, and his (or his father's)
wealth.[51] 'Poemata', which contains such recondite achievements as
a translation from Hebrew into Greek verse (p. 69), continues the
tactic of documenting how others perceived him by printing by way
of preface some of the Italian encomiums that he had received
during his tour (pp. 3–9).

A rich circumstantiality surrounds many of the poems, for
example detailing among other things the author's age when they
were composed. The Puritan tendency of the more mature items
emerges distinctly,[52] and Milton underlines it: 'Lycidas' is introduced
as foretelling 'the ruine of our corrupted Clergy then in their height'
(p. 57).

In part the volume vividly documents the cultural complexities
surrounding the English Civil War. How could a figure that had
negotiated a position quite close to the heart of Caroline court
culture now be ranked so uncompromisingly among its enemies?
But Milton has worked to dramatize that complexity and to
provoke such questions. Moseley has permitted him to produce a
fascinating species of autobiography which at once documents the
growth of the poet's mind and its radicalization. This elegant
volume of early verse eloquently validates the positions he has
assumed, on episcopacy, on divorce, on tolerationism. It proclaims
that Milton's politics are not the politics of envy. By defining his
progressive detachment from the cultural establishment of the 1630s
it has him emerge as an insider (and beneficiary perhaps) alienated
by episcopalian malpractice, rather than an outsider destroying a

---

[51] The tour is the one he undertook in 1638–9; the letter refers to a meeting at
Eton between Milton and Wooton in the spring of 1638.

[52] The political orientation of Milton's poems of the 1630s remains an area of
unresolved critical controversy. See, e.g. Wilding, *Dragons Teeth*, chs. 2 and 3, and
D. Norbrook, *Poetry and Politics in the English Renaissance* (London, Boston,
Melbourne, and Henley, 1984), ch. 10.

culture from which he is socially excluded. Even the neo-Spenserian literary aesthetic espoused in his early verse and explicitly remarked on by Moseley (sig. A4ᵛ) lends a poignancy, proclaiming his poetry's legitimate descent from a consciously archaic English tradition. Milton, though heir to English culture, appears as disinherited in the name of outlandish innovation. His own high level of educational and cultural achievement, and his standing, internationally and domestically, among men of culture are persistently asserted. The poetry collection completes and transcends his earlier attempts, in *The Reason of Church-Government*,[53] at producing a self-image of Milton as bard to complement (and justify) his image as disinterested (and intermittently reluctant) fellow-toiler in the work of completing the English Reformation.

Milton's commitment to using the collection of his poems in a defensive manner appears distinctly in his choice of title-page epigraph: '*Baccare frontem | Cingite, ne vati noceat mala lingua futuro*, Virgil, Eclog. 7. [l. 27–8]' ('Bind the forehead with baccar [an unidentified herb], and do not let the evil tongue harm a future poet'). The lines are highly apposite in poetic terms, part of a pastoral poem prefacing his own frequently pastoral early poetry, and the same eclogue a little later makes reference to the figure of Lycidas (l. 67). But it also shows a concern with the *mala lingua* that had upbraided the future poet frequently since 1643 and which the collection, in some ways, works to silence. One wonders what Thomas Edwards would have made of it.

---

[53] See above, Ch. 2.

4

Lovelace, Herrick, and the Eikon Basilike

IN a sense, the king started to lose in the closing months of the 1630s. Failure to secure a quick resolution to the Bishops' War and the concomitant collapse of his fiscal policies initiated a series of set-backs and disasters. The Civil War began in August 1642, and the royalist war effort, despite some early encouragement, quite quickly fell apart. Marston Moor in July 1644 was a terrible defeat, which shattered the king's Northern forces and drove their commander, the Marquis of Newcastle, into exile. It was Cromwell's victory. Though Fairfax, the commander-in-chief, had fallen back, Crom-well had broken through the right wing and had destroyed the battle-line from behind: 'Only Cromwell, moving across the darkening moorland like some bright-eyed beast of prey, seems to have . . . acted the part of a general.'[1] On 14 June 1645 'the Royalist cause committed suicide at Naseby',[2] leaving Charles with no credible force with which to confront the remodelled parliamentary army. 'By December 1645 it had become obvious to most observers that the king was losing the war':[3] no doubt to the more perceptive it had been obvious for a while.

Propertiless men had composed most of the rank and file of the king's army, and those who survived the fighting ended much as they began, with little or nothing. What they thought of the defeat is unrecorded (so far as I am aware), but we do know that several hundred of them enlisted in the New Model Army and served, at least initially, to Fairfax's satisfaction.[4] Theirs were the simple, abiding problems of staying alive: for people of property who had underwritten the king's war effort and provided nearly all his officer corps, issues were more complicated.

Many had been embroiled only reluctantly in the king's war[5] and

---

[1] P. Newman, *The Battle of Marston Moor* (Chichester, 1981), 122.
[2] Hutton, *Royalist War Effort*, 178.
[3] Ibid. 191.
[4] Hardacre, 33.
[5] On neutralism, see above, Ch. 1.

probably gave up and settled with their enemies as expeditiously as possible, though such a course occasioned the contempt of die-hards. Sir Edward Dering, who had joined the king's cause late and with hesitation,[6] was among the first to seek terms, deserting beleaguered Oxford and making his peace by paying £1,000. His apostasy rendered him odious to the royalists, not least because it seemed the beginning of the disintegration of the king's cause: in a pattern of response that was to be repeated often, a former comrade remarked, 'I fear there be more of his mind undiscovered, but time will make them known to be knaves.'[7]

Defeated supporters of the king faced two sets of interrelated problems, one material, the other ideological. There were two kinds of material disaster, sequestration and compounding. Under the former, which was based on the sequestration ordinance of March 1643, 'the seizure was ordered of the personal and real estates of all who took arms against parliament, contributed to the king's army or otherwise assisted his cause'. This was adjusted later to 'broaden the definition of delinquency' while allowing one-fifth of the delinquent's estate to be reserved for his wife and children. Hardacre observes that these measures 'came as a thunderstroke to the royalists' and 'would soon have ruined the royalists with estates in areas controlled by parliament'. However, this devastation was avoided by the introduction of the procedure of compounding, which had its origins in a declaration of January 1644, promising free pardon to deserting common soldiers of the king and the offer of an accommodation with propertied supporters who were not principals in his cause. A committee was established to sit in Goldsmiths Hall and assess each case:

One small group was to be denied any pardon. Another, whose malignancy was only one degree less, were fined one-third of their estates, while the penalty imposed on the rest was one-tenth. . . . about half the cases were initiated between the years 1644 and 1649, and the balance thereafter. . . . in 1646 there was a great flurry of business . . . rising again in 1649.[8]

Such exactions were obviously more lenient than sequestration, and delinquents could and did delay settlements of their fines, nor did

---

[6] 'Even before the battle of Edgehill he inquired on what terms he might be allowed to submit to parliament' (*DNB*).

[7] Quoted by Hardacre, 21, who notes the irony that both the writer and his correspondent eventually resorted to the same course.

[8] Ibid. 19–23.

the First Civil War conclude with the summary or judicial executions that characterized the end of the second. The psychological stress, however, was very acute. The royalist had to apply for pardon, to admit that he was wrong, and that he was beaten. It meant accepting the odium Dering had attracted, a step that must have anguished those who had censured earlier compounders. The problem was individual, resolved after personal crisis.

University teachers and clergymen of all ranks who had acted as ideologues of the Laudian ascendancy were easy targets for economic penalties, and as the area under parliamentary control increased so too did the ejections. About 30 per cent of the Anglican clergy, Herrick among them, were removed from their livings, and both English universities were purged. Those who failed to secure patronage from wealthy royalists or an accommodation with Parliament faced penury, though a policy of paying them a fifth of their livings was introduced.[9]

The ideological crisis for laity and clergy was acute. Old Tudor orthodoxies about God's providential concern for the Government of England persisted into the 1630s and 1640s. The Edwardine 'Homily against Disobedience and Wilful Rebellion', with a confident flourish at the course of world history, had warned:

Turn over and read the histories of all nations; look over the chronicles of our own country; call to mind so many rebellions of old time, and some yet fresh in memory; ye shall not find that God ever prospered any rebellion against their natural and lawful Prince, but contrariwise, that the rebels were overthrown and slain, and such as were taken prisoners dreadfully executed.[10]

Moreover, the splendour of the Caroline court was in part directed towards inculcating (perhaps not always successfully) old notions of the sanctity of kingship. Masques on a new scale celebrated courtly values in a display of wealth. Painting and sculpture extolled the achievements and aspirations of the reign, as Strong has demonstrated, fashioning resonant icons of imperial splendour to fix a Continental image of kingship in the minds of those Englishmen predisposed to receive it.[11]

How, then, could a God who was both providential and a keen

---

[9] Quoted by Hardacre, 43–51.

[10] 'An Homily against Disobedience and Wilful Rebellion', *Second Book of the Homilies* (The Prayer Book and Homily Society; London, 1840), 40.

[11] R. Strong, *Van Dyck: Charles I on Horseback* (London, 1972), 57.

supporter of the English monarchy permit the débâcle of the English Civil War? How could a monarch as serene, potent, and magnificent as Charles had been represented to be, be brought so low? The acuteness of the crisis in royalist ideology was sharpened by the parliamentary response to victory. In any age of belief, there is a tendency for military success to be interpreted as divine validation of the cause. Thus, Shakespeare has his warrior king, after Agincourt, conclude:

> Come, go we in procession to the village,
> And be it death proclaimed through our host
> To boast of this, or take that praise from God
> Which is his only.[12]

This is an easy line to take in victory, and such a response is pervasive on the parliamentary side. Cromwell gave it specific direction when, after the success of Marston Moor, he wrote:

It had all the evidences of an absolute victory obtained by the Lord's blessing upon the godly party principally. We never charged but we routed the enemy. . . . God made them as stubble to our swords. . . . Give glory, all the glory, to God.[13]

Even in the twilight of the republic, Milton could invoke past victories as evidence of a providence that must not be squandered.[14] When Anne, Lady Halkett, an ardent royalist who had participated in the rescue of James, Duke of York, from parliamentary custody, came at the Restoration to write her memoirs, she recalled a conversation, in the shadow of royalist defeat, with Colonel Robert Overton of the New Model Army:

Collonel Overton sitting by mee att dinner said to mee that God had wonderfully evidenced his power in the greet things hee had done. I replied, no doupt butt God would evidence his power still in the great things hee designed to doe. I spoke this with more then ordinary earnestnesse, which made him say, 'You speake my words, but nott I thinke to my sence. . . . I speake . . . of the wonderfull workes that God hath done by his servantts in the late times that are beyond what any could have brought aboutt withoutt the immediate assistance of God and hiss direction.'

---

[12] William Shakespeare, *Henry V*, ed. G. Taylor (Oxford, 1984), IV. viii. 111–14.
[13] *The Writing and Speeches of Oliver Cromwell*, ed. W. C. Abbott (Cambridge, Mass., 1937–47), i. 287. On the attitude of Cromwell and some contemporaries to God's intervention in English political history, see B. Worden, 'Providence and Politics in Cromwellian England', *P & P*, 109 (1985), 55–99.
[14] J. Milton, *The Readie and Easie Way*, 2nd edn., *CPW* vii, rev. edn., 423.

Lady Halkett, more than a decade later, reconstructs her response in terms of God's eventual providence and the final success of the royalist cause: 'you will ever find reason to change what ever governmentt you try till you come to beg of the King to come home and governe you againe.'[15] Maybe she was indeed gifted with such powers of prophecy, though this sounds more like the voice of hindsight. Interestingly, however, she could not slip the parliamentary hook that success betokened moral right, a nasty and painful ideological difficulty which was largely of the royalists' own making. Nor was this merely a polemical problem; God's indifference challenged the most deeply held tenets of royalist belief.

The bitterness of the royalists' experience of defeat sharpened during the decade, and the execution of the king in January 1649, in Lady Halkett's surprisingly evocative phrase, 'putt such a dampe upon all designes of the Royall Party that they were for a time like those that dreamed'.[16] Yet the crisis was met by some publications of a resolute and ingenious defiance. The rest of this chapter considers three such works, two from the months following the king's death, Richard Lovelace's *Lucasta* and the *Eikon Basilike*, seemingly Charles's apologia for his conduct over the decade, and the third, Robert Herrick's *Hesperides*, published in 1648.

II

Lucasta was published as an elegantly printed octavo volume in the summer after the execution of the king (Thomason dated his copy 21 June), though it had been registered for publication in February 1648.[17] It appeared prefaced with poems to the author by a dozen writers, including, as Wilkinson has noted, two or three known parliamentarian supporters.[18] Yet the royalist orientation of the volume is evident. Although the title-page bears the name 'Richard Lovelace Esq.', the prefatory poems frequently address him by his military rank of 'Colonel', and several of the writers give their own military rank, including his brother, Colonel Francis Lovelace, who

[15] *The Memoirs of Anne, Lady Halkett and Ann, Lady Fanshawe,* ed. J. Loftis (Oxford, 1979), 60–1.
[16] Ibid. 28.
[17] Lovelace, *Poems* , p. lxxii. G. Hammond gives 14 May 1649 as its publication date in Lovelace, *Selected Poems,* 7.
[18] Lovelace, *Poems,* 242–54.

had achieved some prominence as commander of the royalist garrison at Carmarthen.[19] Andrew Marvell, the complexities of whose position in the late 1640s are explored later,[20] suggests in his prefatory poem that the volume will be read in hostile fashion by parliamentary supporters:

> The Ayre's already tainted with the swarms
> Of Insects which against you rise in arms.
>
> .   .   .   .   .   .
>
> The barbed Censurers begin to looke
> Like the grim consistory on thy Booke;
> And on each line cast a reforming eye,
> Severer then the yong Presbytery.
>
> .   .   .   .   .   .
>
> Some reading your *Lucasta* will alledge
> You wrong'd in her the Houses Priviledge.
> Some that you under sequestration are,
> Because you wrote when going to the Warre,
> And one the Book prohibits, because *Kent*
> Their first Petition by the Authour sent.[21]

Marvell alludes to Lovelace's imprisonment by Parliament in 1642 for presenting a royalist petition on behalf of his own county of Kent. He does not dispute the coherence of such partisan antipathy, but merely adds that he is 'not of that rout' who express it and that the book will find support among 'valiant men, and fairest Nymphs' (*Luc.*, sig. A7ᵛ).

The volume contains several poems celebrating or commemorating people and incidents associated with the royalist cause. Thus, in a poem he entitles 'Sonnet. *To Generall* Goring, *after the pacification at* Berwicke', he produces a drinking song:

> In ev'ry hand a Cup be found,
> That from all Hearts a health may sound
> To *Goring*! to *Goring*! see't goe round.   (*Luc.* 102)

The poem was probably composed around the time of the event it mentions, the Pacification of Berwick in June 1639. After then, Goring secured a place in parliamentary demonology only slightly below that of Prince Rupert. He was prominent in the royalist war

---

[19] Ibid. 242.
[20] See below, Ch. 6.
[21] *Luc.*, A7ʳ⁻ᵛ; all references are to this edn.

effort, had commanded the left of the line at Marston Moor, where his rout of Fairfax had given a temporary advantage to the royalists, and since late 1645 had been an *émigré*. Moreover, he had attracted the interest of parliamentary propagandists, whose attacks on him had highlighted his alcoholism.[22] Perhaps Lovelace echoes the opening of Horace's ode on the victory at Actium, 'Nunc est bibendum' (*Odes*, I. xxxvii), but there is also a jaunty indifference to the familiar attack on Goring's depiction in the way in which he celebrates a royalist hero in terms that make no concessions. Drinking with Goring appears as a Cavalier imperative. Lovelace speaks to royalists within a royalist value system. Moreover, the poem gives not the slightest hint of regret at the inception of the campaign it commemorates, a campaign which could easily have been perceived as the cause of sequential disasters. Rather than bemoaning the overreaching Caroline policy towards Scotland, it suggests that a more bloody, confrontational approach might have succeeded. The opening lines, 'Now the *Peace* is made at the Foes rate, | Whilst men of Armes to kettles their old Helmes translate', imply disappointment that Charles has not unleashed his army in an adventure to settle the Scottish Puritans.

Similar points may be made about the poem entitled 'To his [*sic*] Deare Brother Colonel F. L. immoderately mourning my Brothers untimely Death at Carmarthen'. Once more, there is no regret, no reappraisal. Wilkinson helpfully provides the note that 'William Lovelace, the third son, was killed at Carmarthen, probably in 1644, when under the command of his brother Francis, to whom the poem is addressed'.[23] On William, his merits, and his extinction the poem itself is significantly silent. Unusually for a seventeenth-century elegy, the poem does not mention the deceased at all. Rather it addresses itself to placating grief with a call for self-discipline and a productive resolution:

> IV
> Then from thy firme self never swerve;
> Teares fat the Griefe that they should sterve;
> I'ron decrees of Destinie
> Are ne'er wipe't out with a wet Eye.

---

[22] *DNB*. On drunkenness as a motif in royalist writing see Potter, *Secret Rites*, 140–3.

[23] Lovelace, *Poems*, 290–1.

v
> But this way you may gaine the field,
> Oppose but sorrow and 'twill yield;
> One gallant thorough-made Resolve
> Doth *Starry Influence* dissolve.   (*Luc.* 111)

The physical suffering, the ugly violence of William's death, is shuffled off. Military allusion remains only as a metaphor about the conquest of grief, retained in the vague term 'gaine the field'.

This manœuvre is wholly typical of Lovelace's procedures for accommodating the experience of the Civil War. Within the broad Western tradition of love poetry, analogies had been drawn from time to time between aspects of sexual relations and various kinds of combat, as in Shakespeare's 'Now is she in the very lists of love, | Her champion mounted for the hot encounter'.[24] In the *Lucasta*, both explicit reference to warfare and the careful fashioning of the poet–lover as soldier work with the reiteration of such imagery to give even the love poems a martial and, indeed, chivalric patina. His mistress's sigh is thus transformed:

> Cold as the winds that blow
> To silver shot descending snow
> LUCASTA sight [i.e. sighed].
> ('Lucasta's World', *Luc.* 116)

Here 'shot', balls or bullets designed to be discharged from a firearm or cannon,[25] is a metaphor embedded in a simile, and is distanced further by the mannered attributive 'silver'. Similarly, in 'To a Lady that Desired Me I would Beare my Part with Her in a Song', allusion to the sounds of the camp are offered as a touchstone for the speaker's inept musical performance in polite society:

> Madam, th' Alarums of a Drumme
> That cals your Lord, set to your Cries,
> To mine are sacred *Symphonies*.   (*Luc.* 118)

A social context is implied—a soldier speaks to a soldier's wife. Indeed, a subtitle names her as 'Madam A.L.', no doubt to be identified by those familiar with the poet's circle as Anne Lovelace, subject of the poem dedicatory and wife of Lord Lovelace of Hurley. Interestingly, the latter had compounded months before

---

[24] William Shakespeare, *Venus and Adonis*, ll. 595–6, *Complete Works*, ed. W. J. Craig (1954; Oxford, 1965), 1080.
[25] *OED*.

Naseby,[26] though the tense of 'cals your Lord', perhaps accurate enough for the point at which the poem was composed, by 1649 suggests that a struggle continues which for Lord Lovelace had ended.

There are points of comparison in these examples with the section in 'Upon Appleton House' in which plants and flowers are described in an elaborate military conceit:

> Well shot ye Firemen! Oh how sweet,
> And round your equal Fires do meet;
> Whose shrill report no Ear can tell,
> But Ecchoes to the Eye and smell.
> See how the Flow'rs, as at *Parade*,
> Under their *Colours* stand displaid:
> Each *Regiment* in order grows,
> That of the Tulip Pinke, and Rose.[27]

Lovelace's military allusion works rather differently. The effect it produces is not this elegiac, nostalgic regret at the intrusion and wastefulness of militarism. Instead, it suggests that the martial perspective is a quality which the courtly speaker of the poems must assume but which he wears lightly. The jaunty equation of the alarum of the drum and a poor singing voice implies an amiable nonchalance about the graver associations of the former.

Lovelace's description of actual military conflict is curiously bookish, closer to the chivalric encounters of romance than news-book accounts of Marston Moor—or, for that matter, the experiences of himself and his immediate family. Consider the central stanza of 'To Lucasta, Going to the Warres':

> a new Mistresse now I chase,
>   The first Foe in the Field;
> And with a stronger Faith imbrace
>   A Sword, a Horse, a Shield.   (*Luc.* 3)

Amid possible echoes of the Pauline 'shield of faith' (Eph. 6: 16), he offers a vision of military encounter much removed from the actualities of mid-century warfare. There is persistent slippage into other frames of reference. 'The first Foe' postulates the single combat of a duel. 'Chase' implies sport or game—and that the

---

[26] *DNB.*

[27] Marvell, 'Upon Appleton House', st. xxxix, *Poems and Letters*, i. 72; see below, Ch. 7.

enemy will be running away. Cavalry tactics in royalist armies did admit some ill-disciplined *élan* should the opposing wing be routed at the first shock, and it was a strong element in Rupert's style of attack. But the first charge, even among the royalist horse, was a concerted and controlled advance, and often gained much of its effect from the discharge of a volley of pistol shot. Indeed, the armaments of the poem, the sword and shield, strike a chord in the imagination of the sympathetic reader, invoking an earlier, more heroic age. Certainly, English cavalry of the Civil War did wear and use swords, but they did not carry shields. The one regiment, nicknamed 'lobsters', to take the field accoutred like old-fashioned heavy cavalry, proved unequal to the rapid manœuvring of mid-century tactics.[28] Elsewhere, the Cavalier voice of the poems speaks, albeit in *risqué double entendre*, of the timid lover who has his 'Launce broke on her [his mistress's] Bed' ('Valiant Love', *Luc.* 123). Actually, English troops were not armed with lances, though they were retained by Scottish cavalry.[29]

Rendering the accoutrements of Cavalierism spuriously antique proves multifunctional. Possibly there is a class point. The Marchioness of Newcastle, a royalist die-hard of the most extreme kind and the wife of the defeated commander at Marston Moor, expatiated at length on the cachet of swordsmanship and horsemanship:

a Peasant or such mean bred Persons, can shoot off Pistols, or Carbines, or Muskets, but they have no skill to use a Sword, nor know not how to manage a Horse, unless a Cart-Horse, & that better in a Cart than when astride.

And she concludes, somewhat improbably:

the only Grief to Gallant, Valiant Gentlemen in the day of Battel or Duel, is, the fear they should be kill'd with a Bullet, against which they can show no Active Valour or Well-bred Skill [i.e. in their swordsmanship].[30]

Besides social prejudice against the ill-bred musketeer and against firearms in general, which Lovelace may well have shared, there were practical anxieties about bullet wounds. The prognosis for a sword cut that was not immediately fatal was much better than for a

---

[28] Firth, *Cromwell's Army*, 113. Abraham Cowley describes the ineptness of these 'mooving *statues*' in *The Civil War*, i. 477–88, ed. A. Pritchard (Toronto, 1973), 86.

[29] Firth, *Cromwell's Army*, 114–15.

[30] Marchioness of Newcastle, *CCXI Sociable Letters* (London, 1664), 143–4.

bullet wound since the bullet carried infected material deep into the wound and occasioned worse infection.[31] Perhaps the poet is avoiding the nastier aspects of the conflict.

However, the most potent effect of such anachronism is to generate connections between Civil War royalism and the chivalric loyalism of the feudal era. The link is made more obtrusively in some of the prefatory poems from soldiers, particularly in that of Captain Dudley Lovelace, the poet's youngest brother:

> ILE doe my nothing too; and try
> To dabble to thy memory:
> Not that I offer to thy Name,
> *Encomiums*, of thy lasting Fame.
> Those, by the Landed have been writ,
> Mine's but a *Younger Brother-Wit*;
> A Wit thats hudled up in scarres,
> Borne like my rough-selfe in the Warres;
> And as a Squire in the fight,
> Serves only to attend the Knight:
> So't is my glory in this Field,
> Where others act, to beare thy Shield.   (*Luc.*, sig. A2ᵛ)

The relationship he thus offers is chivalric, extended in a romance fantasy which invokes a medieval code of unquestioning fealty. Such posturing had been promoted among courtiers in the 1630s. Charles I, interesting himself in the Garter Festival on St George's Day, had removed it from London to Windsor, thus rendering it less of a public spectacle and more of a closed caste-ritual and, in the process, investing it with a new piety.[32] The conscious chivalrism of the *Lucasta* volume, while it distances the battlefield, nostalgically draws upon the ancient loyalties of squire to knight and knight to monarch. The revolutionary alternative, the idea that the subject may indeed question rather than worshipfully obey, is adroitly set aside.

Lovelace's place in the tradition of English poetry is quite complex. Weidhorn over-simplifies when he categorizes him in 'a subgroup of the secular Donne followers, which discards some of the more abrasive metaphysical way of writing—though not the scabrous content of Donne's poems'.[33] This formulation dismisses

[31] Newman, *Marston Moor*, 126.
[32] Strong, *Charles I*, 59–63.
[33] M. Weidhorn, *Richard Lovelace* (New York, 1970), 147.

too readily both Jonsonian and original elements in mid-century secular lyric. But Lovelace clearly retains from Donne two characteristics that potently engage the crises of the 1640s, witty argument, in Lovelace's case characteristically muted into a species of paradox, and an enthusiasm for erotic celebration.

As in Donne's *Songs and Sonets*, a number of attitudes are adopted and relationships implied. Sometimes, Lovelace assumes the perspective of a rich amoralist, as in 'The Faire Beggar', a poem which seemingly extends charity for sexual favours:

> Cheape then are pearle imbroderies
> That not adorne, but clouds thy wast,
> Thou shalt be cloath'd above all prise,
> If thou wilt promise me imbrac't;
> Wee'l ransack neither Chest nor Shelfe,
> I'l cover thee with mine owne selfe.   (*Luc.* 132)

Other poems of a similar indecency are premissed on relationships of social equality. 'Sonnet' (*Luc.* 10), a seduction poem, adopts the strategy of Donne's 'Flea': here a ring can be borrowed, worn, and returned shining 'as innocent as before', so too may the mistress be penetrated with no loss to herself. The song 'To Amarantha, that She would Dishevell her Haire', set to music by Henry Lawes, offers elegant smut, rendered a little poignant by a concern for the transience of happiness:

> Heere wee'l strippe and coole our fire
>   In Creame below, in milke-baths higher:
> And when all Well's are drawne dry,
>   I'le drink a teare out of thine eye.   (*Luc.* p. 7)

In the 1640s such poetry is not ideologically neutral. This was, after all, the era of an ascendant Puritanism that required strictness in sexual mores. Indeed, the Rump's ordinance of 10 May 1650 relating to such issues, which 'epitomized the triumph of Puritanism in England', provided for the death penalty for adultery and three months in gaol for fornication, though sentences of such severity were rarely exacted.[34] In 1652 Gregory Clement, a regicide, was expelled from the Rump for sleeping with his maidservant, and his name was erased from the king's death warrant as unworthy of such

[34] K. Thomas, 'The Puritans and Adultery: The Act of 1650 Reconsidered', in Pennington and Thomas, 257–82.

an illustrious setting.[35] The parliamentarian press had persistently emphasized the libidinousness of the royalist army;[36] a concern to escape the charge of sexual libertinism radically shaped Milton's polemical strategy in his divorce tracts; and the attack on Ranterism had its foundations in this repressive Puritan consciousness. Lovelace's erotic poetry challenges both Puritan morality and propagandists' stereotyping in its rehearsal of a value-system remote from the ideology of the new masters. As in the poem to Goring, he ignores the easy target he offers to potential enemies, addressing himself to those who share his perspectives. Furthermore, in not responding to the challenge of the new ascendancy, he implies that the tradition of courtly eroticism abides.

Of particular interest are the poems that treat the consequences of the Civil War—going to battle, imprisonment, exile—but also admit erotic elements. Thus, 'To Lucasta, Going beyond the Seas' (*Luc.* 1), which in the context of royalist experience invites interpretation as allusion to exile, refashions the topos of Donne's 'Valediction, Forbidding Mourning' to a new political concern. Similarly, in 'To Althea, from Prison', Love brings his mistress to the incarcerated Cavalier so that he may 'lye tangled in her haire, | And fetterd to her eye' (*Luc.* 97). Dishevelled hair, a common enough emblem in the Western tradition for the unbridling of female sexual appetite, figures prominently in the Lovelace canon, as, for example, in 'To Amarantha, that She would Dishevell her Haire':

> See 'tis broke [her ribbon]! Within this Grove
> The Bower, and the walkes of Love [i.e. her unbound hair],
> Weary lye we downe and rest,
> And fanne each others panting breast.   (*Luc.* 7)

Poems like 'To Lucasta, Going beyond the Seas' and 'To Althea, from Prison' suggest a connection at a sub-logical level between the excitements of courtly eroticism and the responsibilities of the Cavalier. Within the volume is constructed a single synthesizing voice which offers itself as the expression of quintessential Cavalierism. What it articulates is not the crude thesis that Cavaliers have a richer sex life than Roundheads. Rather, it suggests that being

---

[35] C. Hill, *The Experience of Defeat: Milton and Some Contemporaries* (London, 1984), 73.
[36] See above, Ch. 1; below, Ch. 8.

the sort of person who is capable of sensuous and devotional passion brings with it an unqualified love for the king which must express itself in a boundless self-sacrifice, much as the lover sets no limits to his devotion for his mistress. The connection between erotic and political codes of conduct is not arrived at logically: rather, it appeals profoundly to Cavalier modes of self-perception and representation. As Lovelace puts it, in perhaps his most quoted lines, 'I could not love thee (Deare) so much, | Lov'd I not Honour more' ('To Lucasta, Going to the Warres', *Luc.* 3). Thus, the concern with erotic love, central to Donne's secular poetry, in Lovelace assumes a more partisan significance.

The witty argument of the model Donne offers is similarly transformed. Sometimes Lovelace uses paradox in turning neat compliment, as in 'To Ellinda, Upon his Late Recovery: A Paradox', where he develops the argument that the lover was better when he was ill, because then he was close to his beloved nurse:

> How I grieve that I am well
> All my Health was in my sicknes,
> Go then Destiny and tell
> Very Death is in this quicknes.   (*Luc.* 134)

This same structure of argument is imposed with brilliant effect in poems that deal with imprisonment. Just as the speaker was better when he was ill, so he is freer when in prison. Why? Because at liberty one must accept the anguish of submitting to what is wrong, whereas in prison one retains the freedom to hold fast to one's love without compromise. The interrelatedness of Cavalier as lover and loyalist is particularly pertinent:

> Stone Walls doe not a Prison make,
>   Nor I'ron bars a Cage;
> Mindes innocent and quiet take
>   That for an Hermitage;
> If I have freedome in my Love,
>   And in my soule am free;
> Angels alone that sore above,
>   Injoy such Liberty.
> ('To Althea, from Prison', *Luc.* 98)

The deprivations of imprisonment are sloughed off and the values of Cavalierism triumphantly and transcendently rehearsed:

> Live then Pris'ners uncontrol'd;
> Drink oth'strong, the Rich, the Old,
> Till Wine too hath your Wits in hold;
>   Then if still your Jollitie,
>   And Throats are free;
>
>   *Chorus*
> Tryumph in your Bonds and Paines,
> And daunce to th' Musick of your Chaines.
>   ('The Vintage to the Dungeon', *Luc.* 45)

Hammond has argued for a rather different reading of Lovelace, one which locates his political complexity not in a strenuous and ingenious partisanship, but rather in a Marvellian ambivalence in the political perspectives it assumes.[37] Whatever its merits with regard to *Lucasta: Posthume Poems* (London, 1659), Hammond's case finds little support in this reading of Lovelace's first collection.[38] Yet 'Aramantha', the lengthy pastoral narrative with which the first *Lucasta* ends, raises some complications.

Certainly, it plays over some games familiar from elsewhere in the volume. Thus, in 'the jolly Bird of Light | Who sounds his third Retreat to Night' (*Luc.* 145) the military image, of giving the signal to retire,[39] once more accommodates the civil conflict to the cosy associations of a rural idyll, distancing the horrors of battle. The war, thus transformed, is an undisturbing presence. Again, in what I take to be a compliment on the heroine's nipples, we encounter a version of a paradisal wood:

> Garnisht with Gems of unset fruit,
> Supply'd still with a self recruit;
> Her bosom wrought with pretty Eyes
> Of never-planted Strawberries.   (*Luc.* 153)

As Hammond notes, 'recruit' had just entered the language in a number of chiefly military senses.[40] Here, the military metaphor nests within the metaphor of breasts-as-fruit, as, with a disconcerting and distinctly mannerist eroticism, Aramantha's strawberry-nipples, like willing volunteers, hang among other succulent fruits of the forest.

---

[37] G. Hammond, 'Richard Lovelace and the Uses of Obscurity', The Chatterton Lecture on Poetry, 1985, *Proc. Brit. Acad.* 71 (1985), 203–34, *passim.*

[38] Below, Ch. 7.

[39] *OED*, s.v. 'Retreat' sb., 2.a.

[40] Lovelace, *Selected Poems*, 104.

Yet the war and a much more earnest perspective on it abide at the heart of Lovelace's sensuous pastoral. The story relates how Aramantha finds Alexis grieving for the disappearance of his beloved Lucasta; she discloses to him that she is herself Lucasta, in pastoral guise, and that she has fled 'chac'd by HYDRAPHIL . . . The num'rous foe to PHILANACT' from 'this sad storm of fire and blood'; Alexis too, 'His armes hung up and his sword broke, | His Ensignes folded, he betook | Himself unto the humble Crooke' (*Luc.* 161–3). Plainly, Hydraphil and Philanact are to be identified with parliamentarian and Cavalier,[41] and though the former drove Lucasta away, both seem condemned—the text is not completely unambiguous:

> Since seeking thus the remedie,
> They fancy (building on false ground)
> The means must them and it confound,
> Yet are resolv'd to stand or fall,
> And win a little or lose all.   (*Luc.* 161–2)

Throughout *Lucasta* Lovelace, in unqualifiedly partisan terms, has constructed a model for ideological survival which values die-hard intransigence and within which courtly love at once validates militarism and is validated by it. Yet at the end, perhaps as a pointer to another direction remaining open to the Cavalier, his pastoral narrative offers an image of retreat and an escapist fantasy of a lifelong and erotic seclusion, 'Both vowing in her peacefull Cave | To make their Bridell-bed and Grave' (*Luc.* 163).

Read in the context of the crisis in royalist ideology, the *Lucasta* volume of 1649 is resourceful, resilient, and internally coherent. The parliamentary assault on royalism was underpinned by a psychological warfare designed to persuade royalists to consider the cost of the war and to settle. The whole strategy of compounding was to encourage surrender and reconciliation as an alternative to socio-economic obliteration, while with each victory the parliamentarian press presented royalists with grim lists of their casualties. The first *Lucasta*, with some qualification, remains the song-book of the undefeated.

---

[41] Id., *Poems*, 296, and *Selected Poems*, 104.

III

Early in the afternoon of 30 January 1649, Charles I was executed at Whitehall. A troop of horse dispersed the crowd, the body was removed, embalmed, and placed in a lead-lined coffin. Determining its burial place was problematic. The nearest appropriate site was Westminster Abbey, but 'Demonstrators and relic-hunters were alike to be feared, and the new government did not want to see the grave . . . turned into a place of pilgrimage at their very door'.[42] The burial finally took place on 9 February at St George's Chapel, Windsor, in the vault of Henry VIII, which had fallen into such desuetude for royal interment that it had to be located by stamping, in exploratory fashion, on the stones of the chancel. The funeral itself was a maimed rite: Colonel Whichcot, the Governor of the Castle, forbade the use of the Prayer-Book service for the dead, Bishop Juxon declined to extemporize, and so no service was held.

But the image of the king was not so mutely laid to rest. By the day of the funeral, Thomason had received what he endorsed as 'the first impression' of *Eikon Basilike: The Pourtraicture of his Sacred Maiestie in his Solitudes and Sufferings* (1649). The bibliographical history of the book is complex, and the circumstances of its composition remain the subject of rather speculative reconstruction. Thomason's copy was, in fact, the third issue of what was almost certainly the first edition. It is reasonable to assume that the first issue was available very soon after the execution. The volume presents itself as an autobiographical account of the king's conduct since 1640, interspersed with what purport to be his prayers on emergent occasions. The title is curiously ill-fitting, suggesting a portrait or image made of the king, rather than one produced by the king himself. Much of its appeal no doubt rests in its apparently royal origins—late into the nineteenth century it was still customarily called 'The King's Book'. Unsurprisingly, the king's authorship was disputed from the outset, and at the Restoration the claims of John Gauden, a divine who received rapid preferment till his death in 1662, disclose insights into the operations of the royalist underground. Gauden was almost certainly involved in its production, and the most likely account is that he edited and supplemented

---

[42] C. V. Wedgwood, *The Trial of Charles I* (1964; London, 1966), 202, on which my account of the death and burial of the king draws heavily.

material supplied to him by the king.[43] The production was carefully planned. The bookseller who published the first edition, Richard Royston, a committed royalist activist, claimed that he had been told in October 1648 to make ready a press, and that he had received the copy on 23 December.[44] The affair, including its remaining enigmas, has the characteristics of an ingeniously planned and energetically executed propaganda coup.

Its success is difficult to estimate. The book was very widely read, and editions rapidly multiplied: thirty-five were printed in England alone in 1649, and many others, both in English and in translation, were printed abroad. Its direct political effect, however, cannot be determined. Charles's victors, after all, continued to rule for eleven, for the most part untroubled, years, till dismissed through a political manœuvre that owed far more to the internal fracturing of the New Model Army than to popular royalist sentiment. Yet the size of its readership and the vigour with which the new ascendancy both answered and suppressed it indicate its potent impact on the consciousness of the political nation.[45]

Wherein lies its polemical genius? The answer is complex, for this is an ingeniously wrought production. It must rest, in part, in its skilful silences. The book begins at the calling of the Long Parliament. Modern accounts of the Civil War pay considerable attention to the origins of the conflict, and historians of our own era, while they disagree about the causes of the conflict, generally agree that some blame must lie in the social, intellectual, economic, or political history of the nation and more particularly of the period of Charles's personal rule. Certainly, though twentieth-century notions of historical causality are not to be expected from seventeenth-century observers, contemporaries as ideologically

---

[43] This is the conclusion of F. F. Madan, *A New Bibliography of the Eikon Basilike of King Charles the First* (Publications of the Oxford Bibliographical Society, NS 3 (1949); (Oxford, 1950), 133). This has been an invaluable source of information about the early printing history of the text. See also Potter, *Secret Rites*, 171–2. On the context, impact, and imitation of the work, see ibid. 156–70. There is little possibility of further untangling the writing of the king from that of an editor. Even a computer-aided authorship study based on the internal evidence of habits of style would not work since neither Gauden nor Charles produced other extant work in this curious confessional and imprecatory form, and difference of genre and situation would undermine the statistical basis of the investigation.

[44] Madan, *Biography*, 164; on Royston, see Potter, *Secret Rites*, 7–12.

[45] For Milton's response, *Eikonoklastes* (1649), see below, Ch. 6. For an account of the actions against its London publishers, see Madan, *Bibliography*, 164–6.

diverse as Clarendon and Milton found explanations for the conflict in the earlier actions of the king and his agents both civil and ecclesiastical. With a cunning simplicity *Eikon Basilike* initiates its account of Charles's part in the troubles rather later. The years of administration without recourse to Parliaments are set aside, briefly, as wise government (vindicated by the Long Parliament's behaviour on its assembly): 'I was not forgetfull of those sparks, which some mens distempers formerly studied to kindle in Parliaments, (which by forbearing to convene for some yeares, I had hoped to have extinguished).'[46] On the antecedents to the troubles—and Charles's part in them—the *Eikon Basilike* is generally silent, focusing rather on the area of the conflict in which the king was for the most part reacting to events, not initiating or occasioning them.

Very few people are identified by name or title. Besides the king himself, only the queen, the Prince of Wales, Strafford, and Sir John Hotham are thus identified. Madan, who noticed this, related it to its lack of appeal for the modern reader:

> To a more modern age the *Eikon* had lost much of its appeal; whatever its merits as a reflection of the character of King Charles, in the light of the principles to which he adhered, it is lacking both in that breadth of outlook and in those qualities of sympathy and understanding which might have made it one of the most vital and illuminating documents of the age.[47]

Perhaps, but it is that vagueness about the interests, motivations, fortunes—even the identity—of others that is central to the spell the book sought to weave over the consciousness of its contemporaries.

Eikon Basilike divides the opponents of the king into three categories: the multitude, the deluded, and his real enemies. The first category need not detain us. The spectrum of opinion from die-hard royalists to Cromwellian apologists agreed that men outside the enfranchised classes were fickle, stupid, and enemies to property, and that their intervention into politics was wholly malign—though neither side was quite so hostile to the many-headed beast when it acted in their support. Note the complaint about 'those tumultuary confluxes of mean and rude people, who are taught first to petition, then to protect, then to dictate, at last to command and overawe the Parliament' (*EB* 18). The assured

---

[46] *EB* 1. All references are to Wing E268.
[47] Madan, *Bibliography*, 72.

enunciation of received wisdom (the author invokes these comments as endorsed by 'wise men') and the insinuation of morally evaluative terminology are wholly unsurprising in the context of seventeenth-century fear and loathing of the working classes. Unsurprising too is the imprecision: it is in the nature of the vulgar that their names are unknown, and they behave ever thus. Much more fascinating is the juggling with the other categories, the enemies and the deluded. The polemical context must be remembered. The war had been pursued by a Presbyterian-dominated Long Parliament, and though it was the purged Parliament, predominantly Independent, that had brought the king to trial, the Presbyterians had sanctioned insurrection, open warfare, and, it was often remarked, the training of cannon on the king's position on the battlefield. By 1649 the parliamentary configuration was split, with Presbyterians hostile to the King's trial and execution. While these former supporters of the war against the king were potentially supporters of Restoration, some of them had been initiators of the conflict. It was an apparent contradiction which Milton, years later, exploited with, for Presbyterian royalists, a disconcerting insistence.[48]

Eikon Basilike, however, works to fudge these issues. The king's enemies are perhaps to be distinguished from the deluded by the severity of the punishment that, ideally, they would receive. The speaker has much to say about clemency, but remains vague about those to whom it is on offer. Sometimes he seems to hope for a general amnesty: 'The Trophees of my charity will be more glorious and durable over them, than their ill-managed victories over me' (*EB* 264). Pronominalization is a recurrent mechanism for evasiveness in *Eikon Basilike*, but here the reference is clearly to the 'Enemies' mentioned a little earlier (*EB* 259). The book ends with the king's imprisonment at Carisbrooke and purports to have been written in the late autumn of 1648. At times, it seems to look forward in this same spirit of general amnesty to some happy restoration:

If thou [God] *wilt againe put the Sword of Iustice into My hand to punish and protect.*

   Then will I make all the world to see, and my very Enemies to enjoy the benefit of this Vow and resolution of Christian charity, which I now make unto thee O Lord.

---

[48] See below, Ch. 8.

> *As I doe freely pardon for Christ's sake those that have offended me in*
> *any kind; so my hand shall never be against any man to revenge what is*
> *past, in regard of any particular injury done to me (EB 222).*

This is clear: everyone is forgiven, and not only in a spiritual sense: 'If' the king were returned to power and held 'the Sword of Iustice', then the civil courts would exercise his mercy. However, elsewhere it develops the familiar formula of reconciliation with victimization, the policy actually adopted at the Restoration:

> When they have destroyed Me, (for I know not how farre God may permit
> the malice and cruelty of My Enemies to proceed, and such apprehensions
> some mens words and actions have already given Me) as I doubt not but My
> bloud will cry aloud for vengeance to heaven, so I beseech God not to
> poure out his wrath upon the generality of the People, who have either
> deserted Me, through the artifice and hypocrisie of their Leaders, whose
> inward horrour will be their first Tormenter, nor will they escape
> exemplary judgments (*EB* 249–50).

Eikon Basilike must be referring to actual executions. Divine judgement cannot be intended, because such punishment, since it occurs after death, cannot be 'exemplary', in that it cannot be perceived by the living.[49] Is it a question, then, of Presbyterian sheep and Independent-republican goats? One cannot be sure who will escape. At one point, the distinction is made between the malicious (presumably, unforgivable enemies?) and religious fools (the deluded and pardonable?):

> I thanke God, I never found but My pity was above My anger; nor have My
> passions ever so prevailed against Me, as to exclude My most compassionate
> prayers for them, whom devout errours more than their owne malice have
> betrayed to a most religious Rebellion (*EB* 123).

But those motivated primarily by malice are, by implication, excluded from his compassionate prayers. Significantly, this occurs in a chapter dealing with political developments of the early 1640s, when the initiators of action against him—including, presumably, malicious ones—were Presbyterians, the group that, by the late 1640s, was emerging as a potential source of royalist support. The problem is compounded by an approach to the New Model Army:

---

[48] See below, Ch. 8.

[49] 'Exemplary' here almost certainly means 'Of a penalty, damages, etc.: Such as may serve for a warning, or act as a deterrent', a current 17th-cent. signification (*OED*).

For the Army (which is so far excusable as they act according to Souldiers principles, and interests, demanding Pay and Indempnity) I thinke it necessary, in order to the Publique peace, that they should be satisfied, as farre as is just; no man being more prone to consider them than My self: though they have fought against Me, yet I cannot but so farre esteem that valour and gallantry they have sometime shewed, as to wish I may never want such men to maintaine My selfe, My Lawes, and My Kingdomes, in such a peace, as wherein they may enjoy their share and proportion as much as any men (*EB* 228–9).

In some ways, it would seem, *Eikon Basilike* is working towards that intelligent and persuasive formula developed in the Declaration of Breda (1660), which precipitated the Restoration, a general pardon 'excepting only such persons as shall hereafter be excepted by Parliament, those only to be excepted'.[50] But the book is the product of a more uncertain phase. Should the royalists court the now powerless Presbyterians or the powerful but hostile New Model Army? Vagueness keeps the options open—and both options, by 1659–60, remained available. As a whole, the text is curiously removed from the issues that it purports to consider. Terms, categories, and concepts, such as 'Presbyterianism', 'Independency', 'Army Grandee', 'Leveller', that abound in contemporary writing and plainly provide the frame of reference in which most of the political nation perceive recent events, are almost entirely displaced by terms like 'some men', 'My Enemies', 'they'. In support of his argument for Charles's involvement in the writing, Madan claims that Gauden could not have been privy to the affairs of State that the book treats. On the contrary, there is no hard information disclosed in *Eikon Basilike* that would not have been familiar to a moderately well-informed country parson. As has been suggested, such an imprecision served the uncertainty of the immediate political context. It had a further function. If the opponents are not named, then their motivation may not be explored, except in terms of 'malice' or delusion. The lack of specificity serves well to isolate the king from specific particular reproach for his provocation and mishandling of the developing crisis. We are almost never invited to consider individuals' perceptions of and responses to events. The formula used for the chapter headings is significant: '*Upon* His Majesties calling this last

[50] *The Declaration of Breda*, in R. S. Gardiner (ed.), *The Constitutional Documents of the Puritan Revolution*, 3rd edn. (1906; Oxford, 1979), 464.

Parliament', '*Upon* the Earle of Straffords death', '*Upon* His Majesties going to the House of Commons', etc. (*EB*, sig. A2ᵛ, my emphasis). What is offered is not an account of the events themselves but an account of the king's perception of and meditation upon the events. In the process of meditation, awkward hard facts are filtered out.

But malice and delusion cannot constitute a complete explanation for so total a political collapse: the ill-will of a small group of conspirators and the folly of the people could not overthrow an ancient constitution without some *tertium quid*, such as the inherent instability of the State or the incompetence of its ruler. As readers search for this third term, several mechanisms work to deflect them.

As in Milton's *Areopagitica*, iterative imagery contributes power-fully to the polemical effect.[51] One skein of imagery links the events of the Civil War to the spread of fire:

No flames of civil dissentions are more dangerous then those which make Religious pretensions the grounds of Factions (*EB* 3).

What flames of discontent this sparke (though I sought by all speedy and possible meanes to quench it) soon kindled, all the world is witnesse (*EB* 14).

the preposterous rigour, and unreasonable severity, which some men carried before them in *England*, was not the least incentive, that kindled, and blew up into those horrid flames, the sparks of discontent which wanted nor [*sic*] pre-disposed fewel for Rebellion in *Ireland* (*EB* 91).

There are eighteen such occasions where imagery effects this connection between civil disturbance and uncontrolled combustion. A similar group (again, there are eighteen examples) makes an association with wild seas, storms, and dreadful inundations, as in:

But, as it is no strange thing for the sea to rage, when strong winds blow upon it; so neither for Multitudes to become insolent, when they have Men of some reputation for parts and piety to set them on (*EB* 19–20).

But thou O Lord art my refuge and defence, to thee I may safely flie, who rulest the raging of the Sea, and the madnesse of the People.

The flouds, O Lord, the flouds are come in upon me, and are ready to overwhelme me (EB 24).

O Lord, be thou my Pilot in this dark and dangerous storme, which neither

---

[51] T. N. Corns, 'Imagery', 6; see above, Ch. 3.

admits My returne to the Port whence I set out, nor My making any other,
with that safety and honour which I designed (EB 32).

Thus, the forces ranged against Charles and the crises which
develop are expediently depersonalized and equated with natural
disasters, events that are not explicable in terms of human causality
such as economic or political mismanagement by the king or his
agents. Plainly, they cannot be held responsible if there are floods
and storms: nor, it seems, can the specific responsibility for other
disasters be theirs. Moreover, the nature of the disasters, like their
causes, is distanced from the human scale and rendered vague.

This locks into the most important strategy of the text: its display
of piety. The events of the 1640s are meted out to the English king
and people as punishment for 'sin'. The connection with the
imagery of natural disaster is made explicit:

I look upon My sins, and the sins of My people, (which are the tumults of our
soules against thee O Lord) as the just cause of these popular inundations
which thou permittest to overbeare all the banks of loyalty, modesty, Lawes,
Justice, and Religion (EB 24).

But this is not a confession or an admission of his enemies' charges
against him. Rather, we find a complex and subtle response to the
question that confronted the defeated through the whole conflict:
why did God permit failure of his anointed? Cromwell and other
republicans thought or claimed that victory marked the divine
validation of their cause. Anxiety about this argument persistently
surfaces in *Eikon Basilike*. It is the 'fallacy' of those who 'from
worldy successe . . . draw those popular conclusions for Gods
approbation of their actions, whose wise providence (we know) oft
permits many events, which his revealed Word (the onely cleare,
safe, and fixed rule of good actions and good consciences) in no sort
approves' (*EB* 262); 'The prosperous winds which oft fill the sayles
of Pirats, doth not justifie their piracy and rapine' (*EB* 263). *Eikon
Basilike* is a thoroughly orthodox Protestant work, and Protestantism
at the theoretical level can cope with the problem these passages
define. Man as a fallen creature in a fallen world carries with him a
legacy of original sin for which punishment, even eternal punishment, is merited and from which he is redeemed through Christ's
mission and the unmerited extension of grace to the saved. That evil
should be permitted to triumph, then, seems unremarkable. All,
indeed, are sinful, so suffering is not inappropriate: on the contrary,

the sins of the king and people have given the Lord 'just cause' for
dealing so harshly with them.[52] Moreover, suffering and defeat can
be spiritually useful, since they remind the godly of the transience
of worldly glory and their utter dependence on the eternal mercy of
God: 'God was pleased to exercise My patience, and teach Me not
to trust in the arme of Flesh, but in the living God' (*EB* 172).

The pious resignation of the wayfaring Christian is supplemented
by careful invocation of the figures of David and Christ. Charles's
suffering is likened to the suffering incurred by David in punishment for his own sin and by Christ as he takes upon himself the sins
of the world.

A pattern of allusion to the books of Samuel and the Psalms
establishes this first connection. Of all the imagery in the tract
that has its origin in the Bible, over a quarter refers to this material.
Sometimes the author offers explicit analogies between the experiences
of David and those of Charles. Thus we find, 'I never had any
victory which was without My sorrow, because it was on Mine own
subject, who, like *Absolom*, died[,] many of them in their sin' (*EB*
176–7), and 'mens design, like *Absoloms*, is by enormous actions to
widen differences' (*EB* 191). More subtle is the thread of allusion to
Davidic lamentation woven into the inset prayers. The psalmist's
phrasing and imagery are persistently echoed. Thus, 'I will praise
thee: for thou hast heard me, and art become my salvation. The
stone which the builders refused is become the head stone of the
corner' (Ps. 118: 21–2) becomes, in a passage explicitly invoking
parallels with David, '*Though they curse, doe thou blesse, and I shall
be blessed; and made a blessing to my people. That the stone, which
some builders refuse, may become the head-stone of the corner*' (*EB*
137), a reference to the hoped-for rehabilitation of the king or his
reputation. Again, David's predictions for the evil man, 'Behold, he
travaileth with iniquity, and hath conceived mischief, and brought
forth falsehood. He made a pit, and digged it, and is fallen into the
ditch which he made. His mischief shall return upon his own head,
and his violent dealing shall come down upon his own pate' (Ps. 7:
14–16), becomes incorporated into an attack on the king's adversaries,
in another passage which explicitly invokes David's experience:
'*Arise, O Lord, lift up thy selfe, because of the rage of mine Enemies,
which increaseth more and more. Behold them that have conceived*

---

[52] *EB* 24, quoted above.

mischiefe, travelled with iniquity, and brought forth falshood' (*EB* 365).

Such care in intertwining the two royal histories proves polemically ingenious. David, above all, is God's anointed, a king whose divine sanction is manifest and reiterated. He, like Charles, experienced many vicissitudes, including both unpopularity and rebellion, yet God secured his eventual restitution. The pattern of allusion seems to suggest that God will also return the English monarch to his rightful place. David's problems, however, and the apparent occasional withdrawal of God's support are connected with his deviation into sin, the sin of seducing Bathsheba and plotting the death of her husband, one of his soldiers, by having him 'set . . . in the forefront of the hottest battle'. It is stated explicitly in the biblical account that 'the thing that David had done displeased the Lord' (2 Sam. 11: 15, 27). Charles's apologia too needs a sin to explain the vagaries of God's support and to accord with the Davidic myth it so consistently invokes, but not the confession of a sin that would concede the validity of his enemies' case against him. With a perverse genius, *Eikon Basilike* offers as his sin one of the very few actions Charles performed in 1640 which secured the support of his parliamentary opponents, namely the signing of the bill of attainder against his former chief minister, the Earl of Strafford, which permitted his execution. It is represented as the solitary occasion on which Charles allowed some notion of political expediency to overrule what his conscience told him was right:

And indeed, I am so farre from excusing or denying that complyance on My part (for plenary consent it was not) to his destruction, whom in My Judgment I thought not, by any cleare Law, guilty of death: That I never bare any touch of Conscience with greater regret: which, as a signe of My repentance, I have often with sorrow confessed both to God and men, as an act of so sinfull frailty, that it discovered more a feare of Man, than of God (*EB* 7).

Charles appears rather less sinful than David, motivated by a momentary loss of faith and courage rather than by a murderous lust. Nevertheless, 'Nor hath Gods Justice failed in the event and sad consequences, to shew the world the fallacy of that Maxime, *Better one man perish (though unjustly) than the People be displeased, or destroyed*' (*EB* 7–8). Like the repentant David, Charles is represented as acknowledging the justice of God's punishment, together with its spiritual benefit:

those Judgments God hath pleased to send upon Me, are so much the more welcome, as a meanes . . . which his mercy hath sanctified so to Me, as to make Me repent of that unjust Act, (for so it was to Me) and for the future to teach Me, That the best rule of policy is to preferre the doing of Justice, before all enjoyments, and the peace of My Conscience before the preservation of My Kingdomes (*EB* 8–9).

It is a master-stroke. The 'sin' necessary to fulfil the Davidic pattern of deviation, punishment, penitence, and—prospectively—restoration is, in the eyes of enemies, no sin at all and, in the eyes of friends, a miscalculation, largely at the prompting of his aides, reluctantly made and instantly regretted.

The second major area of biblical allusion, paralleling the fate of the king and the suffering of Christ, is more daring and proved to be of abiding influence in the shaping of the cult of King Charles the Martyr. Such allusion clusters towards the end of the book. As Charles is handed to Parliament by the Scots, to whom he had surrendered, he is represented as reflecting, 'if I am sold by them, I am onely sorry they should doe it; and that My price should be so much above My Saviours' (*EB* 201), an allusion to the thirty pieces of silver. As he contemplates his possible execution, he prays in terms which echo Christ's Gethsemane meditation, but which are made to seem more benevolent than Christ's resigned 'thy will be done' (Matt. 26: 42):

I pray not so much, that this bitter cup of a violent death may passe from Me, as that of his wrath may passe from all those, whose hands by deserting Me, are sprinkled, or by acting and consenting to thy death are embrued with My bloud (*EB* 260).

Formulae of forgiveness that echo Christ's 'Father, forgive them; for they know not what they do' (Luke 23: 34) abound, as in, for example:

Let me not so much consider, either what they have done, or I have suffered, (chiefly at first by them) as to forget to imitate My crucified Redeemer, to plead their ignorance for their pardon, and in My dying extremities to pray to thee O Father to forgive them, for they knew not what they did (*EB* 230–1).[53]

Allusion to Christ functions in part as an element in the construction of the king's image as saint and martyr, and is

---

[53] See also *EB* 65–6, 136, 267–8.

commonplace enough in other royalist accounts, in which 'over-night the Church of England found its Counter-Reformation Baroque royal saint'.[54] But such allusion functions well in massaging away that most abiding of royalist anxieties, that failure may be perceived as evidence of divine displeasure. For Charles suffers, like Christ, for the sins of others, and his martyrdom concedes nothing to the theory of endorsement through success. Moreover, it relegates the significance of temporal glory. As the famous engraved frontispiece depicting the king at prayer makes explicit, when Charles assumes Christ's crown of thorns, he spurns the vain crown of earthly success and raises his eyes to the crown of eternal glory. The rules are changed to brilliant effect. The victory in which Cromwell and his associates saw God's hand is dismissed—true victory is in the imitation of Christ's sacrifice: 'If I must suffer a violent death, with my Saviour, it is but a mortality crowned with martyrdome: where the debt of death . . . shall be raised as a gift to faith and patience offered to God' (*EB* 264).

IV

At the expense of chronology the most complex of the royalist texts of the 1640s examined in this chapter has been reserved till last, when some of the issues, attitudes, and strategies will have become familiar in more straightforward manifestations.

We do not know exactly when *Hesperides* was published. The evidence would appear to point to the printing of all except the prolegomenous material before the end of 1647 or at least very shortly afterwards.[55] If so, it was produced in a period of quite extraordinary ambivalence for the supporters of the king.

Herrick's royalist partisanship can scarcely be mistaken. About 30 per cent of ministers were ejected from their livings,[56] and he was certainly one of them.[57] His early ecclesiastical career manifested a close involvement with the Caroline court. He had served the Duke of Buckingham as chaplain on his expedition to the Isle of Rhe in

---

[54] Strong, *Charles I*, 29.
[55] See App. A.
[56] Hardacre, 42.
[57] What is known is recounted in F. W. Moorman, *Robert Herrick: A Bibliographical and Critical Study* (London and New York, 1910), 133–5.

support of the French Huguenots, and would seem to have owed his living at Dean Prior directly to the king.[58] His ideological orientation is plainly inscribed in the many panegyrics to the royal family included in *Hesperides*, and critics have often remarked upon the political dimension to his poetry, and recently to good effect.[59] However, *Hesperides* is characterized by radically different emphases in its political statement. This account has less to say about nostalgia and defeat, much more about the plurality of moods and tones which defies easy reduction. The principal point of divergence is in a fresh perception of the royalist spirit in 1647–8: though 1648 became, by mid-summer, what Marcus calls 'that dark year for royalists',[60] the months before had supported a hope that the nightmare was ending.

Hesperides is the work of a poet who has experienced acutely the bitterness of defeat. Herrick, after all, lost all his ecclesiastical income. Ejected ministers were often granted a fifth of their living to support their families, but as a bachelor he would have qualified for nothing.[61] A dismal, plangent note is often sounded, and at times it takes a personal perspective:

> *The Plunder*
>
> I am of all bereft;
> Save but some few Beanes left,
> Whereof (at last) to make
> For me, and mine a Cake:
> Which eaten, they and I
> Will say our grace, and die.   (*Hesperides*, 200)[62]

'Plunder' in the title prompts us to perceive the poem as a lament for

---

[58] F. W. Moorman, *Robert Herrick: A Bibliographical and Critical Study*, 87.

[59] For other political readings, see esp. R. H. Deming, *Ceremony and Art: Robert Herrick's Poetry* (The Hague, 1974); C. J. Summers, 'Herrick's Political Poetry: The Strategies of his Art', in R. B. Rollin and J. M. Patrick (eds.), '*Trust to Good Verses*': *Herrick Tercentenary Essays* (Pittsburgh, 1978), 171–83; A. Low, *The Georgic Revolution* (Princeton, 1985), esp. 262–74; A. Guibbory, *The Map of Time: Seventeenth-Century English Literature and Ideas of Pattern in History* (Urbana, Ill., 1986), 137–68; and L. S. Marcus, 'Herrick's *Noble Numbers* and the Politics of Playfulness', *ELR* 7 (1977), 108–26, 'Herrick's *Hesperides* and the "Proclamation Made for May"', *SP* 76 (1979), 49–74, and *The Politics of Mirth: Jonson, Herrick, Milton, Marvell and the Defense of Old Holiday Pastimes* (Chicago, 1986), 140–68.

[60] Marcus, '*Hesperides*', 74.

[61] Hardacre, 43–8.

[62] All references are to the Scolar Press Facsimile of the first edn. of *Hesperides* (1969; Menston, Yorks., 1973).

the impoverishment (particularly of the Church) resulting from the Civil War: plunder, the process not the booty itself, has precipitated a catastrophe. It is also a modern sort of tragedy: the word itself is a neologism, much used in Germany in the Thirty Years War and borrowed into news reports, as a verb, from about 1630. Its first recorded substantival use is in 1643. Like 'blitz' or 'blitzkrieg' in the 1940s, it was a new word for an unpleasant new phenomenon.[63] The sacerdotal gesture, '*I* | Will say *our* grace' (my emphasis), while it rehearses a Laudian endorsement of the priest's role among the laity (that is, the priest's duty to direct his flock), nevertheless seems empty, poignant, impotent. Again, in 'Upon the Troublesome Times', a poem of unqualified pessimism, circumstances seem desperate:

> O! Times most bad,
> > Without the scope
> > > Of hope
> Of better to be had!
>
> 2.   Where shall I goe,
> > Or whither run
> > > To shun
> This publique overthrow?
>
> 3.   No places are
> > (This I am sure)
> > > Secure
> In this our wasting Warre.
>
> 4.   Some storms w'ave past;
> > Yet we must all
> > > Down fall,
> And perish at the last.   (*Hesperides*, 247)

The relationship of the historical Herrick to the lyric voices of his poetry defies an easy equation—his final line of the secular section, '*Jocond his Muse was; but his Life was chast*' (p. 398), is as much a comment on the riddling connections between life and art as an exculpatory manœuvre. Yet 'publique overthrow' may safely be interpreted as an allusion to his ejection. The war is perceived as

---

[63] *OED* notes that the word 'plunder' was 'especially associated with the proceedings of the forces under Prince Rupert'. Compare *OED Suppl.* s.v. 'Blitz' and 'Blitzkrieg'. On the plundering of the West Country, see D. E. Underdown, *Revel, Riot, and Rebellion: Popular Politics and Culture in England 1603–1660* (Oxford, 1985), 151–3.

continuing (though hostilities had in effect ceased with the taking of Raglan Castle in April 1646[64]—no place indeed remained 'Secure' from Parliament's armies), and what has been endured proved easier than what will come, a general and pervasive ruin as well as a personal one.

We should be wrong, however, to see this as the prevailing mood of the collection. Consider the evidently late poem 'To the King, upon his Welcome to Hampton Court':

> Welcome, *Great Cesar*, welcome now you are,
> As dearest Peace, after destructive Warre:
>
> . . . .
>
> O *Pompe of Glory!* Welcome now, and come
> To re-possess once more your long'd-for home.
>
> . . . .
>
> Enter and prosper; which our eyes doe waite
> For an *Ascendent* throughly *Auspicate*:
> Under which signe we may the former stone
> Lay of our safeties new foundation:
>
> . . . .
>
> *Chor.* Long live the King; and to accomplish this,
> We'l from our owne, adde far more years to his.
>
> (*Hesperides*, 356)

Herrick must have written this poem within, at most, a few months of 'Upon the Troublesome Times', yet here the war, it is suggested, is concluded, the State may be re-established, the king's supporters may prosper, and the king flourish.

Such conflict of mood precisely matches the royalist position in the period covering 1647 and the first half of 1648, for, despite the defeats and their grave consequences, some signs prompted hopes of a renewal. Throughout 1647, relations between Parliament and the New Model Army deteriorated steadily, and more sapient royalists may well have been aware of both of the king's *rapprochement* with the army leaders after he had been taken into their custody, and his aspirations to profit yet from the discord. Nor were the divisions between the army leadership and Parliament the only evidence of the disintegration of the forces against him. The army itself, which had swept with such cohesion through the later battlefields of the First Civil War, manifested its heterogeneity in peace. The radical movement, especially among junior officers and the lower ranks,

---

[64] P. Young, *Civil War England* (London and New York, 1981), 159–60.

emerged with a heightened political consciousness which by October 1647 was showing itself in dialogue and negotiation, and by November in open mutiny.[65]

Nor was the king beyond liberation. In November he fled Hampton Court, and, though his move to Carisbrooke Castle on the Isle of Wight became another period of imprisonment, he and his supporters thought (incorrectly, as it proved) that further escape would be easy enough, and continued to contrive it throughout the winter and spring. In April 1648 the Duke of York was freed through the ingenuity and daring of royalist agents.[66] Moreover, Charles was in negotiation with Parliament's former allies, the Scots, for his liberation and restoration, and a zealous enmity to the king's enemies was widely resurgent, particularly in Kent, South Wales, and even London. The war in Ireland had ended in a new accord between Catholics, Presbyterians, and the Marquis of Ormond, the royalist lord lieutenant.[67]

The buoyancy of the winter and spring found substantiation in developments of the early summer. By May 1648, Wales was briefly in open insurrection, the Scots had agreed to assemble an army of 30,000 to invade England on the king's behalf, and the Kentish rising, which may well have seemed the start of a nationwide insurrection, threatened to produce an army of 20,000 to march on London, with the further prospect that Kent could be held as a base for pro-royalist French or Danish mercenaries or an Irish invasion force. The New Model Army, riven by internal dispute, openly attacked and clandestinely conspired against by the Parliament it had defended, faced the Second Civil War with the strong possibility of disaster.[68]

The scheming and preparation for the storm that broke in May 1648 provided the probable political context in which Herrick, royal protégé, ejected minister, royalist die-hard, probably completed *Hesperides*, as his world was poised between past horrors and the uncertainties of imminent conflict. By June, optimism would have seemed less well founded: Fairfax had driven back the Kentish rebels. Worse still, in mid-August Cromwell destroyed the Scottish incursion at the Battle of Preston. By late August, Colchester, the

[65] The Leveller movement is considered below, in ch. 5.
[66] Among the conspirators was the future Lady Halkett (see above).
[67] See below, Ch. 6.
[68] For a lucid narrative of events, see Gardiner, iii, esp. 182, 213, 216, 218, 230, 249, 253, 272–4, 336, 344, 356–7, 380, 443, 458.

refuge of the vestigial Kentish rebellion, surrendered to Fairfax.[69] Yet the king and his supporters continued to believe something would be rescued from the catastrophe.[70]

V

'Gather ye Rose-buds while ye may, | Old Time is still a flying' and 'I sing of *Times trans-shifting*'[71] (*Hesperides*, 93, 1): the best-known lines in Herrick allude to a notion of transience that challenges contemporaneously dominant ways of perceiving time. The millenarian impulse, with its emphasis not on flux but on a linear progression to a finity, ran strongly throughout the early seventeenth century, nor was it confined to radicals. Even James I found his thoughts turning to 'the latter dayes drawing on',[72] and to this prospect poetical sensibilities as diverse as Donne's and the youthful Milton's responded variously with awe ('What if this present were the worlds last night?'[73]) and with exhilaration ('Ring out ye crystal spheres'[74]). As Christopher Hill observes, 'Any careful reading of the Bible gives rise to thoughts about the end of the world. In the highly-charged atmosphere of the 1640s, many people expected it in the near future.'[75] Grotius was told that eighty chiliastic treatises had appeared in England by 1649,[76] and the Scot Robert Baillie, learned Presbyterian divine and member of the Westminster Assembly of Divines,[77] wrote home from London, 'The most of the chief divine here, not only Independents but others . . . are express Chiliasts.'[78] Thus, evidently the enthusiasm in England for this mode of thought appeared remarkably strong to outsiders.

Some millenarianism was fed by anxieties that the present order

[69] Gardiner, 386–97, 443, 458.

[70] Ibid. 482.

[71] 'Trans-shift', Herrick's coining, means 'to shift across or away': it seemingly acquired no currency outside the Herrick *œuvre*. For a long and accomplished consideration of the concept in a literary context, see Guibbory, *Map of Time*, 138–59.

[72] Quoted by C. Hill, *Puritanism and Revolution* (1958; London, 1969), 313.

[73] John Donne, *Holy Sonnets*, xiii., *Poetical Works*, 299.

[74] John Milton, 'On the Morning of Christ's Nativity', l. 125, *Poems*, 106.

[75] C. Hill, *The World Turned Upside Down: Radical Ideas during the English Revolution* (1972; London, 1978), 95.

[76] Hill, *Puritanism and Revolution*, 313.

[77] *DNB*.

[78] Quoted by Hill, *Puritanism and Revolution*, 313, *World*, 96.

was in disintegration: James I, for example, would seem to have been prompted by a feeling that the decline in respect for the clergy was ominous.[79] For enemies of the old order, an optimism about the imminence of the millennium fused into confidence about the progress of religious and political change.

In a world in which a broad spectrum of opinion directed its gaze to the millennium, the chiliastic dimension is significantly absent from *Hesperides* and marginal in *His Noble Numbers*. Herrick does not, in any sustained way, perceive time as a linear movement towards an irreversible triumph. In many poems, time withers present beauty, without compensation:

> 3. That Age is best, which is the first,
>   When Youth and Blood are warmer;
>   But being spent, the worse, and worst
>   Times, still succeed the former.
>   ('To the Virgins, to Make Much of Time',
>   *Hesperides*, 93)

Herrick, who was 51 in 1648, lived till 1674, yet poems anticipating his own death, pondering his mortality, observing his decay, and commemorating his demise abound throughout *Hesperides*:[80]

> *His own Epitaph*
>
> As wearied *Pilgrims*, once possest
> Of long'd for lodging, go to rest:
> So, I, now having rid my way;
> Fix here my Button'd staffe and stay.
> Youth (I confess) hath me mis-led;
> But Age hath brought me right to Bed   (p. 253)

Herrick excels at the elegiac subgenre of the epitaph, nor is this the only example written for the living: 'Upon Prew his Maid' (p. 308), a funerary quatrain written for a woman who lived till 1678,[81] perhaps anticipates the journalists' practice of holding obituaries on file.

The mutability motif often finds expression in a perception of

---

[79] Hill, *Puritanism and Revolution*, 313.

[80] L. Stone notes that 'members of the rural élite—wealthy squires and above—who survived to twenty-one could expect to live into the early sixties' (*The Family, Sex and Marriage in England 1500–1800*, abridged edn. (London, 1979), 57), though Herrick was probably a notch or so lower on the social scale.

[81] *The Poetical Works of Robert Herrick*, ed. L. C. Martin (Oxford, 1956), 535.

sexual decline. Thus, 'Age Unfit for Love' concludes in the maxim,
'Ill it fits old men to play, | When that Death bids come away'
(p. 326). The lines gain in power by their possible echo of Henry V's
dismissal of Falstaff, 'How ill white hairs becomes a fool and
jester.'[82] *2 Henry IV* constitutes something of the intertext to
Hesperides, as the poet's remarks 'To his Girles who Would Have
Him Sportfull' and 'His Last Request to *Julia*' (p. 391) suggest the
exchanges between Falstaff and Doll Tearsheet.[83]

The imminence of personal disintegration and the irreversibility
of the process are frequently resolved not in moralizing or
meditation but in a call to epicurean activity, as the poet rehearses
the *carpe diem* topos:

> Much I know of Time is spent,
> Tell I can't, what's Resident.
> Howsoever, cares, adue;
> Ile have nought to say to you:
> But Ile spend my comming houres,
> Drinking wine, & crown'd with flowres.
>
> ('On Himselfe', *Hesperides*, 222)

The passage invokes elements of both the Horatian distinction
between thought for the future and an active relish of present
sensation: 'carpe diem, quam minimum credula postero.'[84] Sometimes Herrick explicitly declares his sense of continuity with
classical tradition. The octet which concludes:

> before that day [of death] comes,
> Still I be Bousing;
> For I know, in the Tombs
> There's no Carousing   (p. 229)

is entitled 'Anacreontike'.[85] Critics have, quite rightly, made much
of Herrick's neoclassicism and of the paganism of the sentiments
borrowed from there and endorsed in his poems. Such sentiments,
though they conflict with the attitudes of nearly all Christian
denominations past, present, and probably to come, are perhaps
rendered rather less shocking by the literariness of the poetry in
which they are inscribed.

---

[82] William Shakespeare, *2 Henry IV*, ed. A. R. Humphreys (London, 1966), V. v.
48.

[83] Ibid. II. iv.

[84] Horace, *Odes*, I. xi. 8.

[85] *Poetical Works*, identifies allusion to *Anacreontea*, 7, 8, 40.

Herrick's poems work through the tradition which they invoke—
they are in imitation of Horace and Anacreon, written from a
posture which simulates the Horatian and Anacreontic stances—
and, as I have argued elsewhere, the ideological implications of
traditional poetic genres are not to be appraised by the simpler
procedures appropriate for prose polemic.[86] Only an innocent in
the ways of reading literature could perceive such poems as, in any
unmediated way, prescriptive or confessional. When Abiezer
Coppe wrote in a pamphlet, 'I can if it be my will, kisse and hug
Ladies, and love my neighbours wife as my selfe, without sin', his
statement could reasonably be perceived as libertine and intentionally
subversive, and its suppression is easy to understand.[87] Although
the literal-minded reader may see them as evidence of his dereliction
of priestly responsibility, Herrick's Horatian and Anacreontic
poems can scarcely be regarded as denials of divine providence or
Christian duty, but, they do have the power to shock. As an
undergraduate Milton too had written facetious and lascivious
erotic poetry (though never in English) in imitation of pagan
classical models.[88] The more puritanical Milton of the mid–1640s
saw fit to disavow such sentiments: 'Haec ego mente olim laeva,
studioque supino | Nequitiae posui vana trophaea meae.'[89] Yet he
nevertheless included them in his collection of 1645.

But there remains an ideological dimension to Herrick's simulation
of neoclassical perspectives, and, perhaps paradoxically, this very
literariness is the key. His own age, brooding on the pace of events,
on the accelerating dynamic of social and political change, saw
evidence of the advent of the millennium, of an end to time and the
physical world: Herrick, regarding human mutability as manifest in
personal decline, eschews the eschatological view in favour of
stratagems older than Christianity. The millenarian perspective is
finite, terminal: the Anacreontic and Horatian may be rehearsed by
poets throughout time as they contemplate the givens of human
mortality. Rather as nightingales become the eternal nightingale in
Keats's 'Ode', so too artists become recurrent manifestations of the

---

[86] Corns, ' "Some Rousing Motions" ', *passim*.

[87] Abiezer Coppe, *A Second Fiery Flying Roule*, in *Ranter Writings*, 107; see
below, Ch. 5.

[88] See esp. 'Elegia Prima', 'Elegia Quinta', and 'Elegia Septima', *Poems*, 18, 80, 69.

[89] *Poems*, 231; see also Thomas N. Corns, 'Ideology in the *Poemata* (1645)', in J.
A. Freeman and A. Low (eds.), *Urbane Milton: The Latin Poetry, Milton Studies*, 19
(Pittsburgh, 1983), 195–203.

eternal artist whose artifice opposes the erosions of time. Herrick's songs about time's trans-shifting resist the process they define.[90] The motifs of hedonism and of the immutability of art come together eloquently in 'To Live Merrily, and to Trust to Good Verses', which ends:

> Trust to good Verses then;
>   They onely will aspire,
> When Pyramides, as men,
>   Are lost, i' th' funerall fire.
>
> And when all Bodies meet
>   In *Lethe* to be drown'd;
> Then onely Numbers sweet,
>   With endless life are crown'd.   (*Hesperides*, 90)

Appropriately, this poem, which invokes the memory of a pantheon of classical poets, does so in a series of echoes of Ovid, Martial, and Catullus.[91]

Yet the notion that time is a process of irreversible decay which can be opposed by the stratagem of art is not the only perspective Herrick develops. Sometimes he explores a cyclic view which conceptualizes time as the regular interchange of natural phenomena and the passing seasons, as in 'Hope Well and Have Well, or, Faire after Foule Weather':

> What though the Heaven be lowring now,
> And look with a contracted brow?
> We shall discover, by and by,
> A Repurgation of the Skie;
> And when those clouds away are driven,
> Then will appeare a cheerfull Heaven.   (p. 218)

'Lowering', 'gloomy, dark, threatening', is sometimes used figuratively of attendant circumstances,[92] and clearly we are to recognize a symbolic aspect to the poem, a contrast between present gloom and future cheer. In the context of the crises of the royalist cause and royalist ideology, Herrick seems to be looking for some cyclic process as certain, as inevitable, as the sequence of sunshine after showers. This political tendency finds a more intricate expression in a much more complex poem, which shares, however, the same symbolic structure, 'Farewell Frost, or Welcome the Spring':

---

[90] Deming explores similar arguments, *Ceremony and Art*, passim; see also T. R. Whitaker, 'Herrick and the Fruits of the Garden', *ELH* 22 (1985), 16–33.
[91] *Poetical Works*, 517.   [92] *OED*.

Fled are the Frosts, and now the Fields appeare
Re-cloth'd in fresh and verdant Diaper.
Thaw'd are the snowes, and now the lusty Spring
Gives to each Mead a neat enameling.
The Palms put forth their Gemmes, and every Tree
Now swaggers in her [h]eavy gallantry.
The while the *Daulian Minstrell* sweetly sings,
With warbling Notes, her *Tyrrean* sufferings.
What gentle Winds perspire? As if here
Never had been the *Northern Plunderer*
To strip the Trees, and Fields, to their distresse,
Leaving them to a pittied nakednesse.
And look how when a frantick Storme doth tear
A stubborn Oake, or Holme (long growing there)
But lul'd to calmnesse, then succeeds a breeze
That scarcely stirs the nodding leaves of Trees:
So when this War (which tempest like doth spoil
Our Salt, our Corn, our Honie, Wine, and Oile)
Falls to a temper, and doth mildly cast
His inconsiderate Frenzie off (at last)
The gentle Dove may, when these turmoils cease,
Bring in her Bill, once more, *the Branch of Peace*.   (pp. 263–4)

The poem is organized around a series of parallels between the natural world and recent English history: as winter gives way to spring so the devastation of war may abate and peace return. Herrick turns the image nicely. 'Northern Plunderer', his term for the north wind—once more, a neologism originating in the recent crises[93]—suggests perhaps the role of the Scottish army fighting in England on Parliament's side. So strongly were the Scots troops associated with looting that when they were about to invade England once more in 1650, this time on behalf of Charles II, Marchamont Needham reminded English neutrals of the thieving antics of the last blue-bonneted incursion.[94] 'A stubborn Oake, or Holme' also carries a political weight. The oak, pre-eminent among trees as the lion was among beasts, no doubt suggests the pre-eminence of kings among men. 'Long growing there' seems more of political than naturalistic significance, a reference to the established and traditional nature of kingship, what Marvell was to call 'the great Work of Time'.[95] I assume the alternative, 'Holme', the

---

[93] First recorded use, 1647 (*OED*).
[94] e. g. *Mercurius Politicus*, 2 (London, 1650), 76.
[95] 'An *Horatian* Ode upon *Cromwel's* Return from *Ireland*', l. 34, *Poems and Letters*, i. 92; on Marvell's use of the symbol of the oak, see below, Ch. 7.

Mediterranean holm-oak, *Quercus ilex*,[96] constitutes part of the pattern of Horatian and Virgilian reference which informs the poem,[97] and which suggests parallels between the poets' experiences of English and Roman civil wars, perhaps even with some oblique aspiration that the English outcome may be as fortunate.

Perceiving war as a natural phenomenon has many advantages for Herrick as it had for that other royalist apologist, the author of *Eikon Basilike*. The onset of winter, though ultimately attributable to the fall of man, is the fault of no living man, and certainly not of the king. Again, the end to the troubles may simply happen in a political universe which, for all the recent discord and present unhappiness, is offered to us as ultimately self-righting. Such a vision, in opposition both to Herrick's other view of progressive decay and to the millenarian perception of the purposeful march of events towards the end of time, accords well with the local mood of hope and uncertainty which characterized the royalist cause through 1647 into the early months of 1648.

VI

A dozen or so poems in *Hesperides* describe or invoke Christmas jollity, and critics have noted that their endorsement of traditional games and customs, like Herrick's praise of May games, constitutes in the context of the English Civil War the expression of a political sentiment: for the most part, his work has been seen as 'a lament for the passing of a moral, ethical, social and religious age that was about to come crashing down under a parliamentary blade'.[98] However, these poems are better interpreted as songs not of lamentation but of protest and resistance, the literary embodiment of a current struggle which did not seem hopeless.

Puritan objections to the traditional celebration of Christmas had a long history. The feast provoked not only familiar hostility to jollity in that it presented opportunities for drinking, dancing, and other abandon, but also antipathy to the paganism of its origins and to the popish superstition implicit in supposedly Christian observance

---

[96] *OED.*

[97] *Poetical Works*, 546.

[98] Deming, *Ceremony and Art*, 155; similarly, Marcus, *'Noble Numbers'* and *'Hesperides'*, *passim*.

of a feast of no biblical authority. As early as 1616, Ben Jonson had mocked such opinions in his *Christmas his Masque*.[99] In the 1640s, however, such long-held distaste was translated into political action as the traditional celebration of Christmas was first discouraged and eventually outlawed. Parliament had decreed that a regular fast should be held on the last Wednesday of each month to mark the solemnity of the nation's troubles:[100] in 1644, this happened to coincide with Christmas Day, but an ordinance of 19 December 1644 insisted that the fast be strictly observed:

this day in particular is to be kept with the more solemn humiliation, because it may call to remembrance our sinnes, and the sinnes of our forefathers, who have turned this Feast, pretending the memory of Christ, into an extreme forgetfulnesse of him, by giving liberty to such carnall and sensuall delights.[101]

As the predominant ideology was further incorporated into the State apparatus, other measures followed, and by an ordinance of 8 June 1647 'for Abolishing of Festivals', 'the Feasts of the Nativity of Christ, Easter and Whitsuntide, and other Festivals commonly called Holy-Dayes . . . heretofore superstitiously used and observed' were forbidden.[102]

The celebration of Christmas became a rallying point for royalists. As one sober, licensed tract of December 1649 remarked, the legislation had been impolitic since it permitted malignants to recruit others to their cause out of 'an holy indignation'.[103] John Taylor, that most spirited of anti-Puritan pamphleteers, in a masterpiece of crude, demotic appeal, produces a fantasy of 'Merry England' which in some ways anticipates the clumsier elements in Herrick's depiction of Christmas. He offers a vision of an England in which 'the Rich relieved the Poore, the Poore had cause to pray for the prosperity of the Rich, one neighbour Feasted another, every one in his degree made good cheere'.[104] Taylor, who would have felt at home in the Fleet Street or Wapping of the late twentieth

---

[99] See Norbrook, *Poetry and Politics*, 242.

[100] *Acts and Ordinances*, i. 580.

[101] Ibid. 954. The same ordinance recognized that such legislation impaired the leisure of 'Scholars, Apprentices and other Servants', and further legislation set aside the second Tuesday of every month 'for Recreation and Relaxation' (Ibid. 985).

[102] Ibid. 954.

[103] George Palmer, *The Lawfulnesse of the Celebration of Christs Birthday* (London, 1649), 10.

[104] John Taylor, *The Complaint of Christmas* (London, 1646), 4.

century, contrasts the pleasures of Christmas past with the austerity of Christmas present and makes the obvious political points:

all the liberty, and harmlesse sports, with the merry Gambolls, dances and friscolls, which the toyling Plowswaine, and Labourer, once a yeare were wont to be recreated [*sic*], and their spirits and hopes reviv'd for a whole twelve month, are now extinct and put out of use . . . Thus are the merry Lords of misrule, supprest by the mad Lords of bad rule at Westminster.[105]

There is, unfortunately, no confirmation from ploughmen and labourers that the festival, as celebrated in their humble wise, had quite such refreshing properties.

Christmas Day in 1647, as *Hesperides* approached publication, was 'marked by an explosion of feeling far more widespread than in any former year'.[106] The Mayor of Canterbury had attempted to ensure it was regarded as a normal business day, insisting that a market be held. A crowd appeared in the street with a football, closed the few shops that had opened, and played in the street. When the Mayor tried to stop them, he was knocked down, and the houses of his supporters were stoned. Rioting resumed on 27 December, when, significantly, the cry was raised, 'Up with King Charles, and down with Parliament and Excise!' Three thousand men from the trained band were needed to restore order. An apologist for the riot made explicit the political connections when he spoke of the tumults as:

provokt by the Mayors violent proceedings against those who desired to continue the celebration of the Feast of Christs Nativity, 1500 years and upwards maintained in the Church. Together with their Resolutions for the restitution of His Majestie to his Crown and dignity, whereby Religion may be restored to its ancient splendour, and the known Laws of this Kingdom maintained.[107]

Disturbances of the same kind occurred in many places.[108]

Herrick's enthusiasm for Christmas festivities as a subject for poetic celebration certainly antedates the Civil War. 'A New-Yeares Gift Sent to Sir *Simeon Steward*', which Martin thinks must have

---

[105] John Taylor, *The Complaint of Christmas*, 7.

[106] Gardiner, iii. 281, on whom my account is based; see also, Underdown, *Revel*, 260–1.

[107] Anon., *The Declaration of Many Thousands of the City of Canterbury* (London, 1647); Thomason dated his copy 'Jan: 5' (i.e. 5 January 1648).

[108] Gardiner, iii. 281–2.

been composed for Christmas 1623[109] and which can certainly have been no later than 1628, since the recipient died in 1629,[110] already rehearses their benefits with a commitment to their powers of social reconciliation and spiritual liberation that reminds the modern reader of Dickens:

> here a jolly
> Verse crown'd with *Yvie*, and with *Holly*:
> That tels of Winters Tales and Mirth,
> That Milk-maids make about the hearth,
> Of Christmas sports, the *Wassell-boule*,
> That tost up, after *Fox-i'th'hole*.[111]
> (*Hesperides*, 145–6)

Very similar sentiments recur elsewhere in his early poetry.

Other poems of indeterminate date of composition articulate the kinds of Christmas sentiment that constituted, by the late 1640s, a militant expression of defiance of the new order. Herrick offers a number of poems dealing with what he terms the 'Ceremonies' of Christmas and associated feasts. The word carries a powerful cultural charge. Perhaps not a little facetiously, he extends the range of application of a term that had previously referred to matters of State and, more significantly, to matters of religion.[112] Whereas the term had a long history of signifying 'an outward rite', 'the performance of some solemn act', 'a solemnity' (*OED*, sig. 1), it had been used disparagingly since early in the sixteenth century to mean mere 'empty form' (sig. 2) and recurs frequently in Puritan propaganda and legislation of the 1640s. For example, the ordinance of 4 January 1645, which prohibited the use in church service of *The Book of Common Prayer* and prescribed, instead, a 'Directory' for public worship, claims that:

the many unprofitable and burdensome Ceremonies, contained in it [*The Book of Common Prayer*], have occasioned much mischief, as well by disquieting the Consciences of many godly Ministers and people who could not yeeld unto them, as by depriving them of the Ordinances of God,

---

[109] *Poetical Works*, 526.
[110] *DNB*.
[111] According to J. Higins, *Junius Nomenclator* (London, 1585), 298, 'A kinde of playe wherein boyes lift up one leg and hop on the other' (cited by *OED*).
[112] *OED* though it seems not to have been alert to Herrick's use of the term in an extended, semi-literal signification.

which they might not enjoy without conforming or subscribing to those Ceremonies.[113]

Once the intertext of such puritanical strictures is reconstructed, poems like the following emerge, uncompromisingly, as the impudent gesticulation of the undefeated:

> *Ceremonies for Christmasse*
> Come, bring with a noise,
> My merrie merrie boyes,
> The Christmas log to the firing;
> While my good Dame, she
> Bids ye all be free;
> And drink to your hearts desiring.
>
> With the last yeeres brand
> Light the new block, And
> For good successe in his spending,
> On your Psaltries play,
> That sweet luck may
> Come while the Log is a teending.
>
> Drink now the strong Beere,
> Cut the white loafe here,
> The while the meat is a shredding;
> For the rare Mince-Pie
> And the Plums stand by
> To fill the Paste that's a kneading.
>   (*Hesperides*, 309–10)

Linguistically, the poem has perhaps an archaic flavour: 'teending' (i.e. 'tinding') is the last recorded intransitive use of the verb and postdates the previous by over 200 years.[114] The sentiment, however, is not archaic: the poem describes how Christmas had been celebrated, how it still was celebrated in contravention of Parliament's ordinances, and how it would be celebrated generally again. Under the gleeful banner of 'Ceremonies' Herrick highlights precisely the aspects of traditional practice that so exasperated his enemies—gluttony, unrestrained drinking, paganism (in the burning of the Yule log[115]), and irrationality. 'Sweet luck', it would seem, is

---

[113] *Acts and Ordinances*, i. 583.

[114] *OED*.

[115] The log was perceived by early 18th-cent. antiquarians as a custom fossilized from pre-Christian times (*OED*), though I am unable to demonstrate the earlier currency of this view. However, Sir Thomas Browne demonstrated the pagan

achieved by playing psalteries as the log ignites and by firing it with the remnants of last year's log. Moreover, 'luck' is an alien concept to those convinced of God's providential care of the godly. A poem like 'Ceremonies for Christmasse' would have struck a Puritan as outrageous, as an utterly unrepentant and unregenerate demonstration of much that had been wrong in pre-revolutionary England. For the royalist, however, it asserts the indomitability of old England: Parliament may outlaw Christmas, but their legislation can be defied, and even if the apparatus of State repression can stop the physical enactment of traditions, they persist in that land which neither mayor nor militia can control, the counter-revolutionary consciousness celebrated in *Hesperides*.

VII

In 'The Argument of his Book', Herrick had announced, among other themes, songs 'of *May-poles, Hock-carts,*[116] *Wassails,*[117] *Wakes*[118]' (*Hesperides*, 1). Other critics have recognized the importance of Puritan Sabbatarianism and opposition to traditional sports as the immediate context for the interesting poems that engage such subjects.[119] Indeed, Herrick has been represented at times as the laureate of the folk customs of Merry England. We must not exaggerate the prominence within *Hesperides* of the customs he lists: the hock-cart is the subject of but one later poem, maypoles of two, and wakes recur in just three poems. Neverthe-

antecedents of some superstitions in *Pseudodoxia Epidemica*, ed. Robin Robbins (Oxford, 1981), i. 424–33. Browne has something to say about (other) Christmas superstitions (ibid. 462).

[116] 'The cart or wagon which carried home the last load of the harvest' (*OED*): curiously, the word, cognate with 'Hockey' 'the old name in the eastern counties of England for the feast of harvest-home', appears first in Herrick and the only other 17th-cent. citation is from Mildmay Fane, the Earl of Westmorland, to whom Herrick addressed 'The Hock-Cart, or Harvest Home' (*Hesperides*, 113). For an account of their relationship, see M.-S. Roestvig, *The Happy Man*, 2nd edn. (Oslo, 1962), i. 114. Possibly Herrick had coined the word: more likely, however, he had adopted it into literary English from a regional and colloquial usage.

[117] 'A custom formerly observed on Twelfth-night and New-Year's Eve of drinking healths from the wassail bowl' (*OED*).

[118] 'The local annual festival of an English . . . parish, observed (originally on the feast of the patron saint of the Church . . .) as an occasion for making holiday' (*OED*).

[119] See esp. Marcus, '*Hesperides*'.

less, the sportive and festive elements are pervasive. As a crude index, we may observe that the words 'feast', 'feasts', and 'feasting' appear twenty-four times in *Hesperides*, 'play', 'played', 'player', 'playing', and 'plays', in their various senses, almost seventy, whereas in *Paradise Lost*, which we may perhaps take as a point of Puritanical comparison, the former group occurs seven times, the latter just eleven.[120] Usually, in *Paradise Lost* 'play' is applied to the behaviour of animals, though Adam and Eve engage in sexual 'play' after their fall. The figures that people *Hesperides* are represented as engaged in diverse sports and pastimes—in stool-ball, a bat-and-ball game of wider regional popularity than cricket, which at that time was still confined to Kent and Sussex;[121] in cudgel-play, a rustic martial art;[122] in cherry-pit, a childen's game of throwing cherry stones into a little hole;[123] in draw-gloves, a parlour game which seemingly consisted in a race at taking off one's gloves at the utterance of certain words;[124] and at push-pin, a children's game in which players push or fillip their pins with the object of crossing those of other players.[125]

By highlighting the ludic, holiday spirit, Herrick once more places *Hesperides* in the ranks of royalist opposition to the Puritan ascendancy. In an age in which even the trivial assumed a high symbolic seriousness, the pursuits he describes and the attitude he defines were the focus of persistent attack. The struggle, as Hill and more recently Underdown have shown, had been long and would continue, and its political significance was explicitly recognized contemporaneously.[126] Local government, when under Puritanical control, attempted to suppress games and festivals; Puritanical ministers discouraged wakes and other holidays and argued for a strict Sabbatarianism; royalist central government and local anti-Puritan sentiment operated to conserve the old ways; and each fared variously in different regions. The major royalist instrument was the so-called Book of Sports, a declaration—what would now be

---

[120] The information is extracted from *A Concordance to the Poems of Robert Herrick*, ed. M. MacLeod, (New York, 1936), and W. Ingram and K. Swaim (eds.), *A Concordance to Milton's English Poetry* (Oxford, 1972).

[121] *Hesperides*, 280; Underdown, *Revel*, 74–5.

[122] *Hesperides*, 300; see the 1636 quotation in *OED*.

[123] *Hesperides*, 17; *OED*.

[124] *Hesperides*, 111, 253, 306; *OED*.

[125] *Hesperides*, 15; *OED*.

[126] C. Hill, *Society and Puritanism in Pre-Revolutionary England* (1964; London, 1966), esp. ch. 5; Underdown, *Revel*, esp. ch. 3.

termed a policy statement—issued in 1618, which explicitly permitted dancing, May games, Whitsun ales, morris dances, and the setting up of maypoles. Underdown notes that it was striking how quickly the inhabitants of small towns and villages appealed to it against the reformers.[127] The struggle against it, both parliamentary and local, continued, and in 1633, after a senior magistrate had reiterated an interdiction against a church wake in Somerset,[128] the county adjacent to Herrick's Devon, the declaration was reissued with a new coda:

in some Counties of Our Kingdome, Wee find that under pretence of taking away abuses, there hath been a generall forbidding, not onely of ordinary meetings, but of the Feasts of the Dedication of the Churches, commonly called Wakes. Now Our expresse will and pleasure is, that these Feasts with other shall be observed.[129]

The year 1634 saw something of a resurgence of the old festive traditions, though once the Civil War started, as region after region fell under the control of parliamentary forces, a Puritan reform was effected. The pertinent governmental instrument was the 'Ordinance for the better observation of the Lords-Day' (8 April 1644), which forbade on Sundays 'any wrastlings, shooting, Bowling, Ringing of Bells for Pleasure or Pastime, Wake, otherwise called Feasts, Church-Ale, Dancing, Games, Sport or Pastimes whatsoever'. It extended its prohibitions to children, insisted 'that no May-pole shall be . . . set up, erected, or suffered', and instructed that the declaration of 1633 be burnt by local magistrates.[130]

Yet resistance continued. There were incidences of the provocative erection of maypoles in Essex in 1647 and in Suffolk in 1648, and, in a demonstration clearly indicative of the political significance of the gesture, at Wolverhampton in 1653 a maypole was set up to celebrate the dissolution of the Rump. Magistrates were active against a variety of feasts and sports in many counties in the late 1640s and the 1650s. As Underdown observes, 'The limited effectiveness of the campaign for godly order is as obvious in the 1650s as in earlier times.'[131] At the Restoration, political change

[127] Ibid. 65.

[128] For a narrative of events, see Gardiner, vii. 319–21.

[129] Charles I, *The Kings Maiesties Declaration concerning Lawfull Sports* (London, 1633), 15–16.

[130] *Acts and Ordinances*, i. 420–2.

[131] Hill, *Society and Puritanism*, 185–6; Underdown, *Revel*, 262.

found symbolic manifestation in the immediate reappearance of maypoles, sometimes tailored to celebrate the triumph of the old order, as in Wells where they were used for posting libellous verses against local Puritans. Rural wakes and revels also revived and appear to have been more freely practised than ever.[132]

Herrick's lyrics are songs not merely of nostalgia but also of a defiant resistance which makes no concession to the Puritans' campaign of repression. The reasons for the incorporation of both the promotion and suppression of maypole raising, dancing, games, and festivals into the rival ideologies are complex, and embedded in the history of English society in the early modern period and more profoundly in the dynamics of mass psychology; they await a proper explanation. Whatever their deeper prompting and more secret motivation, the Puritans' thesis is persistently reiterated throughout the decades: the sportive and festive spirit is pagan and manifests itself in superstitions and idolatrous rites; it facilitates drunkenness and fornication; and it provides, in its unbridled gatherings, a context for civil disorder and threat to property. *Hesperides* relates in curious ways to the newly ascendant ideology of repression. Consider, first, 'The May-Pole' (*Hesperides*, 281). The paganism of the rite was often observed—'a maypole was an idol', as one Puritan convert remarked[133]—and some seventeenth-century observers did note its phallic significance.[134] Its associations with drunken abandon were commonplace. Herrick responds thus:

> The May-pole is up,
> Now give me the cup;
> I'le drink to the Garlandes around it:
> But first unto those
> Whose hands did compose
> The glory of flowers that crown'd it.
>
> A health to my Girles,
> Whose husbands may Earles
> Or Lords be, (granting my wishes)
> And when that ye wed
> To the Bridall Bed,
> Then multiply all, like to Fishes.

There is no warrant for assuming 'Girles' carries necessarily a

---

[132] Hill, *Society and Puritanism*, 186; Underdown, *Revel*, 280–1.
[133] Quoted ibid. 77.
[134] Hill, *Society and Puritanism*, 184.

suggestion of sexual intimacy: that signification seems of eighteenth-century currency.[135] But 'my' gives an almost proprietary air. The lyric acknowledges the role of the rite in courtship—and procreation. Yet the concluding image, for all its flippant charm, is deeply challenging. The Form of Solemnization of Matrimony in *The Book of Common Prayer* comes to mind, with its injunction that marriage 'is not to be enterprised nor taken in hand unadvisedly, lightly, or wantonly, to satisfie mens carnall lusts and appetites, like bruit beasts that have no understanding'.[136] Herrick chirpily offers a view of human sexuality wholly in tune with the coupling of beasts. He further links maypole rituals with drinking: '*Now* give me the cup.' Raising the maypole triggers communal indulgence as '*the* cup' suggests a shared vessel.

'The May-Pole' endorses—albeit in triumphant or defiant mode—many Puritan prejudices. But it disputes one aspect of the familiar diatribe. Far from jeopardizing public order, Herrick's festivals cement it. He persistently invokes images of vertical social cohesion, of practices in which bonds of patronage and duty are consolidated. In this poem, it is limited to the act of the poet sharing the cup with, one assumes, classes including his inferiors, and to the presumably jocular wish that 'my Girles' may effect morganatic marriages. But the theme is fully and more seriously explored in perhaps the best of his festive poems, 'The Hock-Cart, or Harvest Home' (*Hesperides*, 113–15), addressed to Mildmay Fane, Earl of Westmorland, a confirmed royalist, who had been arrested and lodged in the Tower of London from 1642 to 1644, though he had settled with Parliament and was set at liberty thereafter.[137]

Herrick, it has been claimed, 'idealize[s] the innocence of the country scene':[138] perhaps so, but his vision of the hardships of the poorer peasantry is unflinching and unsentimental. 'The Hock-Cart' emphasizes social stratification, only to resolve it or, perhaps more accurately, to accommodate it in the rituals of harvest home:

> Come Sons of Summer, by whose toile,
> We are the Lords of Wine and Oile:

---

[135] *OED*.

[136] *The Book of Common Prayer* (London, 1636), sig. P4^r, my emphasis; this element is omitted from the recommendations for commemoration of marriage in the Directory of Public Worship issued in January 1645 to replace the banned Prayer-Book (*Acts and Ordinances*, i. 599–601).

[137] *DNB*.

[138] Underdown, *Revel*, 14.

> By whose tough labours, and rough hands,
> We rip up first, then reap our lands.   (ll. 1–4)

'We' and 'our' are not categories which include the agricultural labourers, for they, readers are told, are not to drink the wine: 'If smirking Wine be wanting here [at the feast] | There's that which drowns all care, stout Beere' (ll. 36–7). The workers return with the product of their labour and their lord's land to lay it before him as he comes, not from the fields, but from his hall to greet them: 'Come forth, my Lord, and *see* the Cart' (l. 7, my emphasis). '*Tough* labours' and '*rough* hands' emphasize the painful nature of their toil. 'Rusticks' follow the cart 'with their breeches rent' (l. 25), an obvious emblem of indigence. The final lines raise complex political and social issues:

> and as ye eat,
> Be mindfull, that the lab'ring Neat
> (As you) may have their fill of meat.
> And know, besides, ye must revoke
> The patient Oxe unto the Yoke,
> And all goe back unto the Plough
> And Harrow, (though they'r hang'd up now.)
> And, you must know, your Lords word's true,
> Feed him ye must, whose food fils you.
> And that this pleasure is like raine,
> Not sent you for to drowne your paine,
> But for to make it spring againe.   (ll. 44–55)

We need not suppose many contemporary ploughmen read *Hesperides*: yet the explicit, demystifying account of economic relations probably shocks at least some late-twentieth-century readers. Labourers occupy a position in the scale of being only slightly above the beasts of burden. They are similarly rewarded, and, moreover, for the workers as for the animals respite from their painful tasks is only temporary. As others have noticed, the concluding triplet is surely ambiguous. The 'pleasure' promotes the agricultural activity that produces the burgeoning of spring: but 'pleasure' also makes 'pain' spring again. The rustics' toil constitutes the essential ingredient of agricultural production, but its experience is agony: festivities may function to cement social relationships, but the alleviation they offer the workers is utterly transitory. 'The Hock-Cart' confidently and unashamedly asserts the nature of agricultural production in a world *not* turned upside down. Its

assured tone, its refusal to mitigate the inequalities both of effort
and of benefit, proffer a vision of the contemporary social order as
natural, inevitable, and immutable, an order that is most clearly seen
and most warmly celebrated in its ancient festivals. The grateful,
deferential peasant and the benevolent but uncompromising lord
meet in exclusion of any third element, whether upstart tradesman,
radical intellectual, or Puritan preacher. Not riot, but stability and
degree, are produced by harvest home.

Herrick, however, does, somewhat lasciviously, concur in his
enemies' thesis about the proximity of play and sexual abandon, a
thesis he incorporates into his libertarian and oppositional royalism.
In several poems, play between the sexes shades into sexual
foreplay, as in 'Cherry-Pit':

> Iulia and I did lately sit
> Playing for sport, at Cherry-pit:
> She threw; I cast; and having thrown,
> I got the Pit, and she the Stone.   (*Hesperides*, 17)

Presumably we are to recognize the *double entendres* of 'pit'
(meaning target declivity and female pudendum) and 'stone' (meaning
projectile and testicle),[139] though it remains open whether we are to
regard the game of cherry-pit as simply an extended metaphor for
coitus, or rather to read the poem as narrating an episode in which a
game mutates into a sexual encounter. Elsewhere, the narrative
sequence is clearer, as in:

> Pusse and her Prentice both at Draw-gloves play;
> That done, they kisse, and so draw out the day:
> At night they draw to Supper; then well fed,
> They draw their clothes off both, so draw to bed.
>   ('Upon *Pusse* and her Prentice. Epig.', p. 306)

'Pusse', conventionally a proper name for a cat, was contemporaneously applied to girls or women as a term of reproach or
contempt,[140] and both the name and the relationship—she sleeps
with her 'prentice'—indicate a milieu of clandestine licentiousness
among the trading classes. The adjacency of play and sexuality

---

[139] E. Partridge, *A Dictionary of Slang and Unconventional English*, 8th edn., ed.
P. Beale (London, Melbourne, and Henley, 1984), notes that it is 'an open question'
whether 'pit' and its variants are low, colloquial, or euphemistic in the 17th to 19th
cent. *OED*.

[140] *OED*; it was already a slang term for the female genitalia (Partridge, *Slang*).

recurs in all social groups, and, Herrick hints, in its naturalness and transcendence it is essential to human psychology, beyond the reach of Puritan control.

Herrick sets at nothing the moralizing interdictions of his enemies. In 'Corinna's Going a Maying' (*Hesperides*, 74–6), the outrage he provokes explicitly engages those familiar charges of the paganism and irreligion of the old festivals. The poet calls his mistress from her bed to 'fetch in May' (l. 14). Dawn is described in a tissue of classical allusion: the 'Blooming Morne' presents 'the god unshorne', an echo of a Horatian periphrasis for Apollo,[141] and 'Aurora . . . throwes her faire | Fresh-quilted colours through the aire' (ll. 1–4). Such facile mythologizing is not especially interesting in itself—it had constituted a familiar part of poetic texturing throughout the centuries. But here, it ushers in a recurrent pattern of semi-facetious reference to the May rituals in terms of religious observance. Thus, 'all the Birds have Mattens seyd, | And sung their thankfull Hymnes' (ll. 10–11) continues the schema: of itself, the image is conventional enough,[142] but the pseudo-devotional context revives it. Again, ''tis sin, | Nay profanation to keep in' (ll. 11–12) playfully juxtaposes May rites and theological diction. 'Devotion' prompts the decorating of houses with green boughs, so that—and this, in its flippant allusion to the holy of holies, is most striking— 'Each porch, each doore . . . | An Arke a Tabernacle is | Made up of white-thorn neatly enterwove' (ll. 33–5). 'Corinna's Going a Maying' is a complex poem, thematically more concerned with rehearsal of the *carpe diem* motif, but it nevertheless takes some of its power from its impudent invocation of the images and terminology of Christian and pagan religion.

VIII

Two hundred and seventy-three religious poems come after the secular section, following a secondary title-page which bears the title *His Noble Numbers, or, His Pious Pieces, Wherein (amongst Other Things) He Sings the Birth of his Christ, and Sighes for his Saviours Suffering on the Crosse*. We shall consider shortly the Christocentricity he thus emphasizes.

---

[141] *Poetical Works*, 514.
[142] For analogues, see *OED*.

The divine and secular parts of *Hesperides* relate to each other in complex ways. Herrick suggests there is a penitential schema worked out in the piety of his verse:

> *His Prayer for Absolution*
> For Those my unbaptized Rhimes,
> Writ in my wild unhallowed Times;
> For every sentence, clause and word,
> That's not inlaid with Thee, (my Lord)
> Forgive me God, and blot each line
> Out of my Book, that is not Thine.
> But if, 'mongst all, thou find'st here one
> Worthy thy Benediction;
> That One of all the rest, shall be
> The Glory of my Work, and Me.   (*HNN* 1)

We find precedent enough in the seventeenth century for the simultaneous publication of supposed impudent or impious speech-acts together with penitential disclaimers.[143]

Herrick's apologetic posture must be decoded with some care. To keep the poems while asking forgiveness for them cannot pass an analysis of any theological rigour. Like Moll Flanders in old age, the speaker of *Hesperides* seeks absolution while retaining the fruits of sin, an untenable position. Nor is his claim that his 'unbaptized Rhimes' were 'Writ in my wild unhallowed Times' tractable to a biographical interpretation. Some love poems, such as 'Upon his Gray Haires' (*Hesperides*, 226) or 'To his Girles' (p. 392), are premissed on an antithesis between the grey hairs of the male speaker and the youthfulness of his mistresses. By thus dividing the volume into secular and divine poems, Herrick offers his readers two possible constructions. First, a hierarchy of seriousness: whereas much of the secular poetry may embody practices that are no more than rhetorical postures, libertine jokes, or functions of the lyric form, conventions of the genre, the pious material has a transcendent sincerity. Such a construction is perhaps suggested by the epigraph, from Hesiod, affixed to the secondary title-page: 'We know how to speak many false things as though they were true; but we know when we will, to utter true things.' Second, the whole collection exemplifies one of the emphases of *His Noble Numbers*, the inevitability and pervasiveness of sin and the possibilities of its

---

[143] Consider Milton's disclaimer, *Poems*, 231.

expiation through devotional exercise. Herrick offers his own poetic *œuvre* as a model for Christian redemption, almost as if Donne should have published *Songs and Sonets* with the *Holy Sonnets* as a double volume. The voice we hear in *Hesperides*, abandoning licence for prayer, reflects a pattern of conviction and penitence advocated within the divine lyrics. We shall return shortly to consider what specifically *His Noble Numbers* has to say about sin and salvation.

In other ways, however, the religious poems share many of the concerns and values of the earlier section. They are embattled, defiant, and uncompromising rehearsals of a royalist—and in this case Laudian—ideology, sombre in tone, but not despairing.

While supporters of Parliament's side and the Puritan cause, unsurprisingly, saw the success of their endeavours as the divine validation of the struggle, Herrick returns frequently to the topic of affliction, developing the counter-argument that suffering is a process by which God purges and prepares the godly, whereas success marks out the unregenerately sinful. As the poem entitled 'Good Men Afflicted Most' expresses it:

> God makes not good men wantons, but doth bring
> Them to the field, and, there, to skirmishing;
> With trialls those, with terrors these He proves,
> And hazards those most, whom the most He loves.   (*HNN* 38)

In contrast, 'bastard-slips',[144] and 'such as He dislikes, | He never brings them once to th' push of Pikes'. Indeed, the prosperous fall easy victims to Satan, their very prosperity betokening his confidence in possessing their souls: he neglects 'once to cast a frown on those | Whom ease makes his, without the help of blows' ('Satan', *HNN* 41). Earthly suffering functions purgatorially. In 'Persecutions Purifie' Herrick suggests that 'where [God] gives the bitter Pills, be sure, | 'Tis not to poyson, but to make thee pure' (*HNN* 7). Perseverance in adversity receives its reward: 'The lesse our sorrowes here and suffrings cease, | The more our Crownes of Glory there increase' ('Great Grief, Great Glory', *HNN* 41). The pertinent echoes are Old and New Testament. Proverbs cautioned, 'He that spareth his rod hateth his son: but he that loveth him chasteneth him betimes' (Prov. 13: 24), and Paul starkly observed,

---

[144] 'A shoot or sucker springing of its own accord from the root of a tree, or where not wanted. Often *fig.*' (*OED*).

'For whom the Lord loveth he chasteneth, and scourgeth every son whom he receiveth. If ye endure chastening, God dealeth with you as with sons; for what son is he whom the father chasteneth not?' (Heb. 12: 6–7). I have argued that Herrick rarely adopts that millenarian perspective so prominent elsewhere in the religious consciousness of his age. But he does show a strong sense of last things, of judgement, reward, and punishment, though without any suggestion that these stand near at hand. God will indeed punish the guilty, but not here: 'If all transgressions here should have their pay, | What need there then be of a reckning day . . . ?' ('Gods Providence', *HNN* 6). In 'Doomes-Day', less gleefully than Milton contemplating a similar kind of retribution,[145] he offers an epigram: 'Let not that Day Gods Friends and Servants scare: | The Bench is then their place; and not the Barre' (*HNN* 46), that is, they will sit with Christ in judgement and not stand before him.

'The Goodnesse of his God' at once personalizes the issue of affliction and connects with some of the political concerns of Herrick's secular poetry:

> When Winds and Seas do rage,
>   And threaten to undo me,
> Thou dost their wrath assuage,
>   If I but call unto Thee.
>
> A mighty storm last night
>   Did seek my soule to swallow,
> But by the peep of light
>   A gentle calme did follow.
>
> What need I then despaire,
>   Though ills stand round about me;
> Since mischiefs neither dare
>   To bark or bite, without Thee?   (*HNN* 42)

As in 'Hope Well and Have Well: or, Faire after Foule Weather', Herrick finds, in contemplation of the sequence of storm and calm, an image for an element of political optimism. (Much of his nature imagery reflects a city-born alarm at the wildness of weather in the westernmost parts of Britain.) The theological dimension, however, distinguishes the thesis here: the present ills may indeed abate. But if they persist, they do so as it were licensed by God and to serve his

---

[145] See above, Ch. 2.

purpose, presumably chastening and preparing the speaker through suffering. Hence, despair is inappropriate.

Herrick's divine poetry not only accommodates royalist defeats with theories of divine providence, but also works to reassert the values and customs that were ascendant in the Church of England in the Laudian era. As historians have long recognized, much of the emphasis that Archbishop Laud required of his clergy reflected a peculiarly English appropriation of the theology of Jacobus Arminius.[146] Tyacke has argued that Laud's promotion of Arminian doctrine further fissured the Church of England by introducing a new area of discord. Formerly, the prelatical wing and the Puritans, though disagreeing sharply on matters of discipline and church government, had shared a belief in the Calvinist theories of salvation, and particularly in the dogma of predestination. After the rise of Laud, doctrine became a major area of controversy within the Church. Thus, the Scottish divine Robert Baillie observed that English Puritans and episcopalians had been theologically in agreement till Laud stirred 'these unhappy seeds of Arminius'.[147]

What, then, were the characteristics of English Arminianism? Tyacke summarizes them most usefully:

[Arminius] was concerned to refute the teachings on divine grace associated with the followers of Calvin, but he spoke as a member of the fully reformed and presbyterian Dutch Church, whereas his doctrinal equivalents in England were part of a different ecclesiastical tradition. There the most notable survivor of the English Reformation, apart from episcopacy, was the Prayer Book which, as its critics were pleased to point out, was an adapted version of the old Catholic mass book. Consequently Arminianism in England emerged with an additional, sacramental dimension to that in the United Provinces. Arminius was read with approval by anti-Calvinists in England but adapted to the local situation. English Arminians came to balance their rejection of the arbitrary grace of predestination with a new found source of grace freely available in the sacraments, which Calvinists had belittled. Hence the preoccupation under Archbishop Laud with altars and private confession before receiving communion, as well as a belief in the absolute necessity of baptism.

---

[146] For an account of Arminian penetration of the Church of England, see A. W. Harrison, *Arminianism* (London, 1937), 122–56; Tyacke, 'Puritanism', and *Anti-Calvinists*, *passim*. For the development of Arminius's beliefs and teaching, see C. Bangs, *Arminius: A Study in the Dutch Reformation* (Nashville and New York, 1971), *passim*.

[147] Quoted by D. D. Wallace, Jr., *Puritans and Predestination: Grace in English Protestant Theology 1525–1695* (Chapel Hill, NC, 1982), 95.

Tyacke adds that Arminian clergymen, perhaps in part because of parliamentary antagonism to Laudian innovation, revealed themselves 'very hostile to lay intervention' in church matters. Further, 'there was a novel sacerdotal element in their teaching whereby the priestly replaced the preaching function'.[148]

Marcus remarks upon the relationship between *His Noble Numbers* and the doctrine and discipline of the Laudian Church, arguing that '*Noble Numbers* out-Lauds Laud, carrying the conservative Anglican emphasis on set forms and doctrinal uniformity to its furthest possible limit'.[149] Her thesis, however, may invite refinement once we have considered the precision with which Herrick's divine poetry nests within the ideology of Anglican Arminianism.

Many of Herrick's poems assume the form of prayers, or else advice on praying. For example, he writes a couple of 'Graces for Children' (*HNN* 30–1). Quite possibly, such poems were indeed functional, forms of words designed to be used by Herrick's parishioners, as well as abbreviated religious lyrics articulated from within the persona of a simple believer. Marcus refers to an anecdote that some of his poems through oral transmission had been preserved by humble parishioners of Dean Prior as late as 1809.[150] We may easily appreciate how poems like the 'Graces for Children' could be adapted as devotional tools in the instruction of youngsters. Perhaps other prayers of praise and penitence, such as the 'Ode, or Psalme, to God', were made available to fellow-worshippers:

> Deer God,
> If thy smart Rod
> Here did not make me sorrie,
> I sho'd not be
> With Thine, or Thee;
> In Thy eternall Glorie.   (*HNN* 29–30)

The sentiment accords well with the points he makes elsewhere in *His Noble Numbers* about the purposefulness of suffering and its status as an index of salvation. But the prayer remains available for

---

[148] 'Puritanism', 129–30, 139–40. A radically different version of Arminianism was to find a place at the core of the theories of salvation espoused by Milton and John Goodwin.
[149] Marcus, 'Noble Numbers', 111.
[150] Ibid. 110.

the devotional practices of others. Its title proclaims its place in the Davidic tradition. The Psalms were interpreted as lamentations and praise of the historical King David and were adopted into Christian worship as fit medium for devotional expression.[151] So too 'An Ode, or Psalme' at once matches the Herrickian voice and may be used by other, less articulate believers in their own acts of worship.

Other poems instruct how to pray:

> A Prayer, that is said alone,
> Starves, having no companion.
> Great things ask for, when thou dost pray,
> And those great are, which ne're decay.
> Pray not for silver, rust eats this;
> Ask not for gold, which metall is:
> Nor yet for houses, which are here
> But earth: *such vowes nere reach Gods eare*.
>   ('Prayer', *HNN* 52)

Note the declarative and imperative moods: this is priestly instruction delivered with authority. Many poems hit this note, not only about prayer, but about other aspects of doctrine and discipline. Often the format is the epigrammatic couplet. Such couplets constitute about 30 per cent of the secular poems and well over 40 per cent of *His Noble Numbers*. Time and again in his religious verse he adopts the epigrammatic strategy for doctrinal purposes. He gives instruction about aspects of the Godhead:

> God loads, and unloads, (thus His work begins)
> To load with blessings, and unload from sins.
>   ('Loading and Unloading', *HNN* 4)

He cautions patience:

> Whatever comes, let's be content withall:
> Among Gods Blessings, there is no one small.
>   ('Welcome What Comes', *HNN* 17)

He urges a modest, unquestioning faith:

> To seek of God more then we well can find,
> Argues a strong distemper of the mind.
>   ('Sobriety in Search', *HNN* 22)

---

[151] A Psalter was (and still is) published with *The Book of Common Prayer*. W. Schindler has some useful comments on the place of Psalms in 17th-cent. poetry in *Voice and Crisis: Invocation in Milton's Poetry* (Hamden, Conn., 1984), esp. 65–6.

And he encapsulates imperatives:

> Honour thy Parents; but good manners call
> Thee to adore thy God, the first of all.
>   ('God to be First Served', *HNN* 30)

In playing instructor, Herrick further defines his priestly role in Laudian terms, and, by frequently adopting the epigram, he does so in ways which assert the subordination of the laity. The priest gives orders and enunciates general truths and he does so in a form which eschews explanation or justification, precludes lay questioning, and forecloses controversy.

Christian worship, as described or recommended in *His Noble Numbers*, is heavily ceremonial. Herrick does not shy away from the word 'altar', despite its offensiveness to some Protestants. As the *OED* notes, the word itself had been 'the subject of much controversy' in the seventeenth century. In the Prayer Book of 1549 'altar' occurs side by side with 'God's board, Lord's table, Holy table', the two latter of which 'at length displace it in authoritative use'.[152] In Puritan writers, 'altar' carries a taint of popery and perhaps even paganism. Moreover, in the 1630s in particular, questions relating to the status, location, and nomenclature of the communion table occasioned controversy not simply among Puritans but between traditionalists within the Church and those who supported Laudian innovation. Thus, among the Laudians, we find John Pocklington asserting, 'Take wee then a view of the *Christian Church* in the old Testament, and there we finde the name and use of *Altars* is above eight hundred yeares more ancient, than the name of *Tables* in Gods Service.'[153] Again, Peter Heylin emphasizes the antiquity of altars and their distinction in early Christian practice from heathenish ones: 'in the Primitive times, the holy Altars, as they then used to call the Communion Tables (for other Altars they were not) were esteemed . . . sacred.'[154] Laud's old enemy and persistent opponent, John Williams, bishop of Lincoln, whose later career we considered earlier,[155] and some of his junior associates resisted doggedly. The primary element in their

---

[152] *OED.*

[153] John Pocklington, *Altare Christianum* (London, 1637), 4.

[154] Peter Heylin, *Antidotum Lincolniense* (London, 1637), sig. [*] 3ʳ.

[155] See above, Ch. 2. Herrick seemingly felt no animosity towards Williams himself, writing on his eclipse 'Upon the Bishop of Lincolnes Imprisonment', *Hesperides*, 55–6.

case against Laud rested on the innovatory nature of his policy of altars, and they stressed that both the New Testament and the statutes of the English Reformation prefer the term 'Holy Table'.[156] Laud's insistence that the communion table be located, not in the body of the church, but at the east end, across the aisle, and protected by altar-rails, thus physically marking the separation of the minister from his congregation, was profoundly symbolic of the distinction between clergy and laity. Significantly, the word used for the orientation of the communion table at right angles to the congregation was 'Altar-wise'.[157]

Herrick never uses the words '[communion] table' or 'board' in *His Noble Numbers*. The Church services are conceptualized as embodying the imperatives and aspirations of the late archbishop:

> With golden censers, and with Incense, here,
> Before Thy Virgin-Altar I appeare,
> To pay Thee that I owe, since what I see
> In, or without; all, all belongs to Thee.
> ('To God', *HNN* 36)

Altars occur in the imagery of other poems. In the heavily ritualistic 'Dirge of Jephthah's Daughter: Sung by the Virgins', which rehearses the Old Testament account of how Jephthah sacrificed his daughter to fulfil a pledge to God (Judg. 11: 34–40), her gravestone becomes 'The Altar of our love' and the site of pilgrimage and devotion (*HNN* 26). Christ's circumcision is presented as if it were a rite of the Laudian Church:

> Then, like a perfum'd Altar, see
> That all things sweet, and clean may be:
> For, here's a Babe, that (like a *Bride*)
> Will *blush to death*, if ought be spi'd
> Ill-scenting, or unpurifi'd
> ('Another New-Yeeres Gift, or Song
> for the Circumcision', *HNN* 34)

Laud had encouraged worshippers to regard communion as a rite not simply to be participated in, but to be prepared for, much as

[156] John Williams, *Holy Table, Name and Thing, More Anciently, Properly, and Literally used under the New Testament, then that of an Altar* (n. p., 'Printed for the Diocese of *Lincoln*', 1637), *passim*. For an account of the debate, see H. R. Trevor-Roper, *Archbishop Laud, 1573–1645*, 2nd edn. (London, 1962), 315–16.

[157] William Laud, *A Speech concerning Innovations in the Church* (London, 1637), 52.

Roman Catholics prepare for the mass, with introspection and even private confession. Herrick, in a lavishly ritualistic poem which takes the form of an address to 'Alma', presumably his soul, describes what the title terms 'The Parasceve,[158] or Preparation':

> To a Love-Feast[159] we both invited are:
> The figur'd Damask, or pure Diaper,
> Over the golden Altar now is spread,
> With Bread, and Wine, and Vessells furnished;
> The *sacred Towell*,[160] and the *holy Eure*
> Are ready by, to make the guests all pure:
> Let's go (my *Alma*) yet e're we receive,
> Fit, fit it is, we have our *Parasceve*.
> Who to that *sweet Bread* unprepar'd doth come
> Better he starv'd, then but to tast one crumme.
>
> (*HNN* 21)

The 1637 Scottish Communion Service, formulated under Laud's influence and with his endorsement, demanded an enhancement of material trappings, requiring the provision of 'decent furniture meet for the high mysteries . . . to be celebrated'.[161] In January 1645, three years or so before the publication of *Hesperides*, Laud had been executed, but his authority had disintegrated long before. Wherever Parliament's armies had conquered, altar-rails had been smashed, altars desecrated, and the apparatus of Laudian ritual had been destroyed. In his ejection Herrick had felt for himself the implacability of the Puritan ascendancy. Yet, in *His Noble Numbers* he preserves almost a sanctuary for Laudian practice, where tables are still altars, churches are perfumed, and priests perform their sacerdotal rites, untouched by the incursions of iconoclasts.

As we have noted, Laudian doctrinal innovation related primarily to the promotion of an Anglicized Arminian theory of salvation,

---

[158] The parasceve was the day of preparation for the Jewish Sabbath; here, Herrick has extended its signification to mean preparation presumably for Holy Communion (*OED*).

[159] 'Love feast' denoted 'Among the early Christians, a meal partaken of, in token of brotherly love, by the members of the church; app. originally in connexion with the eucharistic celebration' (*OED*). *OED* does not, however, note Herrick's appropriation of the term for the contemporary sacrament of Holy Communion.

[160] 'A cloth, either of linen for use at communion, or of silk or other rich material for covering the altar at other times' (*OED* 'Towel' 2 b).

[161] Quoted by E. P. Echlin, SJ, *The Anglican Eucharist in Ecumenical Perspective: Doctrine and Rite from Cranmer to Seabury* (New York, 1968), 121.

which sets aside the Calvinist dogma of predestination. The issues, however, are far from straightforward. Protestant dogma concerning salvation can perhaps best be conceptualized as a spectrum. One end, represented by the strictest versions of high Calvinism, espoused the dogma of 'double predestination', that is, not only are the elect predestinately saved, but those not especially elect, the majority, are predestined to damnation. Moreover, predestination was deemed to be 'supralapsarian', that is, God performs the double process of determining salvation and damnation even before the Fall. The other end of the spectrum of Protestant belief, associated primarily with Arminius, while acknowledging that some are predeterminately chosen for special election, argues that Christ's Atonement made grace available to all, and that fallen man has sufficient free will to concur with God's saving grace. Various intermediate positions were maintained. From the anti-Calvinist extreme, Laud, who disputed the title of Arminian and claimed rather to articulate the principal tradition of the Christian Church in all ages, dismissed the supralapsarian, double-predestination dogma that God reprobates from eternity the greater part of mankind as an 'Opinioun my very Soul abominates'.[162]

Herrick returns repeatedly to these issues, and his perspective is almost wholly Arminian. He redefines 'predestination' to mean not God's immutable decree, but God's knowledge of the individual's destination:

> Sin is the cause of death; and sin's alone
> The cause of Gods *Predestination*:
> And from Gods *Prescience* of mans sin doth flow
> Our *Destination* to eternall woe.
>
> ('Another [on sin]', *HNN* 63)

That is, God knows who will sin and not achieve subsequent regeneration and so knows our destination. But that destination is determined by our sinfulness and not God's prescience. The concept of predestination is thus redefined here. Predestination, as he puts it a little earlier, is 'the Cause . . . of fall to none' ('Predestination', *HNN* 62). The believer, in one sense, is free 'To make [his] faire *Predestination*': 'If thou canst change thy life, God then will please | To change, or call back, His past *Sentences*'

[162] Quoted by D. D. Wallace, *Puritans*, 96; on the spectrum of Protestant belief, see ibid., *passim*.

('Another [on predestination]', *HNN* 63). The change, however, is a spiritual one. Herrick avoids the Pelagian heresy with which some Calvinists had erroneously charged Arminius,[163] that salvation may be effected through good works: 'In vain our labours are, whatsoe're they be, | Unless God gives the *Benedicite*' ('Gods Blessing', *HNN* 49). Fallen man cannot work his own salvation by himself. As Arminius puts it:

In this [fallen] state, the free will of man towards the true good is not only wounded, maimed, infirm, bent, and weakened; but it is also imprisoned, destroyed, and lost. And its powers are not only debilitated and useless unless they be assisted by grace, but it has no powers whatsoever except such as are excited by divine grace. For Christ has said, 'Without me ye can do nothing.'[164]

Herrick follows the Arminian formula of conceptualizing man's salvation as synergistic, effected through the co-operation of human will and a divine grace which is extended through Christ's atonement and—in a characteristically Anglican version of the dogma—through the sacraments of the Church. Thus, Christ, generously and expansively, '(on the Tree) | Made void for millions', as for Herrick, the debt of man's sinfulness ('The Summe, and the Satisfaction', *HNN* 38). In the church celebration of that sacrifice stands a universal remedy for sinfulness: '*He that is hurt seeks help*: sin is the wound; | The Salve for this i' th Eucharist is found' ('The Eucharist', *HNN* 52).

Arminianism is a profoundly Christocentric theology, and appropriately several of the longer—and finer—poems of *His Noble Numbers* celebrate aspects of the Incarnation and Atonement. Of the Nativity poems, some proclaim their status as the work of more prosperous days. 'A Christmas Caroll, Sung to the King in the Presence[165] at White-Hall' (*HNN* 31–2) refers both in its title and in a note and stage directions to the circumstances of its original presentation. '*The Musicall Part was composed by* M. Henry Lawes', the most prominent court composer of the Caroline period, 'Master of the King's Music', as he frequently styled himself and by 1648 also something of a sufferer for his loyalism. The poem is

---

[163] Bangs, *Arminius*, 215–17; Arminius resisted the charge.
[164] Quoted ibid. 341.
[165] 'A place prepared for ceremonial presence or attendance; a presence-chamber' (*OED*).

arranged as a part-song, with a pause for a 'Flourish' marking off the first section which is sung by the chorus. 'The Star-Song: A Caroll to the King; Sung at White-hall' (*HNN* 35–6) similarly defines the context of its performance in terms which, by 1648, must have seemed very nostalgic. It ends in celebration of the Virgin Mary: 'that His treble Honours may be seen, | Wee'l chuse Him King, and make His Mother Queen.' This distinct whiff of Mariolatry would have seemed decidedly popish to many of his contemporaries.

One of the Nativity poems evokes not only court Christmasses past but also present hardship. 'An Ode of the Birth of Our Saviour' (*HNN* 8–9) explores the paradox between the essential royalty of the Christ-child and the wretchedness of his physical circumstances:

> Thou prettie Babie, borne here,
> With sup'rabundant scorn here:
> Who for thy Princely Port here,
>   Hadst for Thy place
>   Of Birth, a base
> Out-stable for thy Court here.

The poem partially resolves the problem of the indecorousness of the 'Kingly Stranger's' humble lodgings through the promise of devotional artifice. Christ will receive 'a chamber . . . Of Ivorie, | And plaister'd round with Amber', presumably an allusion to some kind of lavish Christmas crib, and as such the sort of idolatry Puritans shrank from. The problem is further resolved in the splendour of religious celebration:

> But we will entertaine Thee
> With Glories to await here
> Upon Thy Princely State here.

The poem is shot through with the values and aesthetics of Laudianism, but in 1648, in the eclipse of the English monarchy, its juxtaposition of what properly belongs to royalty and how in the world it suffers may well have given it a peculiar poignancy for the king's adherents.

His Noble Numbers end in a series of Easter poems. The first and longest, 'Good Friday: *Rex Tragicus*, or Christ Going to his Crosse' (*HNN* 73–4) conceptualizes Christ as a tragic actor:

> The *Crosse* shall be Thy *Stage*; and Thou shalt there
> The spacious field have for Thy *Theater*.

> Thou art that *Roscius*, and that markt-out man,
> That must this day act the Tragedian,
> To wonder and affrightment.

In a theatreless, Puritan England this central image endorses radically oppositional values. As Marcus remarks, what better rebuff for the Puritan play-scourgers?[166] Further, like the spurned Christ-child of 'An Ode of the Birth of Our Saviour', the Christ of these final poems is scorned by the world he lives in:

> the base, the dull, the rude,
> Th' inconstant, and unpurged Multitude
> Yawne for Thy coming [to execution] . . . .
> Amongst this scumme, the Souldier, with his speare,
> And that sowre Fellow, with his *vinager*,
> His *spunge*, and *stick*, do ask why Thou dost stay?
> So do the *Skurfe* and *Bran* too.

That image of the tragic king, baited and hemmed round with a hostile, common people, among them 'the Souldier', expresses the world of anguished royalism in the miserable 1640s. The parallels between Christ's sufferings and those of Charles I are irresistible, and we have seen how they inform *Eikon Basilike*. The voice we hear in these last few poems is that of the die-hard, the unrelenting supporter of Laudian theology and royalist politics who takes up, grieving but not reluctant, the leader's cross:

> When Thou wast taken, Lord, I oft have read,
> All Thy Disciples Thee forsook, and fled.
> Let their example not a pattern be
> For me to flie, but now to follow Thee.
> ('His words to Christ, going to the Cross',
> *HNN* 74)

Suffering—sharing the martyrdom of Christ—becomes the badge of faith:

> But if Thou wilt so honour me,
> As to accept my companie,
> I'le follow Thee, hap, hap what shall,
> Both to the *Judge*, and *Judgement-Hall*.
> ('Another, to his Saviour', *HNN* 74–5)

---

[166] Marcus, *'Noble Numbers'*, 121. On the political significance of the image of the tragic actor, see T. N. Corns, ' "An Horatian Ode upon Cromwel's Return from Ireland," Lines 53–58', *Explicator*, 35 (1976), 11–12.

In characteristically Arminian terms, the Crucifixion is hailed as occasioning an atonement that stands open to all. Christ's blood is 'Pure Balm, that shall | Bring Health to All' ('This Crosse Tree here', *HNN* 77).

Herrick's Easter poems are sombre, but they are not ultimately pessimistic. *Pace* Marcus,[167] they end, not with Good Friday, but with Easter Sunday. 'His Coming to the Sepulcher' celebrates the risen Christ and the empty tomb. Its tone, however, is not exultant but, rather, measured, defiant, and resolute:

> Is He, from hence, gone to the shades beneath,
> To vanquish Hell, as here He conquer'd Death?
> If so; I'le thither follow, without feare;
> And live in Hell, if that my *Christ* stayes there.
>
> (*HNN* 79)

The poet will abide in hell if he may do so in the company of his Lord and in the true faith. That last couplet is a fine, uncompromising flourish, a clenched fist raised against an unremitting adversity.

The royalist response to the crises of the 1640s shapes a range of literature which generically and quantitatively extends far wider than the texts examined in this chapter (and perhaps beyond the range of any primarily critical work). That response pervades Anglican religious poetry, it animates the satire of John Taylor and John Cleveland, it finds defence and expression in royalist journalism and in a myriad of texts imitative of the idiom of *Eikon Basilike*. If royalist generals could have organized their forces as well as royalist poets could marshall their wits the outcome of Edgehill and Marston Moor and Naseby might well have been different.

---

[167] Marcus, '*Noble Numbers*', 124.

5

Levellers, Diggers, and Ranters

So far we have considered the ways in which hostile reportage of the activities and character of radical groups to the left of a staid Congregationalism (in religious terms) or of revolutionary Independency and its antecedents (in political terms) functioned as an aspect of both royalist and, a little later, Presbyterian propaganda.[1] The business of identifying, categorizing, and listing the diversity of sectarian heterodoxy had produced in the mid–1640s that curious subgenre, the catalogue of heresies, perhaps most influentially manifest in the writings of Ephraim Pagitt and Thomas Edwards, whose treatises seem to reflect the tendentious extension of the bestiary genre to English political and religious life, though their roots extend deep into the tradition of anti-heretical writing.[2] Those campaigns provide the immediate context for Milton's publications of 1643–5.

By the late 1640s different groupings emerged, Levellers, Diggers, Ranters, all fading or mutating in the early 1650s, to be supplanted in the English political consciousness by Quakers and Fifth Monarchists. The movements were of profoundly unequal significance in their own age. Levellerism produced demonstrations several thousand strong, provoked serious mutinies in the New Model Army, and occasioned genuine anxiety among members of the Rump Parliament. Cromwell and his associates variously maintained an active dialogue with the Leveller leaders and contrived their suppression through the exercise of the considerable power at their disposal. The Diggers' experimental communism was a much more localized phenomenon, though possibly more extensive than it once seemed, and its termination proved an easy matter. Ranterism, while it produced some fascinating texts, achieved a notoriety disproportionate to its extent.

[1] Above, Chs. 1 and 3.
[2] Edwards, *Gangraena*; Ephraim Pagitt, *Heresiography, or, A Description of the Heretickes and Sectaries of the Latter Times* (London, 1645, 1646).

The Leveller movement originated in the political alliance between some of the more heterodox radicals of the early and mid–1640s and politically animated elements within the New Model Army, particularly (though not exclusively) among the junior officers and the lower ranks. Some of its civilian leaders had a record of campaigning and writing which dates back to the late 1630s and the early 1640s. Lilburne had been prosecuted before Star Chamber in 1637 for importing Puritan publications critical of the Laudian ascendancy.[3] Richard Overton seems to be the most likely author of a short, ingenious mortalist tract, *Mans Mortallitie*, published in Amsterdam in 1643,[4] and his anti-Presbyterian 'Marpriest' tracts of 1645–6 have rightly attracted critical acclaim.[5]

For a period towards the end of the 1640s the Leveller movement's fortunes were intertwined with those of revolutionary Independency, and particularly with the activities of Cromwell and his closest associates. What the Levellers wanted remains surprisingly unclear for a movement which resembled more than other contemporary groupings the structure of a modern political party, with a rank-and-file membership, local organization, rudimentary committee rooms (in taverns), membership contributions, and, most significantly perhaps, manifestos.[6]

The nature of their conflict with Independency has been interpreted as a classical manifestation of class conflict between the bourgeoisie and the *petite bourgeoisie*, in which the Levellers represent the interests of a lower class of craftsmen, small masters, and shopkeepers.[7] The issues, however, seem too confused to admit such confident schematizing and await more detailed research. The Leveller proposals on electoral reform would have widened the franchise but not sufficiently to include women, servants, dependants, or employees in general (though their intentions towards the last category is less certain).[8] They shared far more of the ideology of their rivals than is usually conceded, for example on the central

---

[3] P. Gregg, *Free-Born John* (London, 1961), 53–63.

[4] R.O., *Mans Mortallitie*; see above, Ch. 3.

[5] N. Smith, 'Richard Overton's Marpriest Tracts: Towards a History of Leveller Style', *Prose Studies*, 9/2 (1986), 39–66; reprinted in Corns 39–66.

[6] Brailsford, 25, 312–13.

[7] Brailsford, 9; A. Milner, *John Milton and the English Revolution* (London and Basingstoke, 1981), 82–4.

[8] C. B. Macpherson, *The Political Theory of Possessive Individualism: Hobbes to Locke* (Oxford, 1962), 107–59, addresses the issue of apparent inconsistencies.

issues of religious toleration and the culpability of Charles I. Cromwell's faction too had a concern for social amelioration.[9] The rank-and-file Levellers who mutinied at Burford or demonstrated through the streets of London at the funeral of the martyred Robert Lockyer[10] quite probably were largely of *petit bourgeois* origin— but in all likelihood they were socially indistinguishable from the troopers who remained loyal to Cromwell, Ireton, and the Army Grandees. While most of the leaders of the army Levellers were junior officers or other ranks, Thomas Rainsborough, a very prominent figure in the movement, was a full colonel.[11] Among the civilian Levellers, Walwyn, a younger son of a prosperous landowner, was a successful Merchant Adventurer.[12] John Wildman accepted a majority in the New Model Army in late 1649, though he did not accompany it to Ireland. He became, instead, a large-scale property speculator, owning land in twenty counties, which suggests that he was master of a significant amount of initial capital.[13] Lilburne the Leveller's elder brother Robert was himself an Army Grandee, a colonel and associate of Cromwell and a regicide. His younger brother Henry was lieutenant-governor of Tynemouth Castle until the second Civil War when he declared for the king, and was killed when the castle was retaken, and his head displayed on the castle-gate.[14] John Lilburne was a lieutenant colonel till 1645, and title-pages of his pamphlets (though not his Quaker ones of 1656) bear his military title. His cousin Thomas Lilburne was MP for Durham in the Long Parliament.[15] From the pillory, as he suffered martyrdom under Laud, he asseverated, 'I am the sonne of a Gentle man, and my friends are of rank and qualitie in the Countrey where they live.'[16] Lilburne's final incarceration was precipitated not by an act in defence of general principle but rather by his campaign on behalf of his family's commercial interests in the North-East.[17] Nor were Leveller leaders without culture and education. Overton is a relatively shadowy figure but *Mans Mortallitie* shows a precise familiarity with a recondite aspect of controversial theology. He felt sufficiently secure socially to twit

[9] Worden, 14.
[10] Brailsford, 506–7.
[11] Ibid. 198, 359.
[12] Ibid. 59.
[13] See *DNB*.
[14] Gregg, *Free-Born John*, 247.
[15] W. Dumble, 'Government, Religion and Military Affairs in Durham during the Civil War and Interregnum', M.Litt. diss. (Durham, 1978), 374.
[16] John Lilburne, *The Christian Mans Triall*, 2nd edn. (London, 1641), 31.
[17] Brailsford, 59.

his arresting officer in 1649, Lieutenant Colonel Axtell, with his lowly birth: 'I presume when he was a pedlar in *Harford-shire* he had not so lofty an esteeme of himself.' Walwyn struck Brailsford as a 'surprising figure' in the Puritan age, who 'seems to have strayed into it from the humanist Renaissance'. Clarendon thought Wildman was 'bred a scholar in the university of Cambridge', and the Leveller fellow-traveller, Henry Marten, whose father, a distinguished lawyer, a servant of the Stuart court, and a very rich man, had been knighted by James I, was himself educated at Oxford and the Inns of Court.[18]

There is a tendency, stronger among critics than historians (though Brailsford, too, is guilty), to romanticize and sentimentalize the Leveller leadership. To Haller the young Lilburne was 'a poor lad' making his own way in the world.[19] Webber, comparing Lilburne to Milton, alludes, as if to distinguish him, to the latter's 'respectable middle-class circumstances'.[20] Brailsford's 'guess' that Lilburne failed to enter his trade at the end of his apprenticeship because he could not raise the entrance fee of £100 is difficult to reconcile with his later success as a brewer, which was founded on his uncle's injection of £1,000 of investment capital.[21] Even in exile, despite a financial crisis occasioned by a massive fine, he could afford to buy and run a printing press.[22] The search for heroes often raises the risk of establishing false but agreeable constructs. However the Leveller movement may have articulated a programme consonant with the interests of the *petite bourgeoisie*, their most important spokesmen were not socially or culturally much distinct from Cromwell's circle, nor did they wish to be perceived as such.

For a brief period the Leveller movement was close to the real seat of power. Chronology is important for a proper understanding of Leveller writing and the Lilburne texts which are my concern. The inception of the party is dated by Brailsford as 7 July 1646, when a group of radicals—not including Lilburne, who was in prison at the time—drew up and promulgated *The Remonstrance of Many Thousand Citizens*, which defined its political demands in

---

[18] *DNB*; Brailsford, 59; C. M. Williams, 'The Anatomy of a Radical Gentleman: Henry Marten', in Pennington and Thomas, 118–38.

[19] W. Haller, *The Rise of Puritanism* (New York, 1938), 273.

[20] J. Webber, *The Eloquent 'I': Style and Self in Seventeenth-Century Prose* (Madison, Wisc. and London, 1968), 53.

[21] Brailsford, 80; Gregg, *Free-Born John*, 88.

[22] Ibid. 315.

terms of religious toleration and the radical reform of Parliament and constitution.[23] Their influence grew most pressingly within the ranks of the New Model Army, so that Cromwell and Ireton recognized the need to carry with them at least the passive compliance of the Levellers in the deepening crisis of 1647–8 in the relations between the army and the Presbyterian leadership of the Long Parliament who sought to reduce it substantially and on terms unsatisfactory to the military. It was probably Ireton who produced in the *Solemn Engagement of the Army* (?London, 5 June 1647) 'a sort of military covenant made among the soldiers and with the kingdom'.[24] Throughout the next eighteen months a complicated game was played out between Army Grandees and the Leveller leaders, a game often inscribed in the carefully constructed formulae produced in their respective manifestos. The army leaders' notion for a settlement found fuller expression in the *Representation from Sir Thomas Fairfax and the Army under his Command* (?London, 14 June 1647) and in the *Heads of Proposals* (?London, 1 August 1647), though the latter, again Ireton's work, marked something of a withdrawal from more radical positions which were to be embodied in *The Case of the Army Truly Stated* (?London, 15 October 1947).[25] Something approximating to a dialogue ensued in the debates held in Putney church on 28 and 29 October and 1 November 1647. Ireton's complaint that the Levellers came to the debate with a predetermined position which was not negotiable[26] may perhaps have been ingenuous, though when he and Cromwell address Sexby and Wildman an acerbic edge is apparent from the outset. The debate, however, defined clearly the gaps between the groups and disclosed how far the relative harmony of June 1647 had been broken.[27] It was followed by the first Leveller *Agreement of the People* (?London, 3 November 1647).

Renewed fighting at the outbreak of the Second Civil War interrupted the tempo of events, but by late 1648, when the groups around Cromwell and Ireton perceived the necessity of a decisive move against Long Parliament's hostile leadership, negotiations began again. Ireton produced a new *Remonstrance of the Army* on 10 November 1648, taking the most dynamic grouping within Independency some way towards 'a new alliance with the Left',

[23] Brailsford, 96–102.

[24] A. S. P. Woodhouse, *Puritanism and Liberty* (London, 1938), Introduction, 23.

[25] Ibid. 24–7.   [26] Ibid. 70.   [27] Ibid. 27–8.

resulting in 'Ireton's reluctant acceptance of the Levellers' most cherished principle, settlement by means of an Agreement of the People', in return for accepting a coup to end the Long Parliament and to invest the army's allies in Parliament as a committee for governing the courts till a proper constitutional resolution could be found.[28]

Sections of the New Model Army entered London on 2 December 1648. Four days later, Colonel Pride purged Parliament of the army's enemies, and, in effect, the Levellers' moment of proximity to power had passed. The army officers considered and worked over a second *Agreement of the People*, and, when they had diluted it, they finally presented it to the Rump on 20 January 1649 'with a tepid preamble making it clear that they did not expect the House to implement it'.[29] Leveller leaders produced a third version of the *Agreement* on 1 May,[30] but by then the conflict between Levellerism and revolutionary Independency had entered a new phase. Leveller disaffection found expression in indiscipline and abortive mutiny. On 28 March 1649 Lilburne and other civilian Levellers were committed to the Tower by the Council of State. A month later, Robert Lockyer was shot for mutiny, and his funeral procession occasioned a considerable demonstration in London.[31] A fortnight later a significant Leveller mutiny at Burford was suppressed with limited reprisals by troops loyal to the Grandees, and 'thereafter the Levellers were a broken force', though isolated mutinies rumbled on into the autumn.[32]

Leveller attitudes to the press are quite distinctive. The period from 1647 to the third *Agreement* shows an obsession with encapsulating a political statement within a document, a very literal-minded approach to the concept of a contract between Goverment and the governed. The Army Grandees' various manifestos represent bargaining positions, demands held provisionally, which direct action may alter or carry through to fruition. Leveller publications, in contrast, have a deeper earnestness. The legal contract offers the paradigm for the Leveller manifesto, which accords with the movement's enthusiasm for legal reform and its leaders' (pre-

---

28 A. S. P. Woodhouse, *Puritanism and Liberty*, 31–2.
29 Worden, 76.
30 Woodhouse, *Puritanism*, 365–6.
31 Worden, 188–9; Brailsford, 506–7.
32 Worden, 189, 213.

eminently Lilburne's) frequent invocation of the letter of the law.[33] Both the manifesto and the petition were written by individuals or small working parties, whom Woodhouse and Brailsford frequently identify or at least guess at. But they appear as the voice of 'the Army' or 'citizens and countrymen' or 'many thousands' or 'the people of England'. This has both a practical and a vaguer, ideological implication. The Levellers were England's first political organization to attempt to mobilize popular support from outside those who had traditionally constituted the political nation. In a sense, the Leveller publications work to invent or to call into being political categories that had not previously existed. Some worked well. One petition, presented to Parliament on 1 August 1648, had over 10,000 signatures.[34] Yet a contradiction abided at the heart of Levellerism: it was a mass movement without consistent and reliable mass support. It was committed to election on a widened franchise, but an electorate thus constituted would probably not have elected them. The leadership was an élite embarrassed by its élitism and without a political thinker capable of formulating a coherent notion of the relationship of the leaders to the led. The characteristic idiom, the assumed collective voice, attempts to disguise the central anxiety.

Yet text itself assumes an obsessive, even talismanic, role within Levellerism. In the critical period from November 1648 to January 1649 the energies of key figures were dissipated in honing the formulae of the ill-fated second *Agreement of the People*.[35] At the rendezvous at Corkbush Field between Hertford and Ware on 15 November 1647, the regiments contemplating mutiny appeared wearing in their hatbands copies of the *Agreement of the People*.[36] Lilburne's obsession with the press dated back to the late 1630s. His speech from the pillory includes a descriptive bibliography of Puritan texts—'If you please to read the second and third parts of Doctor *Bastwicks Letany*, you shall find . . . '. He pulled copies of Bastwick's books from his breeches, presumably a tricky task to execute in the pillory, and threw them 'among the people', at once an invocation of popular opinion as witness to his innocence and a symbolic gesture of offensive and pro-

---

[33] Milner, *Milton*, 55–6; Worden, 106.
[34] Brailsford, 347.
[35] Worden, 76.
[36] Brailsford, 295–7.

vocative eloquence, to which Star Chamber responded with an order that he should 'be laid alone, with yrons on his hands and legges'.[37]

II

Lilburne has been the subject of both contemporary and subsequent hagiography. His personal history is indeed a remarkable one, and much of his writing relates directly to his sufferings and his response to them. Though he played a part in the drafting of the petitions and manifestos that dominated Leveller press activity, many of his publications, among them all his most readable, present a species of autobiography, accounts of his trials, interrogations and incarcerations, generally written from prison. He was flogged, pilloried, and gaoled by the Star Chamber. The Long Parliament released him and ordered his compensation, though his subsequent military career was soon interrupted by capture, and in 1643 he was sentenced to death by a court in royalist-held Oxford. Threats of reprisals against royalist prisoners secured his release, but he soon fell foul of Presbyterians and their allies in the Long Parliament. He was arrested three times in 1645 for offences connected with unlicensed printing and for libel, the last time leading to four months' imprisonment without trial. From mid–1646 to late 1647 he was imprisoned, ultimately in the Tower, after sentence by the House of Lords for libelling the Earl of Manchester, and he was incarcerated again by the Commons in 1648 for Leveller activity. The Council of State gaoled him with other Leveller leaders in March 1649, though he was not brought to trial till October, when he was acquitted. In 1651 the Rump fined and banished him for libel and breach of privilege over a family and financial dispute in the North-East. After his return to England, unpardoned, in 1653, he was kept in prison till his death in 1657.[38]

Lilburne's expository technique emerges full-fledged in his account of his trial and punishment in the 1630s, consolidated in the

---

[37] Lilburne, *Triall*, 27, 31, 38. *The Christian Mans Triall*, 2nd edn., which appeared in Dec. 1641, reprints the 1st edn. and incorporates with it *A Worke of the Beast* (London, 1638). All references are to the 1641 edn.

[38] Gregg, *Free-Born John*, *passim*, but esp. 87, 101, 117–24, 138–42, 223, 236–45, 269–70, 294–300, 310–11, 322–34. Lilburne died while on temporary parole (p. 346).

second edition of *The Christian Mans Triall*. Of his conduct at the later trial in Oxford, Clarendon astutely remarks, 'he beheaved with so great impudence . . . that it was manifest he had an ambition to have been made a martyr',[39] a pattern of conduct which recurs both in his manner and in his accounts of himself. Critics have noted his debt to Foxe's *Book of Martyrs*.[40] The nature of that debt is complex. Foxe's martyrology offers a series of paradigms both for enduring and for describing suffering. The account is heavily formulaic, as though saintly martyrdom is a recurrent event, distinguished, from one case to another, only by the changing names of the martyred witnesses to the truth. Indeed, in some editions, such as that of 1641, the illustrative woodcuts of the scenes of martyrdom—burnings and hangings, for the most part—are recycled within the volume, so that the same blocks recur but with the captions changed. In a sense, Protestant martyrdom stood available to Lilburne as a form in which he need only inscribe his own particulars. Foxe calls those who suffer whipping the 'society of the scourged professors of Christ'.[41] It is a society to which Lilburne affiliates himself. Foxe's influence appears strong in the most nasty episodes, such as his flogging from the Fleet to Westminster:

The Cart being ready to goe forward, I spake to the Executioner (when I saw him pull his Corded whip out of his pocket) after this manner; Well, my friend, doe thy office . . . . [I said], I know my God hath not onely enabled me to believe in his Name, but also to suffer for his sake. So the Carman drove forward his Cart, and I laboured with my God for strength to submit my backe with cheerfulnesse unto the smiter, and he heard my desire, and granted my request; for when the first stripe was given, I felt not the least paine, but said, *Blessed be thy Name, O Lord my God, that hast counted mee worthy to suffer for thy glorious Names sake*, and at the giving of the second, I cryed out with a loud voyce, *Hallelujah, Hallelujah, Glory, Honour and Praise be given to thee, O Lord, forever, and to the Lambe that sits upon the Throne*. So wee went up to *Fleetstreet*, the Lord enabling mee to endure the stripes with such patience and cheerefulnesse, that I did not in the least manner shew the least discontent at them, for my God hardened my back and steeled my reynes, and tooke away the smart and paine of the stripes from mee (*Triall*, 19).

---

[39] Edward Hyde, Earl of Clarendon, *History of the Rebellion and Civil Wars in England*, ed. W. D. Macray (Oxford, 1888), v. 306.
[40] e.g. Webber, *Eloquent 'I'*, 68–79.
[41] John Foxe, *Actes and Monuments* (London, 1641), iii. 905.

Lilburne's account transforms the event into a tableau, an icon of suffering, in which the martyred hero turns his eyes beatifically to heaven as his mouth utters speeches which could have been inscribed on balloons and lozenges appended to such figures in woodcuts. But Lilburne, unlike others in the martyrological tradition, not only bears witness of the event: he endures it. Conflicting impulses, to follow the stereotype or to document it experientially, tear at the narrative. A little later on, he recalls he was troubled by the dust of the road, and though God had providentially hardened his body, he had forgotten to moderate the sun which (though it was only April) 'shined very hot upon mee'. By the time he was pilloried, far from being the beneficiary of exceptional providence, he chiefly recalls the agony, 'my backe . . . being very sore, and the Sunne shining so exceeding hot' (p. 20). Both details are to some extent adduced as evidence of his tormentors' perverse and exceeding cruelty—the pillory is too low for his stature, and he is refused his request to be allowed to wear his hat, the latter probably for political reasons—he is being made to stand bareheaded before those who have brought him to punishment. The precise complaints, however, make sense only if they cause suffering. But that suffering seems chillingly real. His shoulders, in the convincingly domestic imagery of a bystander, 'swelled almost as big as a penny loafe with the bruses of the knotted Cords'.[42] We are left to make what we can of the two perspectives—that of the Puritan martyrologist and that of the tortured and resentful young man, but the genre, while gruesomely fascinating, is unstable.

Another element Lilburne could well have taken from Foxe is a commitment to documentation. In Foxe this often takes the form of inset narratives from witnesses and legal documents relating the charging and sentencing of the godly. In *The Christian Mans Triall* it takes a relatively muted form. The pamphlet ends not with a rhetorical flourish, but with the reproduction of the minutes of the Star Chamber act for his strict confinement (pp. 38–9). Later, documentation becomes almost obsessive, further animated by Lilburne's concern with close argument from the precise letter of the charges and warrants against him. When the Council of State rounds him up with the other Leveller leaders in 1649 he chides the arresting officer that 'he ought to have brought his Warrant with him, and to have shewed it me, and given me leave to have coppied

---

[42] Gregg, *Free-Born John*, 65.

it out'.[43] That copy would perhaps have served as an *aide-mémoire* in court: it would certainly have appeared in the published account of the arrest.

Only in limited and rather lifeless fashion does Foxe capture dialogue. In Lilburne the dramatic impulse is deep and eloquent. He finds voices for friends and for foes which characterize them and set them in dramatic conflict as Foxe does not. The hangman who whips him is given a line that makes him strangely likeable: 'I have whipt many a Rogue, but now I shall whip an honest man, but be not discouraged . . . it will be soone over' (p. 20). Even the arresting pursuivant is allowed a voice, to emerge as an affable, if sarcastic, scoundrel, untouched by the ideological complexities of his actions: 'Mr. *Lilburne*, I am glad with all my heart that wee are met for you are the man that I have much desired for a long time to see . . . . Come . . . be not sad, you are but fallen into knaves hands' (p. 1). Yet the admission of other voices persistently subverts the tendency of the tract. As he and his aged co-defendant John Wharton appear before the Star Chamber, their tormentors laugh at their most spirited flourishes. As he asserts that he finds no warrant 'in the Word of God' for an oath of inquiry, 'the Court began to laugh'. When Wharton is offered the oath, he responds with a long harangue. As they press him to answer, he replies that he desires them to let him talk a little and 'he would tell them by and by. At which all the Court burst out laughing' (pp. 13–14). Lilburne locates at the heart of his narrative a dangerous alternative perspective. In terms of Puritan martyrology, Lilburne and Wharton ridiculed by their adversaries present an *imitatio Christi*, reliving the mockery of Christ by his captors. But to another reader the conduct of the Star Chamber could seem plausible and in proportion. After all, why should the greatest men of the country be addressed on equal terms by a young hothead and an old fool? Lilburne's perspective is wholly confined within the frame of the scenes he describes, and absurdities and contradictions, which strike the unsympathetic, emerge unchecked by authorial intervention. A partisan royalist could have read *The Christian Mans Triall* with hearty, if perverse, amusement. As Webber remarks, Lilburne 'often risks personal absurdity without a second thought'.[44]

---

[43] John Lilburne, Richard Overton, and Thomas Prince, *A Picture of the Council of State* (London, 1649), 1.
[44] Webber, *Eloquent 'I'*, 63.

One final element manifest in the early work that recurs later is the absence of sustained and lofty rhetoric. Lilburne, though plainly capable of making himself master of the intricacies of legal procedure and precedent, seems unaware of the classical tradition of forensic oratory. He tells us, 'I am . . . no Scholler, according to that which the world counts Schollership' (p. 30), and the reader may feel acutely the absence of a Ciceronian model in his speeches in court and from the pillory. His persuasiveness owes nothing to the clarity and the driving, overwhelming continuity of exposition that characterizes Cicero. His is the artless and bitty particularity of the English common-law courtroom:

Now, in this Oath he [a hostile witness] hath againe forsworne himselfe in a high degree; for whereas he tooke his Oath that I had printed the Booke called *The Vanity and Impiety of the old Letany*; I here speake it before you all, that I never in my dayes did see one of them in print, but I must confesse, I have seen and read it in written hand (p. 24).

Whenever Lilburne seems to head for the larger and grander statement such passages of close and rather nit-picking argument subvert the tone. The title-page of the 1641 edition of the *Actes and Monuments* shows heroes at the stake trumpeting through the flames. Lilburne's trumpeting seems always compromised by the thinner notes of litigiousness.

Lilburne's persistence with a narrow repertoire of controversial stratagems emerges sharply from consideration of his later prose. His output was prodigious—the *Short Title Catalogue* lists over 120 items, though collaborative authorship and resort to anonymity made the canon uncertain in his own day, as we shall see,[45] and the uncertainty remains. Whatever the interests of this corpus for purposes of historical documentation, the lack of range and sustained skill probably wearies all but the most dogged present-day reader, and only a few have been selected for closer scrutiny here.

The Iust Mans Iustification, or, A Letter by way of Plea in Barre —Thomason dated his copy 10 June 1646—details Lilburne's case against the conduct of his quondam comrade-in-arms, Colonel Edward King, in the parliamentary army's campaign in Lincolnshire. By implication, it questions too the generalship of a persistent adversary of Lilburne (and of Cromwell), the Earl of Manchester,

---

[45] See his interrogation by Prideaux on the issue, discussed below.

who was ultimately responsible for King's conduct. Large issues, about the structure of power within the parliamentary army and, most significantly, about the accountability of its leaders, lie behind the controversy. Lilburne, however, prefers to focus on the personal and the particular. Once more, the litigious spirit prevails. Lilburne is not a prisoner at the Bar, but he organizes his tract as though he were. It is 'A Letter by way of Plea in Barre', directed to Justice Reeves of the Court of Common Pleas (p. 1) and couched not as a letter but as testimony on oath. A close specificity permeates it, and Lilburne carefully emphasizes what he himself did and witnessed: 'I being upon the fourteenth of April last arrested at Westminster' (p. 1); 'Whereupon I went to Alderman *Tilsons*, and asked him whether . . . ' (p. 8). He qualifies his testimony with parenthetic admissions that this is a reconstruction from memory: 'I went to Mr. Major, then as I remember, at Alderman *Tilsons* . . . '; 'we . . . found him obstinate till (as I remember) *Alderman Tilson* told him . . . '; 'he went to Col. *King*, and (as I remember) in Alderman *Tilsons* Hall, debated . . . ' (all p. 7). The pamphlet ends not with an expansive peroration but with appendices of documentation, containing Lilburne's petition to the House of Commons (pp. 17–18), and a list of 'Articles exhibited against Col. Edward King, for his insolencies and misdemenors in the County of Lincoln, to the Honourable House of Commons, in August 1644. by Mr. Messenden, Mr. Wolley, and divers others of the Committee of Lincoln' (pp. 19–20). The latter serves largely to reiterate, in less animated fashion, the charges made in Lilburne's testimony.

Issues of principle break through when Lilburne engages the radical argument that the common law was an instrument of '*the oppressing* bondage . . . since the Norman *yoke*', but such matters are really tangential to the immediate controversy, which is about power and accountability. However, the model of forensic, adversarial debate generally prevails. Lilburne persistently works to particularize and to personalize, assailing, as if he were prosecutor, this 'unjust and troublesome man, commonly called *Colonell Edward King*' (p. 1).

An Anatomy of the Lords Tyranny and Iniustice Exercised upon Lieu. Col. John Lilburne, now a Prisoner in the Tower of London (1646) relates to a later phase in the same campaign, Lilburne's appeal to the House of Commons against his incarceration by the Lords for breach of their privilege in his attack on the Earl of

Manchester. This time Lilburne presents a transcript of his speech before them, 'published to the view of all the Commons of England, for their information' (p. 1). He labours to attest the authenticity of its provenance: the speech is dated, as is the epistle which communicates its transcription, and he details its transmission. It has been 'delivered in writing to the hands of Col. *Henry Martin*' (p. 1). Documentation is nested within the account, transcriptions of the warrant for his arrest (p. 2), a letter he wrote in comment on the warrant (p. 3), an order committing him to Newgate (p. 5), and other documents are invoked which 'you Mr. *Martin* have also in your hands' (p. 17). In *An Anatomy* Lilburne intermittently engages the wealth of evidence with a minute legality, citing 'the expresse Statutes of 9. *H*. 3. 29. 5. *E*. 3. 9. 25. *E*. 3. 4. 28. *E*. 3. 3 [i.e. 9 Henry III c. xxxix, 5 Edward III c. ix, etc.]' (p. 8) and 'Sir *Edward Cooke* that learned Lawyer' who 'doth well and truly observe in the 2. part of his institutes folio. 52 . . . ' (p. 5).

Once more, large issues are central to the controversy, here the role and purpose of the House of Lords and its jurisdiction over commoners. Yet the general is nudged asided by the particular, and the controversy is personalized into Lilburne's combat with individuals, pre-eminently the Earl of Manchester, whose military competence Lilburne had persistently questioned: 'my lord of *Manchester* . . . my grand adversary . . . hath for these two or three yeares thirsted after my blood, for no other crime but that I was faithfull and active in executing the trust reposed in me' (p. 12). Lilburne produces a heroic self-image through recollection of his earlier suffering. As in many of his pamphlets, he reminds his readers of his martyr's status, with a further suggestion that his defiance of his current tormentors, the Lords, is but an extension of the events of 1638: 'But, goe tell their Lordships from me, I understand the liberties of *England* better then so suddenly to be their slave, and to obey their unjust and tyrannicall commands: And therefore tell them, I will whether they will or no, talk with any man that will talk with me, till they out-strip the Bishops (who gagged me for speaking) in cruelty, by cutting out my tongue, or sowing up my lips' (p. 4). Three times (pp. 4, 13, 16) the motif recurs, and he links it with his defiance of the royalist court at Oxford, though, wholly typically, that allusion works to introduce a quotation from his speech there: 'give me leave to say unto you in this particular, as I said unto my Lord *Heath* at *Oxford*, when I was arraigned before him for my life, for drawing my sword for your defence in the kingdomes, when he pressed me to plead unto my indictment. My Lord, said I . . . ' (p. 18). In the spirit of 1638, Lilburne produces (and describes) gestures of symbolic defiance which are sometimes potentially ludicrous. His repeated refusal to kneel at the bar (pp. 4, 13) seems dignified in a way in which his ear-stopping does not: the Speaker of the House of Lords 'commanded the Clerk to read me my Charge; which he began to do. At which I stopped my eares with my fingers, till such time as I perceived the Clerks lips to leave moving' (p. 13). Only occasionally does the discourse reward its readers with some flash of more interesting writing, as in 'if you were in jeast, when you did all this, and never intended, what you declared, but meerly set us a fighting to unhorse and dismount our old Riders & Tyrants, that so you might get up and ride us in their steads' (pp. 14–15). Imagery is rare in Lilburne's prose. Citation of evidence, of documents, of precedence, of statute, of times, dates, places, and people, stifles the imaginative spark as surely as it endlessly defers engagement of the larger argument.

By April 1647 and *The Prisoners Plea for Habeas Corpus* the primary adversaries had changed, though Lilburne's imprisonment in the Tower remained. Once more, the pamphlet is couched as 'an Epistle', this time to William Lenthall, Speaker of the House of Commons, but its format is that of a speech, the speech he would have wished to deliver in person from the Bar of the lower chamber. The image of Lilburne the martyr is elaborated with even greater perseverance, and now the role played by Laud falls to Cromwell, 'who hath forcibly usurped unto himselfe the Office of L.G. [lieutenant-general] . . . and hath tyrannized over the lives Liberties and estates of the freemen of England in a higher manner then ever *Straford* and *Canterbury* did' (sig. A1ʳ). Again, he has exercised worse tyranny 'then ever *Strafford or Canterbury* attempted to doe, for which they lost their heads' (sig. B1ʳ). The larger motives and implications of Cromwell's actions remain marginalized: Lilburne plays the David role in permanent conflict with a procession of Goliaths, scarcely differentiated except by their names. 'Tyranny', a favourite Leveller term, recurs as the charge laid against a series of adversaries.

The final Lilburne pamphlet considered here, *Strength out of Weaknesse*, relates to his incarceration throughout much of 1648 by the Council of State and particularly describes his pre-trial interrogation by Edmond Prideaux, the Rump's Attorney-General. The title-page follows Lilburne's usual practice. It is replete with names, dates, and assertions of the text's provenance. Once more the issues are personalized. Once when his exposition takes a more theoretical turn, he arrests the development with 'Sir, the Designe is easily seene through, which was no more than this; *Cromwell* was resolved to play the knave, and I stood in his way' (p. 6). Lilburne makes no real attempt to understand why Cromwell behaves as he does. He merely constitutes the latest embodiment of tyranny which Lilburne must confront. Once more, he invokes recollection of his earliest trials (p. 20), thus suggesting the continuity of his defiant honesty.

The symbolic action perpetrated and described includes not only familiar hat-symbolism (Lilburne puts his on when Prideaux dons his own—p. 1), but also an element of the absurd. Lilburne declines the invitation to be seated, so he and his adversary stand at opposite ends of a table while he declaims at some length, Prideaux scarcely interjecting a comment. A strong element of repetition creeps in— Lilburne himself remarks upon it—and the reader must wonder what advantages the transcription of a private conversation can hold as a medium for the communication of precise constitutional law and theory. Important points about the constitutional status of the Rump occur in passing and without proper substantiation. As if in recognition of the inadequacy of the exposition, they are set in capitals (p. 11) to achieve typographically the emphasis which cannot be achieved rhetorically within the context of a dialogue.

As in his earliest prosecution by the Star Chamber, Lilburne doggedly maintains a legal quibble, that it cannot be proved that he printed books about which he is interrogated, and he will not admit to them, though he approves of their content and publication. A defendant brought to trial, perhaps for capital offence, can scarcely be blamed for exploiting any inadequacy in the prosecution case. But by emphasizing the intricacies of forensic debate—and evidently celebrating his mastery of them—Lilburne causes his readers to lose sight of the larger issues. Consider:

Sir, I scorn to tell you whether I did or did not [send a book]; it may be I did, it may be I did not, I will not tell you; but if I did, this I aver to you, *I know no evil in so doing*. So he shewed me the *Apprentises Out-cry*; Sir, said he, you had a finger too in the making this book, had you not? Said I, it may I had not onely a finger in it, but also a thumb too; and what then? but it may be I had not, and what then? But whether I had, or had not, I will not tell you (p. 15).

Perhaps to a Leveller loyalist this makes gratifying reading, as Lilburne, matador-like, with a twirl of the cape and a sway of the hips sends the enraged Cromwellian bull thundering impotently past. A less committed reader might see it differently, and a sympathetic image of Prideaux emerges as a well-meaning public servant trying to conduct a reasonable conversation with an unreasonable interlocutor. As in *The Christian Mans Triall*, the openness of Lilburne's discourse permits the construction of alternative and hostile interpretations. At one point, Lilburne glosses Prideaux's behaviour as 'smoothly cunning', but within ten lines he is apprising his readers how cunning he has been:

when I was called into Mr *Prideaux*'s inner Chamber, my friends followed me . . . which Mr *Prideaux* seeing . . . desired them to withdraw, *which because I was resolved not to owne his Attorney Generall-ship, but meerely to talke with him as a private man, I was not solicitour, for them staying in*: but the doore, as I perceived, being left open they stood there, and I am sure the most of them might easily heare mee what I said, for I spake high enough' (p. 1).

The figure of the trickster as hero is as ancient as Homer, but here it subverts Lilburne's image of himself as martyr for the truth, and his adversaries emerge as figures who serve a higher purpose than the minute legalism he espouses. Indeed, readers may feel considerable sympathy with Prideaux's difficulties, not least when he protests (on Lilburne's own account), 'a man doth not know well how to talke to you, you are so subject to print every thing is said to you' (p. 19), a comment which has come to us because Lilburne printed it.

Lilburne's writing can be grimly fascinating, though it perhaps reads best in small doses. Its shortcomings rest largely in the cultural and intellectual inadequacies of Lilburne himself, though they perhaps point to matters central to the Leveller movement. Lilburne frequently invokes 'rights' and 'prerogatives' and 'freedom' in passing, but is reluctant to define or justify those concepts except through the invocation of a legalism which elsewhere he represents as a superstructural feature of a corrupt State founded on the Norman Conquest. Those key issues, about revising the boundaries of the political nation, remain as vague in Lilburne as in the Leveller contributions to the Putney Debates. In place of such argument comes an obsession with reportage, with the display of factuality, and with personalities, both of the Leveller leaders and of their adversaries. Lilburne tries to turn the English State towards democracy on the improbable fulcrum of his own self-image.

Yet, in part, the problems may be inherent in the nature of the discourses available to Lilburne and his associates. Though the 1640s saw the rapid maturation of several genres for polemic and propaganda, pre-eminently the newspaper, more radical voices were persistently drawn to forms ultimately alien to their purpose. For Lilburne, the speech from the dock, the reportage of such speeches, and Puritan martyrology served only in a limited way for the production of Leveller polemic. Such forms as the contract and the agreement could not permit the creation of what the movement ultimately lacked, a vision of a social and political transformation worth fighting for. The problems recur in Digger writing, though Winstanley negotiates them rather differently.

Lilburne's tracts, then, may be perceived as embodying some (but not all) of the shortcomings of the Leveller movement, though they are shot through with attitudes and concerns which are essentially his own. Levellerism, unlike Diggerism, has an ideological diffuseness which defies representation through a single author, and Overton, Walwyn, and perhaps others merit consideration in a study focused solely on the radical milieu.

III

The Digger experiment of 1649–50 was contemporaneously confused with Levellerism, sometimes no doubt in a disingenuous attempt to tarnish Leveller protestations of their own respectability and their commitment to the defence of property. Some activists may have turned to Diggerism from Levellerism, and the rhetoric of the movement persistently represented it as a culmination or continuation. The first Digger manifesto bears the defiant title *The True Levellers Standard Advanced* (London, 1649). However, though a certain vagueness invests much of the writing of 1649–50, the ideological discontinuities between Levellers and Diggers are sharply apparent.[46]

[46] On the relationship between Diggers and Levellers, see Winstanley, *Works*,

A bold praxis characterizes the latter. Thought and action are indivisible. On 1 April 1649 a number of activists began the process of communally cultivating common land on St George's Hill, Cobham, Surrey. The process was at once symbolic and practical. That they should have chosen this site was remarked on as curious by contemporary commentators—the land was not especially promising for the kind of agriculture they favoured. Hill suggests that it may have been in an area of established radical activity, and that proximity to London and its presses was an obvious advantage.[47] He is probably right, though the name may also have been symbolically attractive. George, the ploughman saint, also points to the element of nationalism which sometimes suffuses Digger writing. In a way that anticipated the *modus vivendi* for which George Fox strove for the Quakers at the Restoration, the Diggers persistently stressed their wish simply to live alongside the established order, rarely threatening the property of others. The scheme related, as we shall see, to the millenarian typology at the centre of much of Winstanley's early writing: by cultivating the land communally the Diggers recapture what was lost at the Fall by the first cultivators. It was practical too, providing both a livelihood and a scheme for revolutionary change, but if other landless workers had followed the Digger paradigm, the whole established agricultural economy would have collapsed. If landlords cannot find tenants or day labourers, then large estates cease to be viable. Who would wish for broad acres if one had to work them oneself?

The Diggers' scheme, understandably, was regarded with suspicion and later with an effective hostility by local landowners, who presumably perceived their rights over the common land to have been challenged by the Digger encampment. Fairfax, who was responsible for military control of Surrey, was initially inclined to tolerance, though he displaced the group from St George's Hill and eventually suppressed them by legal action and by physical attacks on their cultivation and their houses. For a while the experiment had attracted some press attention, and Digger communes were

---

2–3, and id., *Law of Freedom*, 26–31, and for a different view M. Goldsmith, 'Levellers by Sword, Spade and Word: Radical Egalitarianism in the English Revolution', in C. Jones, M. Newitt, and S. Roberts (eds.), *Politics and People in Revolutionary England: Essays in Honour of Ivan Roots* (Oxford, 1986), 65–80. On the wilfulness of contemporary confusion between the groups, see Hill, *World*, 121.

[47] Ibid. 110–12.

established elsewhere in England at about a dozen sites, all apparently short-lived, but by the spring of 1650 the movement was at an end.

The chief ideologue of the movement, Gerrard Winstanley, cuts a curious figure within the English literary tradition. His biography, sketchily adumbrated in his writings, has been well supplemented in recent years by historical research. Born in 1609, he would seem to have written nothing before 1648, or after 1652, though he lived till the mid–1670s. His early career was as a rather unsuccessful London cloth merchant, his subsequent career as a fairly prosperous corn-chandler who seemingly achieved a respectability of sorts in the Cobham area. In that curiously short period of political activity and publication, he wrote some of the most interesting controversial prose of that golden age of controversy.[48]

The Winstanley *œuvre* poses interesting problems of interpretation. Despite the abbreviated nature of his writing career, there are crucial shifts of ideology and largely unrecognized complexities which relate to the variety of genres in which he writes. Some of his works appear to be primarily theological treatises, albeit of a heterodox kind. They have about them an atopicality, a sort of timelessness, and an absence of specific allusion to events occurring contemporaneously outside the text. Others are recognizably generically akin to the mainstream of controversial prose. They engage issues of immediate moment, they speak to an audience addressed by name, and are as studded with details of times, actions, and participants as a tract by Lilburne. The distinction is observed in the physical appearance of the texts. The latter group, such as *An Appeal to the House of Commons, Desiring their Answer* (n.p., 1649), or *An Humble Request, to the Ministers of Both Universities* (London, 1650), or *A Letter to the Lord Fairfax, and his Councell of War* (London, 1649), generally are printed in quarto, which is customary for controversial prose. Nearly all Milton's controversial prose is in quarto—his treatise *Of Education* (London, 1644) is in octavo. Leveller pamphlets are usually quarto. Indeed, one Digger tract, *An Appeale to all Englishmen* (n.p., 1650), is a broadside, which perhaps indicates that it was intended for fly-posting. The other group, such as *The Breaking of the Day of God* (London,

[48] *Works*, 5–11; *Law of Freedom*, 10–12, 31–5; P. H. Hardacre, 'Gerrard Winstanley in 1650', *HLQ* 22 (1958–9), 345–9; J. D. Alsop, 'Gerrard Winstanley: Religion and Respectability', *Hist. Jnl.* 28 (1985), 705–9.

1648) or *The Saints Paradise* (n.p., probably 1648) or *Fire in the Bush* (London, 1650), are generally in octavo, though there are exceptions. The controversial pamphlets tend to be considerably shorter than the theological treatises, and their titles rarely have the metaphorical character of the latter.[49]

Again, publishing history differentiates the two groups. Treatises went into a second edition, and five of them appeared in his collection, *Several Pieces Gathered into One Volume* (London, 1649). Winstanley's usual publisher, Giles Calvert, the radical bookseller associated with many heterodox writers,[50] suffixed a list of books by Winstanley still available from his shop (London, 1652) to *The Law of Freedom in a Platform* (sig. M2ᵛ). Since it is a list of the same books reprinted in *Several Pieces Gathered into One Volume* it may be no more than an advertisement for that collection, which he also published. Significantly, though, the controversial pamphlets are neither reprinted nor advertised as still available. Possibly they commanded less of a readership than the treatises. More probably, they may have been perceived as relating only to the immediate developing crisis on which they report and comment. Maybe unsold copies were simply distributed as part of the Diggers' propaganda initiative.

Two works fall outside this genre dichotomy. *A New-yeers Gift for the Parliament and Armie* (London, 1650) synthesizes elements of both genres, and *A Law of Freedom in a Platform* (London, 1652) has been convincingly contextualized in the tradition of Utopian writing.[51]

The coherence and character of Winstanley's thinking, and especially the central elements of it that are concerned with the relationship between religious belief and political action, have been the subject of sometimes heated discussion.[52] The arguments,

---

[49] On the relationship between genre, length, and format, see Corns, 'Publication and Politics', 77.

[50] Plomer; Greaves and Zaller; T. W. Hayes, *Winstanley the Digger* (Cambridge, Mass., 1979), 23.

[51] J. C. Davis, *Utopia and the Ideal Society: A Study in English Utopian Writing 1516–1700* (Cambridge, 1981), esp. ch. 7.

[52] *Law of Freedom*, 35–56; L. Mulligan, J. K. Graham, and J. Richards, 'Winstanley: A Case for the Man as He Said He Was', *JEH* 28 (1977), 57–75; G. Juretic, 'Digger No Millenarian: The Revolutionizing of Gerrard Winstanley', *JHI* 36 (1975), 263–80; J. C. Davis, 'Gerrard Winstanley and the Restoration of True Magistracy', *P & P* 70 (1976), 76–93; C. Hill, 'The Religion of Gerrard Winstanley', *P & P Supplement,* 5 (1978); C. Hill, L. Mulligan, J. K. Graham, and J. Richards,

however, have been informed by a general recognition of three major phases even within so short a career, the pre-Digger period, the period while the Digger experiment is in progress, and the period after it. These divisions inform the following account.

IV

Winstanley's pre-Digger tracts all belong to the genre I have categorized as theological treatises, though their theology is at a considerable remove from Christian orthodoxy. They present, rather, a rich broth of heretical notions current among the more radical strains of contemporary heterodoxy. The earliest ones are effusive, intermittently enigmatic, and are couched at times in an elevated, prophetic idiom.

The title-page of the first well indicates it tenor—*The Mysterie of God concerning the Whole Creation, Mankinde. To be made known to every man and woman, after seaven dispensations and seasons of time are passed over. According to the councell of God, revealed to his servants.* Mystery indeed. In what sense is 'the whole creation' equatable with 'mankinde'? The second sentence flags the tract's place in the millenarian tradition, and the last claims for it the privileged status of prophetic utterance. Again, his second tract, *The Breaking of the Day of God,* with its manifestation that 'The three dayes and a half: or 42 months of the saints captivity under the beast, [are] very nearly expired' (title page), is nested unrelentingly within the currently renascent tradition of apocalyptic writing. In both, to some extent, the voice produced offers to the hostile or unconvinced reader the simpler option of ignoring it: if we do not perceive in Winstanley the voice of the Holy Ghost speaking through a chosen instrument, the simplest conclusion is that we hear, instead, the voice of religious mania, which may safely be ignored.

Others have suggested that an understandable concern with contemporary measures against heresy may have had an influence on Winstanley's expository technique.[53] The exact date of publica-

---

'Debate: The Religion of Gerrard Winstanley', *P & P* 89 (1980), 144–6; G. E. Aylmer, 'The Religion of Gerrard Winstanley', in J. F. McGregor and B. Reay (eds.), *Radical Religion in the English Revolution* (1984; Oxford, 1986), 91–119.

[53] Hill, 'Religion', 21.

tion of *The Mysterie of God*, which Sabine regards as his first tract, is uncertain, though it was some time in 1648. *The Breaking of the Day of God* carries an address dated 20 May 1648, less then three weeks after the passing of *An Ordinance for the Punishing of Blasphemies and Heresies, with the Several Penalties Therein Expressed*. Parts of the ordinance detailing unacceptable doctrine read like a summary of beliefs attributable to Winstanley on the basis of his earliest publications:

that there is no God . . . that . . . the Son is not God, or that the Holy Ghost is not God, or that the Three are not one Eternal God: Or that . . . Christ is not God equal with the Father, or, shall deny the Manhood of Christ, or that the Godhead and Manhood of Christ are several Natures . . . or that shall maintain . . . That Christ did not die, nor rise from the Dead, nor is ascended into Heaven bodily . . . or that the Bodies of men shall not rise again after they are dead, or that there is no day of Judgment after death . . . [or] That all men shall be saved.[54]

Of course the ordinance, which legislated for capital punishment for those who would not recant or who committed subsequent offences, was not designed specifically to trap Winstanley. Indeed, a number of its provisions seem primarily anti-Catholic, though most of the errors are to be found in the lists of the Puritan heresiographers. Winstanley swims the same devotional waters as the more radical and heterodox thinkers of the age. His earliest works boldly bear the name not only of the author but of his intrepid publisher, Giles Calvert. Yet the legislation must surely have been worrying, however motivated one might have felt by millenarian optimism. Plainly, the power of the Beast was not broken. Some very eccentric writers, claiming the ambiguous status of visionaries, survived the rigour of the law quite well, if not wholly unscathed, despite articulating sentiments of a disturbingly seditious or blasphemous kind. There were perhaps advantages in camouflage, in apparently writing the sorts of prophecy that Arise Evans and Lady Eleanor Davis were writing with near impunity.[55]

Whatever the motivation—and Winstanley, coming from the informal seminary of primarily metropolitan radicalism, may simply have brought the idiom with him—the early pamphlets

[54] *Acts and Ordinances of the Interregnum*, i. 1133–5.
[55] Greaves and Zaller.

manifest difficulties in structure, in clarity of exposition, and in the image of the author produced within them, and Winstanley seems to have a poor notion of whom he is addressing and what effect he wishes to have upon them. The points may perhaps be illustrated from his third publication, *The Saints Paradise*, which Sabine thinks was published in the summer of 1648, though the title-page bears no date.[56]

Though the work is about 35,000 words in length, it rehearses a narrow range of concepts, albeit ones that are to remain important in Winstanley's thinking, and it does so in ways which assert them as facts of revelation rather than as proposals to be substantiated by proof or argument. In a sense, the last point is inevitable. Winstanley opens with:

I do not write to teach, I only declare what I know, you may teach me, for you have the fountain of life in you as well as I, and therefore he is called the Lord, because he rules not in one but in everyone (*Works*, sig. A4ʳ).

'You', the object of address, is not unproblematic, for Winstanley seems at this point uncertain of the universality of salvation and of the numbers in whose heart the spirit of God will rise. This passage suggests that spiritual resurrection abides embryonically within all ('not in one but in everyone'). Elsewhere (though the passage is ambiguous) he seems less certain: 'the number of the Saints are limited' (p. 20). Winstanley writes to those in whom the spirit has or will rise. This resurrection, whatever its extent (and the universalist position predominates) lies outside the will of the recipient or of others, much as salvation does in orthodox Calvinist or Lutheran theology, and its epidemic occurrence is perceived as imminent: 'the Father is beginning to work a great mysterie' (p. 46). Winstanley, whose fierce anticlericalism is already apparent, categorizes all theological instruction as either vain, empty book-learning or the reiteration of the spirit by one in whose heart the resurrection has occurred. Even the latter is of uncertain value compared with the personal experience of the saint; it is second-hand, reflective, and of transient significance:

But this teaching in Gods time must vanish too; for this moonlight that is, conveying knowledge to others by helps and mean, is to be swallowed up into the light of the sun, and God shall become all in all, as it is said, ye shall be all taught of God (pp. 2–3).

[56] *Works*, 91.

Winstanley speaks of his 'moonlight' as if in the moments before dawn, so to whom does he speak and why? If he speaks to those in whom the spirit has risen, then his voice is indeed as nothing compared with the inner voice they hear. If to those awaiting the imminent arrival of the spirit, then he acts as precursor to a force which requires no assistance. The dilemma is a familiar one within the prophetic tradition. He says he writes to reassure the former that their current suffering will pass: 'be not troubled you Saints of the most high, though you be hated, reproached, and persecuted' (p. 42). Again, 'this is comfort to the earth, The son or righteousnesse is comming, and hath begun to heal the earth' (p. 121). The late 1640s, before the army seized power, were bleak times for the more extreme sectaries, as the adoption of the Blasphemy Ordinance suggests, so some comfort does not come amiss. Yet a contradiction abides at the heart of Winstanley's tract (as in the prophetic tradition at large): if the resurrected spirit moves so powerfully within the saints, the prophet's ministration is supererogatory.

In truth, Winstanley proselytizes for his own rich blend of contemporary heresies, which, despite the vagueness and repetitiveness which have been remarked upon, emerge frequently and plainly with a simple eloquence:

And friends, doe not mistake as a person resurrection of Christ? you expect he shall come in one single person, as he did when he came to suffer, and die, and thereby to answer the types of *Moses* law; let me tell you, if you look for him under the notion of one single man after the flesh, to be your Saviour, you shall never, never taste salvation by him (p. 82).

Evidently, Winstanley speaks to his 'friends' much as a minister speaks to his flock, however much he may deny that role. What he says is central to his developing theology. For him, the millennium relates to an ethical and spiritual awakening in the hearts of people inhabiting the material world, and to transform that material world into the saints' paradise of his title is to merge the realms of nature and of grace: 'Gods dwelling is not in any locall place above the skies' (p. 97). Nor should people conceive of a divine agency except that which they perceive operating within the saints:

He that looks for a God without himself, and worships God at a distance, he worships he knows not what, but is led away, and deceived by the imaginations of his own heart, which is *Belzebub* the great Devill; but he that looks for a God within himself, and submits himselfe to the spirit of righteousness that shines within; this man knows whom he worships, for he is made subject to, and hath communitie with that spirit that made all flesh, that dwells in all flesh, and in every creature within the globe (pp. 89–90).

V

By the time of Winstanley's next pamphlet, *Truth Lifting up its Head against Scandals*, important shifts have occurred both in the position of sectaries generally and in Winstanley's specific role. The title-page bears the date 1649, the opening epistle to the scholars of Oxford and Cambridge is dated 16 October 1648. Presumably it went to press either in the closing months of 1648—so close to the end of the year that the bookseller felt the 1649 imprint excusable— or early in 1649. The Long Parliament was purged of those elements most actively hostile to sectaries only in December, though the more optimistic radical may well have felt the fragility of their enemies' hold on power somewhat earlier. Moreover, Winstanley writes now as part of a coterie in the making. He writes in part 'as a vindication' of William Everard and himself (Works, p. 103). Everard emerges shortly as one of the Diggers; indeed, he is initially perceived as their leader, but his later history, though somewhat uncertain, evidently leads him towards other groups.[57] Winstanley, for the first time, feels required to engage precisely challenges posed by the practicalities of power. Everard has been arrested by '*the Bayliffs of* Kingston', and Winstanley, who was in his company, has been '*slandered*' by ministers accusing him of blasphemy (pp. 103– 4). For the first time, Winstanley writes with a purpose and to a defined audience, to clarify the nature of his theology both 'To the gentle reader' (presumably, the reader tractable to a sectary's arguments) and, more ambitiously, to the professional clergy, whom he interlocutes throughout in an aggressive vein and whom he invites the more sympathetic reader to judge:

Well, matters of this nature [the nature of the Godhead], are to be judged with a wary and moderate spirit; covetous rashnesse can judge of nothing. I my selfe being branded by some of your mouthes, as guilty of horrid *blasphemy*, for denying all these [orthodox propositions concerning

---

[57] Ibid. 103–4; Greaves and Zaller.

Christ], as you say, though you cannot prove it, was drawn forth by the Spirit to write what here followes; which I leave to the spirituall men all the world over to judge (*Works*, p. 101).

Hill, though usually a reliable guide in the matter of Winstanley's religion, inappropriately attributes a tepidness to *Truth Lifting up its Head*, arguing that he trims his theology out of anxiety about the Blasphemy Ordinance.[58] On the contrary, it is a courageous attempt to clarify what previously had been left vague, for whatever reason. Interestingly, though Calvert put his name to the second edition and to his two previous pamphlets, the first edition appears without a bookseller's imprint, nor does its printer acknowledge it.

After the epistles the tract largely takes the form of questions and answers, as though Winstanley were defending theses in a fair but searching disputation. The tenor of the questions he poses himself disclose, I think, an awareness that previously he may have been misunderstood and that definitions and supplementation perhaps were lacking—'Explaine your meaning', 'Declare more plaine what this first man is?', 'Unfold your meaning in this a little more?', 'I pray explaine this a little more?', 'How doe you mean, make it more clear?' (pp. 116, 118, 133, 135). The questioner occupies the place of sympathetic readers, articulating difficulties as if on their behalf.

The formula allows, albeit still in rather unstructured fashion, the production of the clearest exposition of Winstanley's views to date, and it does so in a way which eradicates whatever remained of the visionary persona. Winstanley patiently explains key concepts, most significantly, perhaps, his equation of God and reason. The word 'reason' related in early modern English to a larger concept than simply the faculty to interpret information logically. It appears represented as one term in an abiding struggle. The other term is 'will'. Reason is that which distinguishes humans from lower animals, which are motivated solely by appetites and emotions. Reason controls the will as a rider controls his horse, an image with some currency in Renaissance iconography. In such a context, Winstanley's equation of God and reason appears more comprehensible. Reason, the sound ethical impulse, opposes the selfish promptings of the lower appetite; in Winstanleyan terms, it is the man of spirit that opposes the man of flesh in the psychomachy

---

[58] Quoted above.

within each human. It works to 'destroy the powers of the flesh; which leades creatures into divers waies of opposition one against another' (p. 110). (Curiously, Winstanley conceives of a lower kind of reason to be found in animals, which is manifest when they behave well and co-operate with humans, though they are unconscious of possessing the faculty (p. 110).)

Winstanley conceives of no pertinent entities outside the primary elements of earth, fire, water, and air. The historical Christ died and his body resolved itself into those elements; what rose was his spirit, that is the impulse towards ethical conduct or reason which he embodied in purest form and which is now being resurrected epidemically throughout mankind in the individual hearts of those who attain to a new purity. The interlocutor within the text poses the obvious objection: 'But it is said that his body rose again and ascended up through the cloudes into the skies, which is called Heaven, or the place of Glory, where the Father dwels?' Winstanley's answer illuminates fascinatingly his way of reading Scripture and also his notion of the concept of 'vision', which has much exercised his interpreters:

And this certainly to me is very cleare, That whereas the Apostles saw Christ arise and ascend, and were witnesses of his Resurrection, it was onely a declaration in vision to them, of the Spirits rising up: for death, and hel, and darknesse, and sorrow, could not hold him under; he saw no corruption; for as soon as that one body, in which he was confined for a time, was laid low; he rose presently up again in the bodies of the Apostles, & so began to spread in the Earth; and when his set time is expired, that the Beast, or flesh shall reign no more: Then he will spread himselfe in sons and daughters from East to West, from North to South; and never cease encreasing till this vine hath filled the Earth (*Works*, pp. 114–15).

Christ is not physically resurrected; that the Apostles believe they have seen and touched him is a 'declaration in vision' of the central but complex truth, that Christ's spirit, that is primarily the ethical system he perfectly embodied, has not died but rather has entered into the Apostles as it will enter into everyone in due course. 'Vision' evidently means the symbolic representation of a complex truth in a form which lends itself to immediate absorption. It is not, as is sometimes said, that he is marginalizing the Scriptures as simply a source of convenient allegory. As he later asserts, 'this is no new Gospel, but the old one; It is the same report that the Pen-men of Scriptures gave' (p. 169). Rather, he takes the Scriptures too seriously to interpret them as supernatural anecdote, as denials of the material properties of the physical world, and strains to find a rational and coherent truth within them. Note too the material nature of the envisaged millennium. The happy resolution leads not to the destruction of the earth but the filling of the earth. When Winstanley records that the central synthesis of Christian ethics and a radical social critique came to him 'in a trance' (p. 190), it is worth recalling how the Apostles too were vouchsafed great truths in a vision. Those truths, however, were imparted not by a supernatural agency but by the embodiment in sensible symbols of a new consciousness arising within themselves.

The social dimension is already present in Winstanley's theology in the radical interpretation of Christian ethical obligations. To live 'in the sight of Reason' is to feed the hungry, clothe the naked, relieve the oppressed (p. 111), while 'the devil' is the impulse that causes people to delight 'in the enjoyment of riches or creatures' (p. 135). But it is in his final pre-Digger pamphlet that a radical social analysis emerges as corollary of the spiritual and ethical account.

The epistle to *The New Law of Righteousnes* is dated 26 January 1648 [NS 1649]. The tract is about 45,000 words long and must have been written in at most three months and quite probably considerably less than that. The defects of poor structure and repetitiveness which it shares with the four earlier tracts may well have their origins as much in haste as in inexperience, though a more accomplished writer would probably have found ways to be briefer. In *The New Law of Righteousnes*, however, Winstanley manifests a more assured grasp of his repertoire, like an artist who has come to know his palette. Two figures, a pair of interrelated dichotomies, organize the exposition, the concept of the two Adams and the distinction between Esau, the man of flesh, and Jacob, his disadvantaged brother:

For assure your selves, this *Adam* is within every man and woman; and it is the first power that appears to act and rule in every man. It is the Lord *Esau* that stepped before *Iacob*, and got the birthright, by the Law of equity was more properly *Iacobs*.

Though *Iacob*, who is the power and wisdom that made flesh did draw back, and give way, that the wisdom and power of flesh should possesse the Kingdom, and rule first; till *Esau*, by delighting in unrighteous pleasures, lost both birth-right and blessing; and left both in the hand of *Iacob* the King, that rule in righteousnesse, that is to rise up next.

The Apple that the first man eats, is not a single fruit called an Apple, or such like fruit; but it is the objects of the Creation; which is the fruit that came out of the Seed, which is the Spirit himself that made all things: As riches, honours, pleasures, upon which the powers of the flesh feeds to delight himself.

And this is the messe of pottage which he prefers before righteousnesse, or before righteous walking in the Creation towards every creature, which is Christ, that power that appears in the fulnesse of time to take the Kingdom and rule next.

Therefore when a man fals, let him not blame a man that died 6000 years ago, but blame himself, even the powers of his own flesh, which lead him astray; for this is *Adam* that brings a man to misery, which is the man of flesh, or the strong man within that keeps the house, till the man of Righteousnesse arise and cast him out, who is the second *Adam* (*Works*, 176–7).

Note that Winstanley does not deny the historicity of Christ or indeed of Adam, accepting, in line with the best contemporary estimates, that the latter lived and died about six thousand years earlier. But for Scriptural accounts of Adam and Christ to relate *only* to discrete, historical individuals would be, for Winstanley, a weakening and an impoverishment of Judaeo-Christian theology. In a sense, he addresses the problem that Milton had to address in *Paradise Lost*: how can the trivial action by one man six millenniums earlier explain all the evil in the world? Winstanley's solution is not so remote from Milton's. That action represents primarily an ethical choice which is to be made by all people throughout history, a choice between godliness and ungodliness (though those concepts differ significantly between Milton and Winstanley). Again, the familiar and ancient typological association of Christ and Adam is ultimately Pauline: 'And so it is written, The first man Adam was made a living soul; the last Adam was made a quickening spirit. . . . The first man is of the earth, earthy: the second man is the Lord from heaven' (1 Cor. 15: 45, 47).

Winstanley veers off from both the Miltonic and Pauline perspective in his association of the appetitive urge of the first Adam with that of Esau, and herein abides the crucial connection between his theology and his political analysis. The impulse to accumulate produces life-threatening disparities of wealth and repressive apparatuses to protect that inequity. The imminent epidemic of Christ's resurrection in the hearts of the people will manifest itself in social and economic revolution:

Christ, the restorer, stops and dammes up the runnings of those stinking waters of self-interest, and causes the waters of life and liberty to run plentifully in and through the Creation, making the earth one store-house, and every man and woman to live in the law of Righteousnesse and peace as members of one houshold (*Works*, 159).

Winstanley's abilities as a phrase-maker had been manifest throughout his early writing. In *The New Law of Righteousnes*, however, literary creativity of a high order manifests itself in more sustained fashion. Spiritual resurrection as an organic process had already been suggested in his characteristic choice of imagery. In *The Saints Paradise*, for example, 'the Father [begins] to pull *Adam* out of selfish flesh again, and to plant him into the pure spirit' (p. 46). In *The New Law of Righteousnes*, the revolutionary consciousness is set to transform society with the irresistibility of spring. His secondary title speaks of 'The New Law of Righteousnes Budding Forth, to Restore the Whole Creation' (p. 155). In a passage which unites the language of the apocalyptic tradition with an incantatory vernal rite of a thoroughly English landscape, Winstanley produces some of the best of his pre-Digger prose:

The windows of heaven are opening, and the light of the Son of Righteousnes, sends forth of himself delightful beams, and sweet discoveries of truth that wil quite put out the covetous traditional bleareyes . . . Light must put out darknesse; the warm Sun wil thaw the frost, and make the sap to bud out of every tender plant, that hath been hid within, and lain like dead trees all the dark cold cloudy daies of the Beast that are past, and silence every imaginary speaker, and declare their hypocrisie, and deceit openly.

Now the tender grasse wil cover the earth, the Spirit wil cover al places *with the abundance of fruit*, that flows from himself (*Works*, 207).

The epistle to the tract is dated days before the execution of the king, and two months before the start of the Digger experiment. *The New Law of Righteousnes* throbs with an excitement at the imminence of change and of the possibilities disclosed by the seemingly epochal resolution of England's political crisis now that the days of the Beast are passed.

VI

The Digger pamphlets, written during the period when cultivation was under way first on St George's Hill and later on Cobham Heath, adopt a curious mode of address. Publication cannot have been conceived as the principal medium of Digger ideology. At that time, the illiteracy level in rural England probably stood at about 70 per cent by a very modest definition of what constituted literacy (namely, the proportion who signed documents rather than made their marks upon them). A considerable range of skill separates the ability to sign one's name from the ability to read controversial prose. Moreover, literacy correlated very strongly with class. In Cressy's phrase, 'literacy was a powerful marker of social and economic position'. Illiteracy was worst among husbandmen and the lowest rural class of agricultural labourers, the 'pitifully poor [who] had neither use for literacy nor opportunities to acquire it'.[59] Such were the likeliest (and, indeed, the most useful) potential recruits to the Digger project, but they must have provided an elusive target for the radical pamphleteer.

Obviously, other mechanisms for political organization, for agitation and propaganda, were available. The first Digger pamphlet appeared over the names of fifteen men, with a suggestion that they were a representative group of a larger body, and we may surmise that many of them would have had spouses. A nucleus of activists had formed before a word was published. Moreover, we know of Digger agents who toured much of southern England in 1649–50 to promote the Digger experiment, to collect funds, and to encourage, with some success, the development of similar initiatives elsewhere.[60]

Word-of-mouth communication played a central role in lower-class radicalism in the early modern period. Indeed, Winstanley himself, quite remarkably for a writer of such power and accomplishment, makes few references to books. Foxe's *Actes and Monuments* and the Bible are the only texts he alludes to, and when he controversially engages an adversary it is, characteristically, in response to something that person has said, rather than written.[61]

[59] D. Cressy, *Literacy and the Social Order: Reading and Writing in Tudor and Stuart England* (Cambridge, 1980), 72, 141, 127.
[60] Hill, *World*, 124–8.
[61] Id., 'Religion', 10; *Works*, pp. 103, 346.

His own grounding in theology, politics, and polemic would seem to have been through debate within radical circles, rather than through close consideration of texts other than the Scriptures. Winstanley's Digger pamphlets do not speak primarily to the propertiless: rather, they speak *for* the poor oppressed people of England *to* the great ones of the earth.

The True Levellers Standard Advanced appeared in late April 1649. A new collectivism characterizes its idiom. An epistle by one John Taylor, a supporter who has evidently absorbed the concepts and vocabulary of *The New Law of Righteousnes*, speaks of 'the Authour of this ensuing Declaration, and the Persons Subscribing' (*Works*, 247), and Winstanley evidently tries to speak not only for himself but for the other fourteen whose names the pamphlet bears. First-person pronominalization is characteristically plural: 'Thus we have discharged our Souls in declaring the Cause of our digging' (p. 266). Occasionally, the singular form breaks in, usually when Winstanley assumes an aggressively prophetic voice:

For do not I see every one Preacheth for money, Counsels for money, and fights for money to maintain particular Interests?

One thing I must tell you more . . . which I received *in voce* likewise at another time; and when I received it, my ey was set towards you. The words were these:

Let Israel go free.

And thou *A-dam* that holds the Earth in slavery under the Curse: If thou wilt not *let Israel go Free*; for thou being the Antitype, will be more stout and lusty then the *Egyptian Pharaoh* of old, who was thy Type; Then know, That whereas I brought *Ten* Plagues upon him, I will *Multiply* my Plagues upon thee, till I make thee weary, and miserably ashamed: *And I will bring out my People with a stronghand, and stretched out arme* (*Works*, 263–6).

Winstanley's radical typology inspires the passage: he adopts the voice of Christ scourging the moneylenders or of Moses addressing Pharaoh because that same spirit animates the believer in whose heart Christ is risen. '*In voce*. . . at another time' invokes recollection of a former period and offers a tantalizing fragment of spiritual autobiography, perhaps to be interpreted in the light of his prefatory comments to the collected edition of his pre-Digger works.[62] In the context of a pamphlet in which a calm, collective (if

---

[62] Discussed below.

rather declarative) rationalism obtains, such passages break in as a more profoundly motivated and deeply experienced testament to the holiness of the undertaking, a liberation theology that relates Diggerism to the Exodus and to the imitation of Christ.

Generally, though, the tone the pamphlet strikes is a balance between, on the one hand, conciliation and coexistence and, on the other, the assertion of a radically challenging egalitarianism:

We are made to hold forth this Declaration to you that are the Great Councel, and to you the Great Army of the Land of *England*, that you may know what we would have, and what you are bound to give us by your Covenants and Promises; and that you may joyn with us in this Work, and so find Peace. Or else, if you oppose us, we have peace in our work, and in declaring this Report: And you shall be left without excuse (*Works*, 257).

A minatory edge trails this statement. The pamphlet functions much as, in *Paradise Lost*, Raphael's visit to Adam and Eve does, 'to render man inexcusable'. The Muggletonians were later to consider that those who had been approached and had rejected the message were certainly beyond redemption.[63]

But the pamphlet simultaneously reassures the Council of State and the army leaders that the events in Cobham should occasion no anxieties about civil order and the rights of property, much in the quietist direction in which George Fox would later lead the Quakers:

Our Bodies as yet are in thy hand, our Spirit waits in quiet and peace, upon our Father for Deliverance; and if he give our Bloud into thy hand, for thee to spill, know this . . . That our Bloud and Life shall not be unwilling to be delivered up in meekness to maintain universal Liberty . . . And we shall not do this by force of Arms, we abhorre it (p. 256).

This embodies something more profound than a mere polemical strategy: rather, Winstanley's group, while defiantly taking upon themselves the title of 'True Levellers', distance themselves in their conduct and expression from the direct-action approach that was to move the Levellers, disastrously, to take up arms at Burford. Thomason dated his copy of *The True Levellers Standard* 26 April, the day on which Robert Lockyer was sentenced.[64] It was probably on sale in one or more of the bookshops (no doubt, in Calvert's)

---

[63] Milton, Argument to *Paradise Lost*, v, *Poems*, 674; C. Hill, B. Reay, and W. Lamont, *The World of the Muggletonians* (London, 1983), 2.

[64] Others have remarked on the coincidence; see Hill, *World*, 113.

around St Paul's, the site of his execution the following day. While the pamphlet proclaims their readiness to die, it does so in terms which would make Cromwell and his group much less likely to give priority to their suppression.

The theology of *The True Levellers Standard* builds on the central tenets of Winstanley's earlier writing, but its political dimension manifests the injection of new thinking from other radical quarters. The arguments of Ireton and Cromwell, that men of no property have no place in the political nation, are tacitly met by the concept that Parliament and army entered into a contract or covenant with the lower classes, promising liberty in return for the expenditure of blood and free quarter (pp. 255, 260), a concept that is rehearsed more powerfully in the pamphlets that follow. Besides a typological explanation for the rise of private property—the curse of the Fall, the crime of Esau—Winstanley adds a familiar historical explanation, again tractable to later elaboration, the theory of the Norman Yoke, whereby the English system of land-tenure is interpreted as a process through which William the Conqueror rewarded his army at the expense of the indigenous people. Lawyers join the clergy as professions to be reviled, and his analysis shows a new subtlety:

For what are all those Binding and Restraining Laws that have been made from one Age to another since that Conquest, and are still upheld by Furie over the People? I say, What are they? but the Cords, Bands, Manacles, and Yokes that the enslaved *English*, like *Newgate* Prisoners, wears upon their hands and legs as they walk the streets; by which those *Norman* Oppressors, and these their Successsors from Age to Age have enslaved the poor People by, killed their yonger Brother, and would not suffer *Iacob* to arise (*Works*, 259).

In an idiom many radicals would have approved of, Winstanley operates from a political theory that regards the law as essentially superstructural, a mere apparatus of the social élite. The passage illustrates other elements which have become important in his writing. Note the first triggering of the patriotism mechanism: English bondage is the consequence of Norman tyranny. The universalism that had inspired his theology eases over to make room for a rather different appeal, and one perhaps more persuasive to the audience to whom he addresses himself.

The passage illustrates too the confident and terse manner in which he synthesizes the major motifs of his symbolical universe.

Now the two Adams, Jacob and Esau, together with the Norman Yoke and, a term to be elaborated, the Common Treasury come together into a close-woven fabric, organized around the central motif of the digging of the common land.

Like many of the most revolutionary initiatives of the sixteenth and seventeenth centuries, the venture is represented not as an innovative rebellion but as a work of restoration. Paradise is regained by taking up, in the spirit of the second Adam, that curse laid on the first: 'The Work we are going about is this, To dig up *Georges-Hill* and the waste Ground thereabouts, and to Sow Corn, and to eat our bread together by the sweat of our brows' (p. 257). Not only does the work achieve an immediate and practical objective, but it also completes a typological schema of redemption. Whereas Milton's fallen men may merely seek a 'paradise within' (*Paradise Lost*, xii. 587), albeit one which is 'happier far' than the first Paradise, Winstanley's theology admits of a material realization of the paradisal state through communal endeavour. The notion becomes the keystone of his symbolic universe.

The pamphlets that appear in quick succession through the summer and autumn of 1649 substantially resemble his first Digger publication, though they are shaped too by the exigencies of their programme of communal cultivation. *A Declaration from the Poor Oppressed People of England*—Thomason dated his copy 1 June—strikes a similar tone, at once reassuring and challenging. Again, Winstanley's name appears with those of others, now grown to forty-four, and they sign it 'on the behalf of all the poor oppressed people of *England* and the whole world' (*Works*, 277). A confident, declaratory voice is heard—Sabine, indeed, finds in the belligerence evidence that others besides Winstanley had a hand in the writing (p. 267): 'we require, and we resolve to take both Common Land and Common woods to be a livelihood for us'; 'the Earth was made for us, as well as for you' (p. 273). Once again, however, men of property receive a general reassurance: 'we shall meddle with none of your Proprieties (but what is called Commonage) till the Spirit in you, make you cast up your Lands and Goods . . . we shall take it from the Spirit, that hath conquered you, and not from our Swords, which is an abominable, and unrighteous power, and a destroyer of the Creation: But the Son of man comes not to destroy, but to save' (p. 272). Yet the immediate problems confronting the Diggers, namely whether they have the right to cut timber on the common land or whether that belongs solely to the lords of the manor, produce an element of muscle-flexing that runs counter to the characteristically passive stance. 'Wood-mongers' are warned off from dealing with the lords of the manor, with the distinct threat 'blame us not, if we make stop of the Carts you send and convert the Woods to our own use, as need requires' (p. 274).

That posture clearly introduces a discordant element within Digger ideology, and also risks the kinds of repression the Levellers were contemporaneously met with. The next pamphlet, *A Letter to the Lord Fairfax and his Councell of War*, dating from the following week, adopts a more modest strategy. Davis has made much of the way in which Winstanley addresses institutions or individuals that control important spheres of influence: 'He was never anti-authoritarian . . . almost all his works contained some sort of appeal to the established authorities or to those he believed to be in command of the power to achieve his purposes.'[65] But, in a sense, he was never in a position to do otherwise. A shrewd grasp of *realpolitik* led him to recognize that his scheme could work only through the tolerance of the victorious republicans, a realism which led him, probably some time in the first half of 1650, to enter the Engagement Controversy as defender of the republic. As Aylmer remarks, paradoxically, his grasp of the central political truth 'that the maintenance of republican rule was a necessary precondition for further economic and social change' manifests a more realistic view than the Levellers could manage.[66] Winstanley knew about power as a horse knows about whips.

He needed pressingly to engage Fairfax's favourable attention to the Digger project. They had met twice, once when he and Everard went to Whitehall on 20 April, and a second time on 26 May, when Fairfax made a site-inspection of St George's Hill. The former exchange, while generally courteous, had been marked by a piece of hat-symbolism of a familiar kind—Winstanley and Everard kept theirs on, much as Lilburne would have done. The latter account was quite vividly reported in a contemporary news-book. Plainly the journalist was not predisposed towards the Diggers, calling their labours 'contemptible', though he remarks on the 'sober answers'

---

[65] Davis, 'Winstanley', 78.

[66] G. E. Aylmer (ed.), '*England's Spirit Unfoulded, or an Incouragement to Take the Engagement*, by Jerrard Winstanley: A Newly Discovered Pamphlet by Gerrard Winstanley', *P & P* 40 (1968), 3–15.

with which Winstanley responded to questions and on how 'civilly and fairly' they conduct themselves. What emerges from the report, however, is a sense of uncertainty about what the Diggers really intend—'they gave little satisfaction (if any at all) in regard of the strangenesse of the action . . . . Some officers wisht they had no further plot in what they did, and that no more was intended then what they did pretend.'[67] Fairfax was obviously the great one with whom the Diggers had established a dialogue, albeit a rather bewildered one on Fairfax's part, and his was the responsibility to maintain law and order in their area of operation.

The new approach to Fairfax in *A Letter to Lord Fairfax* is a response to the powerful intrusion of local politics into the Diggers' world vision. 'Some of your foot souldiers of the Generalls Regiment' have attacked the Diggers, beating two of them badly (*Works*, 284–5). Winstanley, though he proceeds obliquely (p. 284), urgently needs at least a disciplined neutrality from the army. His approach to Fairfax seeks to build upon recent contacts—'we did receive mildnesse and moderation from you and your Councell of Warre, both when some of us were at White-hall before you and when you came in person to *George*-hill to view our works' (p. 281). But the letter, while it addresses Fairfax, is published so that others may read it and thus perceive not only the arguments they present to him but also that the Diggers are, in some senses, in negotiation with the commander-in-chief of the New Model Army. The concluding note, that the letter was delivered 'by the Authors own hand to the Generall, and the chief Officers, and they mildly promised they would read it, and consider it' (p. 292), is a warning that the Diggers are not without influence.

The tract also shows that Winstanley is developing some skill in tuning his argument *ad hominem*. Once more, property-owners are meant to be reassured that 'none of us shall be found guilty of medling with your goods, or inclosed proprieties' (p. 283), and the Diggers are presented as seconding the national endeavour:

And if this you do [leave us alone], we shall live in quietnesse, and the Nation will be brought into peace, while you that are the soulderie, are a wall of fire round about the Nation to keep out a forraign enemy, and are succourers of your brethren that live within the Land, who indeavour to

---

[67] *Works*, p. 15; Anon., *The Speeches of the Lord General Fairfax, and the Officers of the Armie to the Diggers* (London, 1649), sig. E4ᵛ.

hold forth the Sun of righteousnesse in their actions, to the glory of our Creator (p. 286).

Winstanley is never deferential in his addresses to the powerful—witness, for example, the bluntness of his sole surviving private letter, to Lady Eleanor Davis[68]—nor is he artless.

From mid–1649 to the spring of 1650, local issues and the specific legal and practical difficulties the Diggers faced at the hands of local gentry and their dependants predominate in Winstanley's pamphlets. A level of particularity as precise as Lilburne's is added to the larger theoretical and theological perspective. Most pamphlets respond to immediate pressures:

> Upon the 11. day of June 1649, foure men only being fitting and preparing the ground for a winter season, upon that Common called George-hill, there came to them, *William Starr* of *Walton*, and *Iohn Taylor*, two freeholders, being on horseback, having at their heels some men in womens apparell . . . (*A Declaration of the Bloody and Unchristian Acting of William Star, and John Taylor of Walton, Works*, 295).

> there be three men (called by the people *Lord or Manors*) viz. *Thomas* Lord *Wenman*, *Ralph Verny* Knight, and *Richard Winwood* Esquire, have arrested us for a trespass in digging upon the Commons (*An Appeal to the House of Commons*, ibid. 302).

Winstanley, however, soon manifests considerable skill in using the particular as the fulcrum on which to turn a humane irony. Nor is that the only literary quality. Like Bunyan in *Pilgrim's Progress*, Winstanley has a fine ear for epiphanic dialogue, for the phrase that discloses a way of perceiving the world:

> Then they came privately by day to *Gerrard Winstanleys* house, and drove away foure Cowes; I not knowing of it and some of the Lords Tenants rode to the next Town shouting the diggers were conquered, the diggers were conquered. Truly it is an easie thing to beat a man, and cry conquest over him after his hands are tied, as they tyed ours (*A Watch-Word to the City of London*, ibid. 328).

That odd phrase compulsively repeated, 'the diggers were conquered, the diggers were conquered', suggests the unfreedom of those whom, with a Miltonic flourish, he terms 'the snapsack boyes and ammunition drabs' who second the gentry's efforts (p. 331).

Yet while the enemies are rooted utterly in the narrow perspectives

---

[68] Hardacre, 'Winstanley in 1650', 345–9.

of local politics, Winstanley's vision persistently relates the local struggle to the larger issues of the rising of the second Adam. While the gentry sit in the White Lion in Cobham 'to find out who are our backers, and who stirs us up to dig the Commons', Winstanley, shifting from the specific to the universal, can respond, 'Ile tel you plainly who it is, it is love, the King of righteousnes ruling in our hearts, that makes us thus to act that the creation may be set at liberty.' Digging is represented simultaneously as a rational economic activity and as an act of profound spiritual significance, albeit within the context of his markedly materialist theology: 'I tell thee thou *England*, thy battells now are all spirituall. Dragon against the Lamb, and the power of love against the power of covetousnesse' (p. 336).

Winstanley's retention of the larger dimension contrasts sharply with the one publication by the Digger colony established at Wellingborough, Northamptonshire, which passes perfunctorily from the rehearsal of Winstanley's notion of taking up the curse of Adam, to a much fuller account of how their Digger colony is serving to reduce the number of indigent people dependent on the parish and how warmly it had been welcomed and assisted by local gentry (p. 650).

Winstanley's most ambitious Digger pamphlet, *A New-Yeers Gift for the Parliament and Armie* (London, 1650)—Thomason dated his copy 1 January—seems to be, in genre terms, a hybrid, parts of which closely resemble his pre-Digger theological tracts. Approximately 20,000 words long, it marks a new return to an expansiveness uncharacteristic of other Digger pamphlets. It falls into three sections, each with a separate heading. The first, like other Digger pamphlets, attempts to address a politically useful audience with some close regard to polemical tactics. Winstanley evidently aims to convince the Rump and the Army Grandees that their victory over Charles I was closely analogous to the Diggers' problems with the Surrey gentry. Each represents the struggle against 'Kingly power', for just as Charles was heir to the conquest of William I, so too the rights that the lords of the manors claim over the common land are the rewards bestowed by William on his Norman associates (p. 356). Winstanley's appeal stresses the loyalty of the Diggers to the new republic (at a time when it appeared relatively friendless) and may be appropriately related to his contribution to the Engagement Controversy:[69]

---

[69] Discussed above.

hereby our own Land will be increased with all sorts of Commodities, and the People will be knit together in love, to keep out a forreign Enemy that endeavours, and that will endeavour as yet, to come like an Army of cursed Ratts and Mice to destroy our inheritance (p. 356).

Moreover, the opening section looks for common ground between the Diggers and the more radical of the Cromwell faction. Winstanley rehearses once more his anticlericalism, attacking the tithe-funded clergy as another vestige of the Conquest and as a politically unstable element—'The Clergie will serve on any side, like our ancient Laws, that will serve any Master' (p. 358). A republican of Milton's outlook would have liked that point. Moreover, it links the professional clergy with the legal profession as another obstacle to the work of reformation now facing the new republic. Cromwell was to spend some energy in the spring of 1650, before turning to the Scottish military campaign, in building bridges with more radical elements through the promise of legal reform, and indeed some of his rhetoric after the Battle of Dunbar, in the spring of 1650, approaches Winstanley's assertion that '*England* is a Prison; the variety of subtilties in the Laws preserved by the Sword, are bolts, bars, and doors of the prison' (p. 361).[70]

The central section, which carries the heading 'The Curse and Blessing that is in Mankinde', rehearses once more Winstanley's characteristically materialist theology, though with more emphasis on the notion of 'imagination', a concept quite close to the Marxist notion of ideology. Under 'imaginary light', people misperceive the world largely in terms of self-seeking and of a non-materialist spiritual abstraction, in contrast with the way in which those in whom the son/sun of righteousness has arisen perceive more clearly (p. 378). The tract ends rather perfunctorily, with 'A Bill of Account of the Most Remarkable Sufferings that the Diggers Have Met With', essentially a list of fifteen outrages, most of which had been reported in other tracts, followed by a further appeal to the army, which is punctuated with scraps of defiant verse (pp. 392–6).

VII

Winstanley's last and finest theological treatise, *Fire in the Bush*, for a while occasioned some scholarly controversy about its date of

[70] C. Hill, *God's Englishman: Oliver Cromwell and the English Revolution* (London, 1970), 124–5.

publication. Published by Calvert, it carries '1650' on its title-page. Sabine accepted that only reluctantly, since to him it seemed to fit into a schema of intellectual development somewhere between *The New Law of Righteousnes* and the beginning of cultivation. A pamphlet published in spring 1649 would not bear a 1650 imprint (though a very late 1649 one might), and it could hardly be a printer's error. Calvert was reissuing the early theological treatises in a compendium edition in early 1650, so there is an outside chance that it is a second edition of a 1649 pamphlet of which the first edition has not survived, a hypothesis which bibliographical evidence may be able to confirm or confute. Certainly we now know that the edition that survived came into Thomason's hands on 19 March 1650. If that edition is the first, Thomas is surely right to conclude that 'its composition must have been around the beginning of March 1650, since Winstanley says in his preface that he delayed publishing his revelation for a fortnight'.[71]

I find the later dating unproblematic. Winstanley's writing throughout the Digger experiment, most significantly in *The New-yeers Gift*, had shown the complex interdependence of theological and political modes of thought, and we know how in late 1649, his attention returned to the writing he first produced. Calvert issued, presumably early in 1650, *Several Pieces Gathered into One Volume*, which reprints his first five works together with a fascinating preface by Winstanley.[72] Each constituent tract is printed separately, with its own title-page, and could have been sold separately. Some tracts carry '1649' on their title-page, others '1650', which indicates that printing probably began late in 1649— the preface is dated 'Decemb. 20th 1649' (*Law of Freedom*, 156). The preface, written roughly as he was writing *The New-Yeers Gift* and as he was thinking again about his earliest writing, provides an account of how, first, he wrote obsessionally, scarcely eating, 'writing whole winter days from morning till night' so 'when I have risen I was so stark cold that I was forced to rise by degrees and hold by the table, till strength and heat came into my legs' (p. 155). He describes how depressed the reverses of the Diggers have made him and how that inspiration seemed dead within him till 'I learned

---

[71] *Works*, 443; K. Thomas, 'The Date of Gerrard Winstanley's *Fire in the Bush*', *P & P* 42 (1969), 161.

[72] Intact, the volume is extremely rare; Manchester Central Library holds a seemingly unique copy.

to wait upon the spirit, and deliver that to the creation which he
revealed in me' (p. 156).

Fire in the Bush may be coherently contextualized in this revival
of his inspiration. The copy in the Manchester Central Library is
bound in with *Several Pieces*, and it looks virtually uniform with
that edition, published by the same bookseller, in the same format,
with a title-page of similar design. His concluding remarks in the
compendium's preface, 'I was restless in my spirit till I had
delivered all abroad that was declared within me. And now I have
peace', is in the same idiom as his opening comments in *Fire in the
Bush*, that he wrote by inspiration and that he issued his text by
command, 'the voyce was in my very heart and mouth, ready to
come forth; goe send it to the Churches' (*Works*, p. 445).
Disappointment is evident enough in the preface, but he writes
much in his old manner, because he felt he could do no other.

Fire in the Bush marks the fullest elaboration of Winstanley's
theology, though its central notions have appeared before, albeit
sometimes differently expressed and with a different emphasis.
The materialism of Winstanley's theology receives its clearest
expression. The battles of Michael and the Dragon and the
millennium to be established by the second Adam are conceived not
as historical events or events located in an apocalyptic future but as
a process currently under way in the hearts and minds of
individuals, and the redemption of creation consists of a politically
and economically defined resolution:

Oh, say men, if this power of universal love be advanced; this will destroy
all propriety, and all trading . . . . It is true, he shall be advanced for that end
. . . that the Creation may be no longer deceived, but now at length may
come into him, and rest quiet for ever (p. 488).

The text echoes 1 Corinthians 15: 28, 'God may be all in all', but we
must recall how Winstanley equates divinity with the spirit of
reason. That vision of last things is of an abiding state in which self-
seeking is laid aside in favour of a distribution of resources
consonant with the spirit of the second Adam. The fire in the bush
is 'The Spirit burning, *not consuming*, but purging Mankinde'
(p. 451, my emphasis). The vocabulary of the political struggle
permeates this theological writing. The denominations he addresses
are 'like the inclosures of Land which hedges some in to be heires of
Life, and hedges out others'. The son of righteousness 'properly . . .

is called the restorer, Saviour, Redeemer, yea and the true and faithfull Leveller' (pp. 445–6, 454). Juretic's argument, that 'Winstanley's social radicalism can become intelligible only by seeing him as a product of two virtually distinct phases: a pre-Digger and a Digger period', seems unsustainable in view of the complex relationship between his theological and political modes of expression and thought.[73]

VIII

Winstanley's final publication, *The Law of Freedom in a Platform or True Magistracy Restored* (London, 1652), has been perceived as his most paradoxical or quixotic publication. It is a blueprint (or 'platform') for the establishment of a controlled, socialist economic and political system, addressed to Cromwell, with the explicit wish that he implement at least some of it. Even Hill, who has written most persuasively on how Cromwell was perceived by some radical elements in the early 1650s, remarks that 'It is difficult to believe that he had great hopes of converting the Lord General to communism, or that Cromwell would carry out at one blow from above the revolution which the Diggers had failed to bring about from below.'[74] Indeed, Winstanley himself discloses the kind of pessimism which partially subverts his purpose. In the grim poem that concludes the work he muses, 'Knowledg, why didst thou come, to wound, and not to cure? | I sent not for thee, thou didst me inlure' (*Works*, 600). But Winstanley always wrote in the consciousness that the godly needed the protection of the mighty, at least until the resurrection of the second Adam proved more epidemic, and his epistle to Cromwell stresses that partial implementation would be a worthwhile achievement: 'I pray you read it, and be as the industrious Bee, suck out the honey and cast away the weeds' (p. 510). As Hill shrewdly notes, it is a 'gradualist document'.[75] Using the sorts of polemical guile he had developed in, for example, his *Letter to the Lord Fairfax*, he works to fashion an appropriate instrument of persuasion and address.

Between the Battle of Worcester in September 1651 and the

---

[73] Juretic, 'Digger', 280.
[74] *Law of Freedom*, 32.
[75] Hill, 'Religion', 41.

dissolution of the Barebone's Parliament in December 1653 Cromwell appeared not only as an irresistibly powerful figure but also as a potential patron or agent of radical change. It was a perception which he fostered and probably believed. He greeted the inception of the Barebones Parliament with 'This may be the door to usher in the things that God has promised . . . You are at the edge of the promises and prophesies.'[76] Winstanley is careful to contextualize his tract in the scheme of radical optimism that obtained within the Cromwell circle at the time. Cromwell's epochal role is heavily underlined: 'God hath honored you with the highest Honor of any man since *Moses* time, to be Head of a People, who have cast out an Oppressing *Pharaoh* . . . . And God hath made you a successful Instrument to . . . recover our Land and Liberties' (p. 501). This, the easy rhetoric of Cromwellian panegyric, suggests a notion of divine providence remote from Winstanley's more considered theological writing. The compromise is apparent. He again develops the argument used in *The New-Yeers Gift*, that his socialism is of a part with the removal of kingly power, 'To see the Oppressors power to be cast out with his person' (p. 501). The elements he emphasizes, especially in the epistle to Cromwell, are those aspects of legal and ecclesiastical reform where he shared common ground with Cromwell's own more radical instincts (p. 505), and he links his own suggested legal code with the thinking of Cromwell's close aide Hugh Peters, though, as Sabine notes, Winstanley felt only a limited agreement with Peters's idea of searching the Scriptures for pointers towards legal reform (p. 509).

The blueprint for a socialist commonwealth that Winstanley produces has been variously interpreted.[77] Certainly, it is much less libertarian than one might have expected from his Digger tracts. There remains a role for the hangman, punishing the unregenerate and the indocile, and the political nation is redefined in terms which Milton could have approved, to exclude the scandalous and the malignant (p. 542). His ideal is thoroughly patriarchal, indeed modelled in part on the patriarchal family (p. 545). His notion of the common stock and of the storehouse, like other aspects of manufacturing and distribution, incorporates some features of the structure and organization of the London livery companies (pp. 582–5). He stresses, too, the integrity of the family—'Every

---

[76] Hill, *God's Englishman*, 128–45.
[77] Hill, 'Religion', 42–3; Davis, 'Winstanley', 92–3.

Family shall live apart, as now they do; every man shall enjoy his own wife, and every woman her own husband, as now they do' (p. 515)—in ways which echo his earlier strictures on the sexual licence attributed to the Ranters (pp. 349, 399–402). Winstanley is working to produce a vision of society in which Cromwell and his more radical associates could find a kind of godliness fitting the republic of the saints.

Winstanley may, of course, have reassessed his notion of the possible in the light of the Digger experience. Perhaps he simply realized that the executioner's keen whip provided a simple control of the unregenerate snapsack boy or ammunition drab. Or the vision may have been trimmed to a shape possibly more acceptable to those he was addressing. The shift may be the product both of the change in expectation and of the polemical impulse. But Winstanley is more in control of his material, more aware of his audience, than most accounts would credit. The regicides in 1660 could have reflected on the shrewdness of his warning to Cromwell: 'If you, and those in power with you, should be found walking in the Kings steps, can you secure your selves or posterities from an overturn? Surely No' (p. 502).

IX

The term 'Ranter' has none of the straightforwardness of 'Leveller' or 'Digger'. Morton, Hill, and McGregor, the historians associated with the rediscovery of Ranterism as an area of enquiry, are hesitant about the precision of the category. McGregor observes, 'The simultaneous emergence of a number of prophets preaching an almost identical creed led to the impression that the Ranters were a distinct sect of enthusiasts, such as the Quakers. In fact [the term "Ranter"] better describes a climate of opinion.'[78] The title of Morton's study, *The World of the Ranters*, well reflects his concern with describing a larger radical milieu rather than with charting the course of a movement. He observes, 'It would probably be incorrect to speak of the Ranters as a church, or even as a sect', and he notes the theological inconsistencies between leading figures to whom the term was applied.[79] Hill remarks on the way in which the

---

[78] J. F. McGregor, 'The Ranters, 1649–1660', B.Litt. diss. (Oxford, 1969), 59.
[79] A. L. Morton, *The World of the Ranters: Religious Radicalism in the English Revolution* (1970; London, 1979), 92, 78.

word 'Ranter' was used loosely as a pejorative and on the difficulty of identifying 'what "the Ranters" believed, as opposed to individuals who are called Ranters', though he concludes that 'for a brief period between 1649 and 1651 there was a group which contemporaries called Ranters, about which they felt able to make generalisations'.[80] Perhaps more definitely still, Smith's collection of tracts and other material, while admitting the difficulties acknowledged by Morton and others in identifying a core of Ranter belief, offers the writings of what he terms a 'movement' with a community of 'ideas and practices'.[81]

Davis sees in the position of Hill, Morton, Smith, and to a lesser extent McGregor, 'contradictions' between the admissions of difficulty in establishing a certain core of Ranter belief or practice or even personnel and the assertion that the category 'Ranterism' has an objective usefulness for historians of seventeenth-century radicalism, that it defines a real phenomenon. Rather than a 'movement', a 'group', or a 'climate of opinion' Davis identifies only a 'sensation', what might be termed a media event unconnected with reality.[82]

Davis's account certainly chronicles the way in which a tendentious construct, generated in lurid press accounts, offered an image of 'the Ranters' in politically useful terms. We have considered earlier the ways in which the stereotyping of the roundhead presented a legacy of beliefs and images which were exploited by Presbyterians and their associates in attacks on Independency in the mid–1640s.[83] Both Government and opposition activists exploited the Ranter scare of 1650–1. To the opposition, it gave the opportunity to present Independency, and with it the Rump, as the patron of the wildest sectaries, under whose misguided toleration increasingly extravagant theological heterodoxies could spawn. In response, a series of pamphlets, apparently emanating from Government circles, tried to suggest that Ranterism was predisposed to the restoration of the Stuarts. Most significantly, as Worden demonstrates, Government action against specific pamphlets contemporaneously deemed Ranter accorded with the Rump's major initiative of 1650 towards the re-establishment of a broad

---

[80] Hill, *World*, 197, 203, 204.
[81] *Ranter Writings*, 8.
[82] J. C. Davis, *Fear, Myth and History: The Ranters and the Historians* (Cambridge, 1986), 11, 83.
[83] Above, Chs. 1 and 3.

Puritan consensus through the enactment of legislation, at least in part Draconian, against ignoring the sabbath, against adultery, incest, and fornication, against swearing, and against blasphemy. To be seen to be suppressing Ranterism, presented as a serious threat to religious decency, suited well the Rump's manœuvrings to assert its own respectability to Presbyterians who might otherwise incline towards the royalist cause.[84] *Mercurius Politicus*, the Government newspaper, noted that the severity of the action against Ranters 'may serve to stop the slanderous mouths of those that publish abroad such vile reports of this Commonwealth, as if [the Rump] intended to countenance impious and licentious practices, under pretence of religion and liberty'.[85]

Evidently, Ranterism constituted, at the least, a convenient construct for politically sophisticated activists within the mainstream of Puritanism. But what of its status as a movement? The proposition that Ranterism was inchoate or internally incoherent does not preclude the qualified interpretations which Hill and Morton advance. While Davis convincingly shows how the Ranter sensation related not only to immediate exigencies of debate but also to larger questions about the production of hostile mythologies,[86] he does not consider that such constructs could, simultaneously, constitute attempts by people outside a closed and (to them) baffling grouping to understand and give order to their perception of a curious and unfamiliar phenomenon. There is firm evidence that some prominent individuals to whom the term 'Ranter' has been applied had at least some sense of their affinities with each other. Certainly Joseph Salmon sought out Abiezier Coppe after the latter was arrested in Coventry, and he himself was incarcerated in the same gaol.[87] We have extant a letter from Coppe to Salmon and two of his associates, beginning 'My Quintessence, my heart, and soule' and continuing in similarly fulsome, if opaque, terms.[88] Lawrence Clarkson describes in his autobiography *The Lost Sheep Found* (1660) how he had frequented circles in which Coppe had moved.[89] A letter from Salmon makes it plain that he had heard of Jacob Bauthumley and regarded their problems as closely

---

[84] Worden, 232–4.
[85] Quoted ibid. 239.
[86] Davis, *Fear*, esp. ch. 5.
[87] McGregor, 'Ranters', 64–5.
[88] 'Letter from Coppe to Salmon and Wyke', in *Ranter Writings*, 117.
[89] Lawrence Clarkson, *The Lost Sheep Found* (London, 1660), ibid. 181.

analogous: 'Cop[pe], my, thy, own hart is gone to London; No other note from the Vulgar but hanging at least for him. The last week save one, a Souldier [almost certainly he means Bauthumley] was burnt through the tongue for a businesse of the same nature.'[90] The most plausible interpretation of the available evidence is that a number of individuals, of some media notoriety and the targets of judicial procedure, saw themselves as sharing both a common danger and a community of theological or ideological assumptions. Perhaps not a movement, and indeed the persecution meted out to Coppe, Salmon, and Bauthumley indicates a political climate in which such a movement would scarcely have survived; nevertheless, we may identify a looser configuration of mutual interests and sometimes compassion within a section of the radical milieu of 1649–51.

Smith explores particularly well the relationship between members of this configuration and both the beliefs and idiom of religious radicals of the 1640s and earlier.[91] The Ranter *œuvre* itself— the unrepentant theological writings of Clarkson, Coppe, Bauthumley, Salmon, and (provisionally) the anonymous *Justification of the Mad Crew*[92]—is slim and diverse but all the tracts hold at least a few theological heterodoxies in common, mostly of an antinomian kind. A spirited engagement with received dogma about the nature of sin runs through all of them.

Yet the *œuvre* is decidedly uneven, and as striking as the theological diversity of these tracts, on which Davis and others have remarked, is their literary diversity. They represent writings of very different kinds and qualities. The anonymous *Justification of the Mad Crew* could be regarded as a brilliant exercise in black propaganda. It is much more straightforwardly outrageous than the other Ranter publications, and could well have served to exemplify the wisdom of the Rump's legislative programme against such deviancy in a way that the more elusive works of Coppe or Bauthumley could not. The title may be a pre-emptive tactic by a Ranter author, producing a self-image of the wise fool—or a reductive, satirical ploy by a more orthodox enemy. Politically, the

---

[90] 'Letter from Salmon to Thomas Webbe', ibid. 201.

[91] N. Smith, *Perfection Proclaimed: Language and Literature in English Radical Religion 1640–1660* (Oxford, 1989), *passim* but esp. chs. 6 and 8.

[92] All references are to *Ranter Writings*, except for *A Justification of the Mad Crew*, which is edited by Davis, in *Fear*, 138–55.

pamphlet would seem to confirm the assertions of Government propagandists that Ranterism assumes a sympathy to the royalist cause. Associated with this is a plain enunciation of the heresy attributed to Coppe and others—a heresy which Coppe explicitly denied and which runs counter to the moral force of his writing— that God endorses or is manifested in acts conventionally perceived as sinful:

[God] sees dancing, lying with one another, kissing pure and perfect in him . . . He loves as dearly with an infinite unchangeable love the *Cavileer* as the *Round-head*, and the *Round-head* as the *Cavileer*: the *Army* as abundantly as the *Levellers*, and the *Levellers* as the *Army*: For with him is no distinction (Davis, *Fear*, 145).

Good and evil, like the polarities of political life, evaporate in a theological perspective in which God, within the Ranter, may perpetrate any action sinlessly. Taking a hint from an enigmatic verse of Exodus, where God says he will permit Moses to 'see my back parts' (Exod. 33: 23), the author provocatively asserts that 'the devil and [God] are one, that the devil is but a part of Gods backsides' (Davis, *Fear*, 139). Both the blasphemous sentiment and the impertinent phraseology seem designed to outrage. He signs himself 'myself, who am, Jesus the Son of God' (p. 139), a much more blatant formula than, for example, Coppe's references to 'his most Excellent MAJESTY dwelling in and shining through' the author (*Ranter Writings*, p. 80).

In *A Justification of the Mad Crew* the author writes of sexual promiscuity in a way that suggests it had the potent practical and symbolic significance that communal agricultural activity had for Winstanley:

These mad Crew . . . are married all, to every woman is their wife, not one woman apart from another, but all in one, and one in all: There is not this voice heard at this fast, whose wife is this woman, and whose that? and whose husband is such a one? for there is but one Husband, and one Wife: and this man and wife, though made up of many thousands, ly with one another every night, the bed is large enough to hold them all . . . . They have attained resurrection from the dead, yea from that death which saith, these twain, these two, such a one, and such a one, and they are come to this life that in power [pure?] faith, they shall be no more twain, but one flesh . . . (Davis, *Fear*, 147-8).

No other putative Ranter pamphlet so celebrates sexual promiscuity as the manifestation of the sinlessness of those in whom God abides, and thus the pamphlet serves the case for repression rather better than those that bear the name of known individuals who may and do deny blasphemies attributed to them which they do not acknowledge.

Yet if this is black propaganda, a tract written by the enemies of religious radicals sailing under false colours to discredit them, then it is perpetrated with great skill and panache by an author who has produced a credible unified voice capable of a bizarre and ecstatic enunciation. An alternative surmise is worth consideration. In *The Lost Sheep Found* Clarkson describes how, through the agency of Giles Calvert, the radical publisher of Coppe's earliest antinomian pamphlet (and of much of Winstanley's writing), he made contact with a shadowy group called My One Flesh, about whom nothing is known except for Clarkson's account. He describes how he gained admission to this group, whom Coppe visited but of which he was, apparently, not a member, by asseverating that 'none can be free from sin, till in purity it be acted as no sin' and that 'till you can lie with all women as one woman, and not judge it sin, you can do nothing but sin'. Plainly he hit upon the formula, for on his sensationalist account one Sarah Kullin 'did invite me to make trial of what I had expressed', and others follow so that 'I was not able to answer all desires' (*Ranter Writings*, 180–1). Clarkson's account, ten years on, is scarcely an unmediated transcription of events, yet the name of the group, My One Flesh, is deeply reminiscent of *A Justification of the Mad Crew*. It echoes Genesis 2: 24–5: 'Therefore shall a man leave his father and his mother, and shall cleave unto his wife: and they shall be one flesh. And they were both naked, the man and his wife, and were not ashamed.' Not only does the tract make much of the notion of 'one flesh', but it also asserts the Adamite heresy, that the believer is as free from sin and shame as Adam and Eve: 'Shame . . . flyes before them, they are not ashamed of ought they do: they are naked as *Adam* and his wife was in Paradise and are not ashamed, they are past shame' (Davis, *Fear*, 146). The formula that gained Clarkson entrance sounds very close to the phraseology of the tract.

Two alternative and necessarily speculative interpretations may be advanced, one attributing extreme polemical guile and stylistic control, the other suggesting instead the political naïvety of its author. On the former account, *A Justification of the Mad Crew* appears as a cunningly constructed fabrication of evidence against those religious extremists whom the Rump sought to suppress. On the other, it appears as a fascinating but rather ill-judged publication, eloquently documenting a fusion of religious and erotic stimulation.

Of the remaining Ranter pamphlets, Jacob Bauthumley's constitutes the most ambitious in theological terms. It is a tract of the highest seriousness, without humour, without any ludic dimension, for the most part without polemical strategy, without disguise. He represents himself as vouchsafing his work to its audience without any clear sense of who may read it or with what understanding: 'I know the most unto whose hand it may come cannot read it' (*Ranter Writings*, 228), and he claims to offer it in a wholly amicable spirit: 'I leave the Discourse, and thee together; and if you happyly agree, it is all the fruite of my labour that I expect to Reape; If not, I shall willingly waite an opportunity, to make you both Friends, As I am to every man' (p. 230). Thereafter follows a treatise which operates almost entirely at the cutting edge of theological speculation, engaging variously, among other heterodoxies, the immanent and pervasive nature of God (pp. 232–4); the relationship between God and his creation (p. 234); the Trinity (a 'mystery of Iniquity . . . there being nothing in Scripture or reason to countenance such a grosse and carnall conceit of God' (p. 234)); the notion that heaven is not 'any locall place, because God is not confined' (pp. 235–6); the idea that the devil is not 'a creature' for 'there is nothing hath a Being but God' (p. 241); the idea that sin 'is a nothing' other than 'the defect of Grace', 'the Cloud that interposes betwixt God and us' (pp. 242–3). Bauthumley functions consistently at the highest level of theological abstraction. In its level of intellectual intensity and its radical application of reason to piety, his work stands comparison with Winstanley and, indeed, with Milton's great treatise, *De Doctrina Christiana*, with which it shares some common ground. The phrase 'Scripture or reason' captures the Miltonic habit of mind. But note the idiom. Bauthumley, who writes throughout as though this is to be the first of several treatises on cognate themes, does not outrage nor does he disguise his position. Perhaps in that lay his folly. A serving soldier, he met with the full rigour of military law. His book was burnt, his tongue was bored with a red hot iron, he was cashiered from the service, and for decades he apparently eschewed publication. Davis crassly undervalues his work with the trivializing remark that his writings and his fate 'are illustrations of the difficulties and dangers of flirting' with the themes of God's immanence and imminence.[93] Carey's judgement that *The Light and Dark Sides of God* constitutes 'a neglected masterpiece of seventeenth-century devotional prose' is more sound.[94] It is extraordinary that a work of such quality should be produced by a man to whom no earlier publication has been attributed. The underworld of provincial religious radicalism—both he and his father had been activists in Leicester long before the outbreak of the Civil War[95]—had proved a fine seminary. Bauthumley lived on till the 1680s, holding various local government offices in Leicester, including that of librarian, though poignantly (and understandably) he published nothing further, except for a collection of abstracts from Foxe's *Book of Martyrs* (London, 1676).

X

The Lost Sheep Found, Clarkson's autobiography, tendentious as it probably is, shows a literary accomplishment that resides in an engaging power of narrative, a vivid, Nashean imagery, and a capacity to produce a coherent image of himself as a moderately fortunate traveller over the wide terrain of mid-century religious radicalism:

Mrs. *Star* and I went up and down the countries as man and wife, spending our time in feasting and drinking, so that Tavernes I called the house of God; and the Drawers, Messengers; and Sack, Divinity; reading in *Solomons* writings it must be so, in that it made glad the heart of God; which before, and at that time, we had several meetings of great company, and that some, no mean ones neither, where then, and at that time, they improved their liberty, where Doctor *Pagets* maid stripped her self naked, and skipped among them, but being in a Cooks shop, there was no hunger, so that I kept my self to Mrs. *Star*, pleading the lawfulness of our doings as aforesaid, concluding with *Solomon* all was vanity (*Ranter Writings*, 182–3).

Clarkson tells a good tale, though not only is it uncorroborated but also he writes with a larger purpose relating to his immediate

[93] Ibid. 48.
[94] J. Carey, Foreword, *Ranter Writings*, 2.
[95] Biographical information about Bauthumley from *DNB* (forthcoming).

ambitions in 1660.[96] The idiom is characteristic of Clarkson's strengths. The author is emphatically hero of his story; other people are but a supporting cast of supernumeraries, mentioned for the nonce. For the most part, he tells us no more than their names and what he did to them or saw them do. Indeed, she that skipped naked we know only as 'Doctor *Pagets* maid'. The imagery suggests the unsentimental amorality he represents himself as espousing at that time. He declines the offer of sexual congress that her behaviour implies simply because his appetite has been jaded by the availability of others, especially 'Mrs. *Star*'—much as people who live in 'a Cooks shop' feel no hunger. The idiom is analogous to Bunyan's Mr Badman favouring prostitution over marriage with 'Who would keep a Cow of their own, that can have a quart of milk for a penny?'[97]

Clarkson's one Ranter tract, *A Single Eye* (London, [1650]), shows some of the same strengths. It is firmly centred on his own putative experience, describing his seeking for an understanding of the nature of God as a physical quest in real time:

I have travelled from one end of England to another, and as yet could find very few that could define unto me the Object of their Worship, or give me a character what that God is, so much professed by them; yet notwithstanding I could come into no City or Town, Nor Village, but there I heard the name of God under one Form or another, worshipped that for God, which I had experience was no God: So that in the period of my Pilgrimage, I concluded there was gods many, and lords many, although to me but one God (*Ranter Writings*, 163).

With this active role, anecdotally expressed, come other tactics of the stump orator (or tub preacher?). Smith observes, not quite accurately, that in Bauthumley's tract 'the reader is not mentioned but is assumed to be engrossed in following the discourse':[98] rather, I suggest, Bauthumley attempts a pre-emptive irenic address before leaving his reader to contemplate the clarity and logicality of his case, presented without rhetorical mediation. But Clarkson persistently buttonholes his audience, demanding attention, expecting dissent, requiring response: 'having . . . only presented to you a

---

[96] Davis, *Fear*, 64–75.

[97] John Bunyan, *The Life and Death of Mr Badman*, ed. J. F. Forrest and R. Sharrock (Oxford, 1988), 145. As the editors note, the expression is proverbial (Tilley C 767).

[98] *Ranter Writings*, 28.

Map, in which you may take full view what that God is thou pretends to Worship' (p. 163); 'Yet say you, there is a sinful act, or acts that are sinful . . . As I have said, so I say again, that those acts . . . ' (p. 169); 'Alas, friend, let me tell thee, whatever thy tongue saith, yet thy imagination in thee declares against thee' (p. 171). The imperative and interrogative moods entrap the reader into an active relationship with the text: 'Why dost thou wonder? why art thou angry? . . . Observe not the act nakedly, as the act, for we find . . . ' (p. 170).

An earthy (and rather reductive) imagery animates the whole. This works well at a relatively trivial level, as in 'the censures of Scripture, Churches, Saints and Devils, are no more to me than the cutting off of a Dog's neck' (p. 164). But when he addresses the central areas of controversy within antinomian theology this same earthiness, for all that it echoes the idiom of Christ's parables, seems inadequate to the complexity of the issues, despite the *élan* with which he advances it:

> the Lord declares that those filthy abominable works of darkness (by thee so apprehended) shall be destroyed and damned; But how, or where they shall be damned? that is in the saying of the Text, *I will make darkness light:* Oh that this were purely minded, then thou wouldst see that sin must not be thrown out, but cast within, there being in the Vat, it is dyed of the same colour in the liquor; as Saffron converts milk into its own colour, so doth the fountain of light convert sin, hell and devil into its own nature and light as it self; *I will make rough waies smooth* (p. 172).

Clarkson's analogy is of dubious value. It relates to the transformation of one, relatively superficial, characteristic: the milk remains milk, albeit yellow milk. Saffron does not convert it 'into its own nature', so how may we conceptualize the transformation of sin into that which is not sinful in such terms? But then Clarkson persistently seems deeply troubled when he attempts to operate at such levels of abstraction. His syntax, often uncertain, deviates wildly from the norms of English usage, producing passages that are simply incomprehensible. Consider the opening paragraph:

> Having experience that his Majesty, the Being and Operation of all things, appeareth in and to the Creature under a two-fold Form or Visage, by which that becometh real with the Creature, which is but a shadow with this Infinite Being: So that from hence it ariseth, the Creature supposeth God to be that which is not, and that not to be, which is God (p. 163).

At once there is a problem with terms used in a way peculiar to the theological discourse of radical theology, though quite probably the jargon, for such it is, is accessible enough to those who may have constituted his target audience. But the syntax defies understanding. The participial phrase 'Having . . . Visage' supports a relative clause, 'by which . . . Creature', which supports a further relative clause, 'which . . . Being', and a clause of result, 'So that . . . ariseth', which supports a whole skein of further subordinate material: but there is no main clause to which the participial phrase can be related. Nor can we resolve the issue by repunctuating. The main clause of the following sentence, which follows a paragraph break, could not possibly support the unrelated participle. Clarkson cannot handle the syntax of complex expression. Nor can he operate within the conventions of biblical exegesis. He launches into a sort of sermon on the text 'I will make Darkness Light before them' (Isa. 42: 16), which produces passages verging on the ludicrous:

You have heard the Scripture holds forth but one God, which God is Light; yet the same Scripture holds forth not only light but lights; as [Gen. 1.] *verse 14 Let there be Lights, and that Lights in the Firmament of the Heaven*: So that God made two great Lights, that is to say, The light of the Sun, the light of the Moon, Stars, fire and candle. From hence take notice, that though but one God, yet divers Lights, and that all made by God; for he that said *Let there be light*, said *Let there be Lights*: therefore he is called *The Father of Lights*, &c.

But then how shall we do with that place, *for God is light*, not lights; either he must be as well lights as light, or else, that all other lights but one hath a Being and Original besides God (p. 165).

And so on for another 500 words. This hardly approximates to reason, and his confusion of literal and metaphorical categories and of individual manifestations of a pervasive abstraction are as tedious as they are perplexing. Clarkson verges so closely on self-parody that we may entertain the notion that he does so not inadvertently but with some comic intent. To subvert his own discourse in this way may seem absurdly dangerous, although, as we shall see, it is a manœuvre Coppe adopts. But whatever the motivation, it points to a basic insubstantiality in Clarkson at the level of speculative theology: intellectually, he proves underpowered whatever his more superficial attractiveness.

Joseph Salmon's *A Rout, a Rout, or some part of the Armies Quarters Beaten Up, By the Day of the Lord Stealing upon Them*

(London, 1649) embodies elements missing from Bauthumley but present in greater measure in Coppe's most notorious publications, which it antedates by almost a year.[99] Salmon's argument is by no means a straightforward one. He seems to contend that God was immanent in all previous forms of government, but in a 'veiled' form, and that the sequence of power, from king to Parliament and from Parliament to army, will reach its conclusion in some further transformation in which Christ is resurrected epidemically in a much wider community of saints, among which the army, or at least its rank and file, may be numbered. There are elements in common here with Winstanley's theology. What links Salmon to Coppe is the sense of imminence, of the proximity of this transformation, together with an aggressive political stance and the production of a baffling, wise-fool persona.

A Rout persistently engages the immediate political context. It begins with an challenging address to the Army Grandees, explaining to them, in rather minatory fashion, 'My speech is intended especially . . . to my fellow-Souldiers, those of the inferior rank and quality; I have very little from the Lord to declare to You as yet', and adding that, though they have acted as the instrument of God's revolutionary transformation of the State, as his 'Rod', 'the Lord will ere long cast his Rod into the fire of burning and destruction: It will be a sweet destruction, wait for it' (*Ranter Writings*, 190). Any appeal over the heads of commanders to the rank and file is potentially dangerous: in the context of early 1649, against the background of Leveller activity in the months following the execution of the king, that tactic must have seemed particularly alarming. Salmon seeks out the constituency persistently addressed by Lilburne and his associates. His pamphlet, possibly significantly, was printed and distributed not only by Giles Calvert but also by 'T.N.', almost certainly Thomas Newcomb, a figure who would be imprisoned by the Council of State later in 1649 for publishing a Lilburne pamphlet, though he was later to be reconciled to the republican Government.[100]

Salmon at once engages bluntly the nature of political power and attempts to extricate himself from the consequences of that engagement. To the army he writes:

[99] See ibid. 12–13, on Salmon's *œuvre* and his relationship with Coppe.
[100] Smith uses Calvert's edition as copy text. Newcomb is the only printer known to be active in the period whose initials fit (Plomer).

You are led forth in a way of vengeance upon your adversaries; you sentence and shoot to death at your pleasure; it little moves you to trample upon the blood of your enemies; this is your Victory, Glory and Triumph. All this is well; you must tarry here till God moves higher amongst you (pp. 196–7).

'All this is well' seems a curious, contradictory, perhaps even incoherent conclusion to the starkness of 'sentence and shoot to death', the vivid goriness of 'trample upon the blood', and the irony of 'this is your Victory'. Salmon's pose may well be defensive, and he concludes his pamphlet by explicitly assuming the relatively unthreatening role of the wise fool:

I have here offered a few things to a publique view, I know the wise ones amongst you will light it, and dis-regard it; the form, method and language invites not the curious and nice spirit of anie man; it hath no beautie upon it, though a great deal in it, which the Princes of this world cannot discern. It is indeed the foolish language of the Spirit; if you do not like it, retort it again, and I will carrie it where I had it; you are like yet to have no better from me. I was once wise as well as you, but I am now a fool, I care not who knows it: I once also enjoyed my self, but I am now carried out of my wits, a fool, a mad man, besides my self; if you think me any other, you are mistaken, and it is for your sakes that I am so (p. 200).

By demanding the privileges of the wise fool, Salmon achieves two objectives. He exculpates himself from the charge of incoherence which his central, rather opaque thesis may invite. Moreover, he requires the licence accorded the fool, both as a teller of truth *per se* and as a truth-teller who enjoys a freedom not extended to others. He offers himself as court jester to the New Model Army.

XI

Abiezer Coppe was generally perceived as the most significant of the Ranters, in terms of his following, his influence, and the attitude of others, such as Joseph Salmon, towards him.[101] His best writing presents complex problems of interpretation relating to an extreme antinomian perspective on the relationship between language (particularly, the privileged discourse of the Scripture) and the risen Christ within the saints. On to this very problematic issue is

[101] Hill, *World*, 210.

superimposed an aggressive and simultaneously ludic idiom, which transforms Salmon's wise fool into something altogether more elusive and disconcerting.

Coppe's exposition of the problem of the inadequacy of language for communication by the saints is perhaps fullest, though not always clearest, in the eleven-page preface he supplies to Richard Coppin's *Divine Teachings* (London, 1649), a twenty-four-page tract published by Giles Calvert. Of the principal author, Hill writes, 'Richard Coppin denied being a Ranter, but his *Divine Teachings*, published in September 1649, was influential among Ranters; and it is difficult to think of any label which would describe him better.'[102] His tract is primarily concerned with the issue of how truth may best be known. He argues strongly for the subordination of Scripture to the knowledge imparted by those in whom Christ is risen. With a radical inversion of customary hierarchy, he suggests that those who know the texts in Hebrew and Greek are disadvantaged, their knowledge standing below the 'New Man', who characteristically is uneducated: 'God now comes forth from the great and learned of the world, and exalts himself in the poor and ignorant.' Moreover, such believers perceive truth better than prophets, apostles, and even angels; the most profound truth, hidden from them, 'God hath revealed . . . more fully to us in his latter age by his spirit.'[103] This truth, however, is wholly internalized, not to be embodied in any outward form:

to know the Original of Truth, is to know God himself, for the Original is the truth of all things; and God is the Original and this Truth: for he is before all things and is all things, and is the end of all things; as it is said, *The end of all things is at hand*; and this end is God, who is not seen, not comprehended by anything, but by himself.[104]

Coppin offers a lucid expression of an extreme and ultimately paradoxical notion; using language, he explains the limitations of language and the transcendence of the divine. The lower, minor truth he advances in *Divine Teachings* is that the larger truth may not be taught, may not be expressed in any form but itself, which can be absorbed only through the entry of God into the New Man,

---

[102] Ibid. 220.
[103] Richard Coppin, *Divine Teachings*, preface by A. Coppe (London, 1649), 3, 8, 24.
[104] Ibid. 1–2.

or rather the entry of the New Man into the status of Christ, having the Truth of God within him.

Coppe's preface plays over the themes not to clarify but to explore the larger linguistic abyss that opens beneath the argument.[105] His title, 'An Additional and Preambular Hint: As a General Epistle Written by ABC' (*Ranter Writings*, 73), [106] hints at the difficulty. 'By ABC' means, most superficially, 'by Ab[iezer] C[oppe]'; but it also means that the epistle is, in some sense, written by or through the medium of the alphabet, and it may refer to the letters sprinkled like footnote references, tying phrases and words to their biblical source, listed in the margin. Moreover, the constituent letters of that alphabet are capable of alternative interpretation, as if they were the physical emblems or hieroglyphs of the large truths which people seek to relate by them.

In his earlier *Some Sweet Sips, of Some Spirituall Wine* (London, 1649), Coppe speaks of 'A call, to arise out of Flesh into Spirit, out of Form into Power, out of Type into Truth, out of Signes into the thing signified' (*Ranter Writings*, 43). With a similar millenarian urgency, the 'Additional Hint' suggests that the sign system in which divinity had been encoded is superseded by the emergence of the divine in the hearts of the saints: 'All things are returning to their Originals, where all parables, dark sayings, all languages, and all hidden things, are known, unfolded, and interpreted' (p. 73). Thereafter follows a riot of biblical allusion, juxtaposing seemingly contradictory or paradoxical ways of defining the Godhead—'The Servant, and the Lord of all, who is the Prince of Peace, and a Man of War. A jealous God, and the Father of Mercies', and so on—as if illustrating the opacity of received terminology, unillumined by the spirit. Over the opening pages, Coppe meditates, opaquely, on the ways in which the shape of Roman and Hebrew letters may be perceived as representing relationships within the Godhead.

Coppe disappears behind the bewildering persona that speaks in the text. But how is that persona defined? Logically, if Coppin's thesis is right, the New Man who speaks the Truth embodies and in a sense is the Truth, that is, is Christ himself. Coppe appends a letter

---

[105] Smith, *Perfection Proclaimed*, Ch. 7, richly contextualizes Coppe's discussion in contemporary and earlier discussion among religious radicals of the character of divine signification.

[106] While all references to Coppe's work are to Smith's edition, it would be useful also to consult the opening pages of his epistle.

(within the epistle) 'written in Heaven—(in the heart of those, whose heart is in the Lord, who are taught of God, and who have their Teacher in them)', and he signs the letter 'thy Maker . . . in His and Thine ABIEZER COPPE' (p. 78). But he shies away from a straightforward identification of his own prophetic voice with Christ, introducing a third and mediating term, a wise fool more complex than Salmon's. The 'Additional Hint' ends with two poems:

> My heart, my blood, my life, is Thine:
> It pleases me that thou art mine
> I'l curse thy flesh, and swear th' art fine
> For ever thine I mean to be,
> As I am that I am, within A.C.

> Before God, this one of the Songs O *Zion*,
> Before holy man (whose holiness stinks above ground)
> Its at least whimsey, if not Blasphemy;
> But wisdom is justified of her children.   (p. 79)

The riddling humour, the uncertain balancing act between the vatic and the banal, contrasts sharply with the straightforwardness of Coppin's text which immediately follows. Who is the implied speaker and who the addressee of the first poem? Presumably the speaker is Christ in Coppe, speaking as it were to Coppe's flesh; it is also Christ in Coppe speaking to others in whom Christ is risen. But it could be Coppe speaking to Christ within himself. The pronominalization erodes the boundaries of the self. Yet the seriousness of such propositions is impugned within the text. What he offers may be perceived by the unholy holy man as 'whimsey', that is 'a fantastic or freakish idea',[107] or as blasphemy. It may be regarded as wisdom only by its children, presumably those already convinced that it is wisdom. The circularity of the argument appears undisguised.

Coppe's early writing characteristically violates the reader's textual expectations. His preface to Coppin is about a third of the length of the work it introduces, and it operates to obscure Coppin's argument. *Some Sweet Sips* begins with a table of contents which is about 15 per cent of the length of the whole work, and which lists sixty items some of which are related only tenuously to

---

[107] *OED.*

the ensuing text. The text itself consists of letters, some of which are subdivided into chapters, though these in turn are usually only about 500 words long. His most notorious publications, *A Fiery Flying Roll* and *A Second Fiery Flying Roule* (both 1649), are usually perceived as separate items, and indeed they have a discontinuous signature. Yet the contents page of the second is printed in the first, coming between the contents page for the first and the body of the text. The rules and conventions of printing-house practice, which are generally observed in most contemporary publications, are persistently violated in Coppe's works. Obedience to the inner light and indifference towards formalism permeates even the design and layout of the printed book.

The two *Flying Rolls* evoke something stronger than the puzzlement occasioned by the 'Preambular Hint'. The millenarian urgency is yet more keenly felt, though the second coming remains that of Christ resurrected epidemically within the hearts of his saints. The dead world of outward form, the grave in which the spirit has been buried, gives up that spirit: 'the sea, the earth, yea, all things are now giving up their dead. And all things that ever were, are, or shall be visible—are the Grave wherein the King of Glory (the eternall, invisible Almightinesse, hath lain as it were) dead and buried. But behold, behold, he is now risen with a witnesse' (*Ranter Writings*, 81). Both the notion and the idiom perhaps recall Winstanley's *New Law of Righteousnes*, with its incantation to the 'windows of heaven' opening to disclose the sun/son of righteousness (see above). As in Winstanley, the spiritual transformation asserts political imperatives for immediate action, though Coppe's idiom has a guileless confrontational violence. Like Digger rhetoric, his assumes the imagery of levelling, but he relates it more closely to the political catastrophe of Levellerism and to a socially destructive formula for political action. His pamphlet assails those who hold power, attacking them for their suppression of the Levellers and relating his own challenge to theirs: 'You have killed Levellers (so called) you also (with wicked hands) have slain me the Lord of life, whom am now risen and risen, indeed, (and you shall know, and feele it with a witnesse) to Levell you in good earnest' (p. 94). Though he announces 'Sword-levelling is not my principle', yet he engages the immediate circumstances with a closeness of reference that suggests this is political as well as spiritual discourse. The 'one hundred spent in superflous dishes (at your late great *London* Feast, for I know what——)' (p. 94) alludes to the banquet at which city leaders entertained prominent Rumpers and the victorious commanders after the suppression of the Burford rising,[108] and Coppe refers several times to 'the blood of the last Levellers that were shot to death' (p. 88).

Moreover, for the first time in his writing, Coppe enunciates a recurrent sense of social outrage, at 'the Beast (without you) what do you call 'em? The Ministers, fat parsons, Vicars, Lecturers' (p. 88), and at the wealthy of all political hues (p. 105), contrasting conspicuous expenditure and the fortunes made by some through the war with the sufferings of the poorest, of the 'poore prisoners' whose 'Newgate, Ludgate cryes (of late) are seldome out of mine eares . . . Bread, bread, bread for the Lords sake' (p. 90).

Coppe's dialectic, however, runs counter to Winstanley's. While the latter worked (albeit unsuccessfully) to establish a *modus vivendi* with the new ascendancy, asserting the quietism and respectability of the Digger project, Coppe courts and provokes suppression. Challenging conventional sexual morality assumes in these tracts a perverse political value. He attempts to contrast the relative innocence of drunkenness and fornication with the exploitations of the Rump and the Grandees: 'we had as live [lief] be dead drunk every day of the weeke, and lye with whores i' th market place, and account these as good actions as taking the poore abused, enslaved ploughmans money from him' (p. 89). This is perhaps mere rhetorical flourish: he does not advocate drunkenness and fornication, but suggests they are less pernicious than social and economic exploitation. However, his attacks on the propertied and his associated advocacy of the poorest and in a sense most degenerate elements gradually assume a disconcertingly purposeful quality, especially when his exposition assumes an anecdotal or autobiographical form.

Antinomian principle combines unstably with political and social critique. His advocacy of the value of the poor finds expression in a bizarre *imitatio Christi* as he speaks of himself kissing the feet of the poor, seeking out and kissing the grotesque (p. 105), and most outrageously in eating and drinking and dallying with 'she-Gipsies', 'putting my hand in their bosomes' (p. 106). The point remains primarily social:

[108] Worden, 195.

But at that time when I was hugging the Gipsies, I abhorred the thoughts of Ladies, their beauty could not bewitch mine eyes, or snare my lips, or intangle my hands in their bosomes; yet I can if it will be my will, kisse and hug Ladies, and love my neighbours wife as my selfe, without sin (p. 107).

He favours the poor over the rich, but envisages a time when, with the spirit raised epidemically, he may embrace both in equity. Yet the political and spiritual statement finds the most outrageous expression. The equity he offers and the liberation he extends are symbolized (and seemingly acted out) in sexual promiscuity. The passage concludes with an impudent juxtaposition of the Pauline text 'Thou shalt love thy neighbour as thyself' (Rom. 13: 9) with a recollection of the commandment against coveting 'thy neighbour's wife' (Exod. 20: 17). 'Loving my neighbours wife . . . without sin' offers a sexual threat.

But then this text is persistently subverted by the intrusion of the self-image Coppe constructs and of the eccentric and linguistically deviant voice he finds. When he asserts that he is wholly serious, 'there's no jesting with it, or laughing at it' (p. 86), presumably he is joking. For all its manifest and alarming vehemence, it is a text peppered with jokes. When he writes 'a poor Rogue should ask for it' (p. 110), his margin improbably declares, '*A rogo*, to ask'. The text opens with a bizarrely rhythmical section, once more teetering between the voice of the shaman and the voice of the fool:

> My Deare One.
> All or None.
> Every one under the Sunne.
> Mine Own.
> My most Excellent Majesty (in me) hath strangely and variously
>   transformed this forme.   (p. 81)

He speaks of himself imitating the divine madness of David, 'by skipping, leaping, dancing, like one of the fools' (p. 106). Moreover, his anecdotes, powerfully self-dramatizing, represent himself as behaving eccentrically, in what he terms a 'strange and lofty carriage towards great ones', which for the most part consists of looking reprovingly at coaches:

> my charging so many Coaches, so many hundreds of men and women of the greater rank, in the open streets, with my hand stretched out, my hat cock't up, staring on them as if I would look thorough them, gnashing with my teeth at some of them (p. 105).

Arguably, he acts out roles validated by Bible history, the roles of Christ, of David, of the prophets. Yet the text firmly locates that action in the everyday and untransformed world of early republican London, and does so in terms which leave the eccentricity of Coppe's actions—on his own account—unaccommodated. He himself remarks on the strangeness of his conduct.

Coppe's subversion of his polemic leaves me ultimately puzzled and uncertain both about his status and his seriousness. Possibly that may have been his intention. Such confusion may have been generated to deflect the hostile enquiry of readers who would include the Council of State and its agencies of repression. Yet that, ultimately, is foolish. To disguise a political threat by affecting the role of a dangerous and outrageous madman does not necessarily protect the author from repression. Coppe was soon arrested and not released till he had fully and explicitly recanted. Yet this writing is millenarian prophecy; while the total transformation of the spiritual consciousness of the nation seems imminent, the kinds of larger coherence the reader expects are perhaps an irrelevance, a formalist's commitment to old pedantries which are to be swept away by the risen Christ.

6

Milton and the English Republic

THE victory of the revolutionary Independents broke Milton's long silence. He had concluded his advocacy of theological heterodoxy and of the toleration of such heterodoxy with a politically symbolic act, the publication of *Poems* (1645). He returned to print, neither as a poet nor as an apologist for a persecuted minority position but as ideologue of a successful revolution. By the time of the first edition of his *Tenure of Kings and Magistrates*—Thomason dated his copy 13 February—the king had been killed, though it is usually argued that composition of the pamphlet had extended back to the time of the trial.[1] Perhaps as significantly for Milton, his enemies of the mid-decade, Presbyterians and other Puritans similarly intolerant of his kinds of deviance, had endured a devastating political eclipse. Power resided with the leaders of the New Model Army and, underwritten by the military, with the Rump and Council of State. Men like Edwards, Featley, and Pagitt now neither spoke for the ascendancy nor retained a dialogue with it. Prynne had been purged by Pride from his seat in the Commons.[2]

The Tenure is Milton's last pamphlet before his acceptance of Government employment, and it already is clearly marked by a tactical advocacy of a sectional position. But other elements, most especially a vehemence against Presbyterian divines, rage within it in ways that jeopardize its polemical coherence and run counter to the level of theoretical abstraction to which it intermittently lays claim.

Other critics have viewed it rather differently. It has been represented, in qualified ways, as an eloquent statement of ideals of an abiding significance, the values of a dignified and theoretically sound republicanism. The title of John Shawcross's essay, 'The

---

[1] The issues are reviewed in *CPW* iii. 101–6.
[2] For the best account, see D. E. Underdown, *Pride's Purge: Politics in the Puritan Revolution* (Oxford, 1971).

Higher Wisdom of *The Tenure of Kings and Magistrates*', suggests well the tenor of his argument:

> True, there is the overply of debate, of contemporary issues and men, of rebuttal of specific statements and actions—and in these things Milton's effect was short-lived and gnat-like. But there is more: there is philosophic and enduring significance.[3]

In some ways, Shawcross's judgement—for once, strangely off the mark—reflects some of the anxieties of the period in which he wrote, which are disclosed in an unusual concern with demonstrating that Milton 'is amazingly modern in his views' and that 'the driving forces behind his work clearly agree with the so-called radical views of the youth of the last decade [the 1960s]'.[4]

Any such agreement is probably mere coincidence: although *The Tenure* more than any other of Milton's secular writing presents itself as a work of theory, it offers only a modest contribution to the major theoretical issue facing England after the execution of the king, namely the case for republican government. Instead, it mainly engages the secondary and in some ways rather belated argument that rulers are ultimately responsible to their subjects for their actions. The issues that animated the groups of whom Shawcross speaks concerned the distribution of power and the challenge to those institutions in which it was invested. Such issues, indeed, assumed a central significance in the events of 1649, though Milton's pamphlet, like others of a similar political tendency, is curiously deflected from those concerns.

Regicide, not republicanism, predominates in the pamphleteering of revolutionary Independency throughout 1649. The vision is trained backwards, on the act and on events leading to it, rather than forwards to the new ideological terrain of government without kingship. In *King Charls his Case*, by the prosecution's lawyer, John Cook, issued, if Thomason's date is accurate, in February 1649, the case against him, such as would have been made at the trial, is rehearsed forensically. In John Goodwin's *The Obstructours of Justice*, received by Thomason in May, the argument again rests on accountability, not constitutional reconstruction. The movement's actions plainly outran both their theory and their propaganda.

---

[3] J. T. Shawcross, 'The Higher Wisdom of *The Tenure of Kings and Magistrates*', in Lieb and Shawcross, 143.

[4] Ibid. 143.

Milton, disappointingly, shares his confrères' incapacity to advance his readers' gaze from judicial retrospection. His theoretical concerns rest wholly with the legitimacy of the king's trial, and in ways which side-step the central question of the legitimacy of the tribunal that tried him, though Charles had explicitly questioned his judges' mandate.[5] Milton sometimes talks as though the Parliament that brought Charles to trial was the same body in whose name the war had been prosecuted from the outset. Thus, he urges disenchanted parliamentarian supporters 'not to startle from the just and pious resolution of adhering with all thir [strength] assistance to the present Parlament & Army, in the glorious way wherin Justice and Victory hath set them' (*CPW* iii. 194—material added to the second edition is in square brackets). This seems a feeble stratagem to obscure the parliamentary discontinuity of the purge. Presumably the success of which Milton speaks is not merely the victories of the Second Civil War. Parliament and army had been set on its 'glorious way' by the victories of 1644–5; '*present* Parlament' clumsily confuses that issue, suggesting that the power structure obtaining in 1649 was posited on the successes of the mid-decade, and if support had been appropriate then, it remained appropriate later.

Elsewhere, he merely asserts the righteousness of the revolutionaries' actions:

if men . . . have don justice upon Tyrants what way they could soonest, how much more milde & human then is it, to give them faire and op'n tryal? To teach lawless Kings, and all who so much adore them, that not mortal man, or his imperious will, but Justice is the onely true sovran and supreme Majesty upon earth. Let men cease therfore out of faction & hypocrisie to make out-cries and horrid things of things so just and honorable (iii. 237).

Note the way in which Milton tries to incorporate into his argument as premises elements which his enemies would fiercely contest.

How, indeed, may one know that 'Justice', this celestial abstraction, was so surely embodied in Bradshaw's court? In *The Tenure* Milton is forced back on to a rather commonplace and circular argument to which his confrères were often attracted—his party have been favoured by God because they are godly, and they

[5] Wedgwood, *Trial*, 137–8.

are known to be godly because they have been favoured by God, and those thus distinguished are specially and particularly privileged to complete God's work: 'If God and a good cause give them Victory . . . then comes the task to those Worthies which are the soule of that enterprize, to be swett and labour'd out amidst the throng and noises of Vulgar and irrational men' (iii. 192). Revolutionary Independents have command because they are 'worthies' and they are recognizably 'worthies' because 'God and a good cause' has given them that ascendancy. There are two implications. The first is that this group requires no other mandate. It is a revolutionary élite that need justify itself only to God, who gave it victory. The notion is at the heart of Independent ideology, and Milton reiterates it triumphally. The regicidal faction are the 'good men', the only ones who 'can love freedom heartilie' (iii. 190). But in a sense it is a poor position from which to work to convince the unconvinced of the morality of the action. Only his political associates would accept that designation.

The theoretical component, however, should not be dismissed. Milton develops an argument, the antecedents of which have been well documented by his editors and others,[6] about the origins of kingship and magistracy. Indeed, he readily stresses the antiquity of some elements of his case, and moreover the theoretical parts of the tract demonstrate a new care in explicitly working through the argument from the common ground of first principles with a considerable parade of apparent logicality:

It being thus manifest that the power of Kings and Magistrates is nothing else, but what is only derivative, transferr'd and committed to them in trust from the People, to the Common good of them all, in whom the power yet remains fundamentally, and cannot be tak'n from them, without a violation of thir natural birthright, and seeing that from hence *Aristotle* and the best of Political writers have defin'd a King, him who governs to the good and profit of his People, and not for his own ends, it follows from necessary causes, that . . . (iii. 202).

The terms are probably chosen with care—'it follows from necessary causes, that' seemingly shepherds in, not the prejudice of faction, but an inevitable conclusion drawn by an agreed process of logical reasoning from an agreed set of premises. Aristotle and others confirm the antiquity of the argument within the Western

[6] *CPW* iii. 65–80.

philosophical tradition. Milton's case, however, can be made to match the circumstances of 1649 only with the goodwill of the partisan. Concepts like 'the People' and 'the Common good' are open to question both from the left and right of Milton's position. Levellers work towards a rather different notion of the political nation. How the 'poorest He' may be accommodated within this grouping is dubious. Moreover, Milton, like others of his political persuasion, distinguishes persistently between the better part of the people, that is the godly who make up their faction, and others who by reason of their ungodliness are excluded from consideration, certainly all malignants, no matter what their property qualifications, and effectively, by Pride's Purge, Presbyterian royalists and those similarly inclined.

As long as Milton can function at a level of abstraction that precludes the intrusion of the political realities of 1649, his arguments retain some cogency. However, those elements constitute only about a quarter of the text of the first edition. Milton devotes more attention to a very different kind of writing, his vilification of the Presbyterians, which accords curiously with the probable polemical intentions of the pamphlet. Primarily, it is a question of audience. Shawcross surmises, 'Milton's audience . . . is not the Royalists; they are neither persuadable nor in a position to act at this time. It is only hopefully those . . . who have resisted Charles only to balk at reasonable outcomes of their prior actions because of custom and self-interest; they are neither sincere nor honest with themselves. Rather his audience consists of those who "begin to swerve and almost shiver" through false argument and emotional tugs upon them.'[7] Milton says as much himself. He avows that he is writing to Presbyterian royalists: 'As for that party calld Presbyterian, of whom I believe very many to be good and faithfull Christians, though misledd by som of turbulent spirit, I wish them earnestly and calmly not to fall off from thir first principles' (iii. 238). That was, of course, the sensible audience to address. Old royalists would scarcely be placated so soon after the execution, and Independents had no options left but to support the Rump. But Presbyterian opinion was worth playing for. Indeed, Worden has analysed the insistency with which the Rump and Council of State made overtures to their erstwhile associates, a policy which became clearer as the year progressed.[8]

[7] Shawcross, 'Higher Wisdom', 146.   [8] Worden, 80, 191–2.

Milton does produce an argument of sorts addressed to that audience, most persuasively, perhaps, in his suggestions that their complicity in the parliamentary actions of the early and mid–1640s precluded any easy acceptance of 'kingified' presbyterians by the royalist old guard:

> they certainly who by deposing him have long since tak'n from him the life of a King, his office and his dignity, they in the truest sence may be said to have killd the King: nor onely by thir deposing and waging Warr against him, which besides the danger to his personal life, sett him in the fardest opposite point from any vital function of a King, but by thir holding him in prison, vanquishd and yielded into thir absolute and *despotic* power, which brought him to the lowest degradement and incapacity of the regal name. . . . they, which I repeat againe, were the men who in the truest sense kill'd the King (iii. 233).

Implicating the Presbyterians in a common responsibility with the Independents may serve to prompt a re-examination of where their true interests lay, though Milton's formulation of the proposition has a tetchy quality about it. On the same page, he declines to discuss Cromwell's role in the military victory 'lest the story of thir [the Presbyterians'] ingratitude thereupon carry me from the purpose in hand', which is a curiously explicit admission of the difficulty with which he addresses the immediate polemical objective.

Indeed, Milton's vehemence persistly carries him from 'the purpose in hand'. Worden argues that the Rump's initiatives towards the Presbyterians were aimed at placating the laity rather than at persuading the more actively embattled clergy.[9] Milton, as we shall see, later comes into line, and even *The Tenure* shows some sensitivity to the tactic. But his seething animosities overspill the exigencies of the debate. He had vented his fury in the unpublished political poems of the mid–1640s, Sonnets XI and XII and 'On the New Forcers of Conscience under the Long Parliament', which emphasize the ignorance and cupidity of his enemies:

> you have thrown off your prelate lord,
> And with stiff vows renounced his liturgy
> To seize the widowed whore plurality
> From them whose sin ye envied, nor abhorred.[10]

---

[9] Ibid. 81–3.

[10] *Poems*, 296.

The sentiments and the vocabulary recur, not now rehearsed privately but in public and full-throated denunciation:

For while the hope to bee made Classic and Provincial Lords led them on, while pluralities greas'd them thick and deep, to the shame and scandal of Religion, more then all the Sects and Heresies they exclaim against, then to fight against the Kings person, and no less a Party of his Lords and Commons, or to put force upon both the Houses, was good, was lawfull, was no resisting of Superior powers (iii. 196).

It would be good also they liv'd so as might perswade the people they hated covetousness, which worse then heresie, is idolatry; hated pluralities and all kind of Simony; left rambling from Benefice to Benefice, like rav'nous Wolves seeking where they may devour the biggest (iii. 241).

The attractions of the flourish appear irresistible, and an element of gleeful retribution pervades these passages. Note the way in which Milton, rather spuriously, links the Presbyterians' commonplace charge of heresy with his equally commonplace charge of covetousness. Neither, really, can appropriately be equated with idolatry, but it allows a triumphal table-turning. Milton recalls occasionally his polemical objectives, as in his aspiration that 'God . . . will put other thoughts into the people, and turn them from . . . these Mercenary noisemakers' (iii. 236). But to suggest to Presbyterian readers that the ministers they have followed and trusted are as wolves salivating over carrion is an uncertain way of convincing them.

Milton tinkered considerably with *The Tenure* before issuing a second edition towards the beginning of 1650 or perhaps a little earlier—Thomason dated his copy 'Feb 15'. The principal innovation was the inclusion of a long coda demonstrating that Reformed divines as irreproachably respectable as Luther, Zwingli, Bucer, and Calvin had endorsed the concept that monarchs are in various ways answerable to their subjects and that tyrants may be deposed. He had used a similar tactic at the end of *Tetrachordon* (1644) (ii. 692–718), and probably it is a more effective argument to more open-minded Presbyterians than the vituperation he favours elsewhere. Yet it should be noted that it is an argument that functions by moderating the revolutionary claims of Independency.

II

The Council of State, constituted in the weeks immediately following the king's execution, determined on 27 February 1649 'Mondays and Fridays to be the days for considering Irish affairs'.[11] But the pressure of events overwhelmed that tidy resolve. Problems posed by the newly configured alliance of the Catholics, associated with the Confederacy of Kilkenny and notionally in rebellion since 1641, with the Marquis of Ormond, the royalist lord lieutenant, who had been engaged in suppressing them, were compounded by the defection from parliamentary allegiance of Baron Inchiquin and his hitherto fiercely anti-Catholic army and by uncertainties about the loyalties and intentions of the newer settlers of predominantly Scottish ancestry and predominantly Presbyterian faith. Troops loyal to the Rump were confined to Dublin and its environs and to a few coastal enclaves. The necessity of the expeditious dispatch of a relieving force was apparent, as was the potential such an initiative might give to the public apologists of the new regime.[12]

Throughout February and into March the proceedings of most days on which the Council sat have some item of at least indirect significance for the Irish preparations. On 15 March, amid a crowded agenda, two resolutions of particular interest were taken, one appointing Milton to the post of foreign secretary to the Council, the other appointing Cromwell to lead the expeditionary force to Ireland. The latter led to the reconquest of Ireland, and in the process in the autumn of that year to the storming of Drogheda, where a garrison of 2,600 were given no quarter, and of Wexford, where in almost indiscriminate slaughter about 2,000 people were killed.[13] The former resolution led to Milton's first entry, at the age of 41, into salaried employment. Within a fortnight, the Council of State commissioned him 'to make some observations' on the

/ Q

P.T.O.

[11] M. A. E. Green (ed.), *Calendar of State Papers, Domestic Series, 1649–1650* (London, 1875), pp. xii–xiii.

[12] For the historial context, see P. J. Corish, 'The Cromwellian Conquest 1649–53', in T. W. Moody, F. X. Martin, and F. J. Byrne (eds.) *New History of Ireland*, iii. (Oxford, 1986), 336–86; R. Bagwell, *Ireland under the Stuarts and during the Interregnum* (1909–16; London, 1965), ii. 179–80; S. R. Gardiner, *History of the Commonwealth and Protectorate, 1649–1660* (London, 1901), i. 79–177; and K. S. Bottigheimer, *English Money and Irish Land: The 'Adventurers' in the Cromwellian Settlement of Ireland* (Oxford, 1971).

[13] Green (ed.), *Calendar*, 40–1; Corish, 'Cromwellian Conquest', 340–1.

developing crisis in Ireland as documented by various papers they resolved to have published.[14]

The result is Milton's least studied polemic, the 'Observations' he appends to *Articles of Peace, Made and Concluded with the Irish Rebels, and Papists* published in May 1649 'by Autority'—the pamphlet bears neither Milton's name nor initials but has the appearance (for such it was) of an official Government document.[15]

That format eloquently symbolizes Milton's maturity as a political activist prepared to submerge his own personality in the collective endeavour. It also shows a new level of political guile. The predominant strategy of the pamphlet follows the successful exploitation of the papers that had fallen into Parliament's hands after the capture of the king's Cabinet at Naseby. Just as that highly successful tract *The Kings Cabinet Opened* (London, 1645) made public the damning documents, their significance pointed up in the appended annotations of very competent civil servants, so too Milton's brief was to use the material so fortunately come into Parliament's possession. As in the case of *The Kings Cabinet Opened*, the happy chance permits Parliament to demonstrate the involvement of its enemies in negotiation with Catholics.

The principal documents contained in *Articles of Peace* are Ormond's treaty with the rebels, his letter to Colonel Jones, parliamentary commander in Ireland, urging his defection, and a statement by 'the *Scotch* Presbytery at *Belfast*' (title-page), condemning the republic and 'the insolent, and presumptuous practises of the Sectarian party in *England*' (iii. 296). Milton's strategy is to demonstrate Ormond's complicity with the Irish Catholics responsible for the alleged massacres of Protestant settlers, an easy enough task, and thereafter to associate the Presbyterian leadership in Ireland with dividing the endeavours that should straightforwardly and concertedly be brought to bear on the settlement of the continuing rebellion. By speaking in the English national interest he attempts to speak for all Protestant and godly Englishmen, and in so doing he closely follows the purposes of the Rump in its policy towards Ireland. As the Rump set out to widen

---

[14] Green (ed.), *Calendar*, 57.

[15] Apart from Hughes's generally excellent introduction (*CPW* iii. 168–89) and a scattering of comments in Corns, *Development*, the tract is largely undiscussed except for T. N. Corns, 'Milton's *Observations upon the Articles of Peace*: Ireland under English Eyes', in Loewenstein and Turner, 123–34.

its basis of support among the Presbyterian laity, Worden has observed, it regarded its Irish campaign as a valuable part of that initiative. It assured its financial backers that the campaign 'would be conducted on behalf not merely of the Rump's interest but of the united Protestant interest, in which presbyterians of all kinds were involved'. Cromwell saw the confrontations with the Irish (and the Scots) as a means of uniting a majority of Englishmen against 'barbarous races' which were 'the enemies of the nation rather than merely the Rump, and campaigns against them offered the government its best hope of securing the tolerance, if not the support, of Presbyterian opinion in England'.[16]

Milton's hand is a strong one, and he plays it with accomplishment. Those 'kingified' Presbyterian leaders who would oppose the new republic are exemplified by the Belfast group whose eccentric change of loyalty threatens the interests of all the godly:

the Sympathy, good Intelligence, and joynt pace which they goe in the North of *Ireland*, with their Copartning Rebels in the South, driving on the same Interest to loose us that Kingdome, that they may gaine it themselves, or at least share in the spoile: though the other be op'n enemies, these pretended Brethren (iii. 317).

Milton has earned that pronominalization. His pamphlet works to establish a new 'we' of godly Englishmen, from a wider spectrum of religious belief, who share an interest in retaining Ireland—and in retaining a united opposition to the malignant forces with which the Presbyterian leadership would now parley.

The texts that Milton had to engage, and the polemical context in which he had to work, presented him with only limited difficulties with which he could cope admirably. Protestant hatred of Catholicism remained an accessible resource for parliamentarian apologists throughout the Civil War period, and its potency found hideous manifestation in the Irish massacres of 1649 as it had in the mutilation of the supposedly Irish camp-followers in the aftermath of Naseby.[17] However, his second work produced to the commission of the Council of State, his answer to *Eikon Basilike*, posed a challenge of a higher order.

---

[16] Worden, 190–2.
[17] A. Woolrych, *Battles of the English Civil War* (London, 1961), 136.

III

An anecdote of dubious reliability records an overheard conversation between Milton and John Bradshaw, president of the court that
condemned Charles I and probably Milton's closest friend among
leading civilian revolutionary Independents. Congratulating themselves on the ruse, they 'laugh at their inserting a Prayer out of
Sidney's *Arcadia*' into *Eikon Basilike*.[18] The solitary, perhaps
apocryphal, detail points sharply to an element generally missing
from Milton's writings of 1649 and from most of the propaganda
initiatives of the regicide faction in the first year of the republic.
There is little humour and almost no triumphalist laughter about the
dead king. The rank-and-file soldiery may have nicknamed Charles
'Stroker', after the supposed magical properties of the King's
Touch, but Bradshaw in the trial, Milton in print, and Cromwell
in private meetings scrupulously observed a high seriousness.
Seemingly only Charles laughed during the trial, though later a
hysterical levity on rare occasion breaks through, as when Cromwell and Henry Marten smut each other's cheeks with ink as they
sign the death warrant.[19]

Eikon Basilike was not the first tract Milton had confuted using
the quasi-disputational form of quotation and commentary. He had
done the same with Bishop Joseph Hall's *Defence of the Humble
Remonstrance* and with the anonymous response to his *Doctrine
and Discipline of Divorce*. The comparison is highly instructive. To
Hall's assurances that 'No one Clergie in the whole Christian world
yeelds so many eminent schollers, learned preachers, grave, holy
and accomplish'd Divines as this Church of *England* doth at this
day', he responds in Marprelate-fashion—literally, with a laugh—
'Ha, ha, ha' (i. 726), and he urges him and his colleagues, 'Wipe
your fat corpulencies out of our light' (i. 732). For his adversary in
Colasterion he urges ridicule and humiliation, hoisting from the
legal bar for a good blanketing (ii. 754). Moreover, it is not simply
that Milton has lost the knack (or matured), as Salmasius, arraigned
for 'the chicken-hearted stupidity of an unsuccessful dabbler in
letters' (iv. 333–4), will shortly feel. Where once, in the first edition,

---

[18] *LR* ii. 227.
[19] Wedgwood, *Trial*, chs. 5–7; Anon., *A Perfect Narrative of the Whole
Proceedings of the High Court of Justice* (London, 1649), 4; Anon., *The Royall
Legacies of Charles the First* (n.p., 1649), 8.

Milton does invite 'derision' (in fact, for the Pamela prayer), in the second edition he works over the passage, softening the sally considerably (iii. 364).

The avoidance of an eager and gloating triumphalism is profoundly politic, though it makes the 240 quarto pages of *Eikonoklastes* less straightforwardly rewarding to their readers. Milton's text works to kill emotion, and by forgoing celebration of the victory of his faction he simultaneously avoids stimulating pity or anger. The programme is set from the opening sentence (one of the least interesting opening sentences in his prose *œuvre*): 'To descant on the misfortunes of a person fall'n from so high a dignity, who hath also payd his final debt both to Nature and his Faults, is neither of it self a thing commendable, nor the intention of this discours' (iii. 337). Milton works to suggest that both pity and anger are irrelevant in the case of a person who is beyond feeling benefit of either. But he scrupulously avoids outraging an unsympathetic or neutral readership. 'The King', 'this King', 'the late King' are the terms he persistently uses; only twice does he call him 'Charles' (iii. 439, 509), in each case to distinguish him from another monarch. It shows a determined politeness that is abandoned only carefully, preparedly, and temporarily.

The point may also be, in part, social. With the author of *An Answer to a Book, Intituled, The Doctrine and Discipline of Divorce*, he had or claimed a social edge. His opponent apparently had been a serving-man. With Hall, he had another contrived advantage. Hall and all bishops on his account are scarcely human, let alone his equals. With Salmasius he can play the liberal humanist confronted with a hired pedant. With Charles he is doing well if he can assume a footing of equality, and a citizen-to-citizen politeness, stopping well short of deference, is a subtly subversive tone to hit.

Violence is another significant absence. Milton had frenziedly relished the prospect of bishops squirming in the lowest circle of hell (i. 616–17). He declines all consideration of the fate of Charles's soul. At one points he observes, 'With his Orisons I meddle not, for he appeals to a high Audit' (iii. 405). Indeed, he recurrently chides Charles for his presumption in claiming to know the will of God (and to know that the will of God corresponds closely with his own). What he terms 'the high and secret judgements of God' are not to be so confidently asserted (iii. 430). He complains that Charles writes 'as if the very manuscript of Gods judgements had bin delivered into his custody and exposition' (iii. 564). Human justice has been done on Charles: divine justice belongs to God alone and for his secret workings.

But not only the fate of Charles's soul escapes comment. Very rarely does Milton make reference to his execution, and when he does, it comes as a shock, though it is encased in a metaphor:

it needs must be ridiculous . . . that they whose profess'd Loyalty and Allegeance led them to direct Arms against the Kings Person, and thought him nothing violated by the Sword of Hostility drawn by them against him, should now in earnest think him violated by the unsparing Sword of Justice . . . . The onely grief is, that the head was not strook off to the best advantage and commodity of them that held it by the hair; an ingratefull and pervers generation, who . . . first cry'd to God to be deliver'd from thir King (iii. 346).

This is the solitary allusion to Charles's decollation. Only metaphorically (and somewhat dubiously) could Presbyterian activists be deemed to have held the head by the hair, but the grisliness of the image breaks starkly into a text which otherwise avoids it. The 'Sword of Justice' sounds a clean abstraction, remote from the axe and the chopping block.

Milton avoids the corpse, much as his republican associates avoided it. It was carried off, undisplayed, to a relatively obscure and safe resting place. It was an age obsessionally concerned with dismemberment. Montrose's finest poem, written on the eve of his own execution (and quartering), meditates on the grisly process:

> Let them bestow on ev'ry Airth[20] a Limb;
> Open all my Veins, that I may swim
> To Thee my Saviour, in that Crimson Lake;
> Then place my par-boil'd Head upon a Stake;
> Scatter my Ashes, throw them in the Air:
> Lord (since Thou know'st where all these Atoms are)
> I'm hopeful, once Thou'lt recollect my Dust,
> And confident Thou'lt raise me with the Just.[21]

Popular representations both of the execution of Laud and of the regicides at the Restoration dwell gloating on the severed head (in

---

[20] i.e. north, south, east, and west.

[21] James Graham, Marquis of Montrose, 'His Metrical Prayer (On the Eve of his Own Execution)', in T. Scott (ed.), *The Penguin Book of Scottish Verse* (1970; Harmondsworth, 1988), 239.

Laud's case) or the quartered limbs.[22] The Restoration saw the exhumation of Cromwell, Bradshaw, and Ireton and the impaling of their skulls on the top of Westminster Hall.[23] It was a brutal business, and the images shocked the contemporary consciousness as deeply as they do ours. It is not that the seethed pieces were posted up and forgotten about. Dryden, in 1666, in the most bizarre section of *Annus Mirabilis*, has 'The Ghosts of Traitors' descend from London Bridge, where their heads were posted, to dance about the Fire of London and 'sing their Sabbath Notes with feeble voice'.[24]

In sharp contrast, Milton and his confrères make nothing of the physical nature of the king's execution. Marvell was right—the 'bleeding Head' probably did 'fright the Architects' of the new republic.[25] But, fascinatingly, it is a squeamishness shared by royalists and neutrals. The visual representation of martyrdom was central to the English Protestant tradition through its most widely disseminated text. Foxe's *Actes and Monuments*, from its first edition to its most recent (1641), had been richly and disturbingly illustrated with sometimes brilliantly executed woodcuts depicting the sufferings of the saints, exposed in their frail and tremulous mortality to the power of their tormentors. Yet Charles's hagiographers sought different images to represent his suffering. The famed frontispiece shows him whole, fully dressed and perfectly composed, and the funerary etching, *Charles I Lying in State*, has him once more intact and curiously reanimated. Another engraving shows him on a bed, propped on a pillow, looking heavenward and supporting his head with his hand, and a fourth, with decorous obliqueness, has him standing by a death's head, holding a cap like the one he wore to keep his hair from the executioner's blade.[26] Perhaps they feared the taint of the felon would adhere to the image of the king decapitated. Perhaps its assertion of his common humanity disturbed notions of the essence of kingship. Interestingly,

[22] e.g. Anon., *A Prognostication upon W. Laud* (London, 1641), a broadside with a crude woodcut anticipating his execution; reports, sometimes illustrated, of the execution of the regicides are commonplace.

[23] Wedgwood, *Trial*, 216.

[24] John Dryden, *Annus Mirabilis*, st. 223, in *The Poems and Fables of John Dryden*, ed. J. Kinsley (1958; Oxford, 1961), 91.

[25] 'Horatian Ode', ll. 69–70, *Poems*, i. 93.

[26] Strong, *Charles I*, 28, 31; John Quarles, *Regale Lectum Miseriae, or, A Kingly Bed of Miserie* (n.p., 1649), facing sig. B1ʳ; Anon., *King Charles the 1st's Defence of the Church of England* (The Hague, n.d.), facing title-page.

the most graphic depictions of the scene of execution were done by
foreigners.

The most violent element of Milton's tract is its title. But it is the
image of the king—the hagiographer's image—that he destroys, not
the king himself. No sympathetic magic obtains. Though he breaks
that image, there is little that hints at the breaking of the king's own
body. Just as Cromwell's cavalry drove witnesses from the place of
execution, Milton too forbids his readers' gaze to rest for long on
the severed head.[27]

The third major absence from *Eikonoklastes* is a developed
theoretical dimension. Though *The Tenure of Kings and Magistrates* intermittently functions at a level of some abstraction,
Eikonoklastes works much more closely to the text it attacks,
operating within terms of reference *Eikon Basilike* is allowed to
define. Nor, despite its later date, does it address the changes in
constitutional circumstances consequent upon the execution. The
English Republic had been proclaimed, but Milton still does not
engage the issue of the theoretical justification of the constitutional
change. The word 'republic' does not occur in *Eikonoklastes*. The
other term contemporaneously available, 'commonwealth', occurs
frequently, but never in reference to a system of government, rather
as a collective term for the whole body of the people constituting a
nation (*OED* sig. 2 rather than 3). He frequently uses the term 'a
free Nation', though in ways which avoid the specific. Presumably,
the freedoms that are important to Milton may exist under a godly
monarch as well as under a godly republic. Kingship as such is not
the issue: this king and the punishment of this king are. The people
may effect 'the taking away of King-ship itself, when it grows too
Maisterfull and Burd'nsome' (iii. 458), but the constitutional
advantages of the republic remain unexplored. Even the name
'Iconoclastes', as Milton acknowledges, is 'the famous Surname of
many Greek Emperors', godly ones who 'in thir zeal to the
command of God . . . broke all superstitious Images to peeces' (iii.
343).

IV

Masson, in a delicate footnote, described one of the copies of *Eikon
Basilike* from which he was working:

[27] Wedgwood, *Trial*, 194.

This copy must have been the pocket copy of some devoted Royalist, for it had been bound in black velvet for mourning, and has a clasp and gilt edges. As if by long carrying in the pocket, the floss of the velvet is now nearly worn off, and the diminutive little book looks like the faded model of a coffin.[28]

One can but guess when an old book lost its floss, but the hypothesis is plausible and eloquently points to Milton's major difficulty. As has been argued, *Eikon Basilike* is the cleverest of propaganda initiatives, and it offers a very elusive target to its enemies. The apparent author is dead, and the book itself seems not to be a work of controversy but variously a psalter, an act of devotion, and—most tellingly—an object to be revered, not a text to be read. Milton must transmute it into forms tractable to attack and confutation.

Two principal but curiously contradictory tactics obtain, one accepting but distorting the *Eikon Basilike*'s claim to be judged as something other than polemic, the other transforming the text into an exercise in controversial prose which can be met by the methods of political controversy. One set of Milton's imagery labours to connect Charles's text with drama and more specifically with masque. The frontispiece is 'drawn out to the full measure of a Masking Scene' (iii. 342). Charles and his partisans 'Canonize one another into Heav'n . . . they him in the Portrature before his Book: but . . . Stagework will not doe it' (iii. 530). Loewenstein has recently commented on the effectiveness of the manoeuvre: 'The numerous theatrical tropes . . . suggest that the king's court and his activities have all been skillfully stage-managed. . . . [they] suggest a self and role which have been completely fabricated and are ultimately vacuous.'[29] They also feed on the antitheatrical prejudices of the broad mass of Puritan opinion, including those elements that Milton particularly courts.

The iconoclasm works similarly. The king's book was provisionally entitled *Suspiria Regalia*, 'royal sighs', but the Greek name in Greek script was adopted instead, in part at least to baffle casual enquirers who may have noticed it, presumably in running titles on sheets in print-shops at the early stages of the conspiracy to produce and circulate the text. The change in title was perhaps unfortunate,

---

[28] Masson, *Life*, iv. 129 n.
[29] D. Loewenstein, *Milton and the Drama of History: Historical Vision, Iconoclasm, and the Literary Imagination* (Cambridge, 1990), 57–8.

for, though 'icon' could mean no more than a figure or illustration or likeness, it was associated with idols in the Puritan consciousness, and that too allowed Milton to score relatively easy points with a broad spectrum of Puritan opinion: the book becomes 'the Shrine he dresses out for him' where he would 'have the people come and worship him' (iii. 343). The target is now exposed: Puritans had spent happy hours wrecking such shrines. Acknowledging that he exploits a slip, Milton observes sardonically, 'I must commend his op'nness who gave the title to this Book' (ibid.).

Another transformation knocks *Eikon Basilike* into confutable shape by treating it much like any other controversial prose. Milton is keen to attribute to it an explicit polemical objective which, he claims, it largely works to obfuscate. The Latin motto of its final pages, 'Vota dabunt quae Bella negarunt', he glosses 'That what hee could not compass by Warr, he should atchieve by his Meditations' (iii. 342), and he identifies the instigation of a third civil war in England as its real purpose (iii. 339). Most important, the motif of duelling sets himself and Charles on equal footing, engaged in equal struggle: 'I shall make no scruple to take up (for it seems to be the challenge both of him and all his party) to take up this Gauntlet, though a Kings, in the behalf of Libertie, and the Common-wealth' (iii. 338). In fact, *Eikon Basilike* casts down no gauntlet. In its avoidance of specificity and its pietistic tone it avoids direct challenge to anyone. Milton organizes his tract around a patient, point-by-point, chapter-by-chapter refutation, seemingly following the structure of the king's book. But each chapter of *Eikon Basilike* falls into two typographically distinct elements, historical discourse (in roman) and prayer (in italic). Milton comments on the prayers and meditations, but the layout of *Eikonoklastes* does not preserve the two-part division within chapters. That which differentiated *Eikon Basilike* from ordinary controversial prose is significantly excluded from Milton's refutation. The king's book is a text like any other and may be answered in the same terms.

It has been argued that part of the achievement of *Eikon Basilike* rests in its studied vagueness. Milton works to relate the airy elevation of his opponent to the realities of recent events, in so far as they are reconstructible through the memories of the readers. He persistently represents himself as confronting fantasy with hard fact:

But if these his fair spok'n words shall be heer fairly confronted and laid parallel to his own farr differing deeds, manifest and visible to the whole Nation, then surely we may look on them who notwithstanding shall persist to give to bare words more credit then to op'n deeds, as men whose judgement was not rationally evinc'd and perswaded, but fatally stupifi'd and bewitch'd, into such a blind and obstinate beleef (iii. 346–7).

The passage is wholly characteristic of his method and mode of address. Note that he seeks to assert no fresh evidence, privileged as the knowledge of an insider. His appeal is always to what the reader already knows and can recall. He speaks of himself as 'remembring' to his readers 'the truth of what they know to be heer misaffirm'd' (iii. 338). Again, he suggests of one passage in Charles's account, 'a little memory will sett the clean contrary before us' (iii. 398). He also tries to arouse a suspicion, a close questioning of Charles's more indeterminate phrases, not only 'the plausibility of large and indefinite words' ('*his Conscience, honour, and Reason*') (iii. 456), but also of his refusal to name names:

He would have punisht some . . . . Others he *would have disarm'd*, that is to say in his own time: but *all of them he would have protected from the fury of those that would have drown'ed them, if they had refus'd to swim down the popular stream*. These expressions are too oft'n mett, and too well understood for any man to doubt his meaning. By the *fury of those*, he meanes no other then the Justice of Parlament . . . . Those who would have refus'd to swim down the popular streame, our constant key tells us to be Papists, Prelats, and this Faction . . . (iii. 482).

Charles's text, disingenuously riddling, is annotated by Milton to make it clear to a Puritan readership what those weaseling pronouns really mean.

Milton's account is most striking when some elevated flourish of *Eikon Basilike* is confronted with a different, seemingly more accurate, perspective. Of his attempt to arrest the six members, Charles had remarked, '*I went . . . attended with some Gentlemen*.' Milton's response: 'Gentlemen indeed; the ragged Infantrie of Stewes and Brothels; the spawn and shipwrack of Taverns and Dicing Houses' (iii. 380–1). The phrasing, with that pause after the exclamation, simulates a surprised contempt for a palpable misrepresentation. Milton easily captures the high ground, invoking recollection both of contemporary pro-parliamentarian accounts of the event and the easy stereotypical assumptions about the Cavalier soldiery.[30] Again, the *Eikon Basilike* ends with an irenic illusion, a gesture towards reconciliation and new beginnings, calling on Charles II '*not to study revenge*'. Milton meets the fantasy by invoking the reader's recollection of recent and scandalous events, the assassination of the republic's ambassadors, Dorislaus and Ascham: 'how far he, or at least they about him, intend to follow that exhortation, was seen lately at the *Hague*, & now lateliest at *Madrid*' (iii. 577). Ye shall know them by their fruits.

V

Milton's use of the interrogative mood is persistent and purposeful in *Eikonoklastes*. It occurs as part of his reluctance to assert truths in his own voice when they may be derived instead from the recollection or the reason of the reader. Repeatedly, quotation from *Eikon Basilike* supports not a plain denial but rather a question: how does this square with what else Charles says? how may this fiction be related to what you, my readers, know? how can this coherently be related to what else you, my readers, believe in?

For example, *Eikon Basilike* makes much of Charles's agonies of conscience about the execution of Strafford. Milton teases open contradictions within his account with a series of questions:

> Had he really scrupl'd to sentence that for Treason which he thought not Treasonable, why did he seeme resolv'd by the Judges and the Bishops [persuading him to do so]? And if by them resolv'd, how comes the scruple heer again? It was not then, as he now pretends, *The importunities of some and the feare of many* which made him signe, but the satisfaction giv'n him by those Judges & Ghostly Fathers of his own choosing. Which of him shall we believe? For hee seemes not one, but double; either heer we must not beleeve him professing that his satisfaction was but seemingly receav'd & out of feare, or els wee may as well beleeve that the scruple was no real scruple, as we can beleeve him heer against himself before, that the satisfaction then receiv'd was no real satisfaction: of such a variable and fleeting conscience, what hold can be tak'n? (iii. 371)

Milton could simply have juxtaposed the two constructs that *Eikon Basilike* offers, that Charles was convinced he was acting morally and that Charles was convinced he should act in the interests of

---

[30] See above, Ch. 1.

political expediency. Note the pronominalization: Milton incorporates himself and his readers into an active alliance, 'we', hunting out the truth, considering the alternatives, which leads to the only possible resolution to the issue, if Charles be taken at his word on each occasion, namely that his is an unstable conscience which no one may rely on.

The challenge is to memory as well as reason. *Eikon Basilike* complains of the tumults in London driving Charles to withdraw for *'feare of his own person in the streets'*. Think back, Milton urges his readers: 'Did he not the very next day after his irruption into the House of Commons, then which nothing had more exasperated the people, goe in his Coach unguarded into the City? did hee receave the least affront, much less violence in any of the Streets, but rather humble demeanours, and supplications?' Which leads to the conclusion, 'Hence may be gather'd, that however in his own guiltiness hee might have justly fear'd, yet that hee knew the people so full of aw and reverence to his Person, as to dare commit himself single among the thickest of them, at a time when he had most provok'd them' (iii. 394). Here, the resolution comes through an impersonal construction, 'may be gather'd'.

The interrogative mood is pervasive in *Eikonoklastes*, and to dismiss it as 'rhetorical questions' is to understate its effect in persistently opening a dialogue with the reader and in implicating the reader in the hostile appraisal of the king's book. It even prefaces the sharpest insults. '*But*, saith he, *as Swine are to gardens, so are Tumults to Parlaments. . . .* who knows not that one great Hogg may doe as much mischief in a Garden, as many little Swine' (iii. 396). Charles 'had not there the forbearance to conceal how much it troubl'd him, *That the Birds* [i.e. the six members] *were flowne*. If som Vultur in the Mountains could have op'nd his beak intelligibly and spoke, what fitter words could he have utter'd at the loss of his prey' (iii. 439). A hostile historical analogy to Charles's argument begins interrogatively: 'But did not *Catiline* plead in like manner against the *Roman* Senat and the injustice of thir trial, and the justice of his flight from *Rome?*' (iii. 441). Though Milton introduces *Eikonoklastes* with talk of a duel, of the gauntlet taken up, he is cautious that he should be perceived as acting for a larger community, and that larger community extends beyond the Rump Parliament and the Council of State to embrace a readership whose complicity he works to engage.

Statements in the first person singular are relatively rare in this tract, though Milton sometimes makes them. Towards the end, particularly, the idiom shifts as he occasionally points up the distinctions between Charles, whose version of reality he has discredited, and the truth as he sees it, as in 'He bids his Son *Keep to the true principles of piety, vertue, and honour, and he shall never want a Kingdom.* And I say, People of *England*, keep ye to those principles, and ye shall never want a King' (iii. 581). However, even here, the sentiment operates through the mechanism of using Charles's own words against himself, like a wrestler using an adversary's weight to throw him.

Much more common are general statements that explicitly invoke commonplace knowledge available to all. He opens his chapter-by-chapter refutation with 'That which the King layes down heer as his first foundation . . . is to all knowing men so apparently not true, that a more unlucky and inauspicious sentence . . . hardly could have come into his minde. For who knows not that . . . ' (iii. 350). Which reader would not number himself or herself with the knowing? And, like Socratic discourse, it immediately places the challenge of the argument in the knowledge of the audience. Again, he indicts 'the hideous rashness of accusing God before Men to know that for truth, which all Men know to be most fals' (iii. 447). Offering some assumption of broad ideological sympathy from his readers, he sallies, 'But God and his judgements have not bin mock'd; and good men may well perceive what a distance there was ever like to be between him and his Parlament' (iii. 382). Sometimes a more contemptuous note enters: Charles's explanation for finally calling a Parliament is dismissed with 'not *of his own choise and inclination*, as any Child may see, but urg'd by strong necessities' (iii. 354).

VI

A debate about style runs through *Eikonoklastes*. Milton frequently picks up his opponents on eccentricities and infelicities. The Modest Confuter's 'thum-ring posies', uttered in place of 'well siz'd periods' (i. 908), like Prynne's affectation of the form 'Subitane' (for 'sudden') (ii. 723), come in for bantering comment. In the case of his attack on *Eikon Basilike*, however, a much more concerted critique is developed.

The king's style is a bad style, bad particularly because it is situationally inappropriate, thus revealing the shallowness of his grasp of what becomes a statesman. It reveals too an aesthetic alien to that which obtains among the godly. Alien literary forms break into the king's discourse. Thus, 'He ascribes *Rudeness and barbarity worse then Indian* to the English parlament, and *all vertue* to his Wife, in straines that come almost to Sonnetting' (iii. 420–1). Again, 'petty glosses and conceits' suggest 'the quibbl's of a Court Sermon' (iii. 430), perhaps even evidence a chaplain's involvement.

The aspect of style to which Milton recurs is Charles's use of imagery. Sometimes, he opines, it is gratuitously far-fetched: 'We meet next with a comparison, how apt let them judge who have travell'd to *Mecca, That the Parlament have hung the majestie of Kingship in an airy imagination of regality between the Privileges of both Houses, like the Tombe of Mahomet*' (iii. 453), which allows Milton a smart thrust at the Turkish tyranny of the Stuart regime.[31] Milton, generally, is working towards associating Charles with secular and frivolous writing. One simile 'I was about to have found fault with, as in a garb somwhat more Poetical then for a Statist: but meeting with many straines of like dress in other of his Essaies, and hearing him reported a more diligent reader of Poets, then of Politicians, I begun to think that the whole book might perhaps be intended a peece of Poetrie' (iii. 406). Again, he lashes the extended comparison of his honour and reputation with the rising sun putting to flight owls and bats with 'Poets indeed use to vapor much after this manner' (iii. 502).

The attack on Charles's control of genre decorum ties into the stratagem of the Pamela prayer. The issue defies final resolution, but plainly either the republicans seeded an early edition of *Eikon Basilike* with the prayer, which Milton could then attack, or else the royalists foolishly included it and Milton merely exploited what he found.[32] Milton returns to the opening time and again. Clearly, the prayer is plagiarised closely from Sir Philip Sidney's *Arcadia*. Milton has several options open. He attacks the act of plagiarism itself, but he does so in ideologically sophisticated ways. Charles's other prayers are often very deeply indebted to Davidic models; 'However, this was more tolerable then *Pammela's* Praier, stol'n

---

[31] On references to Oriental monarchies, see S. Davies, *Images of Kingship in Paradise Lost* (Columbia, Mo., 1983), esp. ch. 2.

[32] See Hughes's discussion, *CPW* iii. 153–9. For a rather different view of Milton's attack, see Potter, *Secret Rites*, 183.

out of Sir *Philip*' (iii. 547). Milton does not wholly capitulate to puritanical philistinism. Indeed, Sidney was something of a Puritan hero, and his book is 'in that kind full of worth and witt'; but it is the wrong *kind* for the context, and betrays a larger cultural deficiency. Here is a man who, in his affliction, reaches not for any 'serious Book' but for a 'vain amatorious Poem' (iii. 362–3). Milton clinches the point with a charge not unlike the one which Dr Johnson was to bring against 'Lycidas', that 'with these trifling fictions are mingled the most awful and sacred truth, such as ought never to be polluted with such irreverent combinations'.[33] Milton's phrase is yet more damning: here is a man who thought it appropriate to worship God 'with the polluted orts and refuse of *Arcadia's* and *Romances*, without being able to discern the affront rather then the worship of such an ethnic [that is, pagan] Prayer' (iii. 364).

Milton's biographers have sometimes remarked that his royalist enemies failed to associate the 'I.M.' whose name appears on the title-page of *Eikonoklastes* with the author of the notorious *Doctrine and Discipline of Divorce*, widely censured by Presbyterian divines and their confrères. In a sense, Milton was lucky that his enemies had not associated him with the 'I.M.' whose epitaph on Shakespeare appeared in the 1640 edition of the latter's poems, after first being published, anonymously, in the Second Folio, a copy of which Charles carried with him in his captivity, and which in Milton's words was 'the Closet Companion of these his solitudes' (iii. 361).

Other apologists for regicide, especially John Cook, had anticipated some aspects of this attack. Cook had claimed Charles 'was no more affected with a List that was brought in to *Oxford* of five of six thousand slain at *Edgehill*, then to read one of *Ben: Johnsons* Tragedies', and that 'had he made the Law of God his delight, and studied therein night and day, as God commanded his Kings to do; or had he but studied Scripture half so much as *Ben: Johnson* or *Shakespear*', he might better have understood the duties of kingship.[34] However, Milton not only criticizes the style of *Eikon Basilike* but also textures *Eikonoklastes* in such a way as to differentiate it from the tainted aesthetic which informs it.

[33] Samuel Johnson, 'Milton', in *Samuel Johnson*, ed. D. Greene (Oxford, 1984), 699.

[34] John Cook, *King Charls his Case* (London, 1649), 6, 13.

He speaks of the Rump's right to have the record set straight, 'to speak home the plain truth of a full and pertinent reply' (iii. 341), and *Eikonoklastes* is presented as the plain telling of that plain truth, distinguished by its lack of flourishes and artifice from the 'trimm'd over' account that Charles presents, 'speciously and fraudulently to impose upon the simple Reader . . . by smooth and supple words' (iii. 377). He writes largely in accordance with the aesthetic he develops in his critical observations, and imagery is at the core of the matter. The tracts of 1649, as I have demonstrated elsewhere,[35] mark a crucial shift in Milton's prose style as unusual collocations become much less prominent, the image density falls, and the imagery loses the luxuriance that characterized it earlier. Most significantly, in all the pamphlets of 1641–5 which refute or respond to an adversarial tract directly, Milton's writing is textured by a higher density of imagery than that of his opponent. Yet in his response to the flashiness of *Eikon Basilike* he does not deviate from what has become in the earlier tracts of 1649 his new, leaner style.

Thus, Milton's pamphlet, though grimly absorbing, does not reward its readers with the sort of purely literary pleasure that characterize, say, *Of Reformation* or *Areopagitica*. Literariness, both by implication and by explicit comment on his own practice and the king's, seems somehow suspect, opposed to 'plain truth'. Moreover, Milton offers these rather ascetic and limiting notions in a way that assumes a community of cultural values with his readership.

VII

The subdued style of *Eikonoklastes* serves well its polemical objectives. Most of Milton's tracts from *Of Reformation* to *Readie and Easie Way to Establish a Free Commonwealth* address a broad spectrum of Puritan opinion, though from a position on the radical fringe of that spectrum. The tracts of 1649 address the same audience from the same radical outpost, but, save for lapses in the first of them, they do so with a control and subtlety that distinguish them. In part, Milton is acting on behalf of an organization to whom he owes both corporate allegiance and discipline. In a sense,

---

[35] Corns, *Development*, 83–101.

it is remarkable that *Eikonoklastes*, like *The Tenure of Kings and Magistrates*, carries even his initials on its title-page. It is unsurprising that Milton, once he has made the points about picking up the gauntlet on behalf of Parliament and about the advantages the king enjoys, as adversary, over the private citizen, does very little to produce an intrusive self-image within *Eikonoklastes*.

Most significantly, perhaps, the political context in which he operates in 1649 is uniquely complicated. The revolutionary Independents, Milton's political masters, had achieved power through the ejection of the elements within the Long Parliament that had opposed the demands of the Army Grandees and who resisted the trial and execution of the king. Worden has depicted the early years of the English republic as characterized by conservative and cautious government, which contrived to draw in neutrals, to foster connections wherever possible with Presbyterians, and to offer itself as the guardian of order, decency, and an unfanatical, broad-spectrum Puritanism. As in *Observations*, and rather more responsibly than in *The Tenure*, Milton is constructing an argument to woo the Presbyterian rank and file away from the new royalist orientation of their leaders.[36]

Generally, Milton's tack is to demonstrate that Charles was inimical to Presbyterian and Independent alike. He exercises much energy in rehearsing the arguments against prelacy which all Puritans avowed at the outset of hostilities (e.g. iii. 512–19), and he explicitly declares that Charles 'meanes no good to either Independent or Presbyterian' (iii. 562). He further suggests that dangerous adventurers have tried to exploit differences between the groups in ways that were risky for them all:

> But som of the former Army,[37] eminent anough for thir own martial deeds, and prevalent in the House of Commons, touch'd with envy to be so farr outdon by a new modell which they contemn'd, took advantage of Presbyterian and Independent names, and the virulence of som Ministers to raise disturbance (iii. 560).

'Som' suggests we have here a local phenomenon, a narrow section placing in jeopardy what all, Presbyterian and Independent, have fought for. 'Som of the former Army' have already been dealt with

---

[36] Id., 'Milton's *Observations*', 131.

[37] Men like Holles, Stapleton, Waller, and Massey, as Hughes notes (*CPW* iii. 560 n.).

(at Pride's Purge); 'the virulence of som Ministers', though still a problem, is of manageable proportions. 'Names' makes the difference sound trivial, compared with the shared experience of the early years of the decade. Presbyterian ministers, but not the laity, recur as an object of disdain (e.g. iii. 349, 553).

Milton has a considerable advantage in that *Eikon Basilike* went to press before the royalist leadership started to establish a working relationship with Scots and Irish—and English—Presbyterian leaders. He can demonstrate with facility from the king's book that the king had no affection for those of Presbyterian persuasion: 'This he thrice repeats to be the true State and reason of all that Warr and devastation in the Land, and that *of all the Treaties and Propositions* offer'd him, he was resolv'd *never to grant the abolishing of Episcopal, or the establishment of Presbyterian Government*' (iii. 445). It was probably a convincing point to the Presbyterian waverer.

Milton, however, still develops a clear enunciation of the spirit of a new age. The tract is shot through with the ideology of revolutionary Independency, in its assertion of the godliness of their actions and in its dismissal of those who are not with them as in some senses excluded by their blindness from the newly reformed political nation represented by the Rump and the Council of State.[38] 'The mad multitude', as he terms them, are politically beyond consideration (iii. 345). In a curious version of the 'fit audience though few' topos, the truth of his tract may 'finde out her own readers; few perhaps, but those few, of such value and substantial worth, as truth and wisdom, not respecting numbers and bigg names, have bin ever wont in all ages to be contented with' (iii. 339–40). The peroration dismisses 'the inconstant, irrational, and Image-doting rabble', though he is careful to leave the door open for the hitherto unsympathetic Puritan to reconcile himself to the revolution and rejoin the Independents in the government of the godly: those 'whom perhaps ignorance without malice, or some error, less then fatal, hath for a time misledd, on this side Sorcery or obduration, may find the grace and good guidance to bethink themselves, and recover' (iii. 601).

Milton sacrificed much in the provision of that 'good guidance', foolishly, it is sometimes suggested. But is *Eikonoklastes* quite the

---

[38] On Independent ideology, see Milner, *Milton*, esp. chs. 2–3.

failure that Parker, for example, insists?[39] It went through two editions in 1649–50 and was translated into French. Those editions were probably many times larger than each of the clandestine printings *Eikon Basilike* received, and nowadays it is by no means a rare book, despite the order at the Restoration for its collection and destruction.[40] Moreover, its revival as a Whig or Williamite pamphlet points to the potency that the later seventeenth century felt it had.[41] It was part of a campaign that was to prove ultimately successful. No doubt the awesome successes of Cromwell at Dunbar and Worcester did more to discourage English royalists from taking up arms. There was no flurry of active support for Charles II's Scottish adventures among English Presbyterians, and though there were plots among the leadership and the activists, generally the Rump—and Milton—achieved their objective of establishing a *modus vivendi* with their former allies. In some ways, to the modern reader, *Eikonoklastes* may seem a long, dull tract. Milton evidently knew the aesthetic risks he ran. At one point he complains of the drudgery it takes 'to walk side by side' with the verbosity of some parts of *Eikon Basilike* (iii. 433), but he stuck to the task, mindful of his audience and his purpose.

[39] Parker, *Milton*, i. 361.
[40] *LR* iv. 322.
[41] G. T. Sensabaugh, *That Grand Whig Milton* (1952; New York, 1967), 142–55.

7

Marvell, Lovelace, and Cowley

FOR those members of the propertied classes of royalist, Presbyterian royalist, or neutralist inclination prospects by the end of January 1649 must have seemed a perplexing fusion of dismay, hope, and anxiety. Some cause for optimism lay in the fissured and beleaguered nature of the new republic, threatened by internal dissent and opposed by an Ireland for once united in a common purpose and by a powerful Scotland already in arms for Charles I's successor. The base of support for the Rump Parliament may well have been perceived as exiguous, and the constitutional innovations it intended had an air of desperate improvization. The New Model Army, the real underwriters of the Rump's authority, while still an awesome military force, had perhaps begun to disclose a promising disunity, both within its highest circles, in Fairfax's uncertainties about the direction events had taken, and between its commanders and junior officers and other ranks of Leveller inclination.

Paradoxically, the major cause for anxiety lay in some of those same uncertainties. If more radical elements were to assume the ascendant, if the group around Cromwell were either to lose out to others of more radical political or religious intent or, worse, if they were to throw in their lot with those elements, then the Protestant religion as practised even by Presbyterians could be utterly subverted, the rights of property could be redefined, and the political nation could be unacceptably reconstructed.

By the end of 1653, both hopes and fears had proved unfounded. The Rump had shown an alacrity in suppressing some of the more conspicuous radicals. The leaders of the New Model Army had confronted and broken both civilian Levellers and those in their own ranks. After an apparent flirtation with Fifth Monarchism, Cromwell had emerged as a tolerant but staid figure, committed to defending civil order and socially quite conservative. At the same time, despite a vortex of constitutional uncertainty, the republic had survived, primarily because of an unbroken run of military success.

Ireland had been settled; the Scots, beaten at Dunbar, were crushed at Worcester, and with them ended English royalists' best chance of a restoration through military victory, though plots and conspiracies were to rumble on for another couple of years. Moreover, a new ambitious expansionism had begun to animate English foreign policy, manifest in the vigorous exploitation of reconquered Ireland and in the prosecution of a war, primarily about trade, with the Dutch; it was soon to find expression in the Cromwellian design to make England a world power through confrontation with Dutch and Spanish interests in the New World.

An outsider with hindsight may have viewed the years between the execution of the king and Cromwell's assumption of the title of Lord Protector as an inexorable process in which Cromwell's rise to power secured traditional interests of property against the nightmare that could have overwhelmed them. The Levellers and Ranters had been crushed; the brief experiment of the Barebone's Parliament, a nominated assembly in which some religious radicals assumed a high profile, had imploded through its inherent instability; Fifth Monarchists, in 1652 seemingly in the ascendant, had lost whatever passing influence they may have had.

Insiders would have better appreciated the struggles and uncertainties leading eventually to the settlement of power on Cromwell late in 1653. Worden has charted well the complex internal history of the Rump and Woolrych the complex conflicting impulses and influences that were at work in the forming and abandoning of the Barebone's Parliament. Both outsiders and insiders, however, might have recognized that, in Hill's phrase, 'The Revolution was over.'[1] Cromwell's first Council of State had a conservative and propertied complexion which must have reassured many.

Events of the period 1649–53, pre-eminently the eclipse of the royalist cause and the rise of Cromwell, followed by the various consolidations of his power over the middle years of the decade, provide the vital context for understanding the writings of Marvell and Cowley and the later poetry of Lovelace. In Marvell, initial complexities and confusions, which defy a simple schematization, give way to an increasingly conservative version of Cromwellian

---

[1] Hill, *God's Englishman*, 143; this narrative rests largely on Hill's account, on Worden, and on A. Woolrych, *Commonwealth to Protectorate* (1982; Oxford, 1986). For other historical contextualization, see above, Ch. 5.

partisanship. In Cowley and in Lovelace, the utter failure of the royalist cause for which they had made considerable personal sacrifice occasions in the case of the former an extraordinary demonstration of political and poetic resignation, in the case of the latter a defiance but of a grubby and jaundiced kind.

II

Marvell's political verse, particularly the poems that relate to the Civil War and the establishment of the Republic, has exercised twentieth-century critics with taunting conundrums, compounded by problems of chronology and canon. Other, more literary, issues complicate interpretation of the ideological implications of his poetry. In a manner rivalled in the British tradition only by William Dunbar, Marvell achieves an awesome diversity of accomplishment within a relatively slender output. Several studies have demonstrated his range of genres, of themes, of mode, of influence, and of subject.[2] He variously simulates the libertine wit or metaphysical abstruseness of Donne, the smooth, courtly directness of Lovelace, the elegiac pastoralism of Herrick, and the incision of Cleveland. French and Italian influences flicker through his verse, and Lucan, Horace, and Virgilian georgic are incorporated into new constructs, intermittently and variously mediated by contemporary neoclassicists. Panegyric and satire, heroism and withdrawal, poems of state and poems of retreat, Platonic spirituality and carnal celebration, appear intermingled within the volume, *Miscellaneous Poems*, published posthumously in 1681.

Alongside variety of mode, model, genre, and topos comes variety of sentiment. With an instability that would seem pathological were it not associated with such chameleon literariness, issues from the trivial to the transcendent are conflictingly rendered. Thus, the speaker of 'The Mower against Gardens', in an argument of apparent good sense, rails against the artifice and prodigal expense of gardens: the tulip's 'Onion root' is so absurdly esteemed 'That one was for a Meadow Sold' (*Poems and Letters*, i. 44, ll. 15–16). Yet, in 'Upon Appleton House', the elaborate garden, with its '*Regiment[s]* . . . of the Tulip Pinke and Rose' (i. 72, ll. 311–12)

---

[2] See App. B.

provides a fittingly complimentary context for Fairfax and his daughter, while elsewhere the garden where 'all Flow'rs and all Trees do close | To weave the Garlands of repose' ('The Garden', i. 51, ll. 7–8) prepares the mind for ecstasy. Again, 'The Garden' asserts the advantages of contemplative retreat not only over the active life but also over an active heterosexuality—'Two Paradises 'twere in one | To live in Paradise alone' (i. 53, ll. 63–4)—and offers the possibilities of ecstatic detachment in which 'Casting the Bodies Vest aside, | My Soul into the boughs does glide' (i. 52, ll. 51–2). In sharp contrast, in 'A Dialogue between the Soul and Body' each suffers gruesomely through the inseparability, short of death, of their bond, the soul 'hung up, as 'twere in Chains | Of Nerves, and Arteries, and Veins', while the body 'could never rest, | Since this ill Spirit it possest' (i. 22, ll. 7–8, 19–20). The curiously charged asexuality (or perhaps autoeroticism?) of 'The Garden' obviously invites comparison with the lovers of 'To his Coy Mistress', 'like am'rous birds of prey . . . tear[ing] our Pleasure with rough strife, | Through the Iron gates of Life' (i. 28, ll. 38, 43–4), which in turn contrasts with the delicate adoration of the prepubescent girl in 'The Picture of Little T.C. in a Prospect of Flowers' (i. 40–1). While 'To his Coy Mistress' with a fierce logic approaches human relations through a grim syllogism,[3] the relationship in 'The Picture of Little T.C.' turns on the more ancient, though illogical, impulses of sympathetic magic: if T.C. plucks flowers before their time, she in turn will be prematurely 'nipped' (i. 41, ll. 33–40).[4] Individual poems imply a system of values and a sensibility (sometimes a rather disconcerting one), but sentiment often comes with genre, model, and mode, and no single synthesizing voice may be convincingly postulated. It is significant that Marvell should have sought and accomplished such diversity—as if the task of literary production were an end in itself, a subtle, complex, and private competition with no tangible reward.

Yet if we accept that Marvell may be evasive about sexuality and spirituality, need the evasions and contradictions of his political writings require any more reduction to order, especially when the

[3] A point often noted but perhaps best analysed by R. I. V. Hodge, *Foreshortened Time: Andrew Marvell and the 17th Century Revolutions* (Cambridge and Totowa, NJ, 1978), 22–6.

[4] For a description of analogous beliefs among primitive peoples, see J. G. Frazer, *The Golden Bough: A Study in Magic and Religion*, abridged edn. (London, 1960), 27–36.

problems of interpretation are compounded with uncertainties about dates of composition and revision, about the biographical circumstances that may have shaped them, and about their intended audience (if any)? 'A Poem upon the Death of O.C.' laments that 'we, since thou art gone, with heavy doome, | Wander like ghosts about thy loved tombe' (i. 137, ll. 299–300). A letter to Mayor Richardson of Hull, dated December 1660, reports among other parliamentary business, ''tis ordered that the Carkasses & coffins [of Cromwell, Bradshaw, Ireton, and Pride] shall be drawn, with w[ha]t expedition possible, upon a hurdle to Tyburn, there to be hangd up for a while & then buryed under the gallows' (ii. 7). Each quotation is disconcerting in its way—the former in its unctuousness, the latter in the way the account slips into a series of narratives of Government business and is followed by references to 'his M[ajes]tiyes moderation'. 'Carkasses' jars, as does the laconic manner. What really shocks is that one man could be author of them both, probably within a two-year period. Interpreting such a writer calls for a special strategy. *Miscellaneous Poems* is not tractable to the kinds of reading developed for Milton's *Poems* (1645) or Herrick's *Hesperides* or Cowley's *Poems* (1656). 'Miscellaneous' perhaps gives the best pointer—composed of different kinds, and each to be considered discretely.

III

'To his Noble Friend Mr. Richard Lovelace, upon his Poems' (i. 2–4) appeared among the many commendatory poems prefacing the first *Lucasta*, some of which have been discussed already.[5] Since we know it was published early in 1649 we have a *terminus ad quem* for its composition. A section of the poem, lines 21–32—dubiously, in my view—has sometimes been thought 'to mean that the book was not yet licensed', which, if true, would fix the *terminus a quo* at February 1648.[6] There is no reason in any case to suppose composition much antedates publication.

Marvell finds himself in solidly royalist company: not only Lovelace but several authors of the other prefatory poems had borne arms for the king, though it is the logic of the tyrant to

[5] Above, Ch. 4. [6] *Poems and Letters*, i. 239.

assume guilt by association. Even in times of deep political divisions, one need not share another's views to like his poetry. Indeed, the line 'Our Civill Wars have lost the Civicke crowne' (l. 12) suggests that a major ill consequence of the conflict is that citizens who were formerly rewarded for saving their fellows are rewarded now for attacking them. But the references to 'Our [degenerate] times' (l. 1) and 'th' infection of our times' (l. 4) have by 1649 a decidedly partisan and royalist ring—after all, for revolutionary Independents, 'our times' were regenerate, bliss to be alive. Yet the poem's expressions of regret emphasize especially the broken concord between Englishmen, and particularly English men of letters: 'he highest builds, who with most Art destroys' (l. 13).

Milton, in a poem which Marvell could have read in manuscript, had complained of the response to his divorce writings:

> I did but prompt the age to quit their clogs
> By the known rules of ancient liberty,
> When straight a barbarous noise environs me
> Of owls and cuckoos, asses, apes and dogs.[7]

He refers to the organized assaults of Presbyterians and their allies on his more radical and heterodox theology. Marvell conceptualizes the attack on *Lucasta* in similar terms:

> The Ayre's already tainted with the swarms
> Of Insects which against you rise in arms.
> Word-peckers, Paper-rats, Book-scorpions,
> Of wit corrupted, the unfashion'd Sons. (ll. 17–20)

Interestingly, while Milton had been writing literally of the orthodox Puritan backlash, Marvell took the conservative Assembly of Divines as a metaphor for Lovelace's critics, whose 'grim consistory . . . cast a reforming eye, | Severer then the yong Presbytery' (ll. 22–5). The Miltonic echo, if such it is, hints that not only royalists found the 1640s a repressive decade, and the poem concludes with a further reminder of the ideological complexity apparent to subtle wits.[8] In what seems to be an autobiographical allusion, though of a heavily mediated kind, the poet describes how 'beauteous Ladies . . . though yet undrest'[9] assail him, thinking that

---

[7] *Poems*, 244–5, ll. 1–4.

[8] R. Wilcher, *Andrew Marvell* (Cambridge, 1985), 110, also sees a connection.

[9] 'Undrest' probably means primarily 'naked' (*OED*, s.v. 'undressed' 7, which cites this line), though it may carry some sense of 'dishabille' (*OED* 8).

he belongs to the 'rout' of Lovelace's censurers (ll. 33–44). One scratches at his eyes, knowing how upsetting it would be to lose 'that sight' of the naked women, but 'O no, mistake not, I reply'ed, for I | In your defence, or in his cause would dy' (ll. 45–6). The implication would seem to be that Marvell could (and perhaps had) been 'mistaken' for a political enemy of Lovelace, but that he, too, admits a libertine streak—he likes looking at the women—and shares at least some sense of Lovelace's values and is on his side. Yet the ambiguity remains finally unresolved: 'his cause' for which Marvell would die could be either the cause for which Lovelace fought or else the cause of Lovelace himself. While disputing one over-simple categorization—Marvell the censorious Puritan—he postulates no simple alternative.

Though it could have been subsequently revised, primary composition of 'An Horatian Ode upon Cromwel's Return from Ireland' (i. 91–4) may with some confidence be assigned to the period between May 1650, when Cromwell returned, and July 1650, when he invaded Scotland. We know with near certainty that the poem was not printed in 1650—its first certain publication was in 1681. Hodge offers a plausible guess that its audience may have been 'a group of poets and litterateurs, of a predominantly Royalist but unseditious cast of mind, to whom Marvell showed his work',[10] but that is surmise, and other hypotheses are freely available. Perhaps it was intended for publication, but Marvell thought better of it or was advised against it. Perhaps some revolutionary luminary—Needham, Bradshaw, Milton, Cromwell himself—considered it and rejected it. Or it may have been a wholly private exercise, a working through of a personal crisis, or a game Marvell, most secret of men, played in solitary fashion.

In a sense, our ignorance of its intended audience and of its social context multiplies the difficulties in interpretation. It is variously perceived: 'the most private of public poems'; 'For all its rhetorical appeal to an audience . . . and its address to Cromwell . . . it is essentially a private poem'; 'skilful propaganda for the emergent powerful individual'; 'officially a panegyric to Cromwell'; 'the celebration of a return . . . the obverse of *propempticon*, or congratulatory send off'.[11] Such uncertainty probably fed the

---

[10] Hodge, *Foreshortened Time*, 118–19.

[11] B. Worden, 'Andrew Marvell, Oliver Cromwell, and the Horatian Ode', *Hist. Jnl.* 27 (1984), 525–47; reprinted in K. Sharpe and S. N. Zwicker (eds.), 150; Wilcher,

interpretative diversity. For some, the poem is *Trauerarbeit*, the private transformation of grief into art which effects the healing process of mourning: for others, it serves the political ends of a narrow faction. Certainly the poem would have constituted a scintillating propaganda initiative to coax Presbyterian royalists of a singularly literary inclination into at least acquiescence with the new regime. It requires no compromise in one's regrets for the fate of the king, nor does it ask its readers to *like* Cromwell. Marvell emphasizes the heroism of the king—'*He* nothing common did or mean' (l. 57), with an implication that others did. The constitutional argument appears in emphatically royalist guise—Justice and 'the antient Rights' (or at least some of them) belong to the king's party (ll. 37–8). Norbrook's suggestion that 'the poem gives . . . the impression of facing the fact of regicide coldly and unflinchingly'[12] understates the recurrent sense of horror. Indeed, Marvell accentuates the grisliness of Charles's end. The architects of the new republic, like those of the Capitol in ancient Rome, flinch from a 'bleeding head' (l. 69), he tells us: his source, Pliny or Varro, mentions merely a 'caput humanum', presumably a skull. That it bleeds is Marvell's surreal elaboration.[13] Other macabre and equally surreal details—that the soldiers around the scaffold clapped as at a performance and that their hands were bloody, as if they had bathed in the gore of sacrifice—are wholly Marvell's inventions. *Pace* Wilcher, it is not that he thus reinstates realism after the sentimentalism of the picture of the king, bowing 'his comely head | Down, as upon a bed' (l. 64): rather, Marvell subverts realism with the insistent unpleasantness of nightmare.[14] The horror of the execution and the grief and outrage it may have occasioned are reasserted and validated.

Simultaneously, the poem works to deny the culpability of Cromwell. Imagery insistently associates him with the non-human ('the Falcon'—l. 91) and the inanimate ('the three-fork'd Lightning'—l. 13), and thus with the non-moral. Those acts he perpetrated as a

Marvell, 124; Wilding, *Dragons Teeth*, 134; R. L. Colie, '*My Ecchoing Song'*: *Andrew Marvell's Poetry of Criticism* (Princeton, 1970), 64; A. M. Patterson, *Marvell and the Civic Crown* (Princeton, 1978), 62.

[12] D. Norbrook, 'Marvell's "Horatian Ode" and the Politics of Genre', in Healy and Sawday, 159.

[13] *Letters and Poems*, i. 300; Wilcher, *Marvell*, 120.

[14] Ibid. 120.

human agent are habitually transformed into sport—setting 'a Net' to catch Charles in '*Caresbrooks* narrow case' (l. 52) and laying 'his Hounds in near | The *Caledonian* Deer' (ll. 111–12). Moreover, the emphasis on Cromwell's role as agent of the republic (l. 82) further deflects his moral responsibility for the death of the king: he is servant to a collective and quasi-constitutional body, at whose 'feet' he lays what he has gained on their behalf (l. 85).

Wilding has written well on the signifying silences of the 'Horatian Ode'.[15] By simplifying the political configuration into a polarity between Charles and Cromwell, other, more urgently radical, voices are excluded. The political context for the invasion of Ireland included the militant opposition of Levellers both inside and outside the New Model Army. The swiftness of Cromwell's suppression of the Burford Mutiny, possibly alluded to in the breaking 'through his own Side' (l. 15), is largely marginalized, and the reader faces a crisis simplified. Certainly, Marvell's poem excludes from political consideration voices from outside the established ranks of the political nation. However, much more significant than the exclusion of Lilburne and his associates is the exclusion of Charles II. The dead king's son had straightaway been declared monarch of all his father's kingdoms, and he was acknowledged by republican propaganda to be king of Scotland. The Irish forces Cromwell had suppressed, the Scots he turned to meet, the English royalists still prepared to fight, all took up arms in the name of Charles II. By any objective criteria, the real ideological alternatives were not the diachronic and pre-empted choice between Charles I and Cromwell but the synchronic and pressing choice between Charles II and Cromwell.

Moreover, the political climate in London in the summer and autumn of 1650, the period the ode apparently belongs to, was decidedly uncertain: 'The campaign, expected to be "the work of many years", began inauspiciously. The days of the Commonwealth seemed numbered, and it was with a sense of desperation that Cromwell's forces, both their supplies and their morale seriously depleted, moved to Dunbar at the beginning of September to try to force the Scots to a fight.'[16] Far from coursing his hounds in gentlemanly fashion after the deer, he found himself out-

[15] *Dragons Teeth*, 114–37.
[16] Worden, 226.

numbered two to one and half his men sick: his victory was 'as unexpected as it was spectacular'.[17]

Marvell's ode, were it a 'public' poem, could have worked to disorientate Presbyterian royalists and could even have swayed Englishmen who had formerly supported the king's cause in a more straightforwardly partisan fashion. Their grief is accepted and legitimized, Cromwell is largely exculpated, and his victory in Scotland is represented (rather against the evidence) as inevitable, like his crushing of the Irish. Supporting Charles II does not appear as an option, but readers may still feel sentimental about his father. That the voice produced within the poem is that of an admirer of Charles I who has made a transition to support for the Scottish campaign could in itself be very persuasive: Marvell offers a paradigm for the process of ideological reconciliation the Rump desperately wished to foster.[18]

But suppose the ode is not a suppressed or aborted public poem, but rather an exercise in private ratiocination, or, indeed, rationaliz-ation. Under an interpretative strategy appropriate to those circumstances, the poem appears regrettably impoverished. In opting for Horace's model of the political ode, he necessarily accepts certain restrictions on scale—at 120 lines, his poem is longer than most of Horace's—and a manner that tends to understatement, to enigma, to a restraint which leaves the reader an active role in completing the meaning. Such formal requirements may well serve the exigencies of a subtle polemic, but in the context of private meditation they preclude the sort of detail that an unevasive appraisal requires. We have considered some of the silences in the poem. If they reflect Marvell's profoundly held vision rather than propaganda manœuvres they disclose a limited and unimaginative interpretation of English political life in 1650. Furthermore, his categories for Cromwell's enemies are curiously limited.

> And now the *Irish* are asham'd
> To see themselves in one year tam'd.   (ll. 73–4)

Which 'Irish'? Cromwell's forces engaged Presbyterian royalists, old Protestant supporters of the king, and the Catholic confederates who had constituted the rebels of 1640. Some were former friends

---

[17] D. Smurthwaite, *Battlefields of Britain* (1984; London, 1987), 172; Worden, 226.

[18] Ibid. 80, 240; 'Horatian Ode', *passim*.

of the English Parliament, others Catholics who were perceived as no better than savages.[19] What Cromwell's army accomplished in Ireland was, in terms of English parliamentary thinking, really rather more complex. Again, those '*Caledonian* Deer' (l. 112) included not only traditional supporters of the Stuarts but also Covenanters who had fought with significant effect on Parliament's side in England. If the 'Horatian Ode' is indeed the sort of personal invoice the Puritan mind sometimes produced in the early modern period, then it is a sadly incomplete review of those elements that might have justified a transition from royalism to republicanism. I hesitate to favour an interpretation which perceives as intellectually inadequate what may be regarded as an ingenious artefact. In 1650, only a fool or a clairvoyant would have seen the choice as Cromwell or nothing: but then we do not know what revisions Marvell may have introduced subsequently.

'Tom May's Death' (ll. 94–7) poses a major conundrum for Marvell scholars. May died on 13 November 1650,[20] so its earliest point of composition is four months after the 'Horatian Ode', though Marvell may well have tinkered with it much later. Its political sentiments rest curiously alongside the at least nascent republicanism of the ode, so much so that some—most influentially Lord—have disputed its authenticity.[21] The balance of evidence, in terms of the slightness of the external proof against its authenticity and the strength of internal evidence of its obvious quality and its manner, is with those who endorse its inclusion within the canon: the Gordian knot, in Legouis's phrase, may not so easily be severed.[22]

The poem belongs to a narrow genre, the mock elegy, most familiar, perhaps, from Milton's two poems on the death of Hobson, the university carrier.[23] To modern taste, and perhaps to more fastidious contemporaries, the genre loses much of its charm in the requirement that its subject should indeed have died. Milton's poems work around a simple mechanism. Hobson's trade provides

---

[19] For the Irish context, see above, Ch. 6.
[20] See *DNB*.
[21] *Andrew Marvell: Complete Poetry*, ed. G. deF. Lord (1968; London and Melbourne, 1984), p. xxxii; for a response, see *Poems and Letters*, i. 303–4, and W. L. Chernaik, *The Poet's Time: Politics and Religion in the Work of Andrew Marvell* (Cambridge, 1983), 206–14.
[22] *Poems and Letters*, i. 304.
[23] *Poems*, 124–6.

the basis for a series of quibbles connecting the role of carrier with death's own winged chariot:

> Nay, quoth he, on his swooning bed outstretched,
> If I may not carry, sure I'll ne'er be fetched,
> But vow though the cross doctors all stood hearers,
> For one carrier put down to make six bearers.
> Ease was his chief disease, and to judge right,
> He died for heaviness that his cart went light.[24]

Marvell's poem, though several times the length of either of Milton's, also operates on a single, simple mechanism. May, translator of Lucan, Virgil, and Martial, was the most distinguished neoclassical poet of the mid-century, and the influence of his *Pharsalia* is probably detectable in Marvell's 'Horatian Ode'.[25] The joke in 'Tom May's Death' is the subversion of the neoclassical aesthetic with which he was associated. May wakes from death to find himself indeed in a classical Elysium. Surprised and disorientated, 'with an Eye uncertain, gazing wide' (l. 4), he attempts to make sense of the classical eschatology, a fantasy made real, in terms of that reality with which he was formerly familiar, the taverns of 'Stevens ally', where presumably he had habitually roused from a different torpor. Seeing Ben Jonson at hand, he mistakes him for a publican—a coterie joke about the 'corpulence and port' of Jonson, like that of the stereotypical innkeeper, with perhaps a further private humour that 'Ares'—a particular inn-keeper?— especially resembled him. The incongruities of May's ordinary, if life-threatening, alcoholism and the mode of high classical epic continue in lines closely parodic of May's own rendering of Lucan: 'the Historian of the Commonwealth[26] | In his own Bowels sheath'd the conquering health' (ll. 23–4). May supposedly choked to death in a drunken stupor. Thereafter follow a syllepsis and a pun, much in the manner of the Hobson poems:

> By this *May* to himself and them was come,
> He found he was translated, and by whom.   (ll. 25–6)

Neoclassical fantasy, the clutter of the underworld lumber-room, once more appears subverted, as Jonson dismisses him to hell with ' 'Tis just what Torments Poets ere did feign, | Thou first Historically shouldst sustain' (ll. 95–6), with perhaps a minor quibble on

[24] Milton, 'Another on the Same', ll. 17–22, *Poems*, 125–6.
[25] *Poems and Letters*, i. 295.
[26] An allusion to May's *History of the Long Parliament* (London, 1647).

May's dual role. 'Tom May's Death' is a funny poem, a tight, accomplished exercise in a comic genre. But it is not ideologically transparent. Just as Milton's Hobson poem produces an educated-class contempt for the tradesman class, so Marvell's is premissed on a royalist contempt for the ideological apparatus of republicanism. Neither Wilding's hypothesis that 'the hostility to May could be the result of internecine struggles within the Cromwellian camp', nor Chernaik's conclusion that 'The standards by which May is judged . . . are fundamentally aesthetic and moral . . . the political element is secondary' can be reconciled with the political tone of the poem.[27]

The poet whose judgement banishes May to the underworld is Ben Jonson, Caroline court poet, poet laureate, masque-writer, and persistent satirist of pre-revolutionary Puritanism. He was, more-over, a figure frequently invoked by royalist poets as model, mentor, hero, and an associate whose friendship was the subject of proud recollection.[28] Marvell easily (and perhaps more amusingly) could have had May judged and banished by an ancient poet he had claimed to serve. The choice of Jonson, however, signals a political orientation and moreover allows explicit recollection of a period when May, too, served the Caroline court (ll. 37–8).

Jonson's observations are shot through with royalist values. Brutus and Cassius, heroes to republicans, are, as editors note, borrowed from Dante's Inferno, but the epithet, 'the Peoples cheats' (l. 18) is Marvell's own.[29] It carries a clear implication that those who would speak in the name of the English people do so only to deceive. Jonson, moreover, defines the true poet's role as one of resistance to the new ascendancy:

> When the Sword glitters ore the Judges head,
> And fear has Coward Churchmen silenced,
> Then is the Poets time, 'tis then he drawes,
> And single fights forsaken Vertues cause,
> He, when the wheel of Empire whirleth back,
> And though the World's disjointed Axel crack,
> Sings still of ancient Rights and better Times,
> Seeks wretched good, arraigns successful Crimes.   (ll. 63–70)

In the context of the events of 1649–50, little of this appears ambiguous. '*Successful* Crimes'—only the republicans could really

---

[27] Wilding, *Dragons Teeth*, 115; Chernaik, *Poet's Time*, 176.
[28] Cf. Herrick, *Hesperides*, 173–4, 249, 342–3.
[29] Cf. Lovelace's use of the Cromwell-Brutus motif discussed below; *Poems and Letters*, i. 304–5.

be perceived as successful, which, given the antithetical structure of that line, associates their enemies with 'wretched good'. The silenced 'Churchmen' are probably to be identified with eclipsed episcopalians. Presbyterian divines found opportunity enough to comment on the constitutional developments of the times, though apologists for prelacy had fallen largely silent since the early 1640s.[30] 'Better Times' invokes the now familiar royalist nostalgia which suffused, for example, the work of Herrick. The 'Sword' that 'glitters ore the Judges head' probably refers to the quasi-judicial proceedings against Charles I, made possible by the direct intervention of the New Model Army in parliamentary politics, while the 'ancient Rights' of which the poet should sing echoes Marvell's lines in the 'Horatian Ode':

> Though Justice against Fate complain,
> And plead the antient Rights in vain.   (ll. 37–8)

Presumably, such rights are the rights of kings and the rights of all citizens to due process of law, an objection Charles I had raised to the proceedings against him.

'Tom May's Death' relates in other ways to the earlier ode. It shares some of its imagery. In the ode, the founding of the new republic had been likened to laying the foundations of ancient Rome:

> So when they did design
> The *Capitols* first line,
> A bleeding Head where they begun,
> Did fright the Architects to run.   (ll. 67–70)

Marvell in 'Tom May's Death' subverts that image. Discussing *May*'s habit of linking Cromwell's England to classical Rome, he has Jonson conclude:

> Foul Architect that hadst not Eye to see
> How ill the measures of these States agree.   (ll. 51–2)

Earlier, Marvell had likened English statesmen in the late 1640s to the architects of Rome. Now he likens May to a 'foul Architect' for failing to note disparities between contemporary England and ancient Rome. The image of the architect is not especially apposite in the second poem, but by using it again Marvell further stimulates recollection of his own perpetration of the now criticized mechan-

[30] Worden, 81–4; Corns, 'Publication and Politics', 78–9.

ism of equating contemporary and classical events. In so doing he raises disturbing questions of interpretation about those lines in the ode that predict Cromwell will be 'A *Caesar* . . . to *Gaul*, | To *Italy* an *Hannibal*' (ll. 101–2). He jeers at Tom May,

> thou Dictator of the glass bestow
> On him [some unnamed republican] the *Cato*, this the *Cicero*.
> Transferring old *Rome* hither in your talk.   (ll. 47–9)

Yet May's crime is exactly Marvell's practice in his earlier poem.

The mock elegy, then, is in a complicated relationship to the ode, its tight century of lines commenting on and contradicting the 120 lines of the former poem and in some ways disconcerting the reader. Analogies perhaps suggest themselves with William Blake, another riddling poet. 'Tom May's Death' is as much the parodic counterpart of the 'Horatian Ode' as *The Songs of Experience* are of the *Songs of Innocence*. The questions each raises of the other defy any certain or straightforward resolution.

IV

Marvell probably entered Fairfax's service as tutor to Maria, his only child, in 1650, possibly after June, when Fairfax resigned his command and left London for his Yorkshire estates, and he quit his employment about the end of 1652.[31] 'Upon Appleton House, to my Lord Fairfax' (i. 62–86) was probably composed during that period, which he would seem to have spent in part at least at Nun Appleton.

Organizing and interpreting the relationship between the major arcs of narrative and description of which it is composed poses a recurrent challenge. The poet plays numerous, rather modernist, tricks, which assert its artifice and postulate difficulties about how such artfulness relates to an external reality. A double time-scheme operates. The poet regards the workings of the Appleton estate from 'the Morning Ray' (l. 289) in the garden to the concluding 'Let's in' (l. 775) of evening, but in stanzas xlvii to lix he witnesses the work of several days, as hay is mown, dried, stacked, carted, and the stubble grazed. As his readers organize the events of the poem into the scheme of the events of a day, the poet, with no doubt

---

[31] P. Legouis, *Andrew Marvell: Poet, Puritan, Patriot* (Oxford, 1965), 18, 91.

conscious reference to the potent artifice of his descriptive mode, disorders it:

> No Scene that turns with Engines strange
> Does oftner then these Meadows change.   (ll. 385–6)

Days pass as scenes in an afternoon's entertainment. With a flamboyant reflexivity, Marvell has 'bloody Thestylis' break the dumbshow to address the poet directly about the metaphor he has just applied to her and her colleagues (ll. 406–8). An aesthetic mode bordering on surrealism largely obtains. Architects' plans for porticos twist their minds into vaults (st. i). Appleton House sweats and swells to accommodate its great lord (st. vii). Poet and tree are metaphorically superimposed: 'turn me but, and you shall see | I was but an inverted tree' (st. lxxi).[32] The salmon-fishers carrying their coracles become in the space of a stanza '*Tortoise like . . . rational Amphibii*' and fit emblems for the world, the upper hemisphere of which now carries the zone of night as they their boats (st. lxxxvii). In such an insubstantial pageant, political reference shares the general instability, though a central core of complement and lament is more stable.

'Upon Appleton House', like Jonson's 'To Penshurst', the major model for the country-house poem, develops praise for the patron through praise for his estate. Jonson's poem had emphasized the sense of tradition and proportion characteristic of Penshurst's owner, the Earl of Leiceister, his generosity to his guests ('Where comes no guest but is allowed to eat | Without his fear, and of thy lord's own meat'), and his benevolence to the local community ('There's none that dwell about [thy walls] wish them down'). The poem ends:

> Now, Penshurst, they that will proportion thee
> With other edifices, when they see
> Those proud, ambitious heaps, and nothing else,
> May say, their lords have built, but thy lord dwells.[33]

Consideration of Jonson's poem usefully discloses the panegyric manœuvres open to Marvell, only some of which he chose to follow.

The emphasis on the practical modesty of the architecture is retained. Like Jonson, Marvell remarks on the absence of neoclassical

---

[32] The concept, however, is ancient, *Poems and Letters*, i. 289.
[33] 'To Penshurst', ll. 61–2, 47, 99–102, *Ben Jonson*, ed. by I. Donaldson (Oxford, 1985), 282–5.

columns. By the 1650s, however, architectural style had long since been placed on the political agenda. Laud's advocacy of Romish accretions to Gothic English churches, most spectacularly the neoclassical portico by Inigo Jones affixed to the west end of St Paul's, had outraged Puritan opinion, and Charles I had been an obvious enthusiast for Jones's variety of Palladianism.[34] That his execution was staged before Jones's neoclassical masterpiece, the Banqueting House at Whitehall, was replete with cultural irony. When Marvell observes of Appleton House,

> Within this sober Frame expect
> Work of no Forrain *Architect*;
>
> .   .   .   .
>
> Who if his great Design in pain
> Did for a Model vault his Brain,
> Whose Columnes should so high be rais'd
> To arch the Brows that on them gaz'd.   (ll. 1–2, 5–8)

he is making an ideological point. Unlike Laud, Charles I, and others who would adopt their architectural aesthetic, Fairfax builds in the proper English tradition, unaffected by the imperatives of foreigners like Palladio.

Fairfax's generosity has a mere mention. Just four lines represent what in Jonson had been a major theme:

> A Stately *Frontispice of Poor*
> Adorns without the open Door:
> Nor less the Rooms within commends
> Daily new *Furniture of Friends*.   (ll. 65–8)

Poor people appear in plenty in the poem, though they are not the indigent but workers, gardeners, hay-makers, villagers, salmon-fishers, the other ranks in an agrarian society as ordered as any army, a society over which Fairfax presides as lord of the manor as surely as he presided over the army as Lord General. Marvell's view of Fairfax distinguishes him both from cruder royalist stereotyping and from the radical notion of the Army Grandee, a coterie-member profiting from the war. Fairfax is an aristocrat and descendant of a 'great Race' (l. 248) who bore arms in service of true religion. The prolix episode of family history, which has Fairfax's great-great-grandfather anticipate the English Reformation by

---

[34] Consider e.g. the architectural symbolism of the broadside, *The Sound Head, Round-Head, Rattle Head* (n.p., n.d.).

rescuing his future wife from 'Suttle Nunns' (l. 94), further stresses the antiquity of Fairfacian commitment to a militant Protestantism.

Critics have noted that, by the early 1650s, there was no reason for the 38-year-old Fairfax or others to suppose his public career was at an end.[35] Friedman has written well on the fragile relationship in the poem between active and contemplative roles: 'To see "Upon Appleton House" as a fanciful retreat from political reality into a world of rural mindlessness is to misread a poem which at almost every moment is torn between the divergent demands of the world and the self.'[36] A principal concern of the poem is to demonstrate how profoundly recollection of the conflict invades ways of perceiving in rural retirement. Neither Marvell nor Fairfax can really be free of the political life of the nation since the countryside and the garden appear suffused by recollections of the war. The grimmer images make less demand on the reader's imagination:

> The Mower now commands the Field;
> In whose new Traverse seemeth wrought
> A camp of Battail newly fought:
> Where, as the Meads with Hay, the Plain
> Lyes quilted ore with Bodies slain:
> The Women that with forks it fling,
> Do represent the Pillaging.   (ll. 418–24)

Marvell transforms rural endeavour into the savagery of a Goya print. Fairfax felt a particular antipathy to the pillaging of the dead and actively sought to discourage it among his own troops.[37] The extended conceit of the garden as an army, offering the pleasurable ingenuity of flowers 'as at *Parade*' and the sentinel bee who 'runs you through, or askes *the Word*' (ll. 309, 320), modulates into a more sombre reflection in which Gaunt's demi-paradise becomes a paradise lost:

> Oh Thou, that dear and happy Isle
> The Garden of the World ere while,
> Thou *Paradise* of four Seas,
> Which *Heaven* planted us to please,
> But, to exclude the World, did guard
> With watry if not flaming Sword;

---

[35] Chernaik, *Poet's Time*, 30; Wilding, *Dragons Teeth*, 169.

[36] D. M. Friedman, *Marvell's Pastoral Art* (London, 1970), 228.

[37] M. A. Gibbs, *The Lord General: A Life of Thomas Fairfax* (London, 1938), 52.

What luckless Apple did we tast,
To make us Mortal, and The Wast?

.   .   .   .

War all this doth overgrow:
We Ord'nance Plant and Powder sow. (ll. 321–8, 343–4)

The 'Horatian Ode' concluded with the militaristic imperative to Cromwell, 'thou the Wars and Fortunes Son | March indefatigably on' (ll. 113–14). 'Upon Appleton House', by presenting the war primarily as an ectype of the Fall and by stressing not gain and glory but 'Wast', offers a radically different perspective. Fairfax's retirement presumably implied that hostilities with the Rump's enemies should be ended not by more war but by reconciliation, perhaps based on recognition that all sides had, in some senses, lost by the war. The incipient triumphalism sounded towards the end of the ode contrasts sharply with the poignancy of 'Upon Appleton House', where even the symbols of retirement are tinged with this sense of loss. Again, the mown meadow provokes a further recollection of Fairfax's active life, 'this naked equal Flat, | Which *Levellers* take Pattern at' (ll. 449–50). Suppressing radical dissidents must remain a task and an obligation, however disagreements may develop between Cromwell, Fairfax, and the Rump. The price of social stability at Nun Appleton and elsewhere is a persistent vigilance by the propertied classes. Men like Fairfax have a responsibility to maintain the social fabric against the militant challenge of politically conscious elements seeking to redefine the political nation.

But it remains, in some ways, a puzzling poem. Parts invite interpretation as political allegory, but when the scheme is disentangled it often falls apart. At one point, the poet, contemplating a woodpecker, considers how 'the *tallest Oak* | Should fall by such a *feeble Strok*' (of the bird's bill), and he concludes:

Nor would it, had the Tree not fed
A *Traitor-worm*, within it bred.
(As first our *Flesh* corrupt within
Tempts impotent and bashful *Sin*.)
And yet that *Worm* triumphs not long,
But serves to feed the *Hewels young*.
While the Oake seems to fall content,
Viewing the Treason's Punishment. (ll. 553–60)

A mind trained to reading symbolic modes enters a paroxysm of allegorical decoding. The oak equals, what? Probably the king (common enough) or perhaps the old regime. The woodpecker has an axe, so it equals the revolutionary Independents. So its young are? beneficiaries of the revolution, fed on what? the estates of royalists? Which makes the culprit, the cause of the decay, the 'Traitor-worm', what? Earlier royalists? Early Stuart courtiers? And the king died happy to see their estates gobbled up? No, that doesn't quite hold together . . . Perhaps it is significant that it should not. The poet cuts off the meditation with 'Thus I, *easie Philosopher*, | Among the *Birds* and *Trees* confer' (ll. 561–2). Perhaps such brooding over culpability is exactly that, easy philosophy, a kind of cerebral indulgence that deflects attention away from the simpler truths, that all now inhabit that 'Wast'. Laying blame is neither easy, useful nor pertinent.

V

The poems considered thus far defy any easy schematizing. The 'Horatian Ode' and particularly 'Upon Appleton House' contain within them, unreconciled, conflicting values and aspirations, and collectively they manifest a degree of ideological disparity which matches other elements of instability within the *œuvre*, such as the labile perspective on human sexuality. Though one may produce possibly convincing readings of a declarative kind about individual poems, to reduce all to order is to falsify the ambivalence that lies at the core of Marvell's early poetry. In sharp contrast, the political poems of the mid and late 1650s, whatever innovation they display, present fewer uncertainties about ideological orientation. Marvell develops a voice to articulate, without discernible reservation, a conservative species first of republicanism and then of Cromwellianism.

'The Character of Holland' (i. 100–3) can confidently be assigned to 1653.[38] Though it was not published then, it would have served well as a sharply turned attack on Dutch character and conduct in support of the Anglo-Dutch War of 1652–4. Some evidence of its potential as an instrument of Government propaganda comes from the release of part of it, presumably without Marvell's consent,

[38] *Poems and Letters*, i. 309.

during the Anglo-Dutch War of 1665–7.[39] Marvell's satire labours to produce a Dutch stereotype, ignoble, given to eccentricities of diet, custom, and, most important, of religion:

> Sure when *Religion* did it self imbark,
> And from the *East* would *Westward* steer its Ark,
> It struck, and splitting on this unknown ground,
> Each one thence pillag'd the first piece he found:
> Hence *Amsterdam, Turk–Christian–Pagan–Jew*,
> Staple of Sects and Mint of Schisme grew.   (ll. 67–72)

The writing is characterized by an expressive precision. The 'shipwreck' of religion picks up early comments on the lowness of the land, easily missed by pilots (ll. 1–8). As Chernaik observes, 'Geography is presented as emblematic of character.'[40] Yet the lines, *mutatis mutandis*, could be from John Taylor railing against parliamentarian London:

> The Citizens of all Trades . . .
> Were hardly more in number, then Religions,
> That one may say of *London*, what a Towne ist,
> Is it quite Metamorphos'd, and turn'd *Brownist*,
> Or shivered into Sects? alas, how apt ist
> To be a Familist, or *Anabaptist*![41]

The parallels point to the strategy of Marvell's attack, for, *pace* Patterson, 'The Character of Holland' is not 'simple-minded jingoism'.[42] Rather, Marvell presents the new ascendancy as the active enemy of misrule and disorder, the defender of Protestant orthodoxy against the Dutch nest of sectaries and blasphemers, transferring English perceptions of dissent to the Dutch.

'The First Anniversary Of the Government under O.C.' (i. 108–9) appeared in 1655 as a pamphlet printed by Thomas Newcomb, who by that time was undertaking much work on behalf of the Cromwellian Government, including the publication a few months earlier of Milton's second Latin defence,[43] to which Marvell's poem has been compared.[44] It offers a sustained panegyric to Cromwell.

---

[39] Ibid.   [40] Chernaik, *Poet's Time*, 163.
[41] John Taylor, *Mad Verse, Sad Verse, Glad Verse and Bad Verse* (n.p., [1644]), 2.
[42] *Civic Crown*, 123.
[43] Plomer, 136. The pamphlet was anonymous. Curiously, the title-page has two parallel horizontal rules, about a centimetre apart, of a kind which usually brackets off some other element of a title-page, such as an epigraph—or the author's name. Was the latter withheld at a late stage of production?
[44] Chernaik, *Poet's Time*, 51.

Marvell flirts with the notion that Cromwell may usher in the millennium:

> Hence oft I think, if in some happy Hour
> High Grace should meet in one with highest Pow'r,
> And then a seasonable People still
> Should bend to his, as he to Heavens will,
> What we might hope, what wonderful Effect
> From such a wish'd Conjuncture might reflect.
> Sure, the mysterious Work, where none withstand,
> Would forthwith finish under such a Hand:
> Fore-shortned Time its useless Course would stay,
> And soon precipitate the latest Day.   (ll. 131–40)

A tepid and provisional aspect pervades this version of millenarianism. 'Oft I think' concedes 'oft I don't think', and 'think' implies something more tentative than the robust if vague certainties that usually characterize prophetic utterance. Such heady material rests curiously on conditional clauses, and the mood peters out in:

> But Men alas, as if they nothing car'd,
> Look on, all unconcern'd, and unprepar'd;
>
> .   .   .   .   .   .
>
> Hence landing Nature to new Seas is tost,
> And good Designes still with their Authors lost.
>   (ll. 149–50, 157–8)

The vision fades in recognition that others do not share it. Evidently even the congruent wishes of God and Cromwell, unaided, are insufficient to produce the *annus mirabilis*.

Marvell's Cromwell really offers a political direction far less revolutionary than the half-hearted millenarianism implies. Traditional monarchs regard him primarily with envy of his energy and success. Whatever opposition they show is premised not on constitutional principles but on a pragmatic rivalry, and more sensible ones regard him with high respect: 'by his Beams observing Princes steer, | And wisely court the Influence they fear' (ll. 103–4). Domestically, Cromwell functions to control those who threaten property, order, and religious decency. As he did in 'The Character of Holland', Marvell once more distinguishes those whom he would defend from the old stereotype of the radical *enragé* by demonstrating their own opposition to such firebrands. He plays the familiar game of mixing together a range of heterodox opinion so each seems tarred with the most dubious elements of them all. Thus, the Fifth

Monarchists Christopher Feake and Sydrach Simpson, who had been imprisoned in 1654 for preaching against Cromwell, are associated with Quakers (l. 298), with Ranters (l. 307), with Adamites (l. 319), with Muslims (l. 303), and with 'Wand'rers, Adult'rers, Lyers, *Munser's* rest, ꞁ Sorcerers, Atheists, Jesuites, Possest' (ll. 313–14). How fortunate that Cromwell, 'the great Captain' (l. 321), can make them tremble.

The poem concludes:

> Pardon, great Prince, if thus [foreign ambassadors'] Fear or Spight
> More then our Love and Duty do thee Right.
> I yield, nor further will the Prize contend;
> So that we both alike may miss our End:
> While thou thy venerable head dost raise
> As far above their Malice as my Praise.
> And as the *Angel* of our Commonweal,
> Troubling the Waters, yearly mak'st them Heal.   (ll. 395–402)

'Great Prince' offers Cromwell as a sort of continuity to those who may still have doubts about government without a king. He, like the best tradition of English monarchy, offers stability and a defence of order and property. The apostrophe to Cromwell and the pronominalization ('we . . . our . . . thou . . . thy') repay attention. By the end of this long poem, Marvell ventures to speak to Cromwell on behalf of the broad spectrum of the English political nation.

'On the Victory obtained by Blake over the Spaniards, in the Bay of Sanctacruze, in the Island of Teneriff. 1657' (i. 119–24) consolidates the conservative panegyric of Cromwell, further integrating him into an amended version of a royalist world outlook. Editors note that Cromwell had already declined the proffered crown before news of Blake's victory reached England.[45] Yet Marvell proceeds as if Cromwell's role were straightforwardly that of a king: 'Your worth to all these Isles, a just right brings, ꞁ The best of Lands should have the best of Kings' (ll. 39–40). Indeed, by a curious irony, this Cromwellian panegyric works by attributing to the 'monarch' glory occasioned by the success of his subordinate (ll. 167–8). In 'The First Anniversary' Marvell had suggested that, though ordinary princes may triumph vicariously, Cromwell, in contradistinction, achieves his victories in his own person (ll. 23–8). One could read 'On the Victory' without any

---

[45] *Poems and Letters*, i. 330.

consciousness that the success celebrated is that of a republic. The constitutional issues no longer exercise Marvell's concern. Similarly, his 'Two Songs at the Marriage of the Lord Fauconberg and the Lady Mary Cromwell' (i. 125–9) offer a controlled, courtly pastoral which could as easily have marked a ritual of the Caroline court in the 1630s.

'A Poem on the Death of O.C.' (i. 129–37) was intended for publication with the elegies of Dryden and Sprat, though for reasons that are probably now irrecoverable, it was withdrawn from the collection and replaced by Waller's poem on the same subject.[46] Marvell bases his lament on the paradox that Cromwell, though a lofty, triumphant, almost transcendent, prince, was heir to the mortality of ordinary people, and could be brought to his end by grief for the death of his daughter (ll. 21–88). Thereafter, his achievement is contextualized in a broad view of English history, commemorating a 'Monarch' (l. 169) whose valour 'less[ens] *Arthur's* deeds' and 'For Holyness the *Confessor* exceeds' (ll. 177–8). Cromwell now differs from other monarchs not in kind but in achievement. With further irony, the poem ends in anticipation of the reign of Richard Cromwell (ll. 305–24). Again, 'The First Anniversary' had characterized Cromwellian rule as non-hereditary, unlike the rule of other rulers: 'Well may they strive to leave them to their Son, | For one Thing never was by one King don' (ll. 21–2). Marvell's early ideological wanderings found easy anchorage in the simplicities of a revived (Cromwellian) monarchism.

VI

Gerald Hammond's recent reading of Lovelace, besides doing something to rehabilitate his low artistic reputation, has questioned the simplicity of the poet's political perspective. His attempt to read as 'neutralist' many of the poems of the first *Lucasta* discloses certain misapprehensions about the concept of neutralism in the English Civil War and rests in part on some curious interpretations. His notion that 'To Lucasta, from Prison' 'refuses to deliver its expected cavalier sentiment'[47] runs counter to the reading I have developed above,[48] nor does 'To my Worthy Friend Mr Peter Lilly:

[46] *Poems and Letters* i. 332.
[47] Hammond, 'Lovelace', 213
[48] Ch. 4.

On that Excellent Picture of His Majesty, and the Duke of York' subvert panegyric quite as he suggests. The poem rehearses both the tragic dignity of the king and Lely's skill in depicting it evocatively. The detachment that Hammond claims for Lely and Lovelace is based on a rather perverse reading of the line 'Thou sorrow canst designe without a teare' (Lovelace, *Poems*, 58), which, he claims, refers not only to Lely's ability to penetrate the 'stoical appearance' of his royal sitters, but also to the artist's necessary detachment, that he paints their sorrow without himself feeling it.[49] Yet, if we look at the verse paragraph in which the line occurs, we see clearly that Lovelace addresses questions not about the sympathies of artists but about the semiotics of art, and most specifically of how emotion may be represented in portraiture. Once external emblems or 'Hieroglyphicks', as he calls them, expressed qualities and feelings. Thus, 'a black beard' meant the wearer was a 'Villaine'. But Lely can 'designe' sorrow, that is, point it out with a distinctive sign, mark, or token,[50] without the hieroglyphic device of painting a tear in the subject's eye, because of his capacity to replicate expression. I assume that Lely's sympathy with his subject is not stated because it is taken for granted: the portrait is not a dismissal of royal iconography, but rather an enhancement and deepening of the panegyric tradition, such as we find again in *Eikon Basilike*.

Hammond's assiduous search for the 'neutralism' of the first *Lucasta* probably has much to do with his attempts to make sense of the little we know of Lovelace's biography in the 1640s and 1650s. Why did he go abroad after release from prison in 1642 rather than fighting in the armies of the king? Why wasn't he at Cropredy Bridge in 1644, fighting and perhaps dying with other youngish Kentish royalists?[51] Hammond rather narrows the range of possible explanations to an improbable reluctance to take arms for the king. For all we know, his release in 1642 may have been conditional on an undertaking, which many defeated royalists had to give, that he would not bear arms against Parliament.

But Hammond astutely alerts us to distinctions between the first *Lucasta* and *Lucasta: Posthume Poems* (1659). It has been argued that the former is, with some qualifications arising from the

[49] Hammond, 'Lovelace', 222.
[50] *OED*; Weidhorn, *Lovelace*, has a sounder reading of the poem, 34–5.
[51] Hammond, 'Lovelace', 217.

escapism of 'Aramantha', a solidly partisan enunciation of die-hard loyalism. In the latter, other voices persistently break in.

Once again, we find quite frequently military imagery of a kind that playfully sets aside its horrific associations. Thus, fear 'doth barricadoe Hope' from the ears of Lucasta's admirers ('Lucasta Laughing', *Poems*, 122–3), and, in a familiar kind of conceit, 'Volley of sighs' and 'Grones, like a Canon Ball' are despatched by the frustrated lover at his mistress ('In allusion to the *French-Song*', 124). Some items have a strident partisanship. 'A Mock-Song' (154–5) tipsily parodies the gleeful motifs of parliamentarian propaganda. 'He that Tarquin was styl'd'—a clear allusion, *pace* Hammond, to the familiar republican formula for Charles II[52]—is exiled, while republicans let their voices rise to cry, 'Long live the brave *Oliver-Brutus*', and fatuously conclude their song with the refrain 'our Dragon hath vanquish'd the St. *George*'. A curious minor subgenre of seventeenth-century literature is the dialogue with Charon, a form in which someone recently deceased is presented in negotiation with the boatman *en route* to the underworld. In Lovelace's poem, 'A Mock-Charon' (pp. 161–2), Charon's interlocutor, identified, as in a riddle, as 'W.',[53] is a parliamentarian, for he hails Charon, 'Thou Slave! Thou Fool! Thou Cavaleer!' Lovelace scores a bantering, partisan hit as he has hell's devils greet 'W.' with chagrin at his transcendent villainy:

> *Double Chorus of Divels*
> Welcome to Rape, to Theft, to Perjurie,
> To all the ills thou wert, we cannot hope to be;
> Oh pitty us condemn'd! Oh cease to wooe,
> And softly, softly breath, lest you infect us too.   (*Poems* 162)

Lovelace, even in such twilight of royalist fortunes, writes here with the frank and uncompromising hostility of John Cleveland or John Taylor.

Other poems in the second *Lucasta* catch a tone reminiscent of some of Herrick's *Hesperides*. The classical tradition runs nearer to the surface than in the 1649 volume. The latter part of Lovelace's 'Advice to my Best Brother Coll: Francis Lovelace' is modelled

---

[52] *Selected Poems*, 109, identifies 'Tarquin' with Charles I; *Poems*, 310, associates the line with the recurrent use of 'Young Tarquin' as an epithet for Charles II.
[53] Wilkinson's suggestion (*Poems*, 314), that Lovelace intended Philip, fourth Baron Wharton, seems improbable, since, as Wilkinson observes, Wharton did not die until 1696.

closely on Horace, *Odes*, II. x, but considerably—and evocatively—expanded. Horace's 'informes hiemes reducit I Iuppiter; idem I summovet' ('Jupiter brings back the unlovely winters; he also takes them away')[54] becomes:

> That mighty breath which blew foul Winter hither,
> Can eas'ly puffe it to a fairer weather.
> Why dost despair then, *Franck*? *Æolus* has
> A *Zephyrus* as well as a *Boreas*.   (*Poems*, 176)

The elaboration of Horace's image in terms of the succession of prevailing atmospheric circumstances brings Lovelace's poem close to Herrick's 'Hope Well and Have Well, or, Faire after Foule weather' or, closer still, 'Farewell Frost, or, Welcome the Spring', which makes an explicit political statement.[55] Lovelace's advice to his brother, defeated royalist commander at the siege of Carmarthen, and by implication to other defeated activists urges with guarded optimism that they should sit tight and wait for their fortunes to improve: in Horace's phrase, 'non, si male nunc, et olim I sic erit',[56] or, in Lovelace's, ''Tis a false Sequel, Solecisme . . . to suppose I That 'cause it is now ill, 't will ere be so.'

But other voices, more desperate, more bitter, more uncertain of their loyalties, break through: 'a plague on both your houses' underlies a few poems. Sexual libertinism as a mode of oppositionalism probably inspired some of the more erotic lyrics of the first *Lucasta*, and, even there, the poet's pose assumed at times a disturbing amorality, as, for example, in 'The Faire Beggar'.[57] In his second volume, a sordid carnality pollutes and corrupts the world outlook produced within such works. 'Her Muffe' begins as a celebration of Lucasta's cruel beauty, as her 'polish'd hands' fiercely 'deeper pierce' her muff, to produce which 'Beasts' had to 'strip themselves to make you gay'. Yet this poem of elaborate compliment, couched often in terms of neatly turned heraldic imagery, is subverted by the final stanza:

> This for Lay-Lovers, that must stand at dore,
> Salute the threshold, and admire no more:
>   But I, in my Invention tough,
>   Rate not this outward bliss enough,
> But still contemplate must the hidden Muffe.   (*Poems*, 129)

---

[54] Horace, *Odes*, II. x. 15–17.
[56] Horace, *Odes*, II. x. 17–18.
[55] Above, Ch. 4.
[57] Above, Ch. 4.

Hammond claims that this poem antedates Partridge's (and the *OED*'s) first record of 'Muff' being used as a slang term for the female pudendum. Lovelace's usage, however, does not demonstrate its colloquial currency, nor does it matter much whether the poem here appropriates slang: the metaphor is transparent enough, and the lover's assertion that, for him, looking at his mistress's genitals is more rewarding than looking at her hands is crude both in expression and sentiment: the word 'hidden' saves the reader any puzzlement about what Lovelace's is talking about (and would have been redundant had 'Muff' been widely current as a word for the female genitalia). Hammond, who seeks to identify a theme of autoeroticism in the second *Lucasta* which he would interpret ideologically, asserts that 'Female masturbation is the object' of the poem.[58] It can scarcely be that, for as a metaphoric description of the process the first four stanzas are rather imprecise and not wholly apposite, though in a vague, obliquely suggestive way, the notion may be read into the rest of the poem after the surprise of the final stanza. What matters is the way in which the concluding coarseness abandons both the ethic and the aesthetic of courtly eroticism: the rake has become the lout.

   Such boorishness assumes a political dimension, as though dereliction of aristocratic responsibility and the adoption of an ironic vulgarity are legitimate stratagems for mental withdrawal from a lost cause. The 'loose Saraband' of the second *Lucasta* (pp. 139–41) contrasts sharply with the elegant trifle of the same name in the first book (pp. 32–4), and, indeed, with the defiant invocation of Bacchus in 'The Vintage to the Dungeon' (p. 46) or the central stanzas of 'To Althea, from Prison' (pp. 78–9). In the later poem the poet and his mistress, a 'fair Cripple | That dumb canst scarcely see | Th' almightinesse of Tipple', inebriatedly view the way of the world:

> See all the World how 't staggers,
>   More ugly drunk than we,
> As of far gone in daggers,
>   And blood it seem'd to be.

The poem ends tipsily rehearsing Falstaffian values:

---

[58] Hammond, 'Lovelace', 228–9.

> Now, is there such a Trifle
>   As Honour, the fools Gyant?
>
>   .   .   .   .
>
> Let others Glory follow,
> In their false riches wallow,
> And with their grief be merry;
> Leave me but Love and Sherry. (pp. 140–1)

Not quite the voice which articulated the paradox, 'I could not love thee (Deare) so much, | Lov'd I not Honour more.'

The poems of the first *Lucasta*, though reflective of a temporary discomfort, are premissed upon assumptions of a courtier's affluence. When the speaker addresses people of quality, he does so as a member of their caste, without supplication. Later an esurient edge mars the tone of some poems of compliment, as in the long poem to his benefactor Charles Cotton, 'The Triumphs of Philamore and Amoret' (pp. 169–74).[59] Cotton had retired to his Staffordshire estate as part of the process of his marriage to Isabella Hutchinson. The hymeneal dimension, however, is largely overshadowed by the poet's rehearsal of his regrets for his patron's absence and his eager anticipation of his return. His dream vision of the triumph of the couple terminates in an awakening to the recognition of his indigence while Cotton is away:

> Thus *Poets* who all Night in blest Heav'n dwell,
> Are call'd next morn to their true living *Hell*;
> So I unthrifty, to my self untrue,
> Rise cloath'd with real wants, 'cause wanting you. (p. 174)

It is doubtful that we shall ever know with certainty the accuracy of the accounts in Lovelace's earliest biographies that he spent his later years in destitution,[60] but in his later poems Cavalierism has an unmistakable threadbare aspect.

Indeed, poverty sometimes functions as the badge of probity, as the sure evidence that this poet at least has not prostituted his talents at the court of Oliver-Brutus. Consider that gem of a poem, 'To a Lady with Child that Ask'd an Old Shirt' (pp. 148–9): conventionally, it seems, women preparing for childbirth could solicit gifts of linen from their circle of acquaintance:

---

[59] On Lovelace's debts to Cotton, see *Poems* pp. lvi–lvii.

[60] *Poems* pp. lv–lvii; Hammond, 'Lovelace', 230–4.

And why an honour'd ragged Shirt, that shows,
Like tatter'd Ensigns, all its Bodies blows?
Should it be swathed in a vest so dire,
It were enough to set the Child on fire

.   .   .   .   .

But since to Ladies't hath a Custome been
Linnen to send, that travail and lye in;
To the nine Sempstresses, my former friends,
I su'd, but they had nought but shreds and ends.
At last, the jolli'st of the three times three,
Rent th'apron from her smock, and gave it me,
'Twas soft and gentle, subt'ly spun no doubt;
Pardon my boldness, Madam; *Here's the clout.*

The poverty suggested by his garment seemingly has its origins in
the sacrifices of the Civil War: it is an 'honour'd ragged Shirt', and
the simile, 'Like tatter'd Ensigns' makes the connection more
strongly. The poem's central manœuvre, by which it describes the
gift which the lyric itself becomes, has a disturbing, rather
modernist, reflexivity. Lovelace offers his gift with little apology—
'*Here's the clout*'—for, though it symbolizes his material poverty, it
comes, nevertheless, from the muses, as a token that, though not
with the facility of earlier years (they are 'my *former* friends'), he
retains still his integrity as a creative artist.

VII

In the 1630s Cowley had written frequently in celebration of
occasions for royal rejoicing. In 1639 he published poems on the
birth of Charles's son, the Duke of Gloucester. With a poignantly
inept loyalty he even celebrated the conclusion of the Scottish
campaign with:

Others by *War* their *Conquests* gain,
You like a *God* your ends obtain.
Who when rude *Chaos* for his help did call,
Spoke but the *Word*, and sweetly *Order'd* all.[61]

In March 1642 his play *The Guardian* was staged by Trinity
College, Cambridge as an entertainment for the visiting Charles,

---

[61] Abraham Cowley, *Poems*, ed. A. R. Waller (Cambridge, 1905), 22.

Prince of Wales. The play is premissed on commonplace anti-Puritan stereotyping of enemies, but it manifests a new awareness that performers and audience were destined to live in interesting times. Its prologue, besides praising the 14-year-old guest of honour ('When you appeare, great Prince, our night is done'), perceptively warns that such events would not withstand a Puritan victory: 'We perish if the Roundheads be about.'[62] The tone may be facetious, but the prophecy, unusually for Cowley, was accurate. By the time the Earl of Manchester entered Cambridge in February 1644 to administer the Solemn League and Covenant to members of the university, Cowley had already withdrawn to the royalists' temporary capital, Oxford, where he would seem to have entered into the service of Henry Jermyn, Baron of St Edmundsbury, secretary and aide to Queen Henrietta Maria. He left Oxford some time before its fall in the summer of 1646, and he spent the late 1640s in exile, working as secretary to Jermyn (and thus, indirectly, to the queen), mainly working at the task of enciphering and deciphering clandestine correspondence.[63]

His principal publication of the 1640s was a small, neatly produced volume of love lyrics, *The Mistresse*, published by Humphrey Moseley in 1647. Moseley's preface explains that the text had to be printed without the author's direct involvement, though he does not explicitly mention the author's exile as the source of the difficulty. Though less libertine than Lovelace's *Lucasta* and without the frequency of that volume's direct allusion to the wars, *The Mistresse* assiduously rehearses the values and enthusiasms of the Caroline court. The relationship it posits and seemingly celebrates is carnal and extramarital, and implies a life-style of libertine eroticism among the well-to-do. Thus, the lover attempts to coax the mistress from her clothing:

> Fairest thing that shines below,
> Why in this robe dost thou appear?
> Wouldst thou a *white* most perfect show,
> Thou must at all *no garment* wear.
> ('Clad All in White', *Poems* (1905), *77*).

---

[62] Abraham Cowley, *The Guardian: A Comedie Acted before Prince Charls His Highness* (London, 1650), sig. A2ʳ. The Prologue appears also in 'Miscellanies', *Poems* (London, 1656), 15. Biographical information is from A. H. Nethercot, *Abraham Cowley: The Muse's Hannibal* (London, 1931), 72–89.

[63] Ibid. 80–99.

With a gynaecological intricacy perhaps appropriate to a poet who would later study medicine, Cowley has his lover meditate on the nature and function of the hymeneal membrane:

> Slight, outward *Curtain* to the *Nuptial Bed!*
>
> .   .   .   .   .   .
>
> Thou that bewitchest men, whilst thou dost dwell
>   Like a close *Conj'urer* in his *Cell!*
>   And fear'st the days discovering Eye!   ('Maidenhead', 129)

After a series of lubricious metaphors, the poet concludes, for once in a flippantly martial vein that would not be out of place in Lovelace:

> In vain to honour they pretend,
> Who guard themselves with *Ramparts* and with *Walls*,
> Them only fame the truly valiant calls,
> Who can an *open breach* defend.   (p. 130)

A pun on 'breech', meaning the hinderparts, maintains the tone of smutty gallantry.[64]

After the libertine posture, the principal area of ideological interest in *The Mistresse* comes from casual and sometimes facetious allusion to contemporary political life, particularly in Continental Europe, as in 'The Passions':

> Fear, Anger, Hope, all Passions else that be,
>   Drive this one *Tyrant* [love] out of me,
>   And practise all your *Tyranny*.
>   The change of ills some good will do:
>   Th'oppressed wretched *Indians* so,
> Be'ing slaves by the great *Spanish Monarch* made,
> Call in the *States* of *Holland* to their aid.   (p. 85)

Other examples of equating aspects of sexual love to contemporary political life abound. The effect is to produce an image of the speaker as a man of such political sophistication that connections and analogies between public and private life occur naturally to him: the roles of lover and exiled servant of the royal cause interanimate each other, much as those of soldier and lover do in the first *Lucasta*.

The impeccability of Cowley's previous loyalism defines an

[64] *OED.*

important element in the political and literary context of the publication in 1656 of his *Poems*. The handsome folio volume, published, like *The Mistresse*, by Humphrey Moseley, carries on its title-page an epigraph from Virgil's third *Georgic*, which reads in a modern edition, 'temptanda via est, qua me quoque possim | tollere humo victorque virum volitare per ora', that is, 'I must find a way to raise myself from the earth and fly victorious, my name on the lips of men.'[65] Since the volume contains little in georgic mode, the text must be read, I think, essentially as a psychological marker: this volume raises the poet from the depths and constitutes an attempt in some sense to consolidate the achievement of a literary career which had once promised much. The lines that follow immediately in Virgil's poem may suggest themselves to the alert reader: 'primus ego in patriam mecum, modo vita supersit, | Aonio rediens deducam vertice Musas' ('I will be the first—if only life be long enough—to return to my homeland bringing the Muses down with me from the peak of Mount Aonia [i.e. Helicon]').[66] For this volume represents Cowley's first wholly public act since he returned from exile to his *patria*, bringing with him the fruits of his muse.

The purpose and nature of his return from honourable exile to the England of the Cromwellian ascendancy were clouded and controversial in his own day, and it is unlikely we shall with certainty determine what he really sought to achieve by his change of role. His *Poems* (1656), as we shall see, is, ideologically, a complex and enigmatic volume which needs tentative and sensitive interpretation.

Why had Cowley returned? The Act of Oblivion of 1652[67] had tempted home many of his friends, and by various routes and mechanisms Evelyn and Davenant, Waller and Hobbes had established a *modus vivendi* within Cromwellian England. Cowley's return would seem to have been under a passport issued in May 1654 on the authority of Cromwell himself, instructing 'all our Admirals, &c.' to grant Cowley passage from France to England.[68] Thomas Sprat, Cowley's friend and literary executor, in the introduction he wrote to the collected *Works* he published in 1668,

---

[65] *Georgics*, iii. 8–9, in *Virgil: The Eclogues and Georgics*, ed. R. D. Williams (New York, 1979), 57; trans. G. B. Miles, *Virgil's Georgics: A New Interpretation* (Berkeley, Los Angeles, and London, 1980), 167.

[66] *Georgics*, iii. 10–11; Miles, *Virgil's Georgics*, 167.

[67] *Acts and Ordinances*, ii. 565–77.

[68] Nethercot, *Cowley*, 143.

addresses the matter carefully. It seems possible that Cowley had, indeed, intended to work in the royalist underground. Certainly, Thurloe, responsible for countering such subversion, had been advised that the returned exile was probably suspect by Colonel Bampfield, a former royalist agent now clandestinely in the employ of the Protectorate, and in April 1655 Cowley, along with other royalists then living in London, was arrested at night by a company of Cromwellian soldiers. He was subsequently interrogated by both Thurloe and Cromwell, and was eventually released on bail in the sum of £1,000.[69] The other terms of his release remain obscure and have been the subject of speculation in his own time and later. Some certainly suspected that, like Bampfield before him, he had entered into the service of the new establishment. Contemporary anecdote, frequently cited, reports that, after the Restoration, when Cowley sought preferment in recompense for his sufferings in the royalist cause, Clarendon dismissed him with 'Mr. Cowley, your pardon is your reward.'[70] They had belonged to different factions during the years of exile—Clarendon's group had gradually displaced the influence of the Louvre party of Henrietta Maria and Jermyn, to which Cowley was attached, but the frostiness, if the anecdote is correct, may suggest that Cowley was perceived as tainted, perhaps because of the public stance associated with *Poems* (1656), perhaps, as Underdown suggests, because indiscreet associations with Thurloe's spy Bampfield brought him under suspicion of a more dangerous kind of disloyalty.[71]

The hindsights of the Restoration may have some value, even mediated by unreliable transmission and the prejudices of coterie politicians. The ideological crisis which Cowley faced in the mid–1650s provides a more precise context for interpretation of *Poems* (1656). The year of his arrest, 1655, was a climactic year for the royalist underground. Its opening months witnessed the outbreak and disastrous end of the most important royalist enterprise since the catastrophe of Worcester, what is usually termed 'Penruddock's Rising', though its 'leaders' were many and its organization was scattered and only partially co-ordinated by John Penruddock. Underdown summarizes the rising thus:

[69] Nethercot, *Cowley*, 141, 149–57.
[70] Ibid. 199.
[71] D. E. Underdown, *Royalist Conspiracy in England 1649–1660* (New Haven, 1960), 318. On Bampfield's relationship with the Louvre party, see pp. 62–3.

The most obvious conclusion is that the Royalists were entirely incompetent in both strategy and tactics. 'The truth is,' said Clarendon of
Penruddock's venture, 'they did nothing resolutely after their first action.'
. . . preparations were disastrously inadequate. Liaison between the widely
separated centers of conspiracy frequently broke down. . . . news even of
such an important decision as a change of date [for a general uprising] could
somehow fail to reach the rank and file. There were bewildering
uncertainties and duplications of command. . . . Against this background of
disorganization and incompetence must be set the solid strength and
efficiency of the government's countermeasures.[72]

The rising foundered in March, and Cowley's arrest in the
following month presumably belonged to the wave of repression
that followed. On Underdown's account, the royalist arrests
occurred in two stages: in the first, in March and April, the
authorities were mainly concerned with ringleaders; the second
widened the range to be harried.[73] That Cowley came high on the
list may be chance, it may suggest he was associating with more
serious activists, or even that he himself was perceived as a
significant figure. The rising had owed nothing in its planning to the
faction with which he had been associated in exile, though it is
possible that he had seen himself—and was seen by Thurloe and his
cohorts—as in some ways retaining an involvement with the
royalist underground on behalf of his former masters.

Certainly, he felt much of the force of the repression which
Penruddock's Rising had produced, and from a position of
considerable personal difficulty witnessed the utter bankruptcy of
the cause. Cromwell, who had previously sought a *modus vivendi*
with those royalists prepared to come to terms, became increasingly
convinced that the Cavaliers were irreconcilable, that safety lay only
in repression, and that the commonwealth could be established and
maintained only by a more direct intervention of the army in
Government. By the summer of 1656, the Major Generals had been
established as a regional system of military government which put
an absolute stop to united royalist action.[74] Whatever Cowley had
hoped for on his return, he experienced at first hand the complete
collapse of the royalist cause. *Poems* (1656) is shot through with a
sense of the finality of the events of 1655–6: the fantasies with which
the royalist resistance had fed itself are discredited and abandoned.

[72] Ibid. 153–4.   [73] Ibid. 160.   [74] Ibid. 161, 169.

VIII

Nothing in the volume suggests a conscious wish to effect his rehabilitation through praise of Cromwell. His dedicatory elegy is directed to praise Cambridge, his Alma Mater, though the option was open to dedicate it, politically, to the new establishment. After the dedicatory poem comes a complex prose preface and four sections, 'Miscellanies', 'The Mistress', 'Pindarique Odes', and 'Davideis', each with its own title-page, though the signature runs continuously through the whole volume. At no point does Cowley disguise, mitigate, or apologize for his loyalty to Charles I or his son. The first section includes a number of early occasional poems relating to the Caroline court. The second retains the Cavalier love lyrics published in 1647 with the addition of six new lyrics, much in the same idiom. In his preface he concedes very little to prudish readers:

I speak to excuse some expressions (if such there be) which may happen to offend the severity of supercilious [i.e. 'censorious'[75]] *Readers*; for much *Excess* is to be allowed in *Love*, and even more in *Poetry*; so we avoid the two unpardonable vices in both, which are *Obscenity* and *Prophaness*, of which I am sure, if my *words* be ever guilty, they have ill represented my *thoughts* and *intentions*.[76]

Thus, the volume retains much of his earlier verse, with the ideological values inscribed within it, as an abiding record of cultural royalism. However, other sections pose much greater problems, to which I now turn. As others have recognized, Cowley's pindaric odes offer open, rather enigmatic texts which require a tentative and sceptical reading.[77] Again, 'Davideis' is the second epic undertaking that Cowley abandoned incomplete. Unlike his first, on the Civil War, which survives today only in a fragment published in the Restoration and in rare manuscript copies only recently come to light, Cowley vouchsafed his second epic to

---

[75] *OED.*

[76] Cowley, *Poems* (1656), sig. b1[r].

[77] See esp. A. Patterson, *Censorship and Interpretation: The Conditions of Writing and Reading in Early Modern England* (Madison, Wisc., 1984), 144–58, for a discussion premissed on similar assumptions; also, R. Nevo, *The Dial of Virtue: A Study of Poems on Affairs of State in the Seventeenth Century* (Princeton, 1963), 81–7, 120–1; T. R. Langley, 'Abraham Cowley's "Brutus": Royalist or Republican?' *YES* 6 (1976), 41–52; D. Trotter, *The Poetry of Abraham Cowley* (London and Basingstoke, 1979), 133–8.

the world, though, as we shall see, its incompleteness is part of a set of serious problems in interpretation.[78] In his preface he links this second epic to the first, which he says, was abandoned because 'the succeeding *misfortunes* of the *party* stopt the *work*'. He continues in lines which Sprat saw fit to delete in his Restoration edition:

for it is so uncustomary, as to become almost *ridiculous*, to make *Lawrels* for the *Conquered*. Now though in all *Civil Dissentions*, when they break into open hostilities, the *War* of the *Pen* is allowed to accompany that of the *Sword*, and every one is in a maner obliged with his *Tongue*, as well as *Hand*, to serve and assist the side which he engages in; yet when the event of battel, and the unaccountable *Will* of *God* has determined the controversie, and that we have submitted to the conditions of the *Conqueror*, we must lay down our *Pens* as well as *Arms*, we must *march* out of our *Cause* it self, and *dismantle* that, as well as our *Towns* and *Castles*, of all the *Works* and *Fortifications* of *Wit* and *Reason* by which we defended it. *We* ought not sure, to begin our selves to revive the remembrance of those times and actions for which we have received a *General Amnestie*, as a *favor* from the *Victor*. The truth is, neither *We*, nor *They*, ought by the *Representation* of *Places* and *Images* to make a kind of *Artificial Memory* of those things wherein we are all bound to desire like *Themistocles*, the *Art* of *Oblivion*. The *enmities* of *Fellow-Citizens* should be, like that of *Lovers*, the *Redintegration* of their *Amity*. The Names of *Party*, and *Titles* of *Division*, which are sometimes in effect the whole quarrel, should be extinguished and forbidden in peace under the notion of *Acts* of *Hostility*. And I would have it accounted no less unlawful to *rip up old wounds*, then to *give new ones*; which has made me not onely abstain from printing any things of this kinde, but to burn the very copies, and inflict a severer punishment on them my self, then perhaps the most rigid Officer of *State* would have thought that they deserved (*Poems* (1656), sig. a4^{r-v}).

Patterson sees in this passage at least one element of disingenuousness, in that we know Cowley not to have destroyed all copies of his *Civil War*, though he may have tried to suppress it and failed: once a manuscript copy is in circulation it may not easily be recalled or controlled by its author, as writers often complain.[79] Yet the passage does repay close reading, for it is carefully phrased. Cowley begins with a familiar equation of pen and sword, but the image concretizes around a more precise notion of royalist literature as

---

[78] Abraham Cowley, *The Civil War*, ed. A. Pritchard (Toronto, 1973).
[79] Consider the familiar complaint that poor copies in private circulation have been used as copy-text by pirate printers, e.g. in Sir Thomas Browne, *Religio Medici* ed. L. C. Martin (Oxford, 1964), 1–2.

essentially defensive, the exercise of ingenuity in protection of a threatened value system. His silence on the magnanimity of the enemy is surely significant: the epithetless, unqualified '*favor* from the *Victor*' seems the least he could have said. They have won through 'event of battel' (that is, fate as it works in the context of battle)[80] and the 'unaccountable *Will* of God', that is, the inexplicable[81] will of God, who mysteriously tests the godly. By implication Cowley rejects any concession to the familiar parliamentary or Cromwellian view of events as the manifestation of God's endorsement of their cause. Moreover, the phrase 'neither *We*, nor *They*, ought . . . to make a kind of *Artificial Memory*' of the recent past is as much a requirement that the victors should forgo their triumphalism as an assent that the vanquished abandon their perseverance, if a genuine reconciliation is to be achieved.

Cowley's decision to include this passage may have constituted in itself a submission 'to the conditions of the *Conqueror*'. However, the passage may usefully be juxtaposed with other sections of the preface which disclose, if not an explicit note of surrender, then at least an impulse towards quietism and retreat. Cowley offers his collected works as if they were a posthumous publication, for he is, in some sense, 'a *Dead*, or at least a *Dying Person*', at least in terms of his creativity, his muse now 'appearing, like the *Emperor Charls the Fifth*, and *assisting* at her own *Funeral*' (sig. a2ʳ). The extinction of his poetic genius is related directly to the political climate, because 'a warlike, various, and a tragical age is best to *write of*, but worst to *write in*' (sig. a2ᵛ):

The truth is, for a man to write well, it is necessary to be in good humor; neither is *Wit* less eclypsed with the unquietness of *Mind*, then *Beauty* with the *Indisposition* of *Body*. So that 'tis almost as hard a thing to be a *Poet* in despight of *Fortune*, as it is in despight of *Nature* (sig. a3ʳ).

He concludes this argument with a fantasy—perhaps a seriously intended resolution—of rural retreat 'to some of our *American Plantations*', there, not to rediscover his poetic abilities, but, in a significant variant from the usual georgic topos, rather once more to 'bury' himself and his muse (sig. a3ᵛ). His retreat is not to the muses' bower but to a land without muses. So clear is Cowley's sense of the social and political role of poetry that he finds no purpose in it once

---

[80] *OED*, s.v. 'Event'.   [81] *OED*.

it is divorced from its proper cultural context: '*Doctor Donnes Sun Dyal in a grave* is not more useless and ridiculous then *Poetry* would be in that *retirement*' (sig. a3ᵛ).

Cowley's preface, then, stands grimly before his collected works. A valedictory tone suffuses it, and it is a valediction to both political activism and poetic genius. If in the notorious passage Cowley appears to be wrapping himself in the white flag of surrender, other, equally poignant sections show him trying on his winding-sheet.

IX

We know little of the time and circumstance of the composition of the pindaric odes. Nethercot, extrapolating from Sprat's account, sees their inception in Cowley's personal discovery of Pindar, probably during a protracted visit on Jermyn's business to Jersey in 1651, though his production of odes, and probably his revision of the earliest ones, presumably continued to 1656.[82] Cowley takes pains to indicate that poems in this idiom require readers to have their wits about them.[83] In his general preface, he warns, 'I am in great doubt whether they will be understood by most *Readers*; nay, even by very many who are well enough acquainted with the Common Roads, and ordinary Tracks of *Poesie*' (*Poems* (1656), sig. b1ʳ), an anxiety he returns to in the preface to the odes themselves and in the ode, 'The Resurrection' (*Poems* (1905) 22, 183). Particularly, he emphasizes the tangential, digressive element in Pindar's method. It is, however, an idiom well suited to complex political expression that would both elude the dangers of explicitness and allow the conscious exploration of ideological contradictions. For Cowley the cryptographer and Cowley the activist the pindaric proves a rich resource in a period of crisis.

Sometimes, Cowley seems to be rehearsing the values and aspirations of the royalist underground. 'The Plagues of Egypt', his pindaric setting of the narrative of the exodus from Egyptian bondage, offers a vision of a corrupt nation treated better than it deserved, a people led to freedom through the energetic piety of its leadership, despite its own false perspectives and blindness. It opens:

---

[82] Nethercot, *Cowley*, 128–39. [83] Patterson, *Censorship*, 146.

Is this thy *Brav'ery* Man, is this thy *Pride*?
   Rebel to *God*, and *Slave* to all beside!
Captiv'ed by everything! and onely *Free*
   To fly from thine *own Libertie*!
All *Creatures* the *Creator* said *Were Thine*;
No *Creature* but might since, say, *Man* is *Mine*!
In black *Egyptian Slavery* we lie;
And sweat and toil in the vile Drudgerie
   Of *Tyrant Sin*;
To which we *Trophees* raise, and wear out all our Breath,
In building up the *Monuments* of *Death*;
We, the *choice Race*, to *God* and *Angels Kin*!
In vain the *Prophets* and *Apostles* come
   To call us home

   .   .   .   .   .   .

But, we, alas, the *Flesh-pots* love,
We love the very *Leeks* and sordid *roots* below.
             (*Poems* (1905), 219–20)

The pronominalization and the tense system in this and the second stanza pose a problem: whose voice is speaking here? It cannot be Moses, for he is alluded to in the third person towards the end of stanza ii, and the narrative proper, which starts in stanza iii, is marked by at least an intermittent use of the preterite: 'If from some *God* you come (said the proud *King*) . . . ' (p. 220). 'Thy . . . thine . . . we'—the voice seems simultaneously to speak as if to the enslaved Israelites and to English contemporaries. The meaning of 'Liberty', so much the rallying cry of republican revolutionaries, seems an issue—voluntary bondage to the tyrant (Pharaoh? Cromwell?) appears as the residual and paradoxical manifestation of supposed free will. Again, the despised '*Prophets* and *Apostles*' invite interpretation both historically and in terms of contemporary politics. Once the connections are made through the ambiguities of the opening, the subsequent narrative presents an agreeable fantasy of the English people saved despite themselves. At the seemingly impassable Red Sea, though no obvious route appears, an inspired leadership defies pessimistic expectation: 'No means t' escape the faithless *Travellers* spie | But the great *Guid* . . . saw a *Path* hid yet from humane sight' (p. 229). To a rational assessment the way ahead seems hopelessly blocked: to the illuminati a way stands open.

   A grimmer version of the resistance myth occurs in another pindaric ode on a biblical theme, 'The 34. Chapter of the Prophet

Isaiah'. That, too, begins with a voice seemingly addressing directly his own age: 'Awake, and with attention hear, | Thou *drowsie World*, for its concerns thee near' (p. 211). Though the voice identifies itself quickly—'I, [God's] *loud Prophet*' (ibid.)—the phrasing connects Isaiah's Israel to Cowley's England, 'the *Rebel World*' (ibid.) which deserves God's scourge, the 'cursed *Land*' which the '*Destroying Angel*' surveys with punctilious rapacity.

However, Cowley's view of last things usually offers a desperate sort of comfort. Several odes work towards a longer perspective in which England's sufferings appear trivial and transient, though transcendence sometimes carries a heavy price in reduction of even the best human achievements. 'The Extasie' offers what might be termed an 'out-of-body experience', a spiritual space trip to a point of celestial vision. *En route* a backward glance contextualizes England's suffering:

> Where shall I finde the noble *Brittish* Land?
> Lo, I at last a *Northern Spec* espie,
> > Which in the *Sea* does lie,
> > And seems a *Grain* o'th'*Sand*!
> For this will any *sin*, or *Bleed*?
> Of *Civil Wars* is this the *Meed*?
> > And is it this, alas, which we
> (Oh *Irony* of *Words*!) do call Great *Britanie*?   (p. 204)

'*Sin*, or *Bleed*'—the roles of villain and victim, rebel and conservative martyr, seem matched in equal futility, the worst and best endeavours of the last fifteen years squandered over the grain of sand.

In a poet as eager to assert continuities between his own and classical literary accomplishment as Cowley, deviations from familiar topoi assume a particular significance. Cowley's pindarics offer a highly qualified view of the compensations of friendship and a complete rejection of the immortality conventionally conferred by art:

> We *Poets* madder yet then all,
> With a refin'd *Phantastick Vanitie*,
> Think we not onely *Have*, but *Give Eternitie*.
> > Fain would I see that *Prodigal*,
> > Who his *To-morrow* would bestow,
> For all old *Homers Life* e're since he *Dy'ed* till *now*.   (p. 203)

The easy turn of phrase—'immortal Homer'—and the slack and

wishful thinking behind it are brought to touch a firm reality: Homer is no more and no less immortal than the next person, and 'life' since his death has only been *metaphorically* life, for which no one would literally swap his own. Again, the muse may tell '*pleasant Truths*, and *useful Lies*', she may alter ways of perceiving, and produce imaginative worlds in acts of creation which parallel (ephemerally) the Almighty's ('The Muse', pp. 184–6). Yet poetry's truth-telling capacity cannot work to influence human conduct for the better. Into his rendering of Pindar's 'Olympian Ode', Cowley interpolates an injunction against the '*Voluntary Faults*' of the 'unjust and Covetous', but he comments in his notes that it was 'an *innocent addition* to the *Poet* [i.e. Pindar], which does no *harm*, nor I fear, much *Good*', a gratuitous admission of poets' impotence (pp. 160, 166). No claim here for poets as unacknowledged legislators. Moreover, the poets' trade brings even its most illustrious practitioners a dubious recompense, 'the small *Barren Praise*, I That neglected *Verse* does raise' ('Destinie', p. 193).

Friendship is a curious motif in the odes, and a pessimistic note persistently sounds about bonds of loyalty between people: ''Tis now the *cheap* and *frugal* fashion, I Rather to *Hide* then *Pay* the *Obligation*', observes the 'Olympian Ode' with a directness that seems addressed as much to Cowley's coterie associates as to Pindar's original audience (p. 162). Only in one poem, 'To Dr Scarborough', does Cowley approach a Horatian tone, suggesting that friendship and activity on the personal, human scale can mitigate the surrounding horrors of civil war, but the consolations are severely muted. Charles Scarborough (or Scarburgh, as the *DNB* prefers) had been a Cambridge contemporary who, like Cowley, had been ejected and had moved to royalist Oxford in the mid–1640s. Unlike Cowley, however, he had thereafter chosen not exile but a prosperous coexistence with the parliamentarian and subsequently republican ascendancy. His private beliefs are not recorded, though at the Restoration, like other men of distinction such as Wren and Sprat, his career continued unchecked: he became Charles II's physician and was later knighted.[84] Cowley celebrates how Scarborough's skill repairs the damages of the war—'The *Ruines* of a *Civil war* thou dost *alone repair*' (p. 198). Yet the final stanza anatomizes the complexities and contradictions of Cowley's position:

---

[84] *DNB*; Nethercot, *Cowley*, 81–2, 156.

Ah, learned *friend*, it grieves me, when I think
    That *Thou* with all thy *Art* must dy
        As certainly as *I*.
And all thy noble *Reparations* sink
Into the sure-wrought *Mine* of treacherous *Mortality*.
Like *Archimedes*, hon'orably in vain,
Thou holdst out *Towns* that must at last be *ta'ne*,
And *Thou* thy self their great *Defender* slain.
Let's ev'en *compound*, and for the *Present Live*,
'Tis all the *Ready Money Fate* can give,
    Unbend sometimes thy restless care;
    And let thy *Friends* so happy be
    T' enjoy at once their *Health* and *Thee*.
Some hours at least to thine own pleasures spare.
Since the whole *stock* may soon exhausted be,
    Bestow't not all in *Charitie*.
Let *Nature*, and let *Art* do what they please,
When all's done, *Life* is *an Incurable Disease*.   (p. 200)

The Horatian proposition—'for the *Present Live*' rehearses the *carpe diem* motif—is premissed on the tainted word 'compound', which, while it relates as a financial term to the commercial metaphor continued in 'Ready Money' and 'stock', nevertheless alerts readers to the price of easy living in Cromwell's England: surrender. Similarly, the metaphor of 'hon'orably in vain' holding out in a position which must inevitably be surrendered stimulates recollection of Cowley's prefatory observations on 'marching out of our *Cause* it self' and dismantling 'all the *Works* and *Fortifications* of *Wit* and *Reason* by which we defended it' (*Poems* (1656), sig. a4ʳ). The Horatian good life may be realized only by giving in. Nor may it be long maintained. As he so often does in these odes, Cowley eases into the view of eternity, beneath which all achievements, both personal happiness and public responsibility, are reduced to nothing.

Two of the odes may seem more critical of the conduct of the royalists and perhaps even pro-Cromwellian, though those interpretations prove untenable. 'Destinie', which ends with acknowledgment that it was his fate to have been a poet, begins with a complex figure in which the speaker describes a chess game where the pieces apparently move themselves (though they are, rather, manipulated by unseen and capricious angels). Part demands a political reading:

Here a proud *Pawn* I'admire
That still advancing higher
At top of all became
Another *Thing* and *Name*.
Here I'm amazed at th' actions of a *Knight*,
That does bold wonders in the fight.
Here I the losing party blame
For those false *Moves* that break the *Game*,
That to their *Grave* the *Bag*, the conquered *Pieces* bring,
And above all, th' *ill Conduct* of the *Mated King*.   (p. 192)

'Conduct', it should be noted, contemporaneously meant not behaviour but leadership.[85] The king—either Charles II or his father could be perceived to fit—has made errors (palpably), but of a practical, not ethical, kind. Again, the promoted pawn invites interpretation as Cromwell, changing not only his status, but also his 'Name' (in accepting the title of Lord Protector). 'Thing' seems reductive and 'Pawn' scarcely a panegyric token of respect. Moreover, what had been perceived as blameworthy ineptitude among the losing party, seen aright appears as the eccentric hand of capricious and more potent forces.

Unlike most of his pindarics, 'Brutus' appears without authorial annotation, though its subject matter and area of reference are in some ways more recondite than those of poems Cowley annotated quite copiously. The silence, perhaps, alerts us to an element of enigma, as though the poet would not firmly guide his readers to select one of the alternative constructs which the poem invites. The problem rests in the significance of Brutus. As Langley and others have noted, Cromwell was contemporaneously praised in the figure of the tyrannicidal Brutus, so much so that Lovelace parodied such panegyric in his 'Mock-Song'.[86] For some critics, the poem constitutes a recantation of his royalism and a committed attempt at self-advancement.[87] Langley perceives the equation of Brutus and Cromwell as inconsistent with an intelligent reading of the poem (but available to a gullible one). Such a reading would require us to accept the line 'The best *Cause* and best *Man* that ever drew a *Sword*' (p. 196) as applying to the republicans and specifically to Cromwell as general. It would be inconsistent with the openly

---

[85] *OED.*
[86] Langley, Cowley's ' "Brutus" ', 41–52.
[87] Nethercot, *Cowley*, 153–4; Nevo, *Dial*, 119–20.

royalist poems retained within the volume and would seem bizarrely sycophantic in a poet who elsewhere forwent the opportunity for open praise of the new political ascendancy. After all, if the objective is ingratiation with a tyrant, why do it obliquely and enigmatically in 'Brutus' and not in an epistle dedicatory to the Lord Protector or in straightforward panegyric? Such a policy would be an eccentric strategy in an age and a medium so receptive of open praise of the most abject kind.

We should look, instead, at the values inscribed in the poem and at its relationship to Cowley's other odes. The poem describes another species of political failure. Brutus, though motivated by the highest ideals, falls to 'false *Octavius*, and wild *Antonie*', and the best of political causes perishes through a mixture of chance (or fate) and the malice of corrupt adversaries, through 'odde events, | *Ill men*, and wretched *Accidents*' (pp. 196–7). Should we recall the confusions of Penruddock's Rising? The poem engages that old challenge to royalist ideology: how was it that God, if he endorsed their cause, nevertheless permitted their overthrow? The poem ends by invoking the Christian perspective:

> A few years more, so soon hadst thou [Brutus] not dy'ed,
> Would have confounded *Humane Virtues* pride,
> And shew'd thee a *God crucifi'ed*.   (p. 197)

Under a view of eternity, which sees Christ's Atonement as the only act of abiding significance on the human plane, the agonies of political disaster are reduced and accommodated.

X

In 1681, in another crisis for Stuart conservatism, Dryden produced *Absalom and Achitophel*, the best-known Davidic narrative of the English literary tradition. He did so, with controlled irony, in a manner which offers a witty schema of analogy between Hebrew and English politics, with David/Charles II installed by a fickle populace in succession to Saul/Cromwell and perplexed by his son Absalom/Monmouth. The chief reward of the poem, besides the savage precision of its more critical portraits, rests in the ingenuity with which Dryden turns the analogy. Cowley's 'Davideis' operates within a radically different idiom. It is almost humourless, and its political implication is much less transparent: unlike Cowley, Dryden wrote as an apologist for the political ascendancy, not for an oppressed and largely clandestine Opposition. Indeed, the opacity of 'Davideis' has encouraged some to interpret it as a species of Cromwellian panegyric,[88] and others, more improbably still, to deny any political dimension at all, as Parfitt claims:

> there is little sense in the poem as a whole that it is to be read as comment on the present, and little feeling that its material is fired by any committed response to the political issues inherent in that material . . . It is easier, it seems, to be stylish than to think.[89]

Trotter, however, has developed an oblique and more intelligent political reading.[90] I see the poem as another royalist fantasy, the rehearsal of royalist values in action, and I view its abandonment as a further token of Cowley's political despair, another fortification of wit surrendered to the conqueror.

The *roman-à-clef* of Cowley the cryptographer takes a more oblique trajectory than Dryden's. In 'Davideis' David is (and is not) Charles II, just as Saul is (and is not) Cromwell. No simple equations obtain. Yet when Cowley writes,

> some his [David's] Valour praise,
> Some his free Speech, some the fair pop'ular rayes
> Of Youth, and Beauty, and his *modest Guise*;
> Gifts that mov'd all, but charm'ed the Female Eyes   (p. 339)

cognoscenti may see an allusion to Charles II's womanizing as well as to his relative youth. The point emerges again in the couplet, 'Nature his [Goliath's] Limbs only for *war* made fit, | In thine [David's] as yet nought beside *Love* she' has writ' (p. 336). The lines, 'Well did he [Saul] know how *Palms* by 'oppression speed, | *Victorious*, and the *Victors* sacred Meed' (p. 243), allude to a notion from popular botany, but invoke also recollection of the background emblem from the frontispiece to *Eikon Basilike*, a picture of palms growing under weights to confirm the dictum, central to Stuart ideology, 'Crescit sub pondere virtus' ('Virtue grows under a burden'). The image of Saul brings out exactly those martial qualities that incontrovertibly characterized Cromwell for

---

[88] Nethercot, *Cowley*, 154.

[89] G. Parfitt, *English Poetry in the Seventeenth Century* (London and New York, 1985), 183.

[90] *Cowley*, 83–98.

friends and enemies alike. His role is not that of a naturally gracious monarch comfortable with power, but of an edgy warrior promoted into an alien context. The 'usual *Scepter* that rough hand did bear' is a spear (p. 255). The action of the poem, as far as it goes, carries David by means of a resourceful flight into exile at the court of Moab, a naturally devout king though a pagan:

> [Moab] With lifted hands bow'd towards his shining rise,
> And thrice to'wards *Phegor*, his *Baals* holiest Hill,
> (With *good* and pious prayers *directed ill*). (p. 365)

The lines suggest, perhaps, allusion to some pious but misguided host, most likely Louis XIV.

Not all the pieces fit. Charles II was scarcely 'An unknown *Youth* . . . The seventh-born Son of no rich house' (p. 341); Jonathan cannot be accommodated within the schema; and the description of Saul, exhibiting 'Such *Beauty* as great *Strength* thinks no disgrace' (p. 373), does not accord with familiar royalist jibes at Cromwell's legendary ugliness. Yet if Cowley was writing, as I believe he was, a would-be prophetic account of the triumph of the royalist underground, a little camouflage is understandable.

Controversy surrounds the date of the composition of 'Davideis'. Sprat speaks of it as 'wholly written' when Cowley was at Cambridge, though Nethercot sees it as a work begun young and improved (and politically reorientated) in the 1650s.[91] Had either seen the manuscript of Cowley's *Civil War*, another explanation of what Cowley had led Sprat to believe would perhaps have emerged. For, as Pritchard, editor of the manuscript, observes, Cowley 'appears to have determined that his work should not have been entirely wasted',[92] and in 'Davideis' (and elsewhere) he has quarried his early writing quite extensively. By claiming to have written 'Davideis' in his youth, Cowley (if he indeed is the origin of the notion) may have meant no more than that he wrote parts of it in the early 1640s for a different poem.

But are *The Civil War* and 'Davideis' such different poems? May not 'Davideis' too be 'laurels for the defeated'? He describes how the poem was to have developed, how in twelve books, heroic episode would have succeeded heroic episode, culminating with

---

[91] *The Works of Abraham Cowley* (London, 1668), ed. T. Sprat, sig. b3^r; Nethercot, *Cowley*, 49.
[92] *Civil War*, 52.

David's victory over the fallen Saul (*Poems* (1656), 'The Preface', sig. b1ᵛ). If the poem is a royalist fantasy, a celebration of a process whereby the young and talented Charles II displaces the fierce and morose Cromwell, then, once more, history frustrated Cowley's poetic anticipation of events. However prophetic and comforting it may have seemed in the early 1650s to regard the parallels between English and Hebrew history, by mid–1655 those parallels would have seemed at best poignant and at worst absurd.

'Davideis' provides a fitting coda to Cowley's *Poems* (1656). It marks another attempt at poetic wishful thinking wrecked on the hard reality of Cromwellian domination. It is a poem not so much abandoned as surrendered, an attempt to live within a pleasing fiction that could no longer be maintained. For Cowley imagination, the final bastion, had fallen.

8

Milton and the Good Old Cause

MILTON retained a civil service post throughout the 1650s, drawing his final salary for the third quarter of 1659, though he had written little for the State apart from diplomatic correspondence since his last Latin defence, the *Defensio Pro Se*, published in 1655. Throughout the later years of the decade he was probably preoccupied with compiling *De Doctrina Christiana* and working on *Paradise Lost*,[1] and had produced no vernacular polemic since 1649. He returned to the genre in the Indian summer of the Good Old Cause, as that vague configuration of republicans, Independents, sectaries, tolerationists, and political activists in the New Model Army came to style itself in its terminal phase.[2]

Cromwell's death early in September 1658 had brought no immediate catastrophe. Next day, his son Richard was installed as Lord Protector. By the end of the year the Privy Council, recognizing a variety of pressures and also, presumably, feeling sufficiently confident about the stability of the regime, issued writs for a new Parliament. The election returned considerable numbers of old republicans, who were in some ways critical of the Cromwellian ascendancy, and the early months of 1659 saw renewed debate of many issues close to radical hearts.[3] In this climate of revived controversy Milton issued in February *A Treatise of Civil Power*, arguing for the independence of believers' consciences from the restraint and direction of the magistracy.

Like *Areopagitica* but unlike subsequent vernacular tracts, it is addressed explicitly to the Parliament of England. In both cases, that posture was probably quite seriously intended. We noted

---

[1] *LR* iv. 227, 190; *CPW* vi. 22.

[2] On the origins of the term, see R. Hutton, *The Restoration: A Political and Religious History of England and Wales 1658–1667* (1985; Oxford, 1987), 33.

[3] The narrative of the events of 1659–60 is based primarily on Hutton, *Restoration*, 21–118, supplemented by A. Woolrych's historical introduction to *CPW* vii. rev. edn., 1–228.

earlier how skilfully *Areopagitica* speaks to different groups within the Long Parliament. Milton may well have been prompted to return to vernacular pamphleteering by some sense that now again there was an assembly engaged in rational debate, and furthermore, an assembly ideologically closer to his own position than the Long Parliament had been in the mid-1640s. In tone and style, however, it differs very sharply from *Areopagitica* and from much of his early prose.

It is a prose for the most part without simile or metaphor, and the imagery we find is generally of an undeveloped, even perfunctory, kind: 'how uneffectual and weak is outward force with all her boistrous tooles' (*CPW* vii. rev. edn., 257); 'a far worse yoke of servitude' (vii. 265); 'sins and shipwracks of implicit faith' (vii. 266). Quite a high proportion of the imagery is the unadorned appropriation of the similes and metaphors of proof texts into Milton's own prose, sometimes in ways which show almost an indifference to artistic effect but indicate a pronounced concern in working closely—and in being perceived as working closely—to the Bible:

Solid reasons wherof are continu'd through the whole chapter. [Col. 2] *v. 10. ye are complete in him, which is the head of all principalitie and power.* not completed therfore or made the more religious by those ordinances of civil power, from which Christ thir head hath dischargd us; *blotting out the handwriting of ordinances, that was against us, which was contrarie to us; and took it out of the way, nailing it to his cross, v.* 14: blotting out ordinances written by God himself, much more those so boldly written over again by men. ordinances which were against us, that is, against our frailtie, much more those which are against our conscience (vii. 264).

The passage is wholly typical of the texture of *Of Civil Power*. Note the repetition of the same words for repeated concepts. Note the prominence of proof texts, printed in italics, and accompanied with reference to chapter and verse.

Citation has a new role in this tract. Whereas previously, except where Milton was engaged primarily and explicitly in an exegetical process, as in *Tetrachordon*, biblical texts were much more likely to be incorporated into the fabric of his own prose, now they are highlighted as the authority for his statements. Commenting primarily on *De Doctrina Christiana* but making connections with *Of Civil Power*, Schwartz suggests that such citation has far-reaching implications for the authority Milton assumes to himself: 'the more insistently Milton cites the Bible, the more it becomes clear that he appropriates that authority he also grants . . . . to compose one's own words out of another's is to make them one's own.'[4] Milton's argument appears at times entirely to be grounded on biblical evidence, as whole pages are dominated by the serried, italicized ranks of proof texts.

The texture and the method of exposition may well owe much to his current concerns with his Latin exegetical treatise. The general asceticism of his prose style, still at times quite elegant, but never flamboyant in the old manner, may be determined by other factors too. A psychological explanation may have some validity: no longer does he write the prose of a frustrated poet, for those more creative impulses contemporaneously find straightforward discharge in the composition of *Paradise Lost*. But the plain style also shows a new awareness of the impatience and the limitations of his audience. What he offers resembles a briefing, informed notes and pertinent (albeit textual) information about the issues resurfacing in the ideologically refreshed Parliament of early 1659. Milton concludes with no swelling peroration: rather, he remarks upon both his stylistic restraint and brevity:

Pomp and ostentation of reading is admir'd among the vulgar: but doubtless in matters of religion he is learnedest who is planest. The brevitie I use, not exceeding a small manual, will not therfore, I suppose, be thought the less considerable, unless with them perhaps who think that great books only can determin great matters. I rather chose the common rule, not to make much ado where less may serve. Which in controversies and those especially of religion, would make them less tedious, and by consequence read ofter, by many more, and with more benefit (vii. 272).

Milton produces a self-image of the busy man speaking to busy men who, like himself, have the sophistication to appreciate a straightforward exposition.

The audience which Milton addressed evaporated by late April, dismissed by Richard Cromwell at the behest of army commanders suspicious of Parliament's consideration of plans to control them. The problem of identifying the location of power and securing access to it was to recur throughout the rest of Milton's polemical career. In their place, largely at the prompting of more junior

---

[4] R. Schwartz, 'Citation, Authority, and *De Doctrina Christiana*', in Loewenstein and Turner, 231–2. On the style of the tracts of 1659–60, see Corns, *Development*, chs. 2 and 5.

members of the New Model Army, the purged Parliament, dismissed in 1653, was recalled in early May. The Lord Protector was placed under house arrest, and by the end of the month he had accepted a pension and slipped into political obscurity. The restored Rump—the term became widely current later in the year—mustered only a small proportion of the original Long Parliament, though it resumed quite smoothly the governmental role. It met its first challenge competently, a royalist conspiracy known usually as 'Booth's Rebellion' after its most prominent leader, the Presbyterian Sir George Booth, himself a secluded member of the Long Parliament and a member of the recently dismissed Parliament of Richard Cromwell. With gratifying ease Lambert's troops suppressed the limited and incompetent uprising, and by late August 1659 Booth was in the Tower of London.

Presbyterians had played a prominent part in the conspiracy, urged on by a clergy newly impatient of the sort of *modus vivendi* they had established with Independency and agitated by the rapid expansion of the sects, particularly Quakerism.[5] Milton's *Considerations touching the Likeliest Means to Remove Hirelings out of the Church* hit a vein of anticlericalism that may usefully be contextualized in the republican victory over Booth. Thomason dated his copy 'Aug.', and it was first advertised on 8 September, the day after John Mordaunt, Booth's fellow-conspirator, had slipped from the country, despairing of the royalist cause.[6] Milton, addressing now the restored Rump, builds upon an assumption of impatience with the behaviour of the Presbyterian clergy, though his argument against tithes and benefices extends to include all in holy orders. Thus he assails the 'Simonious decimating clergie', in timely fashion assuring the Rump, which had had a scare from the uprising, that, until tithes are removed and religion is 'set free from the monopolie of hireling' no constitutional model 'will prove succesful or *undisturbed*' (vii. 75–6, my emphasis). Though the pamphlet is stylistically closely akin to *Of Civil Power*, some of its phrasing and its charges against the clergy of the late republic echo his antiprelatical writings. These priests too are monsters of ignorance and indolence, their 'sheep', the laity, 'oft-times sit the while to as little purpose of benefiting as the sheep in thir pues at *Smithfield*', while the minister, 'a lollard indeed over his elbow-cushion', gives

---

[5] Hutton, *Restoration*, 54.
[6] *CPW* vii. rev. edn., 236–7; Hutton, *Restoration*, 59.

but a fraction of the Christian instruction they should receive (vii. 302). Those who would accept their religion from such men take it 'by scraps and mammocks [fragments] as he dispenses it in his sundays dole' (vii. 320); earlier he had observed how 'the obscene, and surfeted Priest scruples not to paw, and mammock the sacramentall bread, as familiarly as his Tavern Bisket' (*Of Reformation, CPW* i. 548). The association of the idle and gluttonous priesthood, 'mammocking', and the distribution of the communion bread suggests that Milton remembers what he had written eighteen years before: beating Booth's uprising ushers in a dawn of radical possibility such as had been felt in the early 1640s. As the Yale editor notes, some of the argument and some of the evidence are repeated from his antiprelatical writing.[7]

Milton's perspective has about it an element of retrospection verging on nostalgia. He begins with an address to the restored Rump:

Owing to your protection, supream Senat, this libertie of writing which I have us'd these 18 years on all occasions to assert the just rights and freedoms both of church and state, and so far approv'd, as to have bin trusted with the representment and defence of your actions to all Christendom against an adversarie of no mean repute, to whom should I address what I still publish on the same argument, but to you whose magnanimous councels first opend and unbound the age from a double bondage under prelatical and regal tyrannie (vii. 274).

Milton has adjusted quickly to the change of regime, and his address endorses some tissue-thin arguments in support of the Rump's restoration. Forty-two members of the Parliament convened in 1640 had reassembled in May; secluded members still living outnumbered them by over 160. Milton writes as though the Parliament remaining since Pride's Purge had been—in fact or theory—the Parliament that had initiated hostilities with the king and purged the Church of bishops. He also writes as though the body whose servant in 1649 he became were simply the continuation of the Long Parliament, the same body that, far from offering him 'protection', had instituted measures against the kinds of heterodoxy his pamphlets of 1643–5 contained. Nostalgia, wishful thinking, and transparently selective recollection could scarcely have carried much conviction outside the narrowing circle of the

---

[7] *CPW* vii. rev. edn., 279 n, 299 n, 311 n.

Rump and its supporters. But they, surely, constituted the target of Milton's argument. Once more, he attempts to speak as an insider briefing insiders.

One obscure phrase has excited a welter of critical interpretation: 'The care and tuition of whose peace and safety, after a short but scandalous night of interruption, is now again by a new dawning of Gods miraculous providence among us, revolvd upon your shoulders' (vii. 274). Several have argued that the 'short . . . night' must allude to the six years since Cromwell dismissed the Rump.[8] Masson had argued that the period referred to is the fortnight between the dissolution of Richard Cromwell's Parliament and the return of the Rump. This seems to be the only interpretation wholly consonant with the sense of the passage, though possibly Milton leaves open to any Commonwealth's-man excluded from the Cromwellian apparatuses of power the alternative, rather flattering, construction. But Milton is, after all, talking about eighteen years of achievement; to dismiss six years as a short night, while such it may be *sub specie aeternitatis*, would be nonsensical in the context of praising eighteen years of success. Those six years, after all, were part of that period, and if they are but a short night, the whole is also an inconsiderable thing. Milton's drift in this passage is perhaps away from thinking in terms of successive Parliaments and more in terms of 'Parliament', a stable, abiding entity embodied in a series of manifestations. Moreover, some of the forty-two Rump MPs had sat in Richard's Parliament, nearly all had belonged to the unpurged Long Parliament, and several had variously served in the constitutional bodies established during the Protectorate, so some notion of governmental continuity is, tenuously, plausible.

Yet the pamphlet does end on an agitated note not previously detected:

Thus much I had to say; and, I suppose, what may be anough to them who are not avariciously bent otherwise, touching the likeliest means to remove hirelings out of the church; then which nothing can more conduce to truth, to peace and all happines both in church and state. If I be not heard nor beleevd, the event will bear me witnes to have spoken truth: and I in the mean while have borne my witnes not out of season to the church and to my countrey (vii. 320–1).

---

[8] The issues are reviewed by A. Woolrych in *CPW* vii. rev. edn., 85–6, and 'Milton and Cromwell: "A Short but Scandalous Night of Interruption"?', in Lieb and Shawcross, 201–12.

In part, he reasserts the brevity of his exposition—this is enough to convince those open to conviction. But he postulates too the possibility of failure, the failure to carry the argument because of the self-interest of others and the much larger failure which would follow as a consequence. 'Thus much I had to say' is an ambiguous phrase, meaning at once 'This is the argument which I developed and wished to say' and 'Thus much I was compelled to say', compelled by some urgent imperative to bear witness to a truth which only history would recognize. Milton is edging towards a desperate and explicitly prophetic mode, which will become stronger. We know from his private correspondence that a sense of foreboding was settling over him. Moreover, though late August was a more confident time for old republicans, the Rump's major debate of the tithes issue, and in a sense Milton's best chance to influence the outcome, had concluded in late June.[9] A pattern is emerging of bad timing. First the body he addressed shortly dispersed; now the body he addresses has already finished its debate.

II

The reconvened Rump lasted till mid-October. By now the central issues which would eventually precipitate the fall of the republic were becoming apparent. Republican civil government was only possible with the protection and permission of the New Model Army, but any such Government was fatally drawn to consider those issues of constitutional legality and fiscal control that threatened the military interest. Yet the army leadership lacked the cohesion to adopt Oliver's solution, though possibly Lambert and Fleetwood were considering the establishment of a military government after Parliament had cashiered the former, just a month after his victory over Booth. Lambert's troops surrounded Westminster and locked the doors of the Commons against the Rump. Power was invested in a Committee of Safety made up of officers and civilians prepared to work with the army. Whatever stability that may have offered was very soon broken by the news that

---

[9] *CPW* vii. rev. edn., 83–4.

Monck had condemned the action and declared his support for the Rump.

Monck commanded the army of occupation in Scotland. His motives and intentions throughout the next six months were to remain a matter of conjecture on the part of his contemporaries; historians remain unsure of why he acted as he did. Possibly he had a long-term intention of restoring the monarchy; perhaps he believed in the subordination of the army to civilian government; perhaps he had been infected by the Presbyterian anxieties of the summer about the rise of Quakerism. The extent to which he planned the unwinding of events remains very uncertain. The elements of accident and of planning defy evaluation.[10] Certainly, his army peers were, in Hutton's phrase, 'completely baffled' by his conduct.[11]

The persona Monck presented increased the enigma in ways that have some implications for Milton's later prose. None of the circle around Lambert or Fleetwood seemed really to know him. Latterly, his military service had kept him in Scotland, and he had served for some time in Ireland. He was an infantry officer in an age in which the highest profiles belonged to cavalrymen. From his vantage point as aide to Edward Montagu, a figure of increasing political importance, Pepys recorded persistently the stages by which the movement towards the Restoration emerged, but to him, and it would seem to his master, Monck appeared utterly enigmatic, though far too uninspiring to be a cardinal figure in the developing crisis. Pepys thought 'he seemed a dull, heavy man', an opinion others shared.[12] He noted too how Monck's motivation was attracting speculation as late as March 1660: 'Many think that he is honest yet, and some or more think him to be a fool that would raise himself, but think that he will undo himself by endeavouring it.'[13]

Monck gradually progressed south, and the army of Lambert, which had advanced to meet him, dispersed in early January 1660. A month later Monck entered London and rapidly sent out orders for displacement and command of other military units in order to

---

[10] Hutton tersely reviews the theories, *Restoration*, 70–1.
[11] Ibid. 71.
[12] *The Diary of Samuel Pepys*, ed. R. Latham and W. Mathews (London, 1970), i. 87 and n.
[13] Ibid. 79.

secure complete control of the capital and its environs. From the
New Year to the Restoration in May all significant power really
rested in the hands of this unknown figure and the close coterie of
his own officer corps with which he had surrounded himself.

The eclipse of the Lambert-Fleetwood group was accompanied
by rapid changes in political institutions. On Christmas Eve 1659 a
body of lower-ranking soldiery forced Fleetwood to allow the
Rump to reconvene, leaving him to voice his sense that the Good
Old Cause was disintegrating in the phrase 'God has spat in our
faces'.[14] The Rump busied itself in cashiering commanders who had
opposed it and excluding MPs who had collaborated with them. A
significant change in the predominant orientation of the Rump
followed, associated with more flexible figures like Sir Anthony
Ashley Cooper, as convinced republicans experienced an erosion of
their eminence. On 11 February Monck ordered the Rump to issue
writs for a new election. On 20 February he ordered the
readmission of the secluded members purged in 1649. This enlarged
Parliament formed, in conjunction with Monck, a new Council of
State, including some old republicans, but also a number of secluded
members and figures of an uncertain loyalty, like Cooper, Arthur
Annesley, and Edward Montagu, together with Monck himself. By
late February the Council had incarcerated Lambert and released
Booth. By 10 March Monck was confiding to intimates that he
would permit the Restoration if the next Parliament approved it.
On 16 March the bill for the dissolution of Parliament was passed.
Elections were conducted on terms which allowed all adult males
satisfying the property qualifications something approximating to a
free choice, though Hutton's claim, that in April 1660 'England was
a democracy', seems extraordinary.[15] The result was the Convention Parliament, a body so committed to the Restoration as to
frustrate any Presbyterian aspirations about constraining the
restored monarchy into granting them a favourable religious
settlement.

The timetable to the catastrophe of the Good Old Cause is central
to an understanding of Milton's remaining pamphlets, as is the
enigma surrounding Monck and the rapidity of constitutional
change. From the period between Lambert's dismissal of the Rump

---

[14] Hutton, *Restoration*, 82.   [15] Ibid. 113.

and Monck's entry into England date two manuscript drafts of what would seem to be aborted publications.

The first, usually called after the title it bore on its eventual publication in 1698 *A Letter to a Friend, concerning the Ruptures of the Commonwealth*, is addressed to an unknown republican activist, evidently of some prominence since Milton alludes to the information he brought (vii. 324). It would seem to have been a briefing intended for that person's use, presumably as a speech or pamphlet: 'With this you may doe what you please: put out, put in, communicate, or suppresse' (vii. 332). The text has a curiously hybrid quality, at once alluding to the circumstances of a private conversation between Milton and the recipient and yet offering arguments of a wholly rhetorical kind, such as the comparison between the New Model Army's political intrusiveness and the obedience of other European armies to their political masters, the sort of argument that belongs in public polemic rather than in the private counsels of a faction.

Fascinatingly, it defines the limited repertoire with which Milton would work till the Restoration, primarily the notion of grounding the stability of Government in some unchanging or scarcely changing council made up of men who will subscribe to two principles, religious toleration and the opposition to monarchy. Other elements, like devolution of power to county committees, are also present.

The text is dated 'Octob. 20th. 1659' (vii. 333), five days before Milton received his last quarterly Government salary payment,[16] but Milton abandons his own pretence to insider status: of the person to whom he writes he remarks, 'you have . . . stirred up my thought by acquai[n]ting me with the state of affaires more inwardly then I knew before' (vii. 324). It shows too an uncertainty about how he may reintroduce himself into the national debate. The recipient may do with the communication what he wishes; Milton had thought that 'God or the publick' had required no more of him than his 'prayers for them that govern' (vii. 324), and the idiom seems hard to hit, the fit audience hard to identify. Power, he notes, now resides straightforwardly with the army (vii. 329), and in the political vacuum in which he writes, with the Rump's sitting suspended, no obvious channels remain open.

---

[16] *LR* iv. 227.

The other manuscript from the autumn of 1659, more straight-forwardly, would seem to be the outline of a pamphlet. Its paragraphs are numbered after a fashion. It bears the title 'Proposalls of Certaine Expedients for the Preventing of a Civill War Now Feard, and the Settling of a Firme Government by J.M.', which strongly suggests it belongs to the period when the rival armies of Lambert and Monck were in the field and likely to fight, should the latter advance. It discloses the almost tragic clarity with which Milton comes rapidly to perceive the issues. As the opening sentence says, this is an argument to be laid 'before them in power' (vii. 336), the very vagueness of which indicates the political uncertainties within which Milton operated. His central argument is that the Committee of Safety established by Lambert and his associates should retain the role of maintaining the defence of the realm, but that they should invite the Rump to resume sitting; the Rump should then secure all army personnel in their offices for life and pass an act of oblivion concerning Lambert's coup; they should constitute themselves into a permanent body, changing their name to 'a Grand or Supreme Counsell' (vii. 337), and they should choose a Council of State to function much as it had done in 1649–53. Two tests relating to religious toleration and to the maintenance of the republic would be required of both the civilian Government and the army. For all his ability in identifying the problems, Milton's outline reveals two areas of naïvety. His scheme rests on the assumption that both army and Rump can be made to see where their own interests lie long enough for them to trust each other. Most significantly, he is silent about Monck. In perceiving the problem to lie in the discord between Lambert's group and the Rump, he takes Monck at his word, that his objection to the Committee of Safety is an objection in favour of the Rump.

III

The first edition of *The Readie and Easie Way to Establish a Free Commonwealth* appeared prefaced with 150 words which Milton obviously added just before sending it to the press. The passage concedes his failure to find fit audience in time, though Milton's political difficulties were more acute than he realized. The Rump, which had been sitting while the body of the treatise was written, was supplemented on 21 February 1660 by the readmission of the old secluded members who had been purged from the Long Parliament in 1648. Milton had written under the assumption that the Rump, properly (as he saw it) augmented by fresh republican MPs, would survive as the seat of legislative authority. On 18 February writs had been issued for by-elections to fill the places left vacant by the purge and by subsequent natural wastage among survivors, but planning for this expansion had begun early in January.[17] Milton was well aware of the Rump's original intentions, which he alludes to in the course of his treatise (vii. 367). Those writs were withdrawn by the Parliament to which the secluded members had been readmitted, after he wrote the pamphlet but before he wrote the prefatory comments to it.

But even Milton's prefatory remarks were outdated by events occurring on the morning of 22 February when Parliament issued writs for the calling of a new Parliament and established a committee to determine what political conditions should be placed on eligibility for election. That those conditions would permit the admission of a parliamentary majority favouring the monarchy came to concern Milton deeply in the weeks that followed. But the circumstances of publication indicate the impossibility of Milton's position: the tempo of political polemic could not match the tempo of political change. He has written a pamphlet premised on a situation which had changed by the time he wrote the preface, and he has written a preface premised on a situation which had changed by the time it had been carried to the press. He concludes his prefatory remarks with:

I thought best not suppress what I had written, hoping it may perhaps (the Parlament now sitting more full and frequent) be now much more useful then before: yet submitting what hath reference to the state of things as they then stood, to present constitutions; and so the same end be persu'd, not insisting on this or that means to obtain it (vii. 355).

Milton, surely, is being disingenuous: he can scarcely have thought that a reconstituted Long Parliament, in which a majority were not republicans, would be more likely than a predominantly republican Rump (or supplemented Rump) to heed what he had to say.

But this is a guileful pamphlet, as resolutely and carefully targeted as *Eikonoklastes*, and in its way a remarkable document,

---

[17] *CPW* vii. rev. edn., 353–4 n, 367 n.

considering the circumstances both political and personal under which Milton laboured. Dr Johnson fatuously jeered that Milton had presumed to halt an overwhelming political impulse towards the Restoration with a mere pamphlet.[18] Courage, not vanity, motivates *Readie and Easie Way*, a resolution to play out the game no matter how poor the cards and how shifting the rules.

Milton bases his argument on the assumptions, values, and coloured recollections of the Commonwealth's-men predominating in the Rump:

The Parlament of *England* assisted by a great number of the people who appeard and stuck to them faithfullest in the defence of religion and thir civil liberties, judging kingship by long experience a government burdensom, expensive, useless and dangerous, justly and magnanimously abolishd it; turning regal-bondage into a free Commonwealth . . . Nor were our actions less both at home and abroad then might become the hopes of a glorious rising Commonwealth (vii. 355–6).

Note Milton says 'a great number of the people', not 'most' or a 'majority', for this pamphlet, as we shall see, revives the notion of the sovereignty of the godly. Note too the pronominalization— 'our actions'. By the time of the second edition, Milton, addressing a different audience and in a different political context, substitutes 'thir' (vii. 420). He proclaims a delight apparently shared by few outside the Rump at its reconstitution, 'wonderfully now the third time brought together our old Patriots' (vii. 356).

Revolutionary Independency's defensive stratagems for the justification of their unrepresentative activity resurface boldly: republicans constitute 'that part of the nation . . . , as I perswade me of a great number . . . reservd, I trust, by Divine providence to a better end; since God hath yet his remnant, and hath not quenchd the spirit of libertie among us' (vii. 363–4). Unsurprisingly, that doctrine of the remnant, credible only to the republican vanguard, will be deleted when the pamphlet is reissued. Similarly, his emphasis on religious toleration as the central purpose of Government (vii. 380–2) was an argument dear to active elements within the Rump as to many army republicans; that too is not carried over into the second edition.

The central strategy of the pamphlet rests on the construction of a

---

[18] Samuel Johnson, *The Lives of the English Poets*, ed. S. C. Roberts (1963; London, 1967), 100.

polarity between the simplicity of the solution Milton would have adopted and the expensive, irreversible complexities of restoring the monarchy. Restoration would admit of no further alteration, however grim it proved (vii. 357). Again:

> a king must be ador'd like a Demigod, with a dissolute and haughtie court about him, of vast expence and luxurie, masks and revels, to the debaushing of our prime gentry both male and female; nor at his own cost, but on the publick revenue; and all this to do nothing but bestow the eating and drinking of excessive dainties, to set a pompous face upon the superficial actings of State, to pageant himself up and down in progress among the perpetual bowings and cringings of an abject people (vii. 360–1).

Restoration would utterly destabilize the fiscal system which had emerged, and would lay open to confiscation private property or else require 'a heavy imposition on all men's purses' (vii. 378).

The alternative is the maintenance of the republic on as permanent a basis as could be devised. Milton adopts in his title the manœuvre he had first used in *Considerations touching the Likeliest Means to Remove Hirelings out of the Church*. Perhaps if one merely asseverates that the work proposed is ready or likely to achieve a difficult objective, some at least may believe it. Milton's scheme for constitutional settlement broadly resembles the blueprint devised in his last manuscript 'Proposals', substantially the settlement of the Rump, supplemented by a new draft of republican MPs, into a permanent Grand or General Council of the godly, with control over legislation, taxation, the army and foreign affairs, together with a Council of State, made up of MPs and others, to carry on 'some particular affairs' which call for more secrecy or expedition (vii. 368).

What is interesting about Milton's model—and there was a similar lacuna in his earliest defences of the republic—is the absence of a viable theoretical component. Where the theory should be, after the outline of the proposal, we find instead a curious metaphoric passage:

> And although it may seem strange at first hearing, by reason that mens mindes are prepossessd with the conceit of successive Parlaments, I affirm that the Grand or General Councel being well chosen, should sit perpetual: for so their business is, and they will become thereby skilfullest, best acquainted with the people, and the people with them. The ship of the Commonwealth is alwaies undersail; they sit at the stern; and if they stear

well, what need is ther to change them; it being rather dangerous? Adde to this, that the Grand Councel is both foundation and main pillar of the whole State; and to move pillars and foundations, unless they be faultie, cannot be safe for the building (vii. 368–9).

Milton tries to suggest the arbitrariness of successive Parliaments, 'a conceit' which has prepossessed men's minds, though the notion that one choice by the electorate should remain definitive throughout the life of the successful candidate begs many issues about changes in the electorate, in the competence or beliefs of the candidate, or in political circumstances. The imagery that replaces the argument is peculiarly inept. No ship, albeit a ship of State, is always under sail. And how many hands should be at the tiller? The spatial metaphor of the Grand Council as the foundation of the State lacks conviction. In some respects, foreign affairs for example, they constitute the State; in others, such as taxation, they control apparatuses of the State. But 'the whole State' does not rest upon them. Milton's purposes are transparent, to give the Rump a justification for perpetuating itself and to avoid the anxieties of finding an electorate that would endorse republicanism and toleration, nor does the imagery successfully disguise the transparent pursuit of interest.

The proposal is better endorsed, however, by his wholly pragmatic argument from history, that republics have better achieved social stability and economic prosperity when constituted around permanent councils, though it involves a robust treatment of the evidence. Yes, in Venice they do change some councils more often than once a year but 'the true Senate . . . is the whole Aristocracy immovable'; yes, in the United Provinces they change the States General, but the town committees which appointed delegates to it are immutable (vii. 371–2). Through it all runs the reiterated assertion that 'The way propounded is plain, easie and open before us; without intricasies' (vii. 374).

Despite the polemical control, Masson detected that 'Throughout the pamphlet there is a sad and fierce undertone, as of one knowing that what he is prophesying as easy will never come to pass',[19] and the best recent discussions of the work, by Knoppers and by Holstun, have identified it as a jeremiad, 'a prophetic lament over the apostasy of a chosen nation'.[20] Developing an argument

---

[19] Masson, *Life*, v. 646.
[20] L. L. Knoppers, 'Milton's *The Readie and Easie Way* and the English

originating with Perry Miller and augmented by Sacvan Bercovitch, who identified the genre in American Puritan writing, Knoppers argues that it figures prominently in earlier defences of the Good Old Cause and that Milton operates consciously within the tradition, mutating it so that it 'takes on a distinctively literary aim, to provide a myth of nation, a story by which the English under the restored monarchy can interpret their tragedy'.[21] She notes that an element of contingency obtains even in the Book of Jeremiah, that the threatened nation may escape through repentance, though she underestimates the significance of that component in her own reading. Moreover, only intermittently does Milton slip into the jeremiad mode, and the term's usefulness is disputable. *The Readie and Easie Way* is simply an exercise in discursive vernacular polemic, much like most of his prose *œuvre*, save for exegetical treatises like *Tetrachordon* or disputations like *Animadversions*. We must beware the generation of redundant genre categories, that obscure the process of writing the genre histories still badly needed for the early modern period. Rather, for the most part, Milton attempts to speak to men's narrower interests, stressing how the restored monarchy's conduct is predictable on the basis of past practice and what is known about Charles II and his circle. That element of proof becomes sharper in the second edition. The Book of Jeremiah is wholly deficient in rational justification. Yet that undertone of sadness which Masson noted certainly obtains, and Milton does consciously echo Jeremiah:

Thus much I should perhaps have said, though I were sure I should have spoken only to trees and stones, and had none to cry to, but with the Prophet, *O earth, earth, earth:* to tell the verie soil itself what God hath determined of *Coniah* and his seed for ever. But I trust, I shall have spoken perswasion to abundance of sensible and ingenuous men: to som perhaps, whom God may raise of these stones, to become children of libertie, and may enable and unite in thir noble resolutions to give a stay to these our ruinous proceedings and to this general defection of the misguided and abus'd multitude (vii. 388).

Note how Milton ends proclaiming a frail confidence in the success of his cause—'I trust, I shall have spoken perswasion'. The problem

Jeremiad', in Loewenstein and Turner, 213–26; J. Holstun, *A Rational Millennium: Puritan Utopias of Seventeenth-Century England and America* (New York and Oxford, 1987), 246–65; the definition is from Knoppers, 213.

[21] Ibid. 224.

is that the negative images, of the restored monarchy, of the problems the Good Old Cause faces, of the onrushing catastrophe, appear so much more potent than the confidence he proclaims and the vision of the permanent republican State he attempts to generate. Knoppers is wrong about Milton creating a myth through which defeat could be understood. He can have had no expectation that either he or his recent writings would survive the white terror he envisaged. Though its contemplation may have concentrated the mind, it overstimulated the imagination in ways that disrupt the polemical strategy. While modern readers can see with hindsight the futility of his efforts, to contemporaries too the cause by late February seemed lost. Milton's was almost a solitary voice by then. 'Thus much I should perhaps have said, *though I were sure* I should have spoken only to trees and stones'—the high imperatives he continues to observe ultimately render attention to personal safety and to the probability of success irrelevant. As Samson will observe, 'Masters' commands come with a power resistless | To such as owe them absolute subjection' (*Samson Agonistes*, ll. 1404–5, *Poems*, 391).

IV

The first edition of *The Readie and Easie Way* was not the pamphlet Milton would have written had he known about the events of 22 February and the subsequent ascendancy of his old enemies, the Presbyterian royalists and their confrères, purged from the Long Parliament and now readmitted under the aegis of Monck. A Parliament elected under the terms of eligibility they were likely to entertain could certainly be expected to readmit the king. Milton revised his tract and he wrote to Monck.

The letter, known as 'Present Means, and Brief Delineation of a Free Commonwealth', survives in draft form in manuscript. It is uncertain whether it was sent; it may have been intended for publication—letters to Monck appear frequently as broadsides in early 1660—but no record survives. Ayers possibly errs in his confident assertion that the missive offers the formula for the management of the forthcoming elections.[22] I think the admittedly

---

[22] *CPW* vii. rev. edn., 393.

ambiguous jottings could be better interpreted as advice on a
military coup should the elections go against the republicans:

First, all endeavours speedily to be us'd, that the ensuing Election be of
such as are already firm, or inclinable to constitute a free Commonwealth
(according to the former qualifications decreed in Parliament, and not yet
repeal'd, as I hear) without single Person, or House of Lords. If these be
not such, but the contrary, who foresees not, that our Liberties will be
utterly lost in this next Parlament, without some powerful course taken, of
speediest prevention? The speediest way will be . . . (vii. 392–3).

Milton writes in the period between Parliament's action of
22 February in calling elections, and the work of that same
Parliament in revising the republican limitations on franchise and
eligibility that the Rump had originally issued for the elections by
which they intended to supplement their numbers. Milton acknowledges the likely outcome of elections without appropriate safe-
guards—'who foresees not' that a Parliament will be returned which
is deeply inimical to the Good Old Cause? The letter is addressing
the problem of what to do when and if that disaster happens. He
advocates a military intervention in which Monck will appeal
directly to the gentry class, or at least such of the gentry class as are
politically acceptable. If they refuse to take over responsibility for a
devolved system of government and a standing Grand Council of
delegates nominated by those local organizations, then Monck
should dismiss them and invite others of the gentry who will.

Again, the letter is not guileless. Milton offers Monck extraordinary
powers. He may retain absolute control of the armed forces, and the
calling and dismissing of the gentry seem wholly at his discretion.
But the address assumes that Monck intended to preserve the republic.
Perhaps Milton believed that still; perhaps he thought the chance,
however slim, was worth exploring; perhaps the fact the letter never
went to press indicates that, on reflection, he thought Monck's
support was not worth courting and that the general would accept
whatever decision the new Parliament made.

Additions to the opening paragraph of the reissued *Readie and
Easie Way* foreshadow the ways in which he is directing his address,
as well as a further shift towards the idiom of Jeremiah:

hoping that it may now be of much more use and concernment to be freely
publish'd, in the midst of our Elections to a free Parlament, or their sitting
to consider freely of the Government; whom it behoves to have all things
represented to them that may direct thir judgment therin; and I never read

of any State, scarce of any tyrant grown so incurable, as to refuse counsel from any in a time of public deliberation; much less to be offended. If thir absolute determination be to enthrall us, before so long a Lent of Servitude, they may permitt us a little Shroving-time first, wherin to speak freely, and take our leaves of Libertie. And because in the former edition through haste, many faults escap'd, and many books were suddenly dispersd, ere the note to mend them could be sent, I took the opportunitie from this occasion to revise and somewhat to enlarge the whole discourse, especially that part which argues for a perpetual Senat (vii. 408–9).

Milton clearly signals that he will develop more fully the details of the constitutional model he is advocating—this, largely, is to answer criticism from the circle around James Harrington, the leading English political theorist between Hobbes and Locke and the advocate of constitutional models in which Parliament is refreshed regularly by the replacement or re-election of a proportion of its membership.

More significant, however, is Milton's unflinching anticipation in this preface that the election will go against the republicans and that the Parliament due to assemble on 25 April will have a Presbyterian royalist majority. The publication date of the second edition can be narrowed fairly well to the period after 28 March, when the Long Parliament had been dissolved, and before the elections were complete. His revised preface suggests it is a tract that can be read as well by the resulting Parliament as by the electorate. Indeed, Milton seems a little vague about whether it will appear before or after the new Parliament has convened, which may owe something to his difficulties in steering his tract through the press. Warrants were issued for the arrest of Livewell Chapman, the bookseller who produced the first edition, on 27 March, and the second edition appeared bearing the name of neither bookseller nor printer, a familiar precaution in periods of persecution. Though at one point in the pamphlet he talks of constraints obtaining to prevent Parliament falling into the hands of the enemies of the republic (vii. 432), that safeguard is generally assumed to have failed. Milton scarcely pretends to like those to whom he speaks. His approach to them is justified only by virtue of the fact that 'any State' and almost 'any Tyrant' may be worth addressing at certain times of 'public deliberation'. Yet the images that resonate are those of the shroving-time before the Lent of servitude and the revolutionary's envoi to liberty, both deeply pessimistic in implication. This is a strange pamphlet, fine-tuned to meet the intricacies of a

Harringtonian critique, cynically pitched to scare Presbyterian royalists away from monarchy, yet permeated with the imminence of the abyss.

To incorporate the Presbyterians into the Good Old Cause Milton drastically revises his account of events leading to the formation of the republic. He pushes it back towards the 1630s and early 1640s, which permits him to describe issues on which all elements of the parliamentary opposition to Charles I were substantially united and to rehearse with some vigour the atrocities perpetrated and duplicity manifested by the king. Anti-Catholic sentiment figures much more prominently in the revisions, a manœuvre Milton had deployed to capture Presbyterian opinion in his 'Observations' on *The Articles of Peace*. Milton reminds his readers that all shades of Puritan opinion have more in common with each other than with Stuart kings. The rupture between Presbyterians and the revolutionary Independents, Milton argues, came through anxieties about stabilizing the State and about the corruption of some of the former. The republicans' caution, thoroughness, and probity, not ideology, fractured the old alliance. The settlement that the Presbyterians were negotiating with the king in 1648 would not have guaranteed the liberties both groups valued and subsequently enjoyed (vii. 409–22).

He reworks the sections that describe the style of the Stuart court, suggesting more strongly that the popery of the queen mother and others would infect more widely the Protestant nobility, who like the Huguenot aristocracy would be seduced from right religion. The passage exudes anti-French, anti-Catholic, anti-court sentiment. Households will multiply to satisfy the rest of the royal family; soon there will be a queen, and she probably a foreign Catholic; they will breed, and the 'royal issue' will need paying for. Meanwhile—a contemptuous flourish—the nobility will vie in the acquisition of the offices of servants, 'stewards, chamberlains, ushers, grooms, even of the close-stool' (vii. 425). The dignity of court life comes down to this dubious honour.

Milton's most powerful weapon to sway the Presbyterians is fear of the retribution to be visited upon them. He had made much of Stuart antipathies to Presbyterian church government in *Eikonoklastes*. Now again he cites the words of *Eikon Basilike*:

no son of *Charls* returning, but will most certainly bring back with him, if he regard the last and strictest charge of his father, *to persevere in not the doctrin only, but government of the church of* England; *not to neglect the speedie and effectual suppressing of errors and schisms;* among which he accounted Presbyterie one of the chief (vii. 457–8).

Moreover, the Presbyterians had been co-authors, indeed in some ways the principal authors, of the war against his father: why would Charles II now excuse them (vii. 453)? Milton reaches into the furthest recesses of the shared political memory of English Puritanism, dragging up the royalist stereotypes with which, in the early 1640s, the parliamentarian propagandists began: there will be 'a standing armie . . . of the fiercest Cavaliers . . . perhaps again under *Rupert*', the oldest target of Puritan character assassination.[23] The Cavalier press had latterly revived with some fairly scabrous attacks on luminaries of the Good Old Cause, among them Milton himself.[24] Milton wittily uses their force against themselves:

Let them [the Presbyterian royalists] but hear the diabolical forerunning libells, the faces, the gestures that now appeer foremost and briskest in all public places; as the harbingers of those that are in expectation to raign over us; let them but hear the insolencies, the menaces, the insultings of our newly animated common enemies crept lately out of thir holes, thir hell, I might say, by the language of their infernal pamphlets, the spue of every drunkard, every ribald . . . (vii. 452).

'Our common enemies' gives the direction to Milton's appeal: these are heirs to the Cavalier bravos who swaggered through the Puritan consciousness in the early 1640s, the sons and younger brothers of that 'ragged Infantrie of Stewes and Brothels' (*Eikonoklastes*, *CPW* iii. 380) who had accompanied Charles I in his attempt to arrest the six members. The pamphlet war against Milton and other old republicans gives him the evidence he needs to demonstrate to Presbyterian royalists that the leopard has not changed its spots. In a witty flourish, he confronts Presbyterian fears of an epidemic of sectaries with another, more imminent fear, of the Cavaliers' return, and again he does so through an invocation of stereotypes of the 1640s, both of the sectary and the royalist bravo, 'these new fanatics of not the preaching but the sweating-tub, inspir'd with nothing holier then the Venereal pox' (vii. 453).

Alongside the assiduous manipulation of Presbyterian anxiety Milton attempts to open a new dialogue with them and with

---

[23] Above, Ch. 1.
[24] See e.g. Sir Roger L'Estrange's *Be Merry and Wise* (London, 1660).

republicans disappointed with the emergence of the Cromwellian ascendancy, a dialogue premissed upon the admission that the constitutional tinkerings of the 1650s had done little to establish a stable republican system of government (vii. 430). Milton also addresses more closely the constitutional proposals of James Harrington and his circle. That Harringtonian republicans may have responded critically to the first edition is evidenced by the publication in late March of *The Censure of the Rota upon Mr Miltons Book Entitled, The Ready and Easy Way*.[25] This anony-mous royalist satire takes the form of a burlesque of a discusssion of Milton's pamphlet by the Harringtonian Rota Club. To the Harringtonian argument for a democratic institution incorporating regular elections of sections of the membership in due order, what is termed 'rotation', Milton advances a newly extended defence of the permanent council drawn from an aristocracy of the godly (vii. 434–5, 441–6). Again, critical elements of the argument are carried through the imagery: 'I could wish that this wheel or partial wheel in State [i.e. Harrington's notion of rotation] . . . might be avoided; as having too much affinitie with the wheel of fortune' (vii. 435); 'what can be expected firm or stedfast from a floating foundation?' (vii. 435–6); 'Militarie men hold it dangerous to change the form of battel in view of an enemie' (vii. 442). That he should eschew a more explicit and logical refutation of the position perhaps reflects a reluctance to disclose too clearly how profoundly anti-democratic his own position had become, how anxious he is about any decision arrived at through an electoral procedure. Fear of 'the noise and shouting of a rude multitude' (vii. 442) stalks these pages.

Milton invokes towards the end of the second edition (as he had towards the end of the first) the spirit of the Good Old Cause: 'What I have spoken, is the language of that which is not call'd amiss *the good Old Cause*' (vii. 462). The italics have been added since the first edition, as has the phrase 'which is not call'd amiss', which, as Ayers perceptively comments, 'connotes both objectivity and proud acceptance of the phrase, and Milton's readiness to be openly identified with that which was now hooted at by so many'.[26] Not only has Milton invoked recollection of the earliest days of the struggle, but he has done something to recapture the idiom of his

---

[25] Thomason dated his copy 30 March; *LR* iv. 308.
[26] *CPW* vii. rev. edn., 462 n.

own earliest pamphlets. In terms of the incidence of imagery, the first edition and more especially the second edition come much closer to practices of his antiprelatical pamphlets than to the austere prose of his tracts of 1659. Masson noted certain points of analogy between Milton's last desperate defences of the republic and Lambert's final campaign, begun on 10 April with his escape from the Tower and ending on 22 April with his capture by the turncoat regicide Ingoldsby after he had failed to rally significant numbers to his standard.[27] It might be added that just as Lambert had attempted to muster his forces on the old battlefield of Edgehill, so too Milton tries to shift the intellectual battleground back to the earliest days of the conflict between king and parliament.

Milton's prose works, over the nineteen years he was writing, produce a number of self-images: the radical intellectual of *Animadversions* or *Of Reformation*, sharper than the bishops, the frustrated poet of *Reason of Church-Government*, the sober, respectable Puritan of *Tetrachordon* and *Areopagitica*, the spokesman of the republic in *Eikonoklastes*. Into the second edition of *The Readie and Easie Way* Milton inserts a passage to revive some sense of his heroic status:

Nor was the heroic cause unsuccesfully defended to all Christendom against the tongue of a famous and thought invincible adversarie [i.e. Salmasius]; nor the constancie and fortitude that so nobly vindicated our liberty, our victory at once against two the most prevailing usurpers over mankinde, superstition and tyrannie unpraisd or uncelebrated in a written monument, likely to outlive detraction, as it hath hitherto convinc'd or silenc'd not a few detractors, especially in parts abroad (vii. 420–1).

He invokes recollection of his first Latin tract for the republic, *Pro Populo Anglicano Defensio* (1651), a tract distributed widely throughout Europe and as such unsuppressible, no matter what happened in England. Holstun comments well of the image Milton produces: 'In the face of near-universal backsliding, he stands as a one-man remnant; in writing an elegy for the lost civic virtue of his nation, he writes the epic song of himself.'[28]

Yet Holstun's contentions that the second edition so straightforwardly assumes that the cause is lost, and that 'Milton as Jeremiah pleads almost suicidally for his own execution, which will

---

[27] Masson, *Life*, v. 688.
[28] Holstun, *Millennium*, 262.

verify his prophecy about his nation's expiring liberty', are debatable.[29] Rather, the tract manifests a riot of contradictory impulses. He shows even *in extremis* a close attempt to manipulate those who could still arrest the Restoration, using their fear as a fulcrum on which to turn Presbyterian opinion, but other roles and perceptions break in, the need for a Jeremiah's lamentation and angry reproach, and the seized opportunity for self-memorialization. 'Monument' is an interesting word. At the closing of the Long Parliament, Thomas Scot the regicide, referring to the execution of Charles I, declared he wanted his part in that event recorded on his tomb, a speech which probably confirmed his place among the regicides later put to death. But Milton had other, more literary models for his final gesture. He presents himself to his enemies much as Coriolanus does to the Volsces, reminding them 'If you have writ your annals true' of the acts he perpetrated against them: 'Alone I did it.'[30]

This account to some extent accords with Lewalski's discussion of Milton's tracts of 1659–60, though where she sees him as 'an extremely practical, able, and realistic polemicist'[31] he may more convincingly be perceived as trying to reassemble those old polemical skills in radically changed circumstances. The audience he seeks to address shifts persistently with shifts of power, the critical moments pass before he can publish, and by the end starker perspectives disrupt the work in hand.

In a sense it is fitting that Milton's contribution to the political literature of the Civil War and Interregnum should have ended not with the heroism of the second *Readie and Easie Way* but with the tetchy irrelevance of *Brief Notes upon a Late Sermon, Titl'd The Fear of God and the King*, published probably between 10 and 15 April. Matthew Griffith, sometime chaplain to Charles I and a royalist activist who had shown his own share of moral courage in the 1650s, had preached a prematurely exultant royalist sermon in late March, which he had published early in April and for which he had been imprisoned.[32] Milton's pamphlet shows an almost comic

[29] Holstun, *Millennium*, 262.

[30] William Shakespeare, *Coriolanus*, ed. P. Brockbank (London, 1976), v. vi. 114–117.

[31] B. K. Lewalski, 'Milton: Political Beliefs and Polemical Methods, 1659–60', *PMLA* 74 (1959), 202.

[32] *CPW* vii. rev. edn., 464–5.

disregard for the polemical context, making much of the errors of fact perpetrated by a royalist divine and doctor of divinity:

The rest of his preachment is meer groundless chat, save heer and there a few granes of corn scatterd to intice the silly fowl into his net, interlac't heer and there with som human reading; though slight, and not without Geographical and Historical mistakes: as page 29, *Suevia* the German dukedom, for *Suecia* the Northern Kingdom: *Philip of Macedon*, who is generally understood of the great *Alexanders* father only, made contemporanie, page 31, with *T. Quintus the Roman commander*, instead of *T. Quintius* and the latter *Philip*: and page 44, *Tully* cited *in his third oration against Verres*, to say of him, *that he was a wicked Consul*, who never was a Consul: nor Trojan *sedition ever portraid* by that verse of *Virgil*, which you cite page 47, as *that of Troy*: school-boyes could have tould you, that ther is nothing of *Troy* in that whole portraiture, as you call it, of *sedition* (vii. 477–8).

What is Milton trying to accomplish? In place of the polemicist comes the pedant and indeed the pedagogue, invoking the knowledge which schoolboys have in order to contextualize the ignorance of the royalist divine. Perhaps this is a last manic flourish. Lambert was still on the loose; Griffith had been imprisoned by politicians still professing an opposition to the restoration of the king. But that construction is dispelled by the extraordinary suggestion Milton suddenly and without preparation inserts:

if we will needs condemn our selves to be [corrupt and idle], desparing of our own virtue, industrie and the number of our able men, we may then, conscious of our own unworthiness to be governd better, sadly betake us to our befitting thraldom: yet chusing out of our own number one who hath best aided the people, and best merited against tyrannie, the space of a raign or two we may chance to live happily anough, or tolerably (vii. 482).

What an eccentric coda to two decades of polemical achievement this pamphlet is. Wrapped inside a nit-picking attack on a minor antagonist comes an invitation to Monck to take the throne, not because it is theoretically or ethically justified, but because the likes of Milton may live 'happily anough, or tolerably' for a while till the Good Old Cause can reassert itself. But, of course, the throne was never in Milton's gift, and by mid-May a knowing schoolboy could have seen that the game was up. Milton's final intended audience, an audience of one, Monck himself, had made other plans.

9

Revolution, Restoration, and the English Literary Tradition

MILTON, of course, was right. The Restoration constituted an almost unmitigated horror for some of the godly. Many of the beneficiaries of the Cromwellian ascendancy managed to scramble aboard the reflagged ship of state. Edward Montagu retained his command in the navy, with a peerage; Monck too became a peer; so did former republican activist Ashley Cooper, the politically more elusive Arthur Annesley, and the leader in the late 1640s of the Long Parliament's Presbyterians, Denzil Holles.[1] Minor functionaries of the republic sometimes realigned themselves with considerable success. Thomas Sprat, whose academic career was premissed on the patronage of major figures of the Cromwellian cultural establishment, soon found other ways to preferment, as did others in the circle which was to become the Royal Society. Thus this former elegist of Oliver Cromwell and panegyrist of Richard could soberly assure potential patrons in the mid-1660s that he and his associates had been drawn to science to take their minds off the sufferings of their nation.[2] Pepys too in the Interregnum had worked for Montagu, his kinsman and patron, while latterly harbouring vaguely royalist leanings, and profited well from the change of regime, though his zeal overran his competence, and the recoil from a cannon he discharged in celebration of the king's return smacked his head.[3]

The valuable, the politically accomplished, the devious and the well-connected survived comfortably. Colonel Richard Ingoldsby,

---

[1] Hutton, *Restoration*, 154; they became, respectively the Earls of Sandwich, Albemarle, Shaftesbury and Anglesey, and Baron Holles of Ifield.

[2] T. Sprat, *History of the Royal Society*, ed. J. I. Cope and H. W. Jones (1959; St Louis, Mo. and London, 1966), 55–6.

[3] Pepys, *Diary*, i. 153.

whose military campaign had frustrated Lambert's last attempt to preserve the republic, though himself a regicide, was made a Knight of the Bath. Rear-Admiral Lawson, though he had been regarded with some suspicion by Montagu and had shown a dangerously late loyalty to the republic, was knighted and retained high command. He, like Montagu, died in combat in Charles's Dutch wars.[4]

Others lost their property, their freedom, or their lives. Nor was it a single episode of white terror. Ten regicides suffered grubby and obscene executions in October 1660, shameful events given a curious retrospective dignity by the courage and piety of the victims. Some, however, may argue that they were treated no worse than the Scots Presbyterians had treated Montrose or the Protectorate would have dealt with the anti-Cromwellian conspirator, Miles Sindercome.[5] For a while in 1660 Milton's fate seemed uncertain. Certainly some expected and wanted him to be executed, and he spent much of the summer of 1660 in hiding until the Act of Indemnity and Oblivion, promulgated in late August, exempted him, at least temporarily, from punishment. Gilbert Burnet thought it an 'odd strain of clemency' that he should escape. He remained anxious about possible assassination, a notion too lightly dismissed by Parker. He well knew the royalists' penchant for such acts, and had discussed the killing of Ascham and Dorislaus in *Eikonoklastes* (*CPW* iii. 577). In the event, he lost his pension and the considerable funds he had lent to the republican Government.[6]

Moreover, as the new regime responded to real or imagined conspiracies, and especially as the fiercely anti-Puritan Cavalier Parliament replaced the more conciliatory Convention Parliament, the arrests and killings continued. Lambert was tried for his life in 1662, despite seemingly having escaped the death penalty in 1660, though again he escaped execution. He remained in prison till his death in 1677. James Harrington was arrested late in 1661 and endured years of incarceration without trial. At the same time one of those to whom Milton felt ideologically close, Sir Henry Vane,

---

[4] Hutton, *Restoration*, 135, 80–1, 110, 223, and *Charles II* (Oxford, 1989), 288.

[5] Above, Ch. 6; Anon., *The Whole Business of Miles Sindercome* (London, 1656), *passim*; Hutton, *Restoration*, 134; Wedgwood, *Trial*, 220–3.

[6] *LR* iv. 305–6; Parker, *Milton*, i. 577; Gilbert Burnet quoted by P. J. Kitson, 'The Seventeenth-Century Influence on the Early Religious and Political Thought of S. T. Coleridge 1790–1804', Ph.D. diss. (Hull, 1984), 248.

was beheaded, in effect at the monarch's whim. Milton's sonnet, 'Vane, Young in Years, but in Sage Counsel Old', was first published in a contemporary account of his life and execution. Colonel Hutchinson, though not proceeded against in 1660, was arrested in 1664 and incarcerated so primitively that damp 'soon killed him as efficiently as the executioner's knife would have done'.[7]

But much less publicly. Grisly ritual characterized the judicial style of the Restoration. The remains of others besides regicides were displayed. The heads of dozens of less distinguished people executed after Venner's Fifth Monarchist adventure of 1660 or the botched Northern rising of 1663 were preserved impaled around London or on the gates of Northern cities. Parliamentary heroes of the 1640s were disinterred from their tombs in Westminster Abbey and consigned to a pit. Bradshaw, Ireton, and Cromwell hung, decaying, in their shrouds at Tyburn, while apprentice-boys vied to steal their toes.[8]

Pepys's diary for the autumn of 1660 shows the jumbled responses of an acute but deeply compromised time-server and minor beneficiary of both the old ascendancy and the new. He watched Harrison's execution with a detached admiration, the victim, he notes, 'looking as cheerfully as any man could do in that condition', and by evening he was more upset at kicking his wife's 'little fine Baskett' than by any recollection of the spectacle. When he climbs a turret at Westminster to look at the heads of Harrison and John Cook, he remarks too that he enjoyed 'a very fair prospect about London'. Yet he is disturbed by the gibbeting of the quarters, 'which was a sad sight to see; and a bloody week this and the last have been, there being ten hanged, drawn, and Quartered', and he regards the exhumation of Cromwell as gratuitously upsetting: it 'doth trouble me, that a man of so great courage as he was should have that dishonour'.[9]

Not only were survivors reminded persistently of what was nearly their fate, but they could scarcely feel certain that they too would not suffer capital punishment. Even Pepys, who had made the switch of loyalty as smoothly as Edward Montagu, whom he served, felt a paroxysm of anxiety at encountering an old school-

[7] Hutton, *Restoration*, 206; *LR* iv. 370.
[8] Hutton, *Restoration*, 134.
[9] Pepys, *Diary*, i. 265, 270, 269–70, 309.

fellow, lest he remember how enthusiastically he had welcomed the execution of Charles I.[10] Pepys risked no more, probably, than a check to his ambitious career. For republicans of a higher profile the danger was more acute. Exemption from punishment, evidently, could be reviewed. Throughout the period from the Restoration to 1667, when *Paradise Lost* was published, Milton lived under the shadow of persecution, of a belated vindictive act that, like the blind Fury, would slit the thin-spun life. Parker sometimes talks of the Restoration as though it calmly returned Milton to the fruitful contemplative life.[11] No old republican who had failed to ingratiate himself with the new order could rest secure in the 1660s, and Milton's political consciousness, as we shall see, remained in a complex dialogue with his poetic creativity.

In *The Readie and Easie Way* he had written both of the threat to freedom of worship and of the waste of the providence shown in past military successes, and he had looked in anticipation to the wastefulness and impiety of the restored court. The first point was felt keenly enough among those ministers of Congregational persuasion who failed to survive in their livings at the initial settlement of 1660, though sectaries, and particularly the Quakers, who had suffered intermittently in the Interregnum, temporarily received only local persecution. The second settlement, following the election of the Cavalier Parliament, occasioned the expulsion of many of those Presbyterian royalists whom Milton had warned about the costs of restoration. Many lost their livings in the St Bartholomew's Day expulsions of 1662. The model of conciliation which Charles II and Clarendon had held out, most probably in all sincerity, in the period immediately before and after the Restoration, had been swept aside by the stringency of the Clarendon Code developed under the Cavalier Parliament. Though Laud's old obsessions with Arminian doctrine and with altar-rails did not revive, the model both for worship and for church government was fiercely and uncompromisingly episcopalian. The classical Presbyterian system found no place within the reaction, and the use of the Prayer-Book and the authority of bishops were as insistently asserted as they had been in the 1630s. Prominent and respectable Presbyterian divines felt keenly by the middle of the decade that they had lost much. They were not without friends, but the

[10] Ibid. 280.　　　　　　　　　　　　[11] *Milton*, i. 577.

promises of Breda had not been honoured. Even Edward Calamy, one of the most respected Presbyterian divines of the age, lost his living. Richard Baxter, to whom Clarendon had looked to play a significant part in conciliation between episcopacy and Presbyterianism, concluded in despair, 'We spoke to the Deaf.'[12] Politically, too, old Presbyterian royalists were eclipsed. William Prynne, the most active propagandist of Presbyterian royalism, was rebuked by the House of Commons in late 1661, and by 1663 had formed the view that the terms under which he had supported the Restoration had been betrayed.[13]

The sectaries soon suffered more than loss of livings and freedom of worship. Once Charles's initial and rather whimsical protection for Quakerism had been withdrawn, savage legislation drove many congregations underground and threatened Quakers, less inclined to clandestine operation than other groups, with wholesale transportation. Probably thousands of sectaries died in the plague- and fever-infested gaols in what is sometimes termed the period of the great persecution.[14]

The tawdry symbolism of the restored court worked to negate directly the misery of their own earlier defeat. Before Charles sailed for England, Montagu's fleet had to be renamed, since many of the ships commemorated parliamentary victories. Much as Milton would have expected, the names of the royal family replaced them. Thus the *Naseby* became the *Charles*, the *Langport* the *Henrietta*, the *Dunbar* the *Henry*. The *Winceby* became the *Happy Return*. God's mercies to the English people gave way to the celebration of individual princes and princesses, among them at least one Catholic. Again, in an attempt somehow to cancel out the past, Vane's execution was scheduled to coincide with the anniversary of Naseby.[15]

The coronation, in contrast with the relative austerity of the Cromwellian court, was marked by unprecedentedly lavish display. 'The nobility competed for position and in ostentation. . . . Buckingham's robes were said to have cost £30,000, Hyde [Clarendon] "shone like a diamond" and an onlooker wondered

---

[12] Richard Baxter, quoted by N. H. Keeble, *The Literary Culture of Nonconformity in Later Seventeenth-Century England* (Leicester, 1987), 30; my remarks on Restoration nonconformity owe much to Keeble's account.

[13] Hutton, *Restoration*, 159, 185.

[14] Ibid., *passim*.

[15] Pepys, *Diary*, i. 154; Hutton, *Restoration*, 163.

how so many ostrich feathers could have been found in England.' Besides opulence, the English court multiplied itself through the establishment of subsidiary courts for the queen mother and for the Duke of York, as Milton predicted. Again, Catholics were entertained in the highest circles, as he predicted. And those courts too were characterized by sexual intrigue, as he predicted. In the year of Milton's death, over £2,000 from Government funds were spent on silver ornaments for Nell Gwyn's bed. Those who failed in their warnings can rarely have so appropriately comforted themselves that they were right.[16]

The Cassandra syndrome, however, offers very limited consolation. Important constitutional shifts had occurred in the relationship between king and Parliament, shifts which were initially obscured by the reactionary nature of the Cavalier Parliament. But by 1662 much of political and religious life had been reconstructed as it was in the 1630s, seemingly quite securely. As Colonel Harrison, the regicide, was jeered to the scaffold, the crowd called out, 'Where is your Good Old Cause now?' He answered, with a metaphoric power as awesome as Montrose's in similar circumstances, 'Here in my bosom, and I shall seal it with my blood.'[17] Save in such terms, the Good Old Cause was utterly eclipsed. The 'Paradise within' becomes an informing motif for Puritan thinking and writing for that decade and the decade to come.

Two points remain to be made about the cultural and more specifically literary implications of the conflict. A literature of an abiding fascination was generated in the middle decades of the century through the interaction of the literary process and political and religious commitment. There is an ethical difficulty: the horror of the wars is not in any sense mitigated by the writing produced at its fringe. Yet that literary achievement survives the conflict, though oil-seed rape and winter barley cover the battlefields of Winceby and Marston Moor, and the communal graves of the fallen have disappeared. Moreover, the overt politicization of so many literary forms transformed the subsequent course of writing in English.

---

[16] The first sexual intrigue to attract a wide public awareness was probably the relationship of James, Duke of York, with Hyde's daughter; among Catholic courtiers George Digby, Earl of Bristol, was most prominent, but the House of Lords had 25 Catholic members (ibid. 149, 167). On the expense of royal mistresses, see id., *Charles II*, 335.

[17] Wedgwood, *Trial*, 223.

Lovelace and Herrick, Caroline court poets who published after the declaration of war, exhibit qualities quite different from the more brittle pleasures of Carew, who died in 1639, and Suckling, who died in exile in 1642. Carew's repertoire largely matches Lovelace's, and he performs the role of the smoother, less worrying heir to the traditions of Donne and Jonson with a technical accomplishment that Lovelace often lacks. The same could be argued for Suckling, though the lyric achievement seems slimmer. Yet the two *Lucasta*s have a kind of resonance which Carew and Suckling cannot offer. The values and the social mores the earlier writers celebrate seem easy and ethically vague. Lovelace fashions instead a heroic lament for a passing culture which in its dominant phase appeared shallow and a little tawdry. Herrick, of course, has qualities unmatched by any of them in his religious writing, in his refreshment of a flagging neoclassicism, and in his incorporation of a vision of bucolic England into the courtly lyric. Yet the poems he writes that come closest to the range of Suckling and Carew, like Lovelace's, are distanced from them by their defiant and embattled assertion of the anti-Puritan culture in an era of Puritan ascendancy.

Moreover, at the Restoration the literary culture of the court could not so easily be re-established where it left off. Panegyric loses its almost unqualified assertion of the primacy of the semi-divine king, at least among the more important poets of the period. Norbrook, among others, has alerted us to the subtle emphases and unexpected silences by which even masque-writers of the 1630s could articulate an oblique criticism of the policies of the king.[18] The primacy of the king as object of regard, however, remained undisturbed. The restored court admitted of few such certainties. A radical decentring had occurred. Pre-war panegyric of the late 1630s frequently celebrated the king through the impact he had on his surroundings, describing the effulgence he irradiated to those who regarded him. Thus Suckling's 'On New-Years Day 1640. To the King' begins:

> Awake (great Sir) the Sun shines heer.
> Gives all Your Subjects a New-yeer,
> Onely we stay till You appear,

---

[18] D. Norbrook, 'The Reformation of the Masque', in D. Lindley (ed.), *The Court Masque*, (Manchester, 1984), 94–110.

> For thus by us Your Power is understood:
> He may make fair days, You must make them good.[19]

In similar vein, Carew's 'Upon the Kings Sicknesse' complains that the king's illness—the allusion is probably to James I rather than Charles I[20]—takes the sun from the courtiers' world:

> The griefe is felt at Court, where it doth move
> Through every joynt, like the true soule of love.
>
> .   .   .   .
>
> That ruddie morning beame of Majestie,
> Which should the Suns ecclipsed light supply,
> Is overcast with mists, and in the liew
> Of cherefull rayes, sends us downe drops of dew. [21]

The best of Restoration panegyric, that of Dryden, is premissed not on the notion of Charles II's undisputed centrality, but rather upon the recognition that his reign replaces that of others and that it has been established after defeat and suffering and largely through the efforts of others. These are elements even in *Astraea Redux* (1661) and *To His Sacred Majesty, a Panegyrick on His Coronation* (1660). Oppositional elements are conceded still to exist within the State. 'Jealous Sects'[22] remain, though now controlled by Charles. The sins of the subjects (among them Dryden, elegist of Oliver) are acknowledged:

> Kind Heav'n so rare a temper did provide
> That guilt repenting might in it confide.
> Among our crimes oblivion may be set,
> But 'tis our Kings perfection to forget.[23]

The spirit of 1660, on Dryden's account, is conciliatory, but the reconciliation is based upon an acknowledgement of past and present opposition, albeit of a subordinate and controlled kind. Whereas opposition to the sunlike power of the king seems unthinkable in Carew and Suckling, in Dryden it is presented, rather, as part of the burden of monarchy: 'What King, what

---

[19] ll. 1–5, *The Works of Sir John Suckling: The Non-Dramatic Works*, ed. T. Clayton (Oxford, 1971), 84.
[20] *The Poems of Thomas Carew*, ed. R. Dunlap (1949; Oxford, 1964), 229.
[21] ll. 25–32, *Poems*, 35–6.
[22] *Panegyrick* ll. 81, *Poems and Fables*, 26.
[23] Ibid. ll. 85–8.

Crown from Treasons reach is free.'[24] Moreover, Charles is not instrumental in determining his own destiny: "Twas *Monck* whom Providence design'd to loose | Those real bonds false freedom did impose.'[25] Dryden knows the memory may not be erased. In mentioning the renaming of the *Naseby* he memorializes its former name.[26]

By the mid–1660s, Dryden's panegyrics have assumed a persistently defensive form. *Annus Mirabilis* (1667) is wholly reactive to the alternative, critical constructs available in the interpretation of mid-decade Government policy. By *Absalom and Achitophel* (1681), towards the end of the reign, a policy of damage-limitation obtains, as Dryden, far from celebrating the monarch, demonstrates his superiority to rivals of decidedly limited or destructive character and he concedes that dissent, contradiction, and the construction of alternatives abide at the heart even of the royal court. By then, a different court poetry had emerged in the inverted panegyric of Rochester. Yet even there, Charles II merely exemplifies particularly strongly the absurdities of his gender and the age. Indeed, 'Restlesse he roalles about from Whore to Whore | A merry Monarch, scandalous and poor',[27] but he is distinguished only by his prominence from the lecherous buffoons of his court.

Rochester also marks the end-point of the fascinating shifts in libertine poetry over the central decades of the century. A clear line of indebtedness links Carew's 'A Rapture' to Rochester's 'The Imperfect Enjoyment', but the changes in tone and attitude are profound. Carew had been buoyant:

> Yet my tall Pine, shall in the *Cyprian* straight
> Ride safe at Anchor, and unlade her fraight:
> My Rudder, with thy bold hand, like a tryde,
> And skilfull Pilot, thou shalt steere, and guide
> My Bark into Loves channell, where it shall
> Dance, as the bounding waves doe rise and fall. [28]

In Herrick and the first *Lucasta*, such libertinism assumes a profounder cultural value as the defiant rehearsal of unreconstruc-

---

[24] John Dryden, *Astraea Redux: A Poem on the Happy Restoration and Return Of His Sacred Majesty Charles the Second*, l. 39, ibid. 17.
[25] ll. 151–2, ibid. 20.
[26] ll. 231–2, ibid. 22.
[27] John Wilmot, Earl of Rochester, '[A Satire on Charles II]', ll. 14–15, *The Poems of John Wilmot, Earl of Rochester*, ed. K. Walker (Oxford, 1984), 74.
[28] 'A Rapture', ll. 85–90, *Poems*, 51.

ted anti-Puritan sentiment. The second *Lucasta* perhaps marks a shift to a seamier sexual perspective. For Rochester sexuality constitutes the most eloquent manifestation of and most potent motivation towards the grossest acts of human folly. Nor are its rewards consonant with the sacrifices it requires. Disgrace persistently is its outcome. Sexuality reduces the monarch to a fool: 'His Sceptre and his Prick are of a Length, I And she may sway the one, who plays with th' other.'[29] All classes and estates are led by their lust through St James's Park in the erotic equivalent to the Dance of Death topos:

> Great Ladies, Chamber Mayds, and Drudges,
> The Ragg picker, and Heiress Trudges;
> Carrmen, Divines, Great Lords, and Taylors,
> Prentices, Poets, Pimps, and Gaolers,
> Footmen, Fine Fopps, does here arrive,
> And here promiscuously they swive. [30]

The speaker of Donne's 'Love's Alchymie' had pondered, 'Ends love in this, that my man, I Can be as happy as I can . . . ?'[31] In Rochester sexual love erodes social distinction, but often ends, not in happiness, but in folly and disgrace. The phallicism which Herrick and Lovelace opposed to the Puritan aesthetic becomes in Restoration love poetry a token of universal humiliation, sometimes appearing, as in the case of 'The Imperfect Enjoyment',[32] as a literal and spiritual impotence.

Paradoxically, the Puritan aesthetic, in the literary context, survives the political reverses of the Restoration far better than the culture of the court, though it survives transformed. Milton's career as a writer of political prose halted abruptly in 1660, to be resumed only briefly with—another paradox, some may think—his fiercely anti-Catholic, tolerationist treatise, *Of True Religion* (1673). But his influence as a political thinker was quite strongly manifest after his death, when Whig writers, constructing the history of their movement, rediscovered and reissued his work, and his political prose is discernible as an important influence on radical writers of

---

[29] Rochester, '[A Satire]', ll. 11–12, *Poems*, 74.
[30] Rochester, 'A Ramble in Saint James's Parke', ll. 27–32, *Poems*, 64.
[31] ll. 15–16, *Poetical Works*, 36.
[32] Rochester, 'The Imperfect Enjoyment', *Poems*, 30–2.

the late eighteenth and early nineteenth centuries, among them Coleridge.[33]

The theological heterodoxy of *De Doctrina Christiana* precluded its publication, but *Paradise Lost* compromises on none of its central doctrinal propositions, though the exposition of them is oblique and implicit rather than discursive and explicit. The Milton who could respond mirthfully to the Pamela prayer incident would perhaps have appreciated the irony that *Paradise Lost* had been accorded a central role in the emerging English canon before the rediscovery of his Latin treatise in 1824 stimulated a wider awareness that his religion is at some remove from conventional Anglicanism.[34]

All Milton's major poetry of the Restoration is replete with recollection of the political crises and negotiates a complex position with respect to the ascendancy. The distinction he makes in *Paradise Lost* between 'wedded love' (iv. 750) and 'the bought smile | of harlots . . . court amours | Mixed dance, or wanton mask' (iv. 765–8) complements neatly Rochester's vision of the private life of the merry monarch and his courtiers. In constructing the visions of futurity in *Paradise Lost* Books XI and XII, Milton not only describes the trials of the godly remnant but also emphasizes, with an abiding confidence, God's regard for them. Noah, the 'one just man alive' (xi. 818), functions as exemplar of the saints' capacity to live untainted amid the lurid corruption of the fallen world. Moreover, 'providence' remains their 'guide' (xii. 647). *Samson Agonistes* probably hits at the received image of the restored court, 'Drunk with idolatry, drunk with wine . . . Chanting their idol' (ll. 1670–2), and the regeneration of the defeated hero, striking them down when they are 'set only on sport and play' (l. 1679), offers the eclipsed radical the gratifying fantasy of 'dearly-bought revenge, yet glorious' (l. 1660), as if one of the botched insurrections of the 1660s and 1670s had at least wiped out the court before its collapse.

The political implications of *Paradise Regained* show Milton at his most complex. An unrepentant anticlericalism surely inspires the jibe—Satan makes it, but Christ does not dispute it—that God 'Suffers the hypocrite or atheous priest | To tread his sacred courts, and minister | About his altar' (i. 487–9). But besides the occasional

---

[33] Sensabaugh, *Grand Whig, passim*; Kitson, 'Coleridge', esp. ch. 7.
[34] *CPW* vi. 3–10.

satirical flourish—at the pomp of power and at the folly of militarism as well as at the Church—*Paradise Regained* explores the problem of the powerlessness of the godly, and resolves it in the paradox of the mightiness of unarmed, unaided Christ, eschewing supernatural intervention in resisting and overthrowing Satan. Christ's victory is a victory in the mind and the heart, arenas where the godly remnant may yet fight on even footing with their enemies. The true *imitatio Christi*, on the model of *Paradise Regained*, takes the form of moral and intellectual perseverance of the kind that Milton could have regarded himself as manifesting. The millenarian impulse, powerful in Milton's writings since 'On the Morning of Christ's Nativity' and strongly felt in *Of Reformation*, is not denied, but consideration of when Christ will assume his rule on earth is exclusively the concern of the fallen angels. In a sense, it is now an issue secondary to the ethical imperatives of Restoration nonconformity, resistance of the surrounding corruption, and the nurture of a paradise within. Not only Harrison carried the Good Old Cause in his bosom.

The later influence of Levellerism and Diggerism is harder to chart. The movements scarcely survived into the 1650s as active elements in English politics, though Lilburne may have influenced Paine and Godwin, and Winstanley's thinking has been identified as a component in Coleridge's early synthesis of Christian ethics and radical politics, and aspects of early-nineteenth-century radicalism seem remarkably close to the principles of the Diggers.[35]

Bunyan's literary reputation offers a paradox as rich as Milton's. Just as *Paradise Lost* functions as the cornerstone of English neoclassicism and its author as its primary representative in the canon of cerebral but respectable literary art, so *Pilgrim's Progress* is eventually appropriated as a rugged, accessible devotional treatise, making the central truths of Christian doctrine available to all classes and cultures. Certainly, its circulation in the seventeenth century and later is impressive. It was frequently reprinted, published in Ireland, Scotland, and New England, and translated into Welsh. In the nineteenth century, translated into various African languages, it became part of the missionaries' spiritual armoury. Yet *Pilgrim's Progress* makes no compromise about the

[35] Kitson, 'Coleridge', 100–2, 257; I. McCalman, *Radical Underworld: Prophets, Revolutionaries and Pornographers in London, 1795–1840* (Cambridge, 1988), 64, 68, 71.

social and political assumptions of the lower-class radical sectaries. Bunyan's pilgrim heroes are ordinary men, distinguished only by their election and their ability to persevere, and those who would torment them invite identification with the gentry class and their agents in the reactionary process of putting the propertiless back in their place which characterized regional aspects of the Restoration domestic policy. Texts that value the lives of indigent and counter-cultural itinerants over those of magistrates necessarily invite a political reading, especially when the author vouchsafes that he writes from prison.[36]

[36] Hill, *Bunyan and his Church*, esp. ch. 18, offers the most convincing account of Bunyan's radicalism and a rather better guide to how his text relates to contemporary suffering of the godly than B. Hammond's '*The Pilgrim's Progress*: Satire and Social Comment', in *The Pilgrim's Progress: Critical and Historical Views*, ed. V. Newey (Liverpool, 1980), 118–31.

Appendix A: *Dating* Hesperides

WE do not know exactly when *Hesperides* was published. George Thomason collected a copy but, as sometimes happened, he failed to date exactly when it came into his possession, and the Stationers Register is similarly unhelpful. Its only reference to an anthology of Herrick's verse comes from 1640, when Andrew Crooke entered for his copy '*The severall Poems* written by Master Robert Herrick'. The entry has been variously interpreted as pertaining to the subsequently delayed *Hesperides*, or else to some other collection which was either withdrawn or perhaps did not survive. The publishers of the 1648 volume, John Williams and Francis Eglesfield,[1] seem to have registered nothing in 1647 and 1648.

Many of the poems in *Hesperides* were written long before publication. Martin assigns dates to forty-five in the collection (leaving aside *Noble Numbers*), and of these four are from the second decade of the century, five from the third, and thirteen from the fourth, and, as we know, a collection was at least planned for publication in 1640. Yet *Hesperides* is not simply a great retrospective: it is, in some senses, a product of the late 1640s. Where earlier manuscripts exist, Martin has demonstrated that Herrick revised assiduously and 'to good purpose'.[2] Moreover, while *Hesperides* almost certainly represents the culmination of decades of creativity, it is no mere repository for the uncritically assembled totality of his output. Herrick would seem to have excluded quite a few items: he may, perhaps, have mislaid them, but their omission could, just as coherently, be regarded as manifestation of his editorial control and discrimination in the production of his book.[3]

Hesperides should be regarded both as a product of many years and as a product of the late 1640s which takes its political significance from the peculiar circumstances of that period. When did Herrick put the parts into a whole? The *terminus a quo* may be fairly easily fixed. The latest

[1] Introductory Note to *Hesperides*; Moorman, *Herrick*, 124; Herrick, *Poetical Works*, pp. xv–xvi. A number of copies bear the imprint 'Printed for *John Williams*, and *Francis Eglesfield*, and to be sold by *Tho: Hunt*, Bookseller in *Exon*': so some were evidently intended for sale by an Exeter bookseller in the conurbation nearest Herrick's Dean Prior living.

[2] Ibid. xxxii.

[3] Ibid. xxxii–xxxiii; L. Schleiner notes that a number of poems are extant in song settings but do not appear in *Hesperides*, which suggests that rather more poems were in circulation than Herrick chose to include ('Herrick's Songs and the Character of Hesperides', *ELR* 6 (1976), 77–8).

contemporary references are to his own ejection and return to London—their precise date has not been determined, but it was in 1647—and to the removal of the captive Charles I to Hampton Court, which occurred on 24 August, 1647.[4] So the editorial process, which may have been continuing for some time, was finalized during the period from late autumn, 1647 to some undetermined point in 1648. The evidence of the secondary title-page suggests that publication was effected fairly early in 1648.

Hesperides, like many seventeenth-century collections of poetry,[5] is arranged and printed in sections. The first and longest, consisting of 1,130 almost entirely secular poems, follows the general title-page, dedication, and errata; the second, the text of which has a discontinuous signature,[6] contains 273 divine poems, and follows a secondary title-page, which entitles them *His Noble Numbers, or, His Pious Pieces*, and the imprint of which reads 'LONDON, Printed for *John Williams*, and *Francis Eglesfield*. 1647'. The secondary title-page is printed on sig. Cc8^r, that is, the last leaf of the last gathering of the first part. The general title-page, dedicatory poem, and errata, which must have been printed last since the errata refer to the other sheets, are contained on the half-sheet [A1]–A2–A4. So it seems quite likely that all except the prolegomenous material was printed before the end of 1647 or at least shortly afterwards.[7] As such, *Hesperides* was produced in a period of quite extraordinary ambivalence for supporters of the king.

[4] *Hesperides* (London, 1648), 356; Gardiner, iii. 187.

[5] Compare e.g. the differentiation of the English poems and the poems in other languages in Milton's *Poems* (1645).

[6] The first part ends with gathering Cc; the second begins with Aa (bibliographical description based on examination of B/L copies E.1090 and G11495, which have variant title-pages).

[7] Printers and booksellers in the early modern period tended, for purposes of determining the date to go on title-pages, to regard 1 January as the start of the year, though Thomason, himself a bookseller, regarded 25 March, for other purposes, as the start of the year.

Appendix B: Marvell: The Canon and the Critics

THE rise of Marvell's poetic reputation after two centuries of neglect constituted one of the more signal achievements of early-twentieth-century criticism, and in recent years he has been better served by the scholarship and ingenuity of the discipline than any of his contemporaries.[1] The forward youth who would appear as Marvell scholar needs to set aside some time to consider the secondary material. Two questions suggest themselves: why should Marvell have become the focus of so much critical attention? and what supplementation or correction may a new study achieve?

In a sense, the answers are interrelated. Marvell's *œuvre* offers singular attractions. It is small—too small, some would argue, for Marvell really to rank with Milton or Dryden in the undisclosed league table most scholars privately entertain—but it contains about 2,000 lines of fascinatingly complex accomplishment. Pedagogically —and maybe this too relates to the slenderness of the output— Marvell is one of the easiest of poets in which to engage undergraduate enthusiasm. But, most significantly, Marvell offers a

[1] T. S. Eliot's influential *TLS* article is reprinted in his *Selected Essays* (New York, 1932), 278–90, and in E. S. Donno (ed.), *Andrew Marvell: The Critical Heritage* (London, Henley, and Boston, 1978), 362–76. Donno offers an excellent overview of the history of Marvell's critical reputation (pp. 1–25). Among the most stimulating accounts of Marvell's poetry are the following: W. Empson, *Some Versions of Pastoral* (1935; Harmondsworth, 1966), esp. ch. 4; M. C. Bradbrook and M. G. Lloyd Thomas, *Andrew Marvell* (Cambridge, 1961); Roestvig, *The Happy Man*, esp. vol. i. ch. 4; J. M. Wallace, *Destiny his Choice: The Loyalism of Andrew Marvell* (1968; Cambridge, 1980); H. E. Toliver, *Marvell's Ironic Vision* (New Haven and London, 1965); Colie, *'My Ecchoing Song'*: J. B. Leishman, *The Art of Marvell's Poetry* (London, 1966); Friedman, *Marvell's Pastoral Art*; Patterson, *Civic Crown*; Hodge, *Foreshortened Time*; Chernaik, *Poet's Time*; J. Goldberg, *Voice Terminal Echo: Postmodernism and English Renaissance Texts* (New York and London, 1986), ch. 2; Wilding, *Dragons Teeth*, chs. 5 and 6; Wilcher, *Marvell*; G. Parry, *Seventeenth-Century Poetry: The Social Context* (London, 1985), ch. 9; M. Stocker, *Apocalyptic Marvell: The Second Coming in Seventeenth Century Poetry* (Brighton, 1986); Worden, 'Andrew Marvell'; and Norbrook, 'Marvell's "Horatian Ode"'. Important collections of essays include J. Carey (ed.), *Andrew Marvell: A Critical Anthology* (Harmondsworth, 1969); M. Wilding, *Marvell: Modern Judgements* (London, 1969); K. Friedenreich (ed.), *Tercentenary Essays in Honour of Andrew Marvell* (Hamden, Conn., 1977); C. A. Patrides (ed.), *Approaches to Marvell: The York Tercentenary Lectures* (London, Henley, and Boston, 1978); R. L. Brett (ed.), *Andrew Marvell: Essays on the Tercentenary of his death* (Hull and Oxford, 1979).

puzzle, or rather a series of puzzles, about levels of seriousness, about areas of allusion and reference, and about ideological inconsistencies, apparent or real.

Synthesizing Marvell, finding a key to explain the political vagaries of his poetry, poses a central and alluring difficulty. Critics, perhaps, like their subject authors to be heroes, and the old dictum (and its variants) that the good poet must first be a good person, remains a common assumption, albeit largely unacknowledged. An occasional jaundiced view may offer a biographical explanation, that Marvell's alternating preferences relate to bids for patronage and advancement, but synthesizers look for a larger motivation. For Patterson, Marvell's political writing embodies the friction between a sensibility close to the personal produced in the lyric poems and the exigencies of political crisis, which manifests itself in 'a pattern of alternating commitment and retreat, of rash involvement followed by self-doubt or apology'. For Tolliver, 'the flexibility and subtlety of Marvell's modes of rejection and withdrawal' find explanation in 'the ironist's indirection'. For Wilding, Marvell's political poems of the 1650s disclose the purposeful narrowing of perspective in service of a new establishment. On Chernaik's account, 'his career provides an impressive and moving example of an artist's realism and courage in facing up to the problems of how to live in a fallen world'. His unflinchingly radical Marvell contrasts neatly with Wallace's 'loyalist', a figure analogous to Edward Hyde, one of 'the thousands and thousands of [loyalists]' who 'turned their coats with the times and followed with a clear conscience the changes of regime'.[2] And there are others. With so many Marvells available, most of them internally coherent and many quite attractive, need another be constructed?

In such hard-won internal coherence abides the problem. Hitherto most accounts of Marvell's writings of the late 1640s and early 1650s overstate its cohesion, often as a result of reading backwards from the reassuringly liberal voice produced in his late prose works, particularly the two parts of *The Rehearsal Transpros'd* (1672, 1673). Marvell's responses to royalist defeat, to constitutional uncertainty, and to the ideological transformations of the republican period are disconcertingly unstable in ways that challenge profoundly the more optimistic assumptions of liberal humanism. Marvell does not hold together.

It is unsurprising that critics so often read backwards from Marvell's career after 1660. His life records become considerably fuller after his election to Parliament in 1659, though numerous enigmas remain.[3] We know more about Dryden and Donne and far more about Milton. Where

---

[2] Patterson, *Civic Crown*, 10; Tolliver, *Ironic Vision*, 58–9; Wilding, *Dragons Teeth*, 114–72; Chernaik, *Poet's Time*, 205; J. M. Wallace, *Destiny*, 4.

[3] Legouis, *Marvell*, a revision of his *André Marvell* (1928), remains the best biography in English. For an excellent account of the limitations of documentation, see J. Kenyon, 'Andrew Marvell: Life and Times', in Brett, *Marvell*, 1–35.

he lived, how he supported himself, whom he knew and sympathized with during the 1640s remains highly conjectural. He certainly spent some time abroad, but exactly where, and for how long, and how he was funded are shadowy. As to the 1650s, we know of his interest early in the decade in entering the civil service of the new republic—Milton (abortively) wrote to Bradshaw, a leading civilian Independent, on his behalf[4]—and we know he entered the service of Fairfax and thereafter Cromwell. In both cases, however, his role was relatively menial, as tutor to Fairfax's daughter and Cromwell's ward William Dutton. He did not live in Cromwell's household and he spent some of the mid–1650s abroad with Dutton. In the late 1650s he finally entered the civil service and thereafter Parliament, and, though 'some mystery' surrounds his first election, it is fairly clear that he was returned as a supporter of the new protectorate of Richard Cromwell.[5] Only a handful of his letters are extant from before the Restoration, and nothing that discloses his private hopes or feelings.

Few of the poems traditionally attributed to the 1650s or late 1640s were printed in his lifetime. We owe the survival of most to the publication in 1681—he had died in 1679—of *Miscellaneous Poems*, which appeared prefaced with this note:

TO THE READER

These are to certifie every Ingenious Reader, that all these Poems, as also the other things in this Book contained, are Printed according to the exact Copies of my late dear Husband, under his own Hand-Writing, being found since his Death among his other Papers, Witness my Hand this 15*th* day of *October*, 1680.

Mary Marvell.[6]

By 'Ingenious' readers 'Mrs Marvell' probably meant no more than 'ingenuous', that is 'well-born' or 'of noble disposition'. However, ingenious readers of the more astute kind have brooded persistently on this passage. We have no documentation to support Mary's claim to be his widow, and the more customary interpretation is that she was merely his landlady who assumed the role for various complicated financial advantages, which presumably included remuneration for providing the copy for *Miscellaneous Poems*.[7] For all we know, the author of 'To his Coy Mistress' may have lived wholly celibate.

The cloudy circumstances of publication have interpretative implications. We do not *know* (though critics often guess) when many poems were

[4] Reprinted by Donno, *Marvell*, 99–100.
[5] Legouis, *Marvell*, 116.
[6] *Poems and Letters*, i. 8.
[7] The issues are most fully rehearsed by Bradbrook and Lloyd Thomas, *Marvell*, 145–8.

Appendix B

written, and we have no documentation about revisions which they may have undergone between composition and Marvell's death. There is some evidence that 'Tom May's Death', apparently composed in 1650, has been updated to take note of May's exhumation in 1661.[8] Again, the poems 'among his . . . Papers' may well have omitted some, now lost, and included works by other authors which Marvell had merely transcribed for his own amusement. Thus, on quite good evidence, some would add to his *œuvre* 'An Elegy upon the Death of my Lord *Francis Villers*' and others, though less convincingly, would exclude 'Tom May's Death' and 'On the Victory obtained by Blake'.[9]

[8] *Poems and Letters*, i. 303.
[9] Ibid. 429–36; Marvell, *Complete Poetry*, pp. xxx–xxxii.

Bibliography

Answer to a Book, Intituled, The Doctrine and Discipline of Divorce (London, 1644).

Articles of Peace, Made and Concluded with the Irish Rebels, and Papists (London, 1649).

A Barbarous and Inhumane Speech Spoken by the Lord Wentworth (London, 1642).

The Book of Common Prayer (London, 1638, 1647).

The Brothers of the Blade: Answerable to the Sisters of the Scaberd, or, A Dialogue betweene two Hotspurres of the Times, Serjeant Slice-Man, alias Smell-Smock of Coney-Court in Chick-Lane, and Corporall Dam-Mee of Bell-Alley neer Pick-Hatch (London, 1641).

The Catholikes Petition to Prince Rupert . . . with a Draught of a Proclamation Presented to His Highnesse, for the More Speedy Recruting his Army, Destroying the Protestants, and Gaining a Crowne (London, 1644).

The Censure of the Rota upon Mr Miltons Book Entitled, The Ready and Easy Way (London, 1660).

The Cities Welcome to Colonell Rich and Colonell Baxter, with their Solemne Invitation to the Sainted Commanders in the Army (n.p., 1648).

The Declaration of Many Thousands of the City of Canterbury (London, 1647).

'An Homily against Disobedience and Wilful Rebellion', in *Second Book of the Homilies* (The Prayer Book and Homily Society; London, 1840).

The Kings Cabinet Opened (London, 1645).

King Charles the 1st's Defence of the Church of England (The Hague, n.d.).

Military Orders and Articles, Established by His Majestie (Oxford, n.d.).

A Modest Confutation of a Slanderous and Scurrilous Libell, Entituled, Animadversions (London, 1642).

New Orders, New, Agreed upon by a Parliament of Round-Heads (London, 1642).

Nocturnall Occurrences, or, Deeds of Darknesse Committed by the Cavaleers in their Rendevous (London, 1642).

A Perfect Narrative of the Whole Proceedings of the High Court of Justice (London, 1649).

Prince Rupert's Burning Love to England: Discovered in Birminghams Flames (London, 1643).

A Private Letter, from an Eminent Cavalier (London, 1642).

A Prognostication upon W. Laud (London, 1641).

The Royall Legacies of Charles the First (n.p., 1649).

Sad and Fearful Newes from Beverley (London, n.d.).

A Short, Compendious, and True Description of the Round-Heads and the Long-Heads (n.p., 1642).

A Short History of the Anabaptists of High and Low Germany (London, 1644).

The Speeches of the Lord General Fairfax, and the Officers of the Armie to the Diggers (London, 1649).

These Tradesmen are Preachers in and about the City of London (London, 1647).

The Whole Business of Miles Sindercombe (London, 1656).

The Wicked Resolution of the Cavaliers (London, 1642).

A Witty Answer to a Foolish Pamphlet, Intituled New Orders New (London, n.d.).

ALMONI, PELONI, *A Compendious Discourse, Proving Episcopacy to be of Apostolicall and Consequently of Divine Institution* (London, 1641).

ALSOP, J. D., 'Gerrard Winstanley: Religion and Respectability', *Hist. Jnl.* 28 (1985), 705–9.

ANGLO, SYDNEY, 'The Courtier', in A. G. Dickens (ed.), *The Courts of Europe: Politics, Patronage and Royalty, 1400–1800* (London, 1977), 33–53.

ANSELMENT, RAYMOND A., *'Betwixt Jest and Earnest': Marprelate, Milton, Marvell, Swift and the Decorum of Religious Ridicule* (Toronto, Buffalo, and London, 1979).

AYLMER, G. E., 'The Religion of Gerrard Winstanley', in McGregor and Reay, 91–119.

—— (ed.), *'England's Spirit Unfoulded, or, An Incouragement to Take the Engagement*, by Jerrard Winstanley: A Newly Discovered Pamphlet by Gerrard Winstanley', *P. & P.* 40 (1968), 3–15.

BACON, FRANCIS, *The Advancement of Learning*, ed. G. W. Kitchen (1915; London, 1965).

BAGWELL, RICHARD, *Ireland under the Stuarts and during the Interregnum* (1909–16; London, 1965).

BAINTON, ROLAND H., *Hunted Heretic: The Life and Death of Michael Servetus, 1511–1553* (1953; Boston, 1960).

BANGS, CARL, *Arminius: A Study in the Dutch Reformation* (Nashville and New York, 1971).

BARKER, ARTHUR, *Milton and the Puritan Dilemma, 1641–1660* (Toronto, 1942).

BLUM, ABBE, 'The Author's Authority: *Areopagitica* and the Labour of Licensing', in Nyquist and Ferguson, 74–96.

BOSSY, JOHN, *The English Catholic Community 1570–1850* (New York, 1976).

BOTTIGHEIMER, KARL S., *English Money and Irish Land: The 'Adventurers' in the Cromwellian Settlement of Ireland* (Oxford, 1971).

BRADBROOK, M. C., and LLOYD, THOMAS M. G., *Andrew Marvell* (Cambridge, 1961).

BRAILSFORD, H. N., *The Levellers and the English Revolution*, ed. Christopher Hill (1961; Nottingham, 1976).

BRAMHALL, JOHN, *The Serpents Salve, or, A Remedie for the Biting of an Aspe* (London, 1643).

BRETT, R. L. (ed.), *Andrew Marvell: Essays on the Tercentenary of his Death* (Hull and Oxford, 1979).

BROWNE, Sir THOMAS, *Religio Medici*, ed. L. C. Martin (Oxford, 1964).

—— *Pseudodoxia Epidemica*, ed. Robin Robbins (Oxford, 1981).

BUNYAN, JOHN, *The Life and Death of Mr Badman*, ed. James F. Forrest and Roger Sharrock (Oxford, 1988).

BURTON, ROBERT, *The Anatomy of Melancholy*, ed. Holbrook Jackson (1932; London, 1972).

CAREW, THOMAS, *The Poems of Thomas Carew*, ed. Rhodes Dunlap (1949; Oxford, 1964).

CAREY, JOHN (ed.), *Andrew Marvell: A Critical Anthology* (Harmondsworth, 1969).

CARLTON, CHARLES, *Archbishop William Laud* (London and New York, 1987).

CHARLES I, *The Kings Maiesties Declaration concerning Lawfull Sports* (London, 1633).

—— (attrib.), *Eikon Basilike: The Pourtraicture of his Sacred Maiestie in his Solitudes and Sufferings* ([London], 1649) (Wing E268).

CHERNAIK, WARREN L., *The Poet's Time: Politics and Religion in the Work of Andrew Marvell* (Cambridge, 1983).

COHN, NORMAN, *The Pursuit of the Millennium*, 2nd edn. (London, 1970).

COLIE, ROSALIE L. *'My Ecchoing Song': Andrew Marvell's Poetry of Criticism* (Princeton, 1970).

COOK, JOHN, *King Charles his Case* (London, 1649).

COPPIN, RICHARD, *Divine Teachings*, preface by Abiezer Coppe (London, 1649).

CORISH, PATRICK J., 'The Cromwellian Conquest 1649–53', in T. W. Moody, F. X. Martin, and F. J. Byrne (eds.), *New History of Ireland*, iii. (Oxford, 1986), 336–86.

CORNS, THOMAS N., ' "An Horatian Ode upon Cromwel's Return from Ireland," Lines 53–58', *Explicator*, 35 (1976), 11–12.

—— 'Imagery in Civil War Polemic: Milton, Overton and the *Eikon Basilike*', *Milton Quarterly*, 14 (1980), 1–6.

—— 'New Light on the Left Hand: Contemporary Views of Milton's Prose Style', *Durham University Journal*, 72 (1980), 177–81.

—— 'Obscenity, Slang and Indecorum in Milton's English Prose', *Prose Studies*, 3 (1980), 5–14.

CORNS, THOMAS N., Milton's Quest for Respectability', *MLR* 77 (1982), 769–79.

—— *The Development of Milton's Prose Style* (Oxford, 1982).

—— 'Ideology in the *Poemata* (1645)', in James A. Freeman and Anthony Low (eds.), *Urbane Milton: The Latin Poetry*, *Milton Studies*, 19 (Pittsburgh, 1983), 195–203.

—— 'Publication and Politics 1640–1661: An SPSS-Based Account of the Thomason Collection of Civil War Tracts', *Literary and Linguistic Computing*, 1 (1986), 74–84.

—— 'Milton's *Observations upon the Articles of Peace*: Ireland under English Eyes', in Loewenstein and Turner, 123–34.

—— ' "Some Rousing Motions": The Plurality of Miltonic Ideology', in Healy and Sawday, 110–26.

—— (ed.), *The Literature of Controversy* (London, 1987).

—— SPECK, W. A., and DOWNIE, J. A., 'Archetypal Mystification: Polemic and Reality in English Political Literature, 1640–1750', *Eighteenth Century Life*, 7 (1982), 1–27.

COWLEY, ABRAHAM, *The Mistresse* (London, 1647).

—— *The Guardian: A Comedie Acted before Prince Charls His Highness* (London, 1650).

—— *Poems* (London, 1656).

—— *The Works of Abraham Cowley*, ed. with an account of his life, by Thomas Sprat (London, 1668).

—— *Poems*, ed. A. R. Waller (Cambridge, 1905).

—— *The Civil War*, ed. Allan Pritchard (Toronto, 1973).

CRESSY, DAVID, *Literacy and the Social Order: Reading and Writing in Tudor and Stuart England* (Cambridge, 1980).

CROMWELL, OLIVER, *The Writings and Speeches of Oliver Cromwell*, ed. W. C. Abbott (Cambridge, Mass., 1937–47).

DAVIES, STEVIE, *Images of Kingship in* Paradise Lost (Columbia, Mo., 1983).

DAVIS, J. C., 'Gerrard Winstanley and the Restoration of True Magistracy', *P&P* 70 (1976), 76–93.

—— *Utopia and the Ideal Society: A Study in English Utopian Writing 1516–1700* (Cambridge, 1981).

—— *Fear, Myth and History: The Ranters and the Historians* (Cambridge, 1986).

DEMING, ROBERT H., *Ceremony and Art: Robert Herrick's Poetry* (The Hague, 1974).

DONNE, JOHN, *Poetical Works*, ed. Sir Herbert Grierson (1933; London, 1968).

DONNO, ELIZABETH STORY (ed.), *Andrew Marvell: The Critical Heritage* (London, Henley, and Boston, 1978).

DRYDEN, JOHN, *The Poems and Fables of John Dryden*, ed. James Kinsley (1958; Oxford, 1961).

DUMBLE, W., 'Government, Religion and Military Affairs in Durham during the Civil War and Interregnum', M.Litt. diss. (Durham, 1978).

ECHLIN, EDWARD P., SJ, *The Anglican Eucharist in Ecumenical Perspective: Doctrine and Rite from Cranmer to Seabury* (New York, 1968).

EDWARDS, THOMAS, *Gangraena, or, A Catalogue and Discovery of Many of the Errours, Heresies, Blasphemies and Pernicious Practices of the Sectaries of this Time* (London, 1646).

—— *The Second Part of Gangraena* (London, 1646).

—— *The Third Part of Gangraena* (London, 1646).

—— *Gangraena*, a facsimile reproduction of all three parts intro. M. M. Goldsmith and Ivan Roots (Exeter, 1977).

ELIOT, T. S., *Selected Essays* (New York, 1932).

EMMA, R. D., and SHAWCROSS, J. T., *Language and Style in Milton* (New York, 1967).

EMPSON, WILLIAM, *Some Versions of Pastoral* (1935; Harmondsworth, 1966).

FALLON, STEPHEN M., 'The Metaphysics of Milton's Divorce Tracts', in Loewenstein and Turner, 69–84.

FEATLEY, DANIEL, *The Dippers Dipt* (London, 1645).

FIRTH, C. H., *Cromwell's Army*, 3rd edn. (London, 1921).

—— and RAIT, R. S. (eds.), *Acts and Ordinances of the Interregnum, 1642–1660* (London, 1911).

FISH, STANLEY E., *Self-Consuming Artifacts: The Experience of Seventeenth-Century Literature* (Berkeley, Los Angeles, and London, 1972).

—— 'Driving from the Letter: Truth and Indeterminacy in Milton's *Areopagitica*', in Nyquist and Ferguson, 234–54.

—— 'Wanting a Supplement: The Question of Interpretation in Milton's Early Prose', in Loewenstein and Turner, 41–68.

—— (ed.), *Seventeenth Century Prose: Modern Essays in Criticism* (New York, 1971).

FIXLER, MICHAEL, *Milton and the Kingdoms of God* (London, 1964).

FORTESCUE, G. K., *Catalogue of the Pamphlets, Books, Newspapers, and Manuscripts relating to the Civil War, the Commonwealth, and the Restoration Collected by George Thomason* (London, 1908).

FOXE, JOHN, *Actes and Monuments* (London, 1641).

FRAZER, J. G., *The Golden Bough: A Study in Magic and Religion*, abridged edn. (London, 1960).

FRENCH, J. MILTON (ed.), *The Life Records of John Milton* (1949–58; New York, 1968).

FRIEDENREICH, KENNETH (ed.), *Tercentenary Essays in Honour of Andrew Marvell* (Hamden, Conn., 1977).

FRIEDMAN, DONALD M., *Marvell's Pastoral Art* (London, 1970).

FULLER, THOMAS, *The Holy State* (London, 1642).

GARDINER, S. R., *History of the Great Civil War* (London, 1889).

GARDINER, S. R., *History of the Commonwealth and Protectorate, 1649–1660* (London, 1901).

—— (ed.), *The Constitutional Documents of the Puritan Revolution*, 3rd edn. (1906; Oxford, 1979).

GIBBS, M. A., *The Lord General: A Life of Thomas Fairfax* (London, 1938).

GOLDBERG, JONATHAN, *Voice Terminal Echo: Postmodernism and English Renaissance Texts* (New York and London, 1986).

GOLDSMITH, MAURICE, 'Levellers by Sword, Spade and Word: Radical Egalitarianism in the English Revolution', in Jones, Newitt, and Roberts, 65–80.

GOODWIN, JOHN, *Anti-Cavalierisme, or, Truth Pleading as well the Necessity, as the Lawfulness of this Present War* (London, 1642).

—— *The Obstructours of Justice* (London, 1649).

GOODWIN, THOMAS, NYE, PHILIP, SIMPSON, SIDRACH, BURROUGHES, JEREMY, and BRIDGE, WILLIAM, *An Apologeticall Narration, Humbly Submitted to the Honourable Houses of Parliament* (London, 1643).

GRAHAM, JAMES, Marquis of Montrose, 'His Metrical Prayer (on the Eve of his own Execution)', in Tom Scott (ed.), *The Penguin Book of Scottish Verse* (1970; Harmondsworth, 1988), 239.

GREAVES, RICHARD L., and ZALLER, ROBERT, *Biographical Dictionary of British Radicals in the Seventeenth Century* (Brighton, 1982).

GREEN, MARY A. E. (ed.), *Calendar of State Papers Domestic Series, 1649–1650* (London, 1875).

GREGG, PAULINE, *Free-Born John* (London, 1961).

GUIBBORY, ACHSAH, *The Map of Time: Seventeenth-Century English Literature and Ideas of Pattern in History* (Urbana, Ill., 1986).

HALKETT, LADY ANNE, and FANSHAWE, LADY ANN, *The Memoirs of Anne, Lady Halkett and Ann, Lady Fanshawe*, ed. John Loftis (Oxford, 1979).

HALL, JOSEPH, *Episcopacie by Divine Right Asserted* (London, 1640).

—— *An Humble Remonstrance to the High Court of Parliament* (London, 1640).

—— *A Defence of the Humble Remonstrance* (London, 1641).

HALLER, WILLIAM, *The Rise of Puritanism* (New York, 1938).

—— *Liberty and Reformation in the Puritan Revolution* (New York, 1955).

HAMILTON, K. G., 'The Structure of Milton's Prose', in Emma and Shawcross, 204–320.

HAMMOND, BREAN, '*The Pilgrim's Progress*: Satire and Social Comment', in Vincent Newey (ed.), *The Pilgrim's Progress: Critical and Historical Views* (Liverpool, 1980), 118–31.

HAMMOND, GERALD, 'Richard Lovelace and the Uses of Obscurity', the Chatterton Lecture on Poetry, 1985, *Proc. Brit. Acad.* 71 (1985), 203–34.

HARDACRE, PAUL H. *The Royalists during the English Revolution* (The Hague, 1956).

—— 'Gerrard Winstanley in 1650', *HLQ* 22 (1958–9), 345–9.

HARRISON, A. W., *Arminianism* (London, 1937).

HAYES, T. WILSON, *Winstanley the Digger* (Cambridge, Mass., 1979).

HEALY, THOMAS, and SAWDAY, JONATHAN (eds.), *Literature and the English Civil War* (Cambridge, 1990).

HEINEMANN, MARGOT, *Puritanism and Theatre: Thomas Middleton and Opposition Drama under the Early Stuarts* (Cambridge, 1980).

HERRICK, ROBERT, *The Poetical Works of Robert Herrick*, ed. L. C. Martin (Oxford, 1956).

—— *The Complete Poetry of Robert Herrick*, ed. J. Max Patrick (New York, 1963).

—— *Hesperides* (London, 1648).

—— *Hesperides* (Scolar Press Facsimile, 1969; Menston, Yorks. and London, 1973).

HEYLIN, PETER, *Antidotum Lincolniense* (London, 1637).

HIGINS, J., *Junius Nomenclator* (London, 1585).

HILL, CHRISTOPHER, *Puritanism and Revolution* (1958; London, 1969).

—— *Society and Puritanism in Pre-Revolutionary England* (1964; London, 1966).

—— *God's Englishman: Oliver Cromwell and the English Revolution* (London, 1970).

—— *The World Turned Upside Down: Radical Ideas during the English Revolution* (1972; London, 1978).

—— (ed.), *The Law of Freedom and Other Writings*, by G. Winstanley (1973; Cambridge, 1983).

—— *Milton and the English Revolution* (London, 1977).

—— 'The Religion of Gerrard Winstanley', *P & P Supplement*, 5 (1978).

—— *The Experience of Defeat: Milton and Some Contemporaries* (London, 1984).

—— *A Turbulent, Seditious, and Factious People: John Bunyan and his Church* (1988; Oxford, 1989).

—— REAY, BARRY and LAMONT, WILLIAM, *The world of the Muggleponians* (London, 1983).

—— MULLIGAN, LOTTE, GRAHAM, JOHN K., and RICHARDS, JUDITH, 'Debate: The Religion of Gerrard Winstanley', *P & P* 89 (1980), 144–6.

HODGE, R. I. V., *Foreshortened Time: Andrew Marvell and the 17th Century Revolutions* (Cambridge and Totowa, NJ, 1978).

HOLSTUN, JAMES, *A Rational Millennium: Puritan Utopias of Seventeenth-Century England and America* (New York and Oxford, 1987).

HUCKABAY, CALVIN, *John Milton: An Annotated Bibliography 1929–1960*, rev. edn (Pittsburgh, 1969).

HUTCHINSON, LUCY, *Memoirs of the Life of Colonel Hutchinson*, ed. James Sutherland (London, 1973).

HUTTON, RONALD, *The Royalist War Effort 1642–1646* (London, 1982).

HUTTON, RONALD, *The Restoration: A Political and Religious History of England and Wales 1658–1667* (1985; Oxford, 1987).
—— *Charles II* (Oxford, 1989).

HYDE, EDWARD, Earl of Clarendon, *History of the Rebellion and Civil Wars in England*, ed. W. Dunn Macray, v. (Oxford, 1888).

ILLO, JOHN, 'Areopagiticas Mythic and Real', *Prose Studies*, 11 (1988), 1–23.

INGRAM, WILLIAM, and SWAIM, KATHLEEN, *A Concordance to Milton's English Poetry* (Oxford, 1972).

JOHNSON, SAMUEL, *The False Alarm*, in *The Political Writings of Dr Johnson*, ed. J. P. Hardy (London, 1963).
—— *The Lives of the English Poets*, ed. S. C. Roberts (1963; London, 1967).
—— 'Milton', in *Samuel Johnson*, ed. Donald Greene (Oxford, 1984), 698–716.

JONES, COLIN, NEWITT, MALWYN, and ROBERTS, STEPHEN (eds.), *Politics and People in Revolutionary England: Essays in Honour of Ivan Roots* (Oxford, 1986).

JONSON, BEN, *Ben Jonson*, ed. Ian Donaldson (Oxford, 1985).

JURETIC, GEORGE, 'Digger No Millenarian: The Revolutionizing of Gerrard Winstanley', *JHI* 36 (1975), 263–80.

KEEBLE, N. H., *The Literary Culture of Nonconformity in Later Seventeenth-Century England* (Leicester, 1987).

KENYON, JOHN, 'Andrew Marvell: Life and Times', in Brett, 1–35.

KISHLANSKY, MARK A., *The Rise of the New Model Army* (Cambridge, 1979).

KITSON, PETER J., 'The Seventeenth-Century Influence on the Early Religious and Political Thought of S. T. Coleridge, 1790–1804', Ph.D. diss. (Hull, 1984).

KNOPPERS, LAURA LUNGER, 'Milton's *The Readie and Easie Way* and the English Jeremiad', in Loewenstein and Turner, 213–26.

KRANIDAS, THOMAS, ' "Decorum" and the Style of Milton's Antiprelatical Tracts', *SP* 62 (1965), 176–87, reprinted in Fish, 475–88.
—— 'Words, Words, Words, and the Word: Milton's *Of Prelatical Episcopacy*', *Milton Studies*, 16 (1982), 153–66.

LAMBERT, SHEILA, 'The Beginnings of Printing for the House of Commons, 1640–42', *The Library*, 6th ser., 3 (1981), 43–61.

LAMONT, WILLIAM, *Godly Rule: Politics and Religion, 1603–60* (London, 1969).

LAMONT, WILLIAM, and OLDFIELD, SYBIL, *Politics, Religion and Literature in the Seventeenth Century* (London and Totowa, NJ, 1975).

LANGLEY, T. R., 'Abraham Cowley's "Brutus": Royalist or Republican?', *YES* 6 (1976), 41–52.

LAUD, WILLIAM, *A Speech concerning Innovations in the Church* (London, 1637).

LEGOUIS, PIERRE, *Andrew Marvell: Poet, Puritan, Patriot* (Oxford, 1965).

LEISHMAN, J. B., *The Art of Marvell's Poetry* (London, 1966)

L'ESTRANGE, Sir ROGER, *Be Merry and Wise* (London, 1660).

LEWALSKI, BARBARA KIEFER, 'Milton: Political Beliefs and Polemical Methods, 1659–60', *PMLA* 74 (1959), 191–202.

—— (ed.), *Renaissance Genres: Essays in Theory, History, and Interpretation* (Cambridge, Mass., 1986).

LIEB, MICHAEL, 'Milton's *Of Reformation* and the Dynamics of Controversy', in Lieb and Shawcross, 55–82.

—— and SHAWCROSS, JOHN T. (eds.), *Achievements of the Left Hand: Essays on the Prose of John Milton* (Amherst, 1974).

LILBURNE, JOHN, *The Christian Mans Triall*, 2nd edn. (London, 1641).

—— *The Iust Mans Iustification, or, A Letter by way of Plea in Barre* (London, 1646).

—— *An Anatomy of the Lords Tyranny and Iniustice Exercised upon Lieu. Col. John Lilburne, now a Prisoner in the Tower of London* (London, 1646).

—— *The Prisoners Plea for Habeas Corpus* (London, 1647).

—— *Strength out of Weaknesse* (London, 1648).

—— OVERTON, RICHARD, and PRINCE, THOMAS, *A Picture of the Council of State* (London, 1649).

LINDLEY, KEITH, 'The Part Played by the Catholics', in Brian Manning (ed.), *Politics, Religion and the English Civil War* (London, 1973), 127–76.

LOEWENSTEIN, DAVID, *Milton and the Drama of History: Historical Vision, Iconoclasm, and the Literary Imagination* (Cambridge, 1990).

—— and TURNER, JAMES GRANTHAM (eds.), *Politics, Poetics, and Hermeneutics in Milton's Prose* (Cambridge, 1990).

LOVELACE, RICHARD, *Lucasta* (London, 1649).

—— *Lucasta. Posthume Poems* (London, 1659).

—— *The Poems of Richard Lovelace*, ed. C. H. Wilkinson (Oxford, 1930).

—— *Selected Poems*, ed. Gerald Hammond (Manchester, 1987).

LOW, ANTHONY, *The Georgic Revolution* (Princeton, 1985).

MCCALMAN, IAIN, *Radical Underworld: Prophets, Revolutionaries and Pornographers in London, 1795–1840* (Cambridge, 1988).

MCGREGOR, J. F. 'The Ranters, 1649–1660', B.Litt. diss. (Oxford, 1969).

—— and REAY, B. (eds.), *Radical Religion in the English Revolution* (1984; Oxford, 1986).

MACLEOD, MALCOLM (ed.), *A Concordance to the Poems of Robert Herrick* (New York, 1936).

MACPHERSON, C. B., *The Political Theory of Possessive Individualism: Hobbes to Locke* (Oxford, 1962).

MADAN, F. F., *A New Bibliography of the Eikon Basilike of King Charles the First* (Publications of the Oxford Bibliographical Society, NS 3 (1949); Oxford, 1950).

MANNING, BRIAN (ed.), *Politics, Religion and the English Civil War* (London, 1973).

MARCUS, LEAH SINANOGLOU, 'Herrick's *Noble Numbers* and the Politics of Playfulness', *ELR* 7 (1977), 108–26.

—— 'Herrick's *Hesperides* and the "Proclamation Made for May"' *SP* 76 (1979), 49–74.

—— *The Politics of Mirth: Jonson, Herrick, Milton, Marvell and Defense of Old Holiday Pastimes* (Chicago, 1986).

MARVELL, ANDREW, *Andrew Marvell: Complete Poetry*, ed. George de F. Lord (1968; London and Melbourne, 1984).

—— *The Poems and Letters of Andrew Marvell*, ed. H. M. Margoliouth, 3rd edn. rev. Pierre Legouis with E. E. Duncan-Jones (Oxford, 1971).

MASSON, DAVID, *The Life of John Milton* (London, 1877–94).

MAY, THOMAS, *History of the Long Parliament* (London, 1647).

MILES, GARY B., *Virgil's Georgics: A New Interpretation* (Berkeley, Los Angeles, and London, 1980).

MILNER, ANDREW, *John Milton and the English Revolution* (London and Basingstoke, 1981).

MILTON, JOHN, *The Doctrine and Discipline of Divorce*, 1st ed. (London, 1643).

—— *The Poems of Mr John Milton, Both English and Latin* (London, 1645).

—— *Complete Prose Works* of John Milton, ed. Don M. Wolfe *et al.* (New Haven, 1953–82).

—— *The Poems of John Milton*, ed. John Carey and Alastair Fowler (London, 1968).

MILWARD, PETER, *Religious Controversies of the Elizabethan Age* (London, 1977).

—— *Religious Controversies of the Jacobean Age* (London, 1978).

MOORMAN, F. W., *Robert Herrick: A Bibliographical and Critical Study* (London and New York, 1910).

MORRILL, J. S., *The Revolt in the Provinces* (London, 1976).

MORTON, A. L., *The World of the Ranters: Religious Radicalism in the English Revolution* (1970; London, 1979).

MUELLER, JANEL, 'On Genesis in Genre: Milton's Politicizing of the Sonnet in "Captain or Colonel"', in Lewalski, 213–40.

—— 'Embodying Glory: The Apocalyptic Strain in Milton's *Of Reformation*', in Loewenstein and Turner, 9–40.

MULLIGAN, LOTTE, GRAHAM, JOHN K., and RICHARDS, JUDITH, 'Winstanley: A Case for the Man as He Said He Was', *JEH* 28 (1977), 57–75.

NETHERCOT, ARTHUR H., *Abraham Cowley: The Muse's Hannibal* (London, 1931).

NEVO, RUTH, *The Dial of Virtue: A Study of Poems on Affairs of State in the Seventeenth Century* (Princeton, 1963).

NEW, JOHN F. H., *Anglican and Puritan: The Basis of their Opposition, 1558–1640* (London, 1964).

NEWCASTLE, MARCHIONESS OF, *CCXI Sociable Letters* (London, 1664).

NEWMAN, PETER R., 'The Royalist Army in Northern England, 1642–5', D.Phil. diss. (York, 1978).

—— 'Catholic Royalists of Northern England, 1642–1645', *Northern History*, 15 (1979), 88–95.

—— *The Battle of Marston Moor* (Chichester, 1981).

NORBROOK, DAVID, *Poetry and Politics in the English Renaissance* (London, Boston, Melbourne, and Henley, 1984).

—— 'The Reformation of the Masque', in David Lindley (ed.), *The Court Masque* (Manchester, 1984), 94–110.

—— 'Marvell's "Horatian Ode", and the Politics of Genre', in Healy and Sawday, 147–69.

NYQUIST, MARY, 'The Genesis of Gendered Subjectivity in the Divorce Tracts and in *Paradise Lost*', in Nyquist and Ferguson, 99–127.

—— and FERGUSON, MARGARET W. (eds.), *Re-membering Milton: Essays on the Texts and Traditions* (New York and London, 1987).

PAGITT, EPHRAIM, *Heresiography, or, A Description of the Heretickes and Sectaries of the Latter Times* (London, 1645, 1646).

PALMER, GEORGE, *The Lawfulnesse of the Celebration of Christs Birthday* (London, 1649).

PALMER, HERBERT, *The Glasse of Gods Providence towards his Faithfull Ones* (London, 1644).

PARFITT, GEORGE, *English Poetry in the Seventeenth Century* (London and New York, 1985).

PARKER, WILLIAM RILEY, *Milton's Contemporary Reputation* (1940; New York, 1971).

—— *Milton: A Biography* (Oxford, 1968).

PARRY, GRAHAM, *Seventeenth-Century Poetry: The Social Context* (London, 1985).

PARTRIDGE, ERIC, *A Dictionary of Slang and Unconventional English*, 8th edn. ed. P. Beale (London, Melbourne, and Henley, 1984).

PATRIDES, C. A. (ed.), *Approaches to Marvell: The York Tercentenary Lectures* (London, Henley, and Boston, 1978).

PATTERSON, ANNABEL M., *Marvell and the Civic Crown* (Princeton, 1978).

—— *Censorship and Interpretation: The Conditions of Writing and Reading in Early Modern England* (Madison, Wisc., 1984).

—— ' "No Meer Amatorious Novel?" ', in Loewenstein and Turner, 85–102.

PENNINGTON, DONALD, and THOMAS, KEITH (eds.), *Puritans and Revolutionaries* (Oxford, 1978).

PEPYS, SAMUEL, *The Diary of Samuel Pepys*, ed. Robert Latham and William Mathews (London, 1970).

PLOMER, HENRY R., *A Dictionary of Booksellers who were at Work in England, Scotland and Ireland from 1641 to 1667* (London, 1907).

POCKLINGTON, JOHN, *Altare Christianum* (London, 1637).

POTTER, LOIS, *Secret Rites and Secret Writing: Royalist Literature, 1641–1660* (Cambridge, 1989).

PRICE, A. F., 'Incidental Imagery in *Areopagitica*', *Modern Philology*, 49 (1952), 217–22.

QUARLES, JOHN, *Regale Lectum Miseriae, or, A Kingly Bed of Miserie* (n.p., 1649).

REED, J. C., 'Humphrey Moseley, Publisher', *Oxford Bibliographical Society Proceedings and Papers*, 2 (1927–30).

R. O. (attributed to Richard Overton), *Mans Mortallitie* (Amsterdam, 1643; London, 1644).

—— *Mans Mortalitie*, ed. Harold Fisch (Liverpool, 1968).

ROESTVIG, MAREN-SOFIE, The *Happy Man*, 2nd edn. (Oslo, 1958, 1962).

ROLLIN, ROGER B., and PATRICK, J. MAX (eds.), *'Trust to Good Verses': Herrick Tercentenary Essays* (Pittsburgh, 1978).

SABINE, GEORGE H. (ed.), *The Works of Gerrard Winstanley* (Ithaca, 1941).

SCHINDLER, WALTER, *Voice and Crisis: Invocation in Milton's Poetry* (Hamden, Conn., 1984).

SCHLEINER, LOUISE, 'Herrick's Songs and the Character of *Hesperides*', *ELR* 6 (1976), 77–91.

SCHWARTZ, REGINA, 'Citation, Authority, and *De Doctrina Christiana*', in Loewenstein and Turner, 227–40.

SCOTT, EVA, *Rupert Prince Palatine*, 2nd edn. (London, 1904).

SENSABAUGH, GEORGE T., *That Grand Whig Milton* (1952; New York, 1967).

SHAKESPEARE, WILLIAM, *Complete Works*, ed. W. J. Craig (1954; Oxford, 1965).

—— *2 Henry IV*, ed. A. R. Humphreys (London, 1966).

—— *Coriolanus*, ed. Philip Brockbank (London, 1976).

—— *Henry V*, ed. Gary Taylor (Oxford, 1984).

SHARPE, KEVIN, and ZWICKER, STEPHEN N. (eds.), *Politics of Discourse: The Literature and History of Seventeenth-Century England* (Berkeley, Los Angeles and London, 1987).

SHAWCROSS, JOHN T. 'The Higher Wisdom of *The Tenure of Kings and Magistrates*', in Lieb and Shawcross, 142–59.

Sion College Ministers, *Testimony to the Truth of Jesus Christ* (London, 1648).

SMECTYMNUUS, *An Answer to a Booke Entituled, An Humble Remonstrance* (London, 1641).

SMITH, NIGEL, 'Richard Overton's Marpriest Tracts: Towards a History of Leveller Style', *Prose Studies*, 9/2 (1986); reprinted in Corns, 39–66.

—— *Perfection Proclaimed: Language and Literature in English Radical Religion 1640–1660* (Oxford, 1989).

—— 'Areopagitica: Voicing Contexts, 1643–5', in Lowenstein and Turner, 103–22.

—— (ed.), *A Collection of Ranter Writings from the 17th Century*, foreword by John Carey (London, 1983).

SMURTHWAITE, DAVID, *Battlefields of Britain* (1984; London, 1987).

SPRAT, THOMAS (ed.), *The Works of Abraham Cowley* (London, 1668).

—— *History of the Royal Society*, ed. Jackson I. Cope and Harold Whitmore Jones (1959; St Louis, Mo. and London, 1966).

STERNE, LAURENCE, and KOLLMEIER, HAROLD H., *A Concordance to the English Prose of John Milton* (Binghamton, N.Y., 1985).

STOCKER, MARGARITA, *Apocalyptic Marvell: The Second Coming in Seventeenth Century Poetry* (Brighton, 1986).

STONE, LAWRENCE, *The Family, Sex and Marriage in England 1500–1800*, abridged edn. (London, 1979).

STRONG, ROY, *Van Dyck: Charles I on Horseback* (London, 1972).

SUCKLING, SIR JOHN, *The Works of Sir John Suckling: The Non-Dramatic Works*, ed. Thomas Clayton (Oxford, 1971).

SUMMERS, CLAUDE J., 'Herrick's Political Poetry: The Strategies of his Art', in Rollin and Patrick, 171–83.

TAYLOR, JOHN, *Mad Verse, Sad Verse, Glad Verse and Bad Verse* (n.p., [1644]).

—— *The Complaint of Christmas* (London, 1646).

THOMAS, KEITH, 'The Date of Gerrard Winstanley's *Fire in the Bush*', *P & P* 42 (1969), 160–2.

—— 'The Puritans and Adultery: The Act of 1650 Reconsidered', in Pennington and Thomas, 257–82.

T. J., *The World Turn'd Upside Down, or, A Briefe Description of the Ridiculous Fashions of these Distracted Times* (London, 1647).

TOLIVER, HAROLD E., *Marvell's Ironic Vision* (New Haven and London, 1965).

TREVOR-ROPER, HUGH R., *Archbishop Laud, 1573–1645*, 2nd edn. (London, 1962).

—— *Catholics, Anglicans and Puritans: Seventeenth Century Essays* (London, 1987).

TROTTER, DAVID, *The Poetry of Abraham Cowley* (London and Basingstoke, 1979).

TURNER, JAMES GRANTHAM, *One Flesh: Paradisal Marriage and Sexual Relations in the Age of Milton* (Oxford, 1987).

TYACKE, NICHOLAS, 'Puritanism, Arminianism and Counter-Reformation', in Conrad Russell (ed.), *The Origins of the English Civil War* (London and Basingstoke, 1973), 119–43.

—— *Anti-Calvinists: The Rise of English Arminianism, c. 1590–1640* (Oxford and New York, 1987).

UNDERDOWN, DAVID E., *Royalist Conspiracy in England 1649–1660* (New Haven, 1960).

UNDERDOWN, DAVID E., *Pride's Purge: Politics in the Puritan Revolution* (Oxford, 1971).

—— *Revel, Riot, and Rebellion: Popular Politics and Culture in England 1603–1660* (Oxford, 1985).

USSHER, JAMES, *The Judgement of Doctor Rainoldes touching the Originall of Episcopacy* (London, 1641).

—— et al., *Certain Briefe Treatises, Written by Diverse Learned Men, concerning the Ancient and Modern Government of the Church* (Oxford, 1641).

VIRGIL, *The Eclogues and Georgics*, ed. R. D. Williams (New York, 1979).

WALLACE, DEWEY D., JR., *Puritans and Predestination: Grace in English Protestant Theology 1525–1695* (Chapel Hill, NC, 1982).

WALLACE, JOHN M., *Destiny his Choice: The Loyalism of Andrew Marvell* (1968; Cambridge, 1980).

WARREN, WILLIAM, *Strange, True and Lamentable Newes from Exceter* (London, 1643).

WEBBER, JOAN, *The Eloquent 'I': Style and Self in Seventeenth-Century Prose* (Madison, Wisc. and London, 1968).

WEDGWOOD, C. V., *The Trial of Charles I* (1964; London, 1966).

WEIDHORN, MANFRED, *Richard Lovelace* (New York, 1970).

WHITAKER, THOMAS R., 'Herrick and the Fruits of the Garden', *ELH* 22 (1985), 16–33.

WILCHER, ROBERT, *Andrew Marvell* (Cambridge, 1985).

WILDING, MICHAEL, 'Milton's *Areopagitica*: Liberty for the Sects', *Prose Studies* 9/2 (1986), 7–38; reprinted in Corns, 7–38.

—— 'Marvell's "Horatian Ode upon Cromwell's Return from Ireland", the Levellers, and the Junta', *MLR* 82 (1987), 1–14.

—— *Dragons Teeth: Literature in the English Revolution* (Oxford, 1987).

—— (ed.), *Marvell: Modern Judgements* (London, 1969).

WILLIAMS, C. M., 'The Anatomy of a Radical Gentleman: Henry Marten', in Pennington and Thomas, 118–38.

WILLIAMS, JOHN, *Holy Table, Name and Thing, More Anciently, Properly, and Literally Used under the New Testament, then that of an Altar* (n.p., 'Printed for the Diocese of *Lincoln*', 1637).

WILLIAMS, ROGER, *The Bloudy Tenent of Persecution for Cause of Conscience* (London, 1644).

WILLIS, HUMPHREY, *Times Whirligig, or, The Blew-New-Made Gentleman Mounted* (n.p., 1647).

WILMOT, JOHN, EARL OF ROCHESTER, *The Poems of John Wilmot, Earl of Rochester*, ed. Keith Walker (Oxford, 1984).

WINSTANLEY, GERRARD, *The Saints Paradise* (London, ?1648).

—— *Several Pieces Gathered into One Volume* (London, 1649).

—— *The Works of Gerrard Winstanely'*, ed. George H. Sabine (Ithaca, NY, 1941).

—— 'England's Spirit Unfoulded, or, An Incouragement to Take the Engagement , by Jerrard Winstanley: A Newly Discovered Pamphlet by Gerrard Winstanley', ed. G. E. Aylmer, *P & P* 40 (1968), 3–15.

—— The Law of Freedom and Other Writings, ed. Christopher Hill (1973; Cambridge, 1983).

WOODHOUSE, A. S. P., *Puritanism and Liberty* (London, 1938).

WOOLRYCH, AUSTIN, *Battles of the English Civil War* (London, 1961).

—— 'Milton and Cromwell: "A Short but Scandalous Night of Interruption"?', in Lieb and Shawcross, 201–12.

—— Commonwealth to Protectorate (1982; Oxford, 1986).

WORDEN, BLAIR, *The Rump Parliament* (1974; Cambridge, 1977).

—— 'Andrew Marvell, Oliver Cromwell, and the Horatian Ode', *Hist. Jnl.* 27 (1984), 525–47; reprinted in Sharpe and Zwicker, 147–80.

—— 'Providence and Politics in Cromwellian England', *P & P* 109 (1985), 55–99.

YOUNG, PETER, *Civil War England* (London and New York, 1981).

Index